LOST CITIES
&
ANCIENT
MYSTERIES
OF THE
SOUTHWEST

Adventures Unlimited Press

LOST CITIES
&
ANCIENT
MYSTERIES
OF THE
SOUTHWEST

DAVID HATCHER CHILDRESS

Lost Cities & Ancient Mysteries of the Southwest

ISBN 10: 1-931882-94-0
ISBN 13: 978-1-931882-94-1

Published by:
Adventures Unlimited Press
One Adventure Place
Kempton, Illinois 60946 USA
auphq@frontiernet.net

www.adventuresunlimitedpress.com

10 9 8 7 6 5 4 3 2 1

LOST CITIES
&
ANCIENT
MYSTERIES
OF THE
SOUTHWEST

In the first place God made idiots.
This was for practice.
Then he made proofreaders.
—Mark Twain (1835-1910)

Thanks to all the many people who helped with this book, including Jennifer Bolm, John Michell, Gary David, Philip Coppens, Christopher O'Brien, Martin Gray, Boomer, Greg Bishop, Mike Marinacci, Jack Kutz, Bill Corliss, and many others.

TABLE OF CONTENTS

1.

NORTHERN MEXICO

AZTLAN AND THE ZONE OF SILENCE

*Twenty years from now you will be more disappointed
by the things you didn't do than by the ones you did do.
So throw off the bowlines. Sail away from the safe harbor.
Catch the trade winds in your sails.
Explore. Dream. Discover.*
—Mark Twain

*The bus came by and I got on, that's when it all began
There was Cowboy Neal at the wheel of the bus to
Nevereverland*
—Grateful Dead, *The Other One*

The afternoon sun was starting to set into the dusty haze in the west. I stared briefly at the orange ball in the sky and then looked up and down the railway tracks.

A taxi driver had called out to me up the street: where was I going?

"I don't know," I told him, and stumbled on down the street. Somewhere, at the bottom, I knew, was the railroad station.

I had been all over the world, having interrupted my college education in Montana to try a stint as an English teacher in Japan and Taiwan. From there it was on to Thailand, Burma, India and Nepal. I had been fascinated by Himalayan climbing and remote Tibetan monasteries and spent some months trekking and exploring in the mountains.

After that, back on the road, I had only a few hundred dollars. I traveled through Pakistan, Afghanistan, Iran, Turkey, Syria, Jordan and Israel to Egypt. From there I went to Sudan where I began looking for a job, and got one with a Kenyan-American catering company. For several years I lived in Sudan making good money managing the catering operations of oil exploration camps.

After traveling through the Indian Ocean, Australia, New Guinea and other remote islands, I decided that I needed to seek the lost cities of South America. I went into those jungles and deserts and then looked at Central America, Guatemala and Mexico.

I was writing books on giant ruins, lost cities and ancient technology. I was living a life on the road like Jack Kerouac, a Dharma Bum drifting from town to town, cantina to cantina. Rifts of Bob Dylan and the Grateful Dead drifted through my head as the sun disappeared below the railroad tracks. Somewhere down those railroad tracks was my life. Where was I going? At 50 years old was I a beatnik on the street? I could afford to buy a ticket, so I didn't need to ride the rails for free.

I dusted off my jacket and then looked around. Where was I?

On the Tracks with Neal Cassady

I was standing on the railway tracks in San Miguel de Allende. Down on the corner was a young girl with

2

a flower cart. Farther up the street was a man selling mariachi guitars. At my feet was where Neal Cassady was found dead in 1968. I kicked some dust against the rail with my boot.

Supposedly, the last thing he said before he died of exposure on that cold February morning was "64,928," the number of crossties he had counted on the railway tracks walking between San Miguel de Allende and the town of Celaya, about 15 miles to the south. Neal Cassady was the protagonist of Jack Kerouac's most famous book, having entered the inner circle of the Beat Generation after meeting Allen Ginsberg and Kerouac in New York in 1947.

Soon Cassady and Kerouac began the series of cross-country adventures that would later become *On the Road*. They raced aimlessly across the U.S.A. and Mexico, with Cassady setting the pace and the agenda. Others joined in their journeys: Alan Ginsberg, William Burroughs, Peter Orlovsky, and more.

William Burroughs, probably more than any of the other "Beats," spent a great deal of time in Mexico. In fact, it was in Mexico City that he shot and killed his wife, Joan, in 1951. Joan Vollmer Burroughs was a very intelligent woman who took an active part in the rambling, intellectual conversations the Beats were prone to, but having become addled by drugs and alcohol, agreed one fateful night to put a glass of gin on her head and let Bill shoot it off "William Tell-style." Later he went on to write *The Naked Lunch* and *The Ticket that Exploded*, among many other works.

Like me, Burroughs traveled to North Africa, Europe, South America and Mexico in search of mystery and adventure. In South America he searched for ayahuasca, which he called yagé, a hallucinogenic plant found in the Amazon. After living in Morocco, Paris and London, he moved to Lawrence, Kansas, where he passed away on August 2, 1997. Burroughs, like all travelers, was a loner. Driven by his addictions,

3

and the need to head down the road to somewhere, he kept moving for over 60 years around the world.

I was driven as well—I was on a quest for the ancient past, a search for the lost cities of all the continents. My special interest has always been archeology, though I feel I belong foremost to the great fellowship of travelers on the open road—like Kerouac, Burroughs and Cassady. The road in front of us goes on forever, and so we walk one step at a time into the future. Now, having spent several years in Europe and South America, I was in Mexico looking north to the U.S.A. What would I find there?

I hesitated, and looked south down the tracks in the dusty light of dusk. It was there that Cassady, well into a night of mixing Seconal pills (downers) with alcohol—a deadly combination—wandered onto the railroad tracks intending to walk to the next town of Celaya in only jeans and a T-shirt. It was a cold rainy night, and Cassady was found beside the tracks the next morning. He arrived at a hospital in a coma and died a few hours later. It was February 4, 1968. Kerouac would die a year later. So did Cassady get to Celaya and back? It would be interesting to count the crossties, I thought for a moment. But my direction was supposed to be north.

There was little movement at the station on that hot late afternoon. A car horn honked in the distance somewhere. I pondered that moment, one that all travelers face, on the crossroads. Different paths lay ahead for me: down the tracks like Neal Cassady, another casualty of "the road," or back up the street to a bar I had seen with the simple words "La Cantina" over the door.

Something stirred in me. Yes, that was where I was headed. A sudden gust of wind blew over the tracks, scattering yet more dust. Mystery and adventure were in the air—they just needed to be sought out.

Up a narrow street toward the main plaza of San

Miguel de Allende was the light green adobe wall with "La Cantina" above the door. Without a further glance around, I kicked the door inward and entered the establishment. It suddenly dawned on me why heading for La Cantina had felt like the right thing to do. There was my partner, Jennifer, sitting at the bar, her blonde hair falling down to her shoulders. She had a shot of tequila in her hand and a longneck bottle of beer on the bar. The bartender gave me a friendly look and soon the flow of lime and tequila had started.

I was on the road, like Neal, Jack and Bill. My quest was for the lost cities and ancient mysteries of the American Southwest. Jennifer and I would head north to the Mexican-American border town of Ojinaga. From there, up through west Texas, New Mexico, Arizona and parts unknown. There were thousands of miles of deserts, mountains and river valleys to explore. Ancient legends claimed that the gold of the Aztecs came from this region, and there were lost mines and other ancient mysteries to investigate.

Legends also claimed that at least one lost civilization was to be found somewhere north of the Mexican border—Gran Quivera or Cibola and the Seven Cities of Gold. Plus, there were strange tales of Egyptians and Romans in the Southwest, as well as other exotic visitors. What was the truth behind these stories? I would drive the back roads in my beat up four-wheel-drive to see these things for myself, exploring the enigmas of living thunderbirds, the Marfa Lights and the mysterious Zone of Silence.

I bought a shot for everyone at La Cantina, to the patrons' great cheer. Sipping a cold beer, I thought of some of the puzzles that surrounded Mesoamerican civilization. At the time of the Conquest most of what is today Mexico was ruled by the Aztecs—but they were newcomers to the region. Before them, several other groups had controlled much of the territory; going backward in time, the land had been ruled by the Zapotecs, the Toltecs, the mysterious Teotihuacan culture, the Maya and, furthest back, by the Olmecs.

My mind wandered. Why had the Spanish come to this particular small town and built a cathedral? Today San Miguel de Allende has become an art colony and attracts many tourists. Curiously, it has been doing that for years. Was San Miguel de Allende some sort of power place? There are ancient mines in the area—had the Spanish come here to resume excavations at these mines once worked by the Toltecs and Aztecs?

The Strange World of Ancient Mexico

In order to understand the early history of the Southwest, we need to understand the early history of central Mexico. For many years archeologists believed that there was very little contact between the northern populations (of Arizona, New Mexico, the Great Plains and the Mississippi Valley) and the highly developed population centers in central Mexico. Now it is known that there was a great deal of contact—both by land and waterway—via established trade routes. The big question is still: how extensive was it? I think it will be shown throughout this book that the sophistication and interconnectedness of the various ancient cultures was much greater than is widely accepted.

The oldest, and probably greatest mystery of early Mexico is the problem of the Olmecs. Most traditional archeologists were amazed at the sudden recognition of the Olmecs as a culture that was apparently older than the Maya, a literal "Mother Culture" for Central America.

According to the famous Mexican archeologist Ignacio Bernal, Olmec-type art was first noticed as early as 1869 and the term "Olmec," or "Rubber People," was first used in 1927. But it was not until a special meeting in Mexico City in 1942 that the matter was largely settled that the Olmecs were a separate culture that predated the Maya. The date for the beginning of the Olmec culture was to remain a matter of great debate, however. Naturally, a number of prominent Mayan archeologists, including Eric Thompson who helped decipher the "Mayan calendar," refused to believe that this new culture called the Olmecs could be earlier than the Mayas. It is now generally conceded, however, that the Olmecs were the source of many advances that had been attributed to the Maya, e.g., the number system, the calendar and even the ball game played throughout Mesoamerica with rubber balls on a standard court.

Bernal continued to research the Olmecs and came out with the first—and for a long time, the only—significant study on this early Central American culture in his 1969 book *The Olmec World*.[5] In that book, Bernal discussed the curious finds attributed to the Olmecs all over southern Mexico and Central America, as far south as the site of Guanacaste in Nicaragua. Even such famous Mayan sites as Uaxactun and El Mirador were thought by Bernal to have been previously occupied by the Olmecs. However, he could not figure out the origin of these strange and distinctive people whose art featured bearded men, Negroid heads, Asian likenesses and undecipherable hieroglyphs.

The idea that these strange depictions of people with widely varied features, which suggest they were of European, African *and* Asian descent, could be the product of a cosmopolitan society where people intermingled as the result of early transoceanic trade and exploration seems totally alien to the historians and scientists who have taken over the archeology of the Americas. Despite the clearly disparate looks of the various lords, kings, travelers and magicians depicted, most professors teaching at our major universities maintain that this is not evidence of ancient pre-Columbian contact. They admit, though, that people might erroneously get this idea from a "superficial" view of these various statues and carvings.[2] So, to mainstream historians, the origin of the Olmecs remains obscure.

In my book *The Mystery of the Olmecs*[9] I maintain that the most logical explanation for the variety of visages is that people crossed both the Atlantic and Pacific oceans to converge on the narrow isthmus of southern Mexico that would be an obvious center for trade. This is substantiated by the fact that Olmec settlements are found on both the Atlantic and Pacific coasts.

The most well known examples of Olmec art are the giant basalt stones carved into heads with typical Negroid features of wide, flat noses and thick lips. Many of the heads feature helmets, and most of the faces are scowling. Many alternative theories exist on how Negroids arrived in Central America. One theory is that they are connected with Atlantis; as part of the warrior-class of that civilization they were tough and hard bitten. Or perhaps they were part of an Egyptian colony in Central America, or from some unknown African empire. Others have suggested that they came across the Pacific from the lost continent of Mu, or as Shang Chinese dignitaries and generals. Interestingly, a Chinese scholar on the Shang Dynasty claims that the Olmec hieroglyphs are an example of the ancient Shang script which goes back to 1300 BC.[9]

Tula, Toltec Capital

Leaving San Miguel de Allende, Jennifer and I decided to take a side trip to the Toltec capital of Tula. The Toltecs were a warrior tribe who eventually filled the leadership void in Mexico left by the collapse of the Teotihuacan culture, which occurred around 700 AD. That culture is credited with building the massive administrative and religious complex that bears its name (now located just a few miles outside Mexico City), including the enormous pyramids of the Sun and Moon. They employed expert craftsmen and produced fine goods that were traded far to the north and south. They had a well-ordered and hierarchical society, but for reasons unknown, the culture went into decline and their power centers were abandoned.

The Toltecs moved into the region about 100 years after the decline of the Teotihuacan. They were fine craftsmen and metallurgists, and picked up some of the pieces of the Teotihuacan culture. The word "Toltec," in fact, means "craftsman" and came to be applied to any people who were carrying on the civilization of the Teotihuacan, as opposed to more barbaric peoples. The Aztecs even sometimes applied the word Toltec to themselves.

As we drove through the countryside, we passed a number of small towns and then came to the modern town of Tula, a prosperous city by the looks of it, guarded by two gigantic statues standing along the highway. Breezing by the Tula monoliths, we continued on to the archaeological site of the same name. The ancient city itself is situated on a hill above the modern city, and is a popular tourist spot.

By noon, we were wandering among the Atlanteans of Tula, the huge stone statues that stand on top of a pyramid in the arid mountains north of Mexico City. "Atlantean" is a term applied in architecture to any load-bearing statues that hold up a roof, referring to the Atlas of Greek mythology who was condemned to hold up the heavens. The roof at Tula is long gone, but the impressive statues and the pyramids they stand on amazed early archeologists when they first discovered the site at the turn of the last century.

For a long time, Tula (which means "the glorious") was thought to be a mythical place, much like Atlantis or Shangri-La. As the respected British archaeologist Michael Coe points out in his book *Mexico*,[85] "It has been the misfortune of modern scholarship that there are not one, but many places named Tula in Mexico— a quite natural circumstance from the meaning of the name. Thus the term was indiscriminately applied to great centers like Teotihuacan and Cholula."

It was the French explorer and historian Claude Joseph Désiré Charnay who first began to suspect that Tula (also called "Tollan") was a real place. He developed an unpopular theory that there had once been a vast Toltec empire in central Mexico which had spread its dominion from a legendary capital called Tollan as far as Teotihuacan, Toluca, Xochicalco, Cholula, and even Chichén Itzá far away in the Yucatán. Charnay eventually became convinced that the site of Tula, 50 miles north of Mexico City in the province of Hidalgo, held the remains of the legendary Toltec capital.

At the time, the village was quite small, and evidenced only a few overgrown mounds, but with the help of local laborers, Charnay soon came across huge basalt blocks more than seven feet long that appeared to him to be the giant feet of statues. Indeed, they were those of the incredible Atlanteans.

Charnay recognized similarities between the objects he found at Tula and those he had seen previously at Chichén Itzá. Charnay was certain that he had found ancient Tula, the legendary city of Mesoamerican myth. The prevailing scholars, high in their ivory towers of academia, firmly denied that he had discovered the ancient capital. However, in the 1930s the archaeologist George Vaillant reexamined the site, and discovered that Charnay was at least correct in his notion that the ruins adjacent to the small village of Tula were Toltec in nature, and indeed, this may well have been the ancient city of Tollan.

Because of their prowess and strength, the Toltecs were the stuff of legend in Mesoamerica. They were particularly reverent of the plumed-serpent god

Quetzalcoatl, a creator god who had many aspects in the various Mesoamerican cultures. He is sometimes known as a light-skinned man with a beard, a Christ-like figure who was said to have journeyed throughout the region bringing wisdom and peace to the people. One of the reasons Tula, or Tollan, was so important was its association with Quetzalcoatl. It was at Tula that Quetzalcoatl lingered and was presented with the "bow string of power."[24] It was to Tula that Quetzalcoatl promised to return. It was of Tula, "the glorious," that the *Song of Quetzalcoatl* was sung by the Yaqui Indians of northern Mexico. Tula was the great Toltec capital, and I believe it was from here that the rubber balls, exotic feathers, chocolate beans, and other goods found in the cities of the Hohokam and Anasazi in what is now Arizona were sent.

Jennifer and I walked around the main pyramid, and examined the gigantic Atlanteans. They were indeed huge, more than 30 feet high, constructed in four sections with stone plugs fitting neatly into corresponding contacts. The statues are dressed as warriors, and they hold some kind of curious device in their hands. Archeologists maintain that these are spear-throwers. These simple devices could project a small spear fairly accurately, and their use was widespread, penetrating into the Southwest as far as California and Nevada. Warfare in many regions, however, was largely hand-to-hand combat using clubs, maces, swords, and, in the case of the Mayans, exotic flint knives. Boomerangs and various other throwing sticks were also used, and spears or lances were also common.

Zechariah Sitchin, in *The Lost Realms*,[151] claims that the strange weapons the Atlanteans hold are plasma guns, used for melting rock in the mining operations

11

that were the main reason for the construction of many of the early cities in North and South America. Sitchin promotes the idea that extraterrestrials, known to the Sumerians as the Annunaki, came to earth, settling the ancient Middle East, constructing pyramids as space beacons, and eventually conquering Central and South America in their quest for gold, which was needed on their home planet.

Another interesting theory linking the ancient civilizations of Asia Minor to Mexico holds that the seafaring Phoenicians, and their cousins the Carthaginians, fled with their fleets to the shores of the Yucatan after their debilitating defeat in the Punic Wars.[35] Here, they established port cities; the Olmec-Mayan-Toltec port city of Comacalco, on the Gulf Coast near Palenque, was probably one of their ports. Indeed, warriors depicted in the excellent murals at Chichen Itza show bearded and heavily mustachioed men with armor, helmets, shields and swords. They appear to be of Mediterranean origin, rather than the traditional American Indian. American Indians are the only race that does not grow facial hair, and pureblooded Indian men can grow neither mustaches nor beards.

The Toltecs are known to have conquered areas quite far away from their capital at Tula, such as the northern Yucatan, where they made Chichen Itza another capital. After they conquered the Yucatan, did they turn their attention north to the territories of central Arizona, New Mexico and California? Why had the Toltecs established themselves at Tula, north of Teotihuacan, in the first place? The Toltecs were known as warriors and metallurgists, using metal swords, helmets and spearheads whenever they could. Were they trying to be closer to the cities farther north where the richest mines were located?

The Mystery of Mexican Metals

As I began researching the subject of lost treasures and mines in the Southwest, I came head-on into a little-known controversy surrounding Mexico and its neighboring areas: allegedly the people there did not know how to work metals until about the time of the Aztecs and their empire, i.e., until the 15th century AD. Incredibly, sophisticated metalworking techniques were known to have been developed in South America as far back as 1200 BC, but such metalwork was not supposedly apparent in Mexico until thousands of years later.

Mexico in 1519, as the archeologist C. A. Burland said, "was where Sumer and Egypt stood in 3500 BC." In other words, mainstream archeologists say that the cultures of Central America were lagging by thousands of years the progress made by the civilizations in Asia, Europe and Africa. South American cultures such as Tiwanaku (Tiahuanaco) and the later Incas did have sophisticated mining and metalworking endeavors over a thousand years before those of Mexico, but still lacked, supposedly, knowledge of the wheel and writing.

Victor von Hagen and other mainstream archeologists claim that none of the early Mexican cultures worked metal, and that this ability came up from South America by slow stages through indirect trade. Says von Hagen in his 1958 work *The Aztec: Man and Tribe*, "It does not appear at Teotihuacán, which was already a memory when the technique of gold and copper working reached Mexico. It was unknown to the early Mayas, and the Olmec craftsman contented himself with making diadems of jade. It was not practiced in Mexico much before the eleventh century."[14]

This assumption that metalworking was non-existent in Mexico until 400 years before the Conquest

13

seems very odd. It seems likely that metalworking in Mexico, as in the Old World and South America, would have been going on for thousands of years. In fact, as we shall see, many of the Toltec and Aztec mines were in parts of Mexico now known as the American states of Arizona, New Mexico, Colorado, Utah, California and Nevada.

In a 1995 article in the *Boston Globe* by journalist David L. Chandler entitled "Ancient Mariners: Strong Evidence of Andean-Mexican Seagoing Trade as Early as 600 AD,"[10] the author echoes mainstream thought on the lack of metals in Mexico and says, "Sophisticated and unique metalworking techniques, developed in South America as far back as 1200 BC, suddenly appeared in Western Mexico in about 600 AD—without ever being seen anywhere in between. The only reasonable explanation, according to archeologist Dorothy Hosler, is seaborne trade."

Discussing Hosler's work, Chandler says, "Centuries after their development in South America, metal objects appeared suddenly on Mexico's west coast. But the absence of any metal artifacts from that period in all of Central America in between, or in the interior and east coast of Mexico, indicates that these casting methods, alloys and designs could not have been exported via overland trade... Unlike the use of metals elsewhere in the ancient world, where the focus was usually on weapons and agricultural tools, much of the emphasis of both the Mexican and Andean metallurgists was on decorative and ceremonial objects such as bells and jewelry, and small tools such as needles and tweezers."

Chandler goes on to mention how the lost wax process was used in both Colombia and Mexico. Hosler's detailed analysis of the metals from both North and South America showed that, rather than Mexican metals having been transported up from the south, virtually all the objects found in Mexico were made from native Mexican ores, so what must have come up from the south was metalworking *technology*. In order to have imparted such knowledge, Hosler concluded, the visits must have been much longer and more extensive than would have been needed simply to trade finished goods.

At the end of the article, Chandler quotes Hosler: "One of the aspects that's very interesting for archeologists is that we tend to think these two great civilizations [Mexican and Andean] grew without much influence from one another... This is fairly unambiguous evidence that there was more extensive interaction than was thought."

So, already there are major cracks in the mainstream archeological dogma that metalworking came late to Mexico. While in 1958 it was thought that metals were not found in Mexico until the 11th century, they are now thought to have occurred by the 7th century AD. While this time frame allows for the Toltecs to have worked metal, it is still a relatively late date in my opinion. One problem with most metal artifacts is that if they are left exposed to the elements they will corrode and deteriorate. In the steamy jungle environment that covers much of the area in question, this would happen very quickly. Gold, on the other hand is indestructible, but is often reused and turned into gold bars or hammered into different objects. Cortez was given gold bars by emissaries of Montezuma when he landed at Veracruz from Cuba in 1519.

But is it true that the Mexican cultures that predated the Toltecs (for example, the Mayas and Olmecs) did not know metals? Mormon archeologists, seeking proof that the *Book of Mormon* gives an accurate account of Mesoamerican history—including early metalworking—have pointed out that language studies help confirm that metallurgy was indeed used in very ancient Mexico. Mayan and Olmec scholars who were reconstructing parts of several

Mesoamerican languages were puzzled to find that a word for "metal" existed as early as 1000 BC, while the language of the Olmecs had a word for metal as early as 1500 BC. (John L. Sorenson, *An Ancient American Setting for the Book of Mormon*, 1985, Deseret Book Company, Salt Lake City)

More importantly, metals that predate 600 AD have been found in Mesoamerica. A pottery vessel dating to around 300 AD (mentioned by Sorenson) might have been used for smelting. A metallic mass within this vessel contained copper and iron. The archeologist who made this find has also found a refined piece of iron in an ancient Mesoamerican tomb.

Much older are the tons of iron that the Olmecs apparently mined. In 1996, a non-Mormon archeologist named Dr. Anne Cyphers asserted that, "a total of 10 tons of iron has been found at San Lorenzo, in several massive hoards, the largest of which was four tons. Before the discovery of these hoards, only a few pieces of iron were known. They were discovered by using metal detectors." (William J. Hamblin, "Talk on the Olmecs by Cypher," posted 9/26/96 SAMU-L). So, the origin and practice of metalworking in Mexico, as we see, is controversial. Like many things in archeology, the use of metals in Mexico is being continually pushed further and further back in time, to a point where metallurgy in Mexico is contemporary with metallurgy in South America.

Tayopa and the Lost Mines of the Toltecs

After a restful night in Tula and breakfast the next morning of beans, eggs and tortillas, Jennifer and I headed north toward the Texas border. With Tula a cloud of dust in the rearview mirror I began wondering about where, exactly, the Toltecs got the metals for their swords and shields and helmets made of copper, silver and gold. Were their ancient mines inherited later by the Aztecs, and then by the Spanish?

It is known that the Toltecs and Aztecs understood the mining and smelting of gold and silver, and used the metals for ornaments with which to adorn themselves, and even to make household utensils. When the early Spanish explorers came to Peru, Central America and Mexico, their greed was heightened by the gold, silver and copper adornments that were common among the indigenous peoples. It is said that many of the great treasures that belonged to the Aztecs and Incas were buried to prevent them from falling into Spanish hands, and it appears true that ancient and valuable collections of gold and silver were stashed away, their locations becoming obscured with the wiping out of the indigenous populations and the later passing of the Spanish Conquistadors, and the decay and destruction of the early Spanish Missions.

These great hoards are scattered all over South America and Mexico and all that part of the Great Southwest that belonged to Mexico at the time of the Spanish Conquest. Northern Mexico and the American Southwest are steeped in stories of Aztec treasure, and stories of Montezuma's lost treasure can be found as far north as Colorado and Utah.

J. Frank Dobie mentions a curious lost city and mining area named Tayopa that was known to exist in northern Mexico, near Chihuahua City, in his classic 1928 book *Apache Gold and Yaqui Silver*.[32] He claims that Tayopa was once a small town, one of the earliest in northern Mexico, that had a great church (now gone) with silver bells and tons of pure silver church accoutrements like candlesticks, columns, brackets and shelves that must have come from a secret mine. The church also owned gold and silver bars, crucifixes and many more precious artifacts.

The great silver and gold treasure was amassed between 1632 and 1646 by the Jesuits who were operating the Tayopa mission and the adjacent mines. During those years, instead of sending the gold and silver to Mexico City (for the Church and a royal one-fifth to the king), the Jesuits hoarded the metals and made wares for their own mission out of them.

The Spanish government had long had problems with the powerful Jesuits in the New World, and accused them of working with Spain's archenemies, the Dutch, to take over large areas of remoter spots in South and North America. Dobie mentions that as early as 1592 Spain passed a law against the owning and operating of mines by priests. He says that this was so grossly violated that that in 1621 Philip III reiterated the law, providing harsh penalties for offenders. Eventually, all Jesuits were expelled from Spanish dominions in 1767, and this naturally included northern Mexico.

Dobie says that Tayopa was located in an exceptionally isolated and inhospitable area of northern Mexico and during the year 1646, according to Jesuit records, only four people were encountered on the trail to the silver mine over a four-month period. Yet, it was a tremendously rich mine, and one that had probably been worked by the Toltecs and later by the Aztecs. Yet, this well known mine has remained lost for over 350 years! Presumably the large silver bells, bars and artifacts, valued today at over 100 million dollars, are still in the ground or inside the mine, even today.

Where is this lost mission, village and mine? Dobie's research indicated that it was somewhere in the eastern part of Sonora State, near the Chihuahua border, near a town named Nacori Chico. This town is easily found on maps. But other coordinates are not so easy to find. According to one source, Tayopa laid "somewhere between Nacori Chico and Guaynopa." Guaynopa is another fabled mine, equally lost.

Dobie says that Tayopa was mentioned in Britton Davis' autobiographical book *The Truth about Geronimo*.

Said Davis, "I first heard of the legend of Tayopa... This mine was said to have been of such wonderful richness that blocks of silver taken from it had to be cut into several pieces so that mules could carry them to the seacoast for shipment to Spain. My informant, the white-haired *presidente*, a man over 80 years of age, told me that his grandfather, who also had lived to be a very old man, had worked in the mine as a boy, and that it was in a mountain range to the east of Nacori."[32]

Davis said that when he came to Nacori Chico, the small town was in "a curious state of affairs. The population was 313 souls; but of these only fifteen were adult males. Every family had lost one or more male members at the hands of the Apache."

Dobie also quotes Davis as saying Mescalero Apaches had moved into the territory, and had always made it a policy to discourage mining and traders. One day they attacked Tayopa when the men were all away at a fiesta and killed everyone there, also setting fire to the town and attempting to destroy the entrance to the mine. For a hundred years after that, no force was strong enough to reoccupy remote Tayopa with the strong Apache bands nearby.

Dobie mentions that during the 1800s, the Apaches terrorized much of the countryside of northern Sonora and Chihuahua. In 1842, a strong band of Mescaleros, almost within sight of Chihuahua City, captured a train of 80 mules bringing freight from Vera Cruz. Only one Mexican escaped the attack. A bounty was set on Apache scalps that eventually attracted a group of adventurers and bounty hunters from north across the border.

The bounty hunters, led by Captain James Hobbs and including 70 Shawnee warriors working for Hobbs, followed the Apaches west into the area of Tayopa and the mountains lining the borders of Sonora and Chihuahua. After some days, they finally caught up with the Apaches near Tayopa, and a battle occurred from which Hobbs and the Shawnees emerged victorious. Having defeated the Apaches and taken scalps for the bounties, the troops explored the area. Dobie quotes from Hobbs' memoir saying that near a lake the group "found some ancient ruins, the cement walls and foundation stones of a church; and a lignum vitae cross, which seemed as sound as it had ever been. We also found remains of a smelting furnace, a great quantity of cinders [slag], and some drops of silver and copper. From the appearance of the ruins, it seemed as if there had been a considerable town there. The lake was at the headwaters of the Yaqui... We left the country with regret... Besides the remains of furnaces, we saw old mine shafts that had been worked, apparently long before. Specimens of gold, silver, and copper ore that we took to the mint at Chihuahua were assayed and pronounced very rich."[32]

The headwaters of the Yaqui, in these modern times, seems to be known as the Rio Aros. This is the same river that goes north from Nacori Chico. Dobie mentions a story from the area that "on a still night one could hear dogs bark and the church bell ring in Tayopa."[32]

I checked my maps of Sonora and Chihuahua as we drove north. Finding the lost mining town of Tayopa seemed a bit much for me on this trip, but this was the sort of thing I was keenly interested in. The Apaches were newcomers to the area, so the mining operation found by the lake was not theirs. It must have been the works overseen by the missionaries. But who showed them the mines? Maybe they were first worked by the Pima-Hohokam people of southern Arizona. Or maybe they were ancient mines of the Aztecs or Toltecs?

The Mysterious Origins of the Aztecs

If the Aztecs and their famous leader Montezuma really commanded a huge treasure at the time of the Conquest, in order to pursue what might have happened to it, we must examine the important questions of who the Aztecs were and where they came from. The wandering tribe today known as the Aztecs came into the Valley of Mexico, known then as Anáhuac, in AD 1168. This date is recorded in their written ideographic histories, known as codexes, and has been synchronized with our Gregorian calendar. This rather late date in history makes the Aztecs, like the Incas, very close to modern times, at least as far as "prehistoric civilizations" are concerned.

The Aztecs did not call themselves such. They said that they came from some fabled land, Aztlan, and apparently because of this the Spaniards referred to them as "Aztec." But it is certain that they neither called themselves that nor were they called that before the Conquest. They called themselves, like many tribes, "the people," or in their Nahuatl language, "Tenochas." Many archeologists called this tribe that dominated central Mexico at the time of the Conquest Tenocha-Aztecs. They named their capital city after themselves, Tenochtitlan: City of the Tenochas. For simplicity's sake, we shall call them "Aztecs."

The Aztecs claimed they came from a land to the north called Aztlan, and according to their origin myths, they emerged from a series of caves. Other cultures have similar myths: the Incas came out of caves; the Hopis came out of caves in the Grand Canyon; Greeks were given divine guidance at Delphi by a priestess in a trance in a darkened sanctuary; and many Christians experienced heavenly happenings in grottoes. According to Aztec history, they encountered the Hummingbird Wizard in one of the caves they traversed. This was the famous Huitzilopochtli (a name the conquistadors never mastered, calling him

Huichilobos, or "witchy-wolves").

Huitzilopochtli became the Aztec god of war, and they revered an idol they made of him. The idol spoke to them and gave them advice: wander, look for lands, avoid any large-scale fighting, send pioneers ahead, have them plant corn and when the harvest is ready, move up to it; keep me, Huitzilopochtli, always with you, carrying me like a banner and feed me on human hearts torn from the recently sacrificed... And the Aztecs did all this, moving southward from an unidentified land in either northern Mexico or in what is today the United States.

We do not know the size of the Aztec tribe when it reached the area of central Mexico, an area formerly controlled by the Toltecs. The Swiss archeologist Victor von Hagen estimates that the group was probably relatively small—perhaps a thousand, perhaps five thousand, not much bigger. In so thickly settled an area as the valley of Anáhuac (the location of present-day Mexico City) the small tribe's arrival probably passed completely unnoticed. Having settled in the valley, on a plain over 7,000 feet in altitude, the Aztecs grew in number. Their clans lacked sufficient women to make wives for all the men so they took to wife-stealing, and now for the first time their neighbors around the valley took notice of these foreigners.

Other tribes around the valley attacked and defeated the Aztecs. One part of the tribe was captured and forced into slavery, while another part escaped to one of the swampy islets out in Lake Texcoco. Says von Hagen, "Those left behind were involved in the wars of their captors, wherein they displayed such valor that when asked to name a boon, they asked for the daughter of the chieftain, so that through her they could form a respectable lineage. It was granted, but they sacrificed the beautiful girl, flayed her, and draped the skin over their head priest that he might impersonate the Nature Goddess. When the chieftain of their captors, the father of the girl, arrived in gorgeous array, he expected, naturally, to attend a wedding ceremony. Instead he found the horrible sight of his flayed daughter. One can somehow understand his wrath. Those Tenochas who escaped the butchery by his warriors fled and joined their tribesmen on the second islet on the lake."[14]

Lake Texcoco wherein the Aztec founded their capital Tenochtitlán, was one of five contiguous lakes that made up one large body of water; the other lakes were Chalco, Xochimilco, Xaltocán and Zumpango. From the high snow-covered mountains that surrounded the valley of Anáhuac there poured the brawling streams that made these lakes, which were fifty miles long, five hundred square miles in surface, and ringed with tall, slender marsh grass. The lakes were deep in some places but shallow in others, especially around the islets that formed the city of the Aztecs. The Aztecs dedicated their first temple in their year 4-Coatl (1325 AD) and began building wattle and daub houses thatched with the marsh grass. In the beginning, through agreements with the tribes that lived on the shore, they had permission to use borderlands for planting. They augmented these lakeside fields with *chinampa* agriculture, a method in which outsized wickerwork oval-shaped baskets were towed to their islets, anchored to the shallow bottom and filled with earth. In these they grew more crops.

During the years 1403-55 (the Aztec III period) the growing city-state, through alliance and war, depressions and recovery, outgrew the primitive stage and filled in the background with new and enlarged cultural horizons. They created artificial islands and causeways along the shallow sections of the lake. The Aztecs became the dominant tribe over much of Mexico and became the principal directors of life within and without the valley of Anáhuac. So they expanded, conquering other tribes and creating a great empire that would greet the Spanish explorer-invaders

23

in 1519. Their island city of Tenochtitlan, ever growing on reclaimed land, would become Mexico City, capital of a new empire.

Montezuma's Gold Sent North

We have already seen that the subject of metallurgy in Mexico is strangely controversial. What concerns us here is to establish that the Aztecs did indeed have gold, silver, copper and other metals, as well as, presumably, mines.

Von Hagen says that mining was rudimentary. "Gold was panned or collected in nuggets; silver, which seldom occurs pure in nature, was more of a problem and was less used. Gold is a metal of great ductility, for a single grain can be drawn into a wire five hundred feet long. It was worked by the Aztecs with the simplest of techniques. It was melted in a furnace, heated by charcoal, draft being supplied by a man blowing through a tube into the charcoal embers. There are few implements extant but we have been left illustrations of goldsmithery. They worked the gold by means of hammering, embossing, plating, gilding, sheathing."[14]

The marketplaces in Mexico typically contained goose quills filled with gold dust. Bernal Diaz, who accompanied the conquistadors on several of their earliest exploits and left invaluable chronicles of his observations, saw gold being freely traded in marketplaces, "placed in thin quills of geese, so that the gold could be seen through it."[4] Goldsmiths had a guild. Those attached to Montezuma's many-roomed household were non-taxpayers; they were supplied with placer gold and busied themselves making pieces for Montezuma and other officials. Bernal Diaz speaks of the "workers in gold and silver... and of these there were a great number in a town named Atzcapotzalco, a league from Mexico [City]."[4] Since the gold was sold in the market, presumably any craftsman who had enough to barter for goose quills of gold dust could work it up into jewelry for himself or else for trade.

Most of the gold extracted by the conquistadors from Montezuma, some 600,000 pesos weight of it, was melted down into ingots; some of it they thought too beautiful to destroy, like the pieces they received at Veracruz at the beginning of the adventure. According to Diaz's account, these included: "a wheel like a sun, as big as a cartwheel with many sorts of pictures on it, the whole of fine gold; and a wonderful thing to behold... Then another wheel was presented of greater size made of silver of great brilliancy in imitation of the moon... Then were brought twenty golden ducks, beautifully worked and very natural looking, and some [ornaments] like dogs, and many articles of gold worked in the shape of tigers and lions and monkeys... Twelve arrows and a bow with its string... all in beautiful hollow work of fine gold."

All this was sent intact to Holy Roman Emperor Charles V (King Charles I of Spain). He being then in Flanders, Cortez's ship was sent after him. He was at last found in Brussels, and, on July 12, 1520, Cortez's ambassadors presented the Aztec treasure to him. His comment, whatever it was, has not been recorded. That gold, like all the rest that came from the Americas, went into his crucibles to be made into ingots to pay the soldiery to maintain him on the tenuous throne of the Holy Roman Empire. Fortunately the great artist Albrecht Dürer was present at the time, and he left impressions of it in his diary. A descendant of a line of Hungarian goldsmiths settled in Nuremberg, Dürer knew what he was seeing. He wrote:

I saw the things which were brought to the King from the New Golden Land [Mexico]; a sun entirely of gold, a whole fathom broad;

25

likewise a moon entirely of silver, just as big; likewise sundry curiosities from their weapons, arms and missiles... of all which is fairer to see than marvels...

These things were all so precious that they were valued at 100,000 gulden. But I have never seen in all my days what so rejoiced my heart as these things. For I saw among them amazing artistic objects and I marveled over the subtle ingenuity of the men in these distant lands. Indeed I cannot say enough about the things which were there before me.

That was the only commentary on these masterpieces by anyone whose opinion meant anything. Emperor Charles V ordered that henceforth all gold and silver coming from the Indies be smelted down on arrival. Little survived—except the wonderful descriptions of the early conquistadors. So little gold was later to be found or seen, historians of the 18th century began to believe that the treasures of the Aztecs had been greatly exaggerated by the conquistadors. While there might have been some gold bars and some nicely worked ornaments, it was nothing like what was earlier claimed, the Aztecs simply not having had much gold or other metals for the conquistadors to loot.

This was proved wrong in 1931 when the Mexican archeologist Dr. Alfonso Caso found the undisturbed tomb of a Mexican chieftain at Monte Albán, south of Mexico City, containing superbly beautiful necklaces, earplugs, and rings. Historians realized that Mexico had, indeed, a vast store of metallurgical treasures.

So here begins the mystery of Montezuma's lost gold. The conquistadors had initially managed to acquire a fortune in gold and jewels from the Aztecs, but shortly afterward, no gold or jewels were to be found in the Aztec lands. So where did all the Aztec gold come from—and where did it go?

Lost Toltec and Aztec Mines of Jade, Turquoise and Emeralds

The Aztecs, Toltecs and other Mesoamericans used gold and silver to inlay precious stones. Lapidaries, workers in precious stones, were many, and "skilled workmen Montezuma employed." Foremost of the stones was jade. This was found in southern Mexico (now Guatemala) and valued more than gold itself, which Bernal Diaz found to his satisfaction, for he took four jades during the first Spanish retreat from Tenochtitlán and they "served me well in healing my wounds and gathering me food."

Jade was an article of tribute and the glyph for it is found in the *Aztec Book of Tributes,* a rare codex. It is utterly amazing how the Aztec craftsman achieved the delicate handling of so hard a stone; it required great patience. Everything of jade was saved, even the smallest pieces of the "precious green," to be put in the mouths of the dead to take the place of the stifled heart.

Jade was the most valuable of all stones to the ancient Chinese, Mayans, Olmecs, Mixtecs, Toltecs and Aztecs. A mystery surrounds the wide use of jade in Mesoamerica, as it was apparently abundant, yet only one source of jade in the Americas has ever been recognized: the jade mines near Quirigua in Guatemala. Von Hagen says that there is a difference, mineralogically, between the jade of America and that of the Orient, which should put to rest the idea that the American Indian got his jade from China; it is "American."

While numerous works of jade have been found, we are not sure where it all came from. Some jade may have come from southern Nevada, where jade mines also exist, but historians fail to accept this. There is also a Jade Cove along the central California coast. Jade is reportedly found here among the many rocks on the beach. Such a spot would be a treasure trove for Olmec or Toltec jade expeditions, or for a Chinese junk looking for the ultra-valuable gem.

It is known that turquoise came by trade from the north. It was much in demand and traveled almost as far as the Yucatan. The Aztecs exacted turquoise as a form of tribute according to records from eleven towns on the tribute rolls; it was used with other materials for the making of mosaics on masks, knives, and even walls.

One of the reasons the Aztecs and other Mesoamerican tribes didn't use metals for spearheads and swords as extensively as in the Old World was because of the high quality obsidian to be obtained near Lake Texcoco. Sharper than any metal, obsidian glass was an Aztec specialty; it was exported as raw material and as finished product. Found close by, a product of volcanic action, obsidian was used for knives, razors, lip plugs, mirrors of high polish, and other objects of immense beauty.

According to Victor von Hagen, emeralds (quetzal-itzli) were the prize gemstone for the Aztec as well as for the Spanish. José de Acosta, an early visitor to the New World wrote, "The Kings of Mexico didde much esteeme theme; some did use to pierce their nostrils and hang them therein, on the vissages of their idolles."[14] As soon as Montezuma was elected Chief Speaker of the Aztecs, the first thing he did was "to pierce the gristle of his nostrils, hanging thereat a rich emerald."

Says von Hagen:

> The conquistadors saw them as a symbol of riches. Hernán Cortez commandeered the whole of them for himself; he knew that Cleopatra wore emeralds and that a Christian pilgrim lately

from India saw them in a temple of Buddha, "flashing their fire two hundred leagues on a cloudless night."

As for the source, Montezuma expressed ignorance; they were from "the south." In fact, they were from only one region, the mountain areas in Colombia, about Muzo, which was the only source of emeralds at that time. They were plenteous in Colombia, where they were used for barter to obtain cotton and gold dust. They were well known in Panama and used to great effect in combination with gold. They were obtained for Montezuma by the activities of his pochteca merchants who penetrated beyond Nicaragua. Emeralds are soft and chip easily, yet the Aztecs cut them in intricate patterns—flowers, fish, fanciful forms of exquisite workmanship. Hernán Cortez got his emeralds directly from Montezuma, one in a pyramidal shape, "broad as the base of the hand," others so fabulous that Charles V is said to have coveted the fantastic baubles. Cortez refused 400,000 ducats in Genoa for them, saving them for Doña Juana de Zuniga, his betrothed, a daughter of a ducal family. He gave her five Aztec-worked emeralds, "one in the form of rose, one like a bell with a pearl for a tongue, one like a fish, one like a trumpet, one like a cup."[14]

So we see that the Aztecs were themselves the center of a vast trading network of jewels and valuable metals. Emeralds are a special mystery—not only are they the most precious of all gems, they are the rarest. Although von Hagen says the only source of emeralds was Colombia, we do not actually know where the Aztecs got their emeralds. Most emeralds even today come from South America, but is there a lost emerald mine somewhere in the American Southwest?

Turquoise came from the American Southwest. Jade came from southern Guatemala and perhaps Nevada. Gold and silver apparently came from many areas in Mesoamerica, including mines in the American Southwest and northern Mexico. Were the mines in the American Southwest ancient Toltec mines that the Aztecs had inherited? Had the Aztecs originally come from the lands of Arizona and New Mexico? Did Montezuma send the remnant of his golden hoard to the American Southwest to keep it safe from the conquistadors?

Toltec and older artifacts have been found as far north as Lake Pyramid in Nevada. Nevada State Anthropologist Donald Tuohy reported on a number of discoveries as early as 1973 and again in his *Nevada State Museum Newsletter* of March/April 1996. Tuohy reported that a fragment of a figurine found on the Walker Lake Paiute Reservation was identified as coming from central Mexico sometime between 300 BC and 300 AD. Another ceramic piece was etched with the figure of a man in a feathered-serpent headdress that was unquestionably from the Teotihuacan area, and was in Teotihuacan IV style which is around 700 AD. Another potsherd was found to be part of a leg of a tripod vessel made by the Toltecs in Mexico between 900 AD and 1500 AD. More on the fascinating subject of Toltecs in Nevada in a later chapter!

Mexcaltitan and the Claim for Aztlan

Over dinner that night in Gomez Palacio, I thought about Aztlan and the origin of the Aztecs. In the early 1990s the small island town of Mexcaltitan declared that it was the Aztlan of Aztec legend. An article in a 1968 issue of *National Geographic* first suggested this connection, but little has happened since then on that archeological front.

Mexcaltitan today lies in a mangrove swamp, and is home to 1,800 people. It contains a tiny museum that houses some pre-Hispanic pottery, but no evidence that it was the place from which the Aztecs took their first step into the history books. Locals are more concerned about shrimp fishing and preparations for the annual festival that takes place at the end of June, when the island's population triples for a few days of dancing and heavy drinking.

This little-known town is very interesting, however, in that it was built on man-made islands surrounded by concentric circles of canals, with causeways allowing access to the inner islands. Its construction is somewhat reminiscent of the Aztec's capital Tenochtitlan, built on reclaimed land in Lake Texcoco. This same configuration was used by the Phoenicians in building Carthage. Atlantis was also described by Plato as having concentric circles of canals with causeways leading in to the core. Recent books have even claimed that Mexcaltitan is the basis for the legend of Atlantis.[74]

In an article on Mexcaltitan entitled "Search for Aztec Homeland Clouded in Myth, Politics," by Alistair Bell (Reuters, June 22, 2004) it was claimed that Aztec legend says Aztlan was a small island on a lake inhabited by herons north of Mexico City.

Says Bell, "The small western state of Nayarit, long neglected by the federal government, declared itself the 'cradle of the Mexicans' in the early 1990s based on an old theory that the marshy island of Mexcaltitan was in fact Aztlan. Little stirs on the mosquito-infested islet nestled in a saltwater lagoon on the Pacific coast. An expected tourism boom to the state has mostly failed to materialize and the islanders still scratch a living from fishing for shrimp and lobsters."

Bell quotes Jesus Jauregui, an expert in western Mexico at the National Institute of Anthropology and History who says, "No serious archeological study has

31

ever been done in Mexcaltitan. Aztlan is a mythical place, not a historical one."

I think that Aztlan *is* a historical place, and its location will someday be determined. Bell says that the best clue to the origins of the Aztecs is their language, Nahuatl. The Aztec tongue is widely recognized by linguists as being part of the Uto-Aztecan family and related to the language of the Ute Indians of Utah as well as the languages of the Hopi and Comanche. These languages, in turn, are probably related to the Hohokam and possibly Toltec tongues.

Mexcaltitan may have been one of the stopping places for the Aztecs coming from farther north, and it may have been a Toltec town before it was Aztec. With Nahuatl speaking tribes found as far as away as northern Arizona, Utah and Colorado, it would seem that we must look farther north for Aztlan.

At the very least, Mexcaltitan shows us that there were important ancient port cities along the Pacific Coast of North America. The Olmecs had Pacific port cities in Guerrero and Chiapas states, which were probably later used by the Zapotecs and Mixtecs. The Toltecs may have also used these port cities, including Mexcaltitan.

Yet an even greater empire existed further north. This was Cibola and its cities of gold. Some legends said that there were seven lost cities of gold in the territories generally thought to be Arizona and New Mexico today. Other areas around these states could also be included, such as west Texas, Colorado and Utah.

One theory that has popped up from time to time is that the mysterious Aztlan of the Aztecs was also the legendary Cibola of American Southwest. Both were somewhere beyond the northern parts of Mexico. What great cities had once existed in the mountains, valleys and plains of the American West? How were they connected to the ancient empires of the Aztecs,

Toltecs and Olmecs?

Driving into the Zone of Silence

Thoughts of the Toltecs and the mysterious Aztlan bounced around my head as we drove along Mexico's Highway 45, going north toward the Zone of Silence and Chihuahua City. We had spent the night in Gomez Palacio and now the early morning sun began to give long shadows to the desert that stretched in every direction. Out there somewhere was the Zone of Silence.

Well, the Zone of Silence could wait until we'd had a big breakfast of *Huevos Rancheros*—fried eggs with tortillas and salsa. Soon the sun was blazing higher in the sky and a rugged desert stretched before us.

Our next stop would be the town of Ceballos, the gateway to the strange Zone of Silence. This bizarre, virtually uninhabited district on the Mexican side of the Rio Grande, across from the Big Bend area of Texas, is a twilight zone of weird animals, strange magnetic and vortex phenomena, mysterious lights and man-made hills.

In the early 1980s, paranormal investigator Gerry Hunt drove from the United States to Chihuahua to investigate the Zone of Silence. What Hunt reported seems fantastic by any standard. Hunt says in his book *The Zone of Silence*[6] that the area has seen gigantic UFOs, is bombarded almost nightly by meteorites and has been the target of government investigations by both the U.S. and Mexico. The area became known as the Zone of Silence because normal radios do not work within the 1,500 square mile area. Some sort of interference generated within the zone jams the signals.

Jennifer looked up from her map and looked around

sharply. "I think we just entered the Zone of Silence," she said. "Its on the map."

Checking it out, I thought the area looked pretty much the same as the others around it: dry scrub brush and rugged hills and ravines. Suddenly, the radio went out, and Jennifer began fiddling with it.

"We've lost radio contact," she joked. "Come in Devil Dog leader, over." We sat in silence after that.

According to Hunt, a U.S. Air Force *Athena* rocket was fired in 1970 from Green River, Utah and was programmed to land in White Sands, New Mexico but instead was drawn 900 miles off course and plunged into the Zone of Silence. The missile carried a deadly radioactive cobalt warhead, and the U.S. Military launched a massive recovery operation, building a special railroad spur into the zone and scooping up hundreds of tons of magnetic earth as well as the remains of the rocket.

Curiously, Hunt reports that rocket pioneer Werner von Braun made a mysterious visit to the zone just two months before the *Athena* rocket went off course. This raises speculation that the U.S. military purposely fired the rocket into the zone so as to be able to conduct special experiments there under the guise of recovering the rocket.

Says Hunt, the largest meteorite ever recorded exploded over the zone in 1969 in an earsplitting series of fireworks that made hundreds of petrified witnesses think that the end of the world was at hand. The meteorite, known as the Allende Meteorite, showered the desert with tons of fragments, portions of which were later recovered by scientists from around the world.

In September of 1976, a gigantic rectangular UFO with lights on its side passed over the small town of Ceballos on the edge of the Zone of Silence. It was witnessed by the population of the entire town, who came out into the streets as the craft passed over.[6]

In exploring the zone, Hunt claims to have seen six mile-long rectangular platforms of earth that are apparently man-made, as well as a man-made hill in the shape of a crumbling pyramid. Small carved stone statues have been discovered in the zone; some of the statues are of pumas, and one is of a man wearing a turban!

That this area of the Sonora desert is some sort of vortex area has been known for the past hundred years. According to an old *Ripley's Believe It or Not* cartoon "huge columns of sand appear suddenly in the Sonora Desert, in Mexico, and mysteriously whirl violently—although there is not the slightest breeze in the area." Ripley's is referring to the Zone of Silence.

Hunt says that creatures living inside the zone are often bizarre mutants, including tortoises and insects that grow three times the normal size. Centipedes are sometimes a foot long with purple heads, and tortoises have strange markings on their backs and no tails. It is the only known place where cactus grows in certain shades of red and purple. There is even said to be a Bigfoot type creature living in the area.

One of Hunt's theories is that the strange magnetism that is part of the zone attracts visitors from outer space who travel to the zone to recharge their silent engines that run on magnetic energy. Hunt likens the zone to the Bermuda Triangle, and says that the instruments of airplanes go crazy when flying over the area.[6]

At Ceballos, the town where the giant cigar shaped UFO had been seen years ago, we filled up the gas tank at the local Pemex station and then turned east and headed for a junction known as El Socorro. As we turned off the main road, we followed a dirt track that was leading east-northeast. I used the compass on the rearview mirror of my SUV.

Other dirt tracks occasionally branched off, and sometimes there was an old, small wooden sign that said, simply, "Zona." There was a flat-topped

35

mountain in the distance that we kept heading for.

After about 37 miles, we came to a sudden green spot, then it was desert again. After driving along the top of an irrigation ditch a short distance more, we abruptly came to the famed field of meteorites. They were everywhere! Millions of meteorites were all around us. Some had letters and symbols scribbled on them. We were definitely in the Zone of Silence!

It seemed incredible—all these meteorites all over the place. We drove to the top of the bluff that was dead ahead. As we came to the top, I stopped the engine and we got out of the SUV. There were stone circles made of meteorites, and the remains of campfires. Maybe we would camp for the night as well. We set up our tent, and later I gazed up at the countless stars in the cloudless night sky. I couldn't help but wonder—were more meteorites going to crash to earth tonight? Maybe we should sleep in the SUV.

I finished my lunch at Sanborn's restaurant in downtown Chihuahua City, the Zone of Silence and our night of watching the sky now fading away into my memory. Nothing particularly remarkable had happened, but it was a strange experience, nonetheless. Next to me was Jennifer, doing the Sudoku puzzle of the day. As I waited for the bill, I thought about the strange world of ancient Mexico—the Olmecs, the Maya, the Zapotecs, the Toltecs, and others. I thought of the enigma of the Aztecs and where they had come from. Somewhere to the north, according to their legends, was their homeland, Aztlan. It was still a lost land, gathering dust in the sands of time.

I helped Jennifer stow her backpack and we steered the SUV north on Mexican Highway 16 for Big Bend and the remote border town of Ojinaga—a town known for its association with the Devil. Most towns don't want to flaunt their problems with the Devil, but Ojinaga is an exception to that rule.

Ojinaga and its Struggle with the Devil

I played with the radio for some time, trying to get a station as we drove north for Ojinaga, on the Mexico-Texas border. It was still a few hours away on Highway 16.

"I can't get a station," I said.

"Maybe we're still in the Zone of Silence," offered Jennifer.

Technically we weren't, but it was still a remote area.

Ojinaga is today a border town with a population of about 10,000, across the Rio Grande from Presidio, Texas. Outside of town is "El Cerrito del la Santa Cruz," the Mount of the Holy Cross. According to legend, the Devil lives inside the mountain in "La Cueva del Diablo," or Devil's Cave, where strange things happened. This cave, with its many side passages, has frightened the local residents for generations.

Four hundred years ago, the Devil terrorized people from time to time by bouncing a gigantic metal ball like a basketball-playing Godzilla, smashing everything in his path. To save the community, a young priest fought with the Devil and forced him back into his cave. He then took a cross and sealed the cave. In Ojinaga they say that the Devil is even now inside the mountain. The steel ball he used to crush people and homes can be seen in the middle of town. It is known as the Devil's Ball and is now cemented into the sidewalk on Zaragosa Street. It has been painted yellow by the city, and is something of a small tourist attraction.

Ojinaga is an old town that played an unlikely part in the history of the earliest Spanish exploration in the New World. In 1528, an official Spanish expedition commanded by Panfilo de Narvaez was shipwrecked in the Gulf of Mexico somewhere near the land that is now Alabama and Florida. Narvaez lost his ships and his life in the incident. Incredibly, the second in command of the expedition, Alvar Nunez Cabeza de Vaca (whose family name means "Head of the Bull"), led a handful of survivors to the Mississippi where they built a raft. They re-entered the Gulf of Mexico and eventually made it to the Galveston area where they were captured by local natives (presumably the Tejas Indians) and made slaves. Cabeza de Vaca and his Moorish servant Esteban began showing a talent for miraculously curing people of diseases and other afflictions, and the captives were set free. They then wandered into southern Texas and, after coming upon the Rio Grande, began to follow it to the west.

Once they got into the rugged and remote Big Bend area, they came to Ojinaga. Along the way the ranks had been whittled away by attacks, accidents, disease and starvation until only four of the original expedition remained to stumble into Ojinaga. The year was 1535 and the town remembers the arrival of these first foreigners to this day. The nearby El Cerrito del la Santa Cruz got its name when Cabeza de Vaca planted his cross, which is the symbol by which he is identified in paintings and drawings, at its summit. Each year in Ojinaga, on the fiesta day of the Holy Cross ("la Santa Cruz") in May, the *matachines* dancers perform in a ceremony commemorating the event. The ritual probably started as a celebration in the old Indian religion, and was adapted into the trappings of Catholicism after the time of Cabeza de Vaca.

Ojinaga again made the history books when Pancho Villa rode on the town in one of the big battles of the Mexican Revolution in January 1914. Ojinaga was one of the last retreats of the *Federales*, the federal troops who fought for the new regime of Victoriano Huerta, a general who had usurped power from Francisco Madero and then had him killed. Madera had successfully opposed long-term dictator Porfirio

Diaz and taken power as leader of Mexico in 1911.

When Villa marched from Chihuahua City to Ojinaga to confront the *Federales*, many of them, including General Salvador Mercado and Pascual Orozco, fled to Texas for safety, as they knew they were doomed. The *Federales* were not welcomed in the United States, where President Woodrow Wilson had refused to recognize the leadership of Victoriano Huerta. They, along with their families, were led on a forced march up to nearby Marfa, Texas. From there, the U.S. Government loaded them into boxcars and sent them off to concentration camps away from the border.

Villa and his army executed any stragglers and suspected sympathizers of the *Federales*. He posed for movie photographers in the streets of Ojinaga, and stocked up on American military supplies. He is also said to have buried a large hoard of gold in a secret location near the Devil's Cave on El Cerrito del la Santa Cruz!

A curious side-note to this story is that the famous American writer Ambrose Bierce, author of *The Devil's Dictionary*, disappeared at the battle of Ojinaga. He had gone to Mexico to "ride with Villa," and was never seen again. His story is told at greater length in a book I co-authored with Stephen Mehler called *The Crystal Skulls*.[8] That book also tells the story of the famous British adventurer F.A. "Mike" Mitchell-Hedges, who also rode with Villa. He was the possessor of the famous crystal skull that bears his name. This controversial life-size crystal skull, said to come from a lost Aztec or Mayan city, is crafted from fine quartz crystal, worked against the grain (which would normally result in breakage) with a movable jaw carved from the same block. Interestingly, the deposed dictator Porfirio Diaz was said to have possessed a number of crystal skulls.

We spent the night in Ojinaga, getting a hotel in the downtown area around Zaragoza Street. That evening we ate in one of many of small restaurants near the main square. We made a toast to the Devil, with his caves, dictionaries, strange metal balls and lost treasure.

Northern Mexico was a land of awesome mountains and deserts. Remote and often hidden mines were still to be found in the Sierra Madre of northern Sonora and Chihuahua. Across the river was the American Southwest, a land that was once so foreign and inaccessible it was actually marked *Terra Incognita* on maps—"the unknown land." Sometimes called *Apacheria* because of the presence of the fierce Apache Indian tribes, it was an area so treacherous that in the 1800s it was considered one of the most dangerous places in the world! Indeed, it is still an enigmatic place—a place of mysterious lights, hollow mountains of gold, strange ruins and bizarre ancient tablets that tell of explorers from across the Atlantic that were searching for a New Jerusalem.

Above: On the tracks with Neal Cassady. The train station and railroad tracks at San Miguel de Allende where Cassady began his fateful midnight walk to the next town. Left: Neal Cassady, circa 1965. The beat goes on…

Heir's Pistol Kills His Wife; He Denies Playing Wm. Tell

Mexico City, Sept. 7 (*AP*).—William Seward Burroughs, 37, first admitted, then denied today that he was playing William Tell when his gun killed his pretty, young wife during a drinking party last night.

Police said that Burroughs, grandson of the adding machine inventor, first told them that, wanting to show off his marksmanship, he placed a glass of gin on her head and fired, but was so drunk that he missed and shot her in the forehead.

After talking with a lawyer, police said, Burroughs, who is a wealthy cotton planter from Pharr, Tex., changed his story and insisted that his wife was shot accidentally when he dropped his newly-purchased .38 caliber pistol.

Husband in Jail.

Mrs. Burroughs, 27, the former Joan Vollmer, died in the Red Cross Hospital.

The shooting occurred during a party in the apartment of John Healy of Minneapolis. Burroughs said two other American tourists whom he knew only slightly were present.

Burroughs, hair disheveled and clothes wrinkled, was in jail today. A hearing on a charge of homicide is scheduled for tomorrow morning.

No Arguments, He Says.

"It was purely accidental," he said. "I did not put any glass on her head. If she did, it was a joke. I certainly did not intend to shoot at it."

He said there had been no arguments or discussion before the "accident."

"The party was quiet," he said. "We had a few drinks. Everything is very hazy."

Burroughs and his wife had been here about two years. He said he was studying native dialects at the University of Mexico. He explained his long absence from his ranch by saying that he was unsuited for business.

Wife From Albany.

He said he was born in St. Louis and that his wife was from Albany, N. Y. They have two children, William Burroughs Jr., 3, and

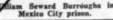

William Seward Burroughs in Mexico City prison.

(Associated Press Wirefotos)
The late Mrs. Joan Burroughs— killed at party.

Julie Adams, 7, who he said was his wife's daughter by a previous marriage. The couple had been married five years.

She had attended journalism school at Columbia University before her marriage to Burroughs.

Burroughs, who also had been married before, formerly lived in

Loudonville, a swank suburb of Albany. He is a graduate of Harvard University and worked for two weeks in 1942 as a reporter for the St. Louis Post-Dispatch.

His paternal grandfather laid the foundation of a fortune when he built his first adding machine in St. Louis in 1885.

News report on the accidental shooting of Joan Vollmer (his common-law wife) by Beat author William Burroughs in Mexico City on Sept. 6, 1951. (Reported in *New York Daily News*, 8 September, 1951 from a Mexico City report the day before.)

42

One of the "Atlanteans" at Tula, the former capital of the Toltecs located north of Mexico City and the Aztec capital of Tenochtitlan.

Top: Toltec panel at Chichen Itza in the Yucatan showing Toltec ships that were used along the Gulf Coast and possibly up large rivers such as the Rio Grande. Below: Toltec panel at Chichen Itza showing apparent human sacrifice with snakes emerging from a severed head. In Hinduism, the seven-headed snake god is Narayana, also known as Ananta.

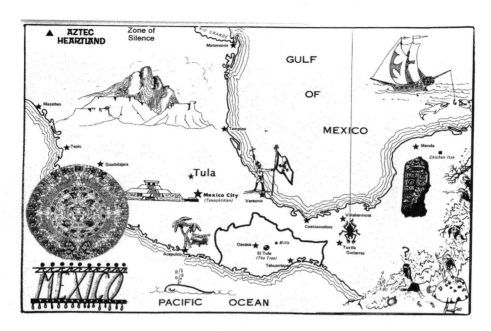

Above: A map of the Mexican heartland showing the Zone of Silence to the north, Oaxaca to the south, Mexico City (Tenochtitlan), and Tula, the Toltec capital. Below: The Mayan bridge at Yaxchilan. Were other sophisticated bridges built by the Toltecs or Hohokam further north?

45

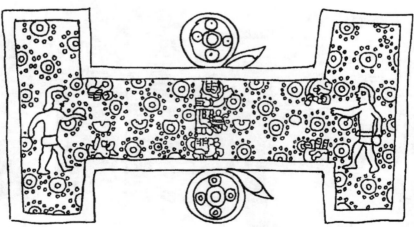

Top: The legendary home of the Aztecs, Aztlan, from an old Spanish manuscript. Aztlan may have been in what is now the American Southwest. Bottom: A diagram of an Aztec ballcourt from the Bourbon Codex. Ancient ballcourts have been found from Central America to northern Arizona and southern Utah. Rubber balls from Central America were prefered, but leather balls stuffed with cotton were also used.

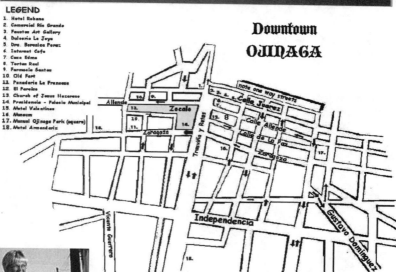

LEGEND
1. Hotel Rohana
2. Comercial Rio Grande
3. Fausten Art Gallery
4. Dulceria La Joya
5. Dra. Berenice Perez
6. Internet Cafe
7. Casa Edma
8. Tortas Real
9. Farmacia Santos
10. Old Fort
11. Panaderia La Francesa
12. El Paraiso
13. Church of Jesus Nazarene
14. Presidencia - Palacio Municipal
15. Motel Valentines
16. Museum
17. Manuel Ojinaga Park (square)
18. Motel Armendariz

Downtown OJINAGA

Top: The island city of Mexcalitan. Center: A map of the border town of Ojinaga. Left: The Devil Ball in downtown Ojinaga.

47

Indian laborers in the silver mine at San Pedro in northern Mexico. Note the ladders cut in a sawtooth pattern typically used in the mines of the Southwest and Mexico (right side of picture).

2.
TEXAS

MYSTERY LIGHTS AND LONE STAR STRANGENESS

West Texas cowboys, all over town
With gold and silver, they're loaded down
Just back from roundup, did seem a shame
So my uncle, starts a friendly game...
—Grateful Dead, *Me and My Uncle*

When the going gets weird,
the weird get going.
—Peter Braniff

Mexico and the eerie noise from the Zone of Silence faded behind us as we pulled out of Presidio, the tiny Texas border town across from Ojinaga. I imagined weird dust devils and strange radio static as the car sped down the road. The gas gauge said full. Things seemed off to a good start, I thought to myself.

Half an hour earlier, we had driven over the Rio Grande to American immigration and customs. I showed the immigration and customs officer my passport and he asked me if I had anything to

49

declare.

"Just some books that I bought and some tequila," I told him.

"How many bottles of tequila?" he asked, raising one of his eyebrows.

"Only two," I said.

"Go on," he said with a nod. He was looking for illegal immigrants, not tequila smugglers.

We stopped briefly to top up the tank. Jennifer decided to get some strawberry milk at the gas station store, while I checked out the map. Soon we were cruising east out of Presidio on Highway 170, on our way into Big Bend country. It was a bright September afternoon, and we looked forward to exploring the weird world ahead of us.

Texas Highway 170 follows the Rio Grande River through the Big Bend Ranch State Park. From its source in Rio Grande, Colorado, the river runs 1,900 miles south and east to empty into the Gulf of Mexico. It goes through Taos and Santa Fe, New Mexico then through Albuquerque and Las Cruces. It passes El Paso and from there, forms the entire southern border of Texas. Right around Presidio, the river takes a big bend, forming the large "spur" that can be seen in the south-western outline of Texas. As we followed the meandering waterway, I thought about this massive river system and the role it played in Southwestern history.

The rivers have always been the highways of any continent, and the Rio Grande is no exception. Tributaries of the upper Rio Grande lead all the way to the Zuni pueblos and Chaco Canyon. On the other side of the Rockies, over the Continental Divide, are the Hopi Mesas. Rivers on that side of the Divide all flow into the Pacific Ocean, including the Verde River which starts near the sacred Hopi mountain of San Francisco and continues due south to the Phoenix area where it turns west.

The Hopi Mesas were linked across the Continental Divide with the pueblos of Zuni and Acoma by an ancient road known as the Palatkwapi Trail. This ancient road spanning two rivershed systems, and connected to the famous Chaco Canyon road system, was first seen by a European in 1583. A Spanish explorer living in Santa Fe, Antonio de Espejo, had heard that a rich gold mine lay far to the west in the *Terra Incognita* (as the Spanish in Santa Fe called Arizona, Utah, California and Nevada at that time). When he set out to find this mine, he came upon the important trade route used by the Indians. More on the Palatkwapi Trail in a later chapter.

But had the Rio Grande River been a major highway of transport in ancient times? Stopped at a rest area, I looked around with my binoculars. Certainly, it was a major source of water in a dry land, but it would also seem likely that over the thousands of years of human discovery, a number of exploration parties must have found their way up from the Gulf of Mexico into this large river. They could have followed it for quite a way, deep into the southern Rocky Mountains of New Mexico.

If ancient explorers such as Egyptians, Phoenicians, Greeks and Romans came into the Southwest, one would think they would have left some evidence. Indeed, one would think that the Big Bend area would have been a noteworthy section of the waterway to these early explorers, as they followed the river around its twists and turns.

In fact evidence of such expeditions has been found. Strange artifacts such as coins, swords and shields (not of American Indian origin) have been found in Mexico and the United States. A small carved head (with a full beard and conical cap) found in 1933 in Toluca Valley west of Mexico City was determined to be of Roman orign.[36, 37] Close to the Rio Grande, the Los Lunas inscription site, near Albuquerque, has a rock shelter where odd carvings have been interpreted

51

to be the Ten Commandments![35] Another important bit of evidence was discovered at Big Bend Hot Springs—rock carved inscriptions on what has been called the Big Bend Mystery Tablet.

The Big Bend Mystery Tablet

We drove eastward through Big Bend Ranch State Park, past La Mota Mountain to our north. Leaving the State Park, the road stops following the river, and heads due east into Big Bend National Park. We drove past Hen Egg Mountain and into the Christmas Mountains. These mountains, and the Chisos Mountains in front of us, were weird, rocky outcrops in a fascinating variety of shapes. Some looked like walls, some had windows; some were giant round eggs and others, human profiles—this was the red, rocky world of Big Bend.

Big Bend, and West Texas in general, has always been sparsely populated. One early business was a health spa at Big Bend Hot Springs, which was eventually sold to the State of Texas in 1942. The State, in turn, ceded it to the Federal government for inclusion in Big Bend National Park. The aging resort in the remote and rugged region was run for a time by private contract, until 1952 when the resort was totally abandoned. The property deteriorated quickly, as the bathhouse had already been almost completely destroyed by floods, which also collapsed the motel veranda. The hot spring continued to flow, but the tourist traffic was down to a few adventurous backcountry hikers. Even today, Big Bend is a large and little visited National Park. It is one of the most remote areas of the continental United States.

Various hikers in the area came and went, and then in January of 1962, four hikers came to the hot springs and made the amazing discovery of the mysteriously inscribed stone tablet. Charles and Bernice Nickles operated a seaplane service in Alaska during the summers, but every winter, they came down to San Marcos, Texas to stay with their son, Donald Uzzell and his wife, Reva.

The two couples had been out searching for petroglyphs when they spotted what they thought might be a cave above them after crossing Tornillo Creek. They decided to investigate it, and Donald Uzzell scaled the steep rocks for 30 feet. He then squeezed himself into a crevice that from below looked like only a shadow on the cliff wall.

Inside this narrow cave Uzzell found seven stacked clay tablets with strange writing on them. Uzzell handed the tablets down one at a time to Charles Nickles, who had climbed partway up the cliff. Soon, they had the clay pieces safely down from the cave, and Donald, sometimes hanging by one hand, also made it down from the cliff.

The seven pieces fit together like a jigsaw puzzle to form a single, long tablet with 13 lines of writing. Fortunately, Donald Uzzell remembered he had a camera in his car and photographed the stone tablet and its very legible writing before placing the pieces carefully in the trunk. Realizing that they had stumbled onto something of major importance, they contacted the Park Service.

The pieces of the tablet were turned in to the Panther Junction Ranger Station, but some months later the Park Service told the Uzzells that they did not know what to make of them. They were clearly not Apache artifacts, but could otherwise not be identified.

Donald Uzzell began to send copies of the photos of the tablet to various people. Among them was the well-known Texas historian J. Frank Dobie, author of *Apache Gold and Yaqui Silver* as well as many other books on lost treasure, mines and other mysteries of the West. Dobie suggested an epigrapher named Dr. Lewis R. Church as someone who could possibly translate the tablet. The Uzzells sent a color print of Donald's photograph of the rock to Dr. Church who then passed it on to Dr. Leo Phillips of the Classical Languages Department at Brigham Young University in Utah. Both these men agreed that some of the characters were similar to very ancient Greek, but they could not actually identify the curious alphabet being used.

The Uzzells then contacted Bernice and Jack McGee, amateur epigraphers who had written several magazine articles on pre-Columbian inscriptions found on rocks in Oklahoma. The McGees immediately became intrigued and wanted very much to see the actual tablet.

The Uzzells and the McGees then began the ultimately futile attempt to get the pieces back from Big Bend National Park. Inquiries to the park headquarters got them in touch with the park's chief naturalist, Rollin Wauer. Wauer expressed interest in the tablet and assured the McGees he would do his best to find out what had become of the pieces.

Unfortunately, Wauer reported back that a search of park records revealed no mention of the tablet. The ranger who had accepted the pieces of clay from the Uzzells had since been transferred to Nevada. When Wauer called him, he did remember the tablet.

"It lay on the floor of the maintenance building for months," the ranger told Wauer. "I showed it to any and all that were willing to look at it, but everybody agreed it hadn't any antiquity nor historical significance. It disintegrated from all that handling and, when we moved it down to the new administration building, it turned into a pile of dust."

The McGees and the Uzzells were shocked and nearly crushed by this sad disclosure. The tablets had apparently been destroyed—not in some official cover-up, but by simple neglect. All they had left was the photograph, so they continued to mail it out. Copies of the photo were sent to the renowned historian Cyclone Covey, and to professor of classical languages John

54

Andronica. Both were very intrigued by the tablet and the strange writing.

Dr. Covey wrote to the McGees and said the inscription appeared to be authentic: "If the tablet were a hoax, Andronica and I would have spotted it at once. If the inscription were pure classical Greek, we could translate it, but there is another language mixed in the Greek letters. A lot of non-Greeks, both pagan and Christian, wrote Greek, including Phoenicians, Egyptians, Jews and Irish monks."[30]

In October 1970, nearly nine years after the tablet was originally brought into the light of day, the Uzzells, the Nickles, the McGees and Rollin Wauer of the National Park Service returned to the hot springs where the tablets had been found. Donald Uzzell reenacted his climb and thoroughly reexamined the narrow cave, but found nothing.

Dr. Covey continued to study the photograph. He consulted with other epigraphers, including Dr. Barry Fell, then the president of the American Epigraphic Society. Through their combined efforts, a translation finally began to emerge. The American Epigraphic Society would later call this "one of the most significant archaeological discoveries of the century."

Fell talks about the Big Bend Tablet briefly in his 1980 book (published by *The New York Times*) *Saga America*,[35] saying the inscription was extremely complex, a rich potpourri of mingled languages. It was written not in Greek, but in a variant of Libyan alphabetic script with repeated refrains in Lycian and Lydian. Says Fell:

For over 2,000 years America has served as a place of refuge for Old World communities driven from their homes by conquest or persecution. A situation only too well known in modern times, it would appear to reflect a historic role of the New World through much of recorded history. Not without justice does the Statue of Liberty bear the immortal lines penned by Emma Lazarus as she watched the immigrants stream ashore in 1903:

> Send these, the homeless, tempest-tost to me,
> I lift my lamp beside the golden door.

A curious clay tablet found in a rock crevice near Big Bend, Texas apparently tells us the Zoroastrians, followers of Mithraic sun worship, came once to America, seemingly from Iberia, though whether as refugees or not we cannot tell. More striking are the evidences from Tennessee and Kentucky, where the combined efforts of Dr. Henriettte Mertz, Professors Cyrus Gordon and Cyclone Covey, and Dr. Robert Stieglitz, have given us the outlines of an immigration there of homeless Jews after the several pogroms of Antiochus in Syria, and Nero and Hadrian in Rome.[35]

Fell goes on to say in all his books, including *Saga America*, that voyagers from the ancient kingdoms of Lycia and Lydia in West Asia Minor and Libya in northern Africa sailed daringly back and forth across the Mediterranean for hundreds of years before the birth of Christ, trading goods, knowledge and skills. It is from Lydia that we get the earliest known form of coinage; these are the gold coins first issued around 700 BC. King Midas reigned in Lydia. Were his ships, manned by the mighty sailors of Hittite, Phoenician and Greek origin, going up the Rio Grande to the gold mines of New Mexico?

Fell attempted to translate the inscription on the Big Bend Mystery Tablet. The lines of characters traversed the tablet in curious ways. Like many ancient texts, it was written in "boustrophedon" style, meaning, "as the ox plows." In this style, the first line is written from left to right, but the second line is written the reverse way, from right to left. Each phrase then alternates down the length of the text. Other oddball ancient languages are also written this way: Doric Greek, Hittite, Indus Valley script, Easter Island Rongo Rongo script, and others.

Fell read the text on the Big Bend tablet alternately left-right and then right-left. The first two sentences read:

Why this suffering?
Oh, what anguish.

The tablet then reads:

A call to prayer, 29th December, year 6
Heal us. Heal us. Heal us.
The faithful are beset by sorrows.
Guide, O Mithras,
Show forth thy strength and promise of aid
As revealed by Ahuramazda

Dr. Fell maintained that the message on the sun-baked clay was in the form of a prayer to the god Mithras asking for his divine intervention in the sorrowful lives of whoever wrote it. Three times the words "Heal us" are repeated in the text. He said that making tablets like this and hiding them in a cave, or perhaps carving an inscription on a rock face not easily reached to be defaced, was a fairly common practice among ancient explorers. They felt they needed to make sacrifices and to call upon the gods for favors, and from time to time, to make a written plea to the gods during a difficult moment in the journey.

Mithra was the Sun God in the pantheon of Zoroastrianism. Zoroastrianism began in about the sixth century BC in Persia, with the divine revelation of the nature of the universe to the prophet Zoroaster.

According to his teachings, the world is the scene of a never-ending struggle between darkness and light, and man has the free will to choose upon which side he will fight. The fight for right is led by Ahura Mazda, and Mithra was said to be the eye of Ahura Mazda, the Master of the World. Zoroastrianism is a very esoteric religion, and the knowledge of the stars and astrology was a key element. The Three Wise Men of the nativity story in the Bible, who followed the Star of Bethlehem for years in search of the king it foretold, were Zoroastrians.

Although it cannot actually be tied to Zoroastrianism, the cult of "Mithras" was a popular religion in the eastern Mediterranean in the early centuries AD, which was adopted and spread widely by the Roman legions. Their places of worship, known as "mithraea," were either modified natural caves, or man-made underground sanctuaries; they have been found from Hadrian's Wall in England to the shores of the Danube and the deserts of Palestine. It is interesting to note that these structures were similar in design to the kivas of the Pueblo Indians, being subterranean rooms with benches built along the sides for a maximum of 30 to 40 people. The central artwork of the mithraea was a work called a tauroctony, showing Mithras slaying a bull. Mithras often had the heavens under his cape, and a snake, a scorpion, a dog and a raven were often part of the picture. It has been postulated that this was not just a representation of some myth, but an allegory for the end of the Age of Taurus, with other key constellations, some from the Zodiac, also represented. The cult of Mithras was a mystery religion, the tenets of which were passed along from initiate to initiate, so no written records of their beliefs exist. It is clear, however, that knowledge of the stars was a specialty.

So the followers of Mithra (and apparently also Mithras) followed the movements of the heavens.

The Zoroastrians, like other ancient Mediterranean cultures, were expert stargazers. They knew all the stars and the lore connected to them. They knew the cyclical changes associated with the seasons, and understood the precession of the equinoxes.

The navigators of the ancient world were also stargazers, and it was by the stars that they navigated across the Mediterranean and then out into the Atlantic. These astrologer-navigators were able to use their knowledge of the stars to guide the many ships that crossed the Atlantic in prehistory. So perhaps it is not unusual at all to find a plea to Mithras inscribed by ancient seafarers moving up the Rio Grande.

Sailors in the Mediterranean were a mixed bunch, and just as today, crewmembers could have hailed from all kinds of backgrounds. The remnants of the seafaring powers would likely mix and match as kingdoms rose and fell. As we have seen, Doric Greek, the oldest known written form of that language, as well as Hittite, was written in the boustrophedon manner, the style used on the Big Bend Mystery Tablet. The famous Hittite port of Byblos, later a Phoenician port, was famous for its ancient books, probably written in boustrophedon pattern. The name of the Bible comes from this ancient port. As an interesting aside, there is now a theory that Homer's epics, *The Iliad* and *The Odyssey*, written about 800 BC, were a combination of star navigation tales and ancient history.

Ancient Hittite, Greek and Phoenician sailors generally sailed out of what is today Lebanon, Turkey (Lydia is today in coastal Turkey) or Cyprus, and these sailors had ports in North Africa, Malta, Spain and other areas near the Pillars of Hercules—the Strait of Gibraltar.

Barry Fell thought it was probable the group that left the Big Bend Tablet sailed from the Spanish peninsula, just like Columbus, crossing the Atlantic and eventually coming to the Gulf Coast. It may have been an isolated exploration mission, but more probably it was just one of many ancient transoceanic voyages. As we picked our way along a trail in the Chisos Mountains, I found myself wondering: Were these explorers and refugees trying to find the seven gold cities of Cibola? Maybe they were to establish them!

> *Well, you're lost in the rain in Juarez,*
> *When it's Easter time, too.*
> *And your gravity fails,*
> *And negativity don't pull you through.*
> —Bob Dylan, *Just Like Tom Thumb's Blues*

The Flying Terror of Texas Thunderbirds

Big Bend is also where the largest of pterosaur fossils has been discovered, the *Quetzalcoatlus*, with a wingspan of over 15 meters (45 feet). Despite its huge size, the skeleton was lightly built and the whole animal probably weighed no more than 100 kilograms (about 45 pounds). Its neck was extremely long, and its head was topped by a long, bony crest. Unlike most other pterosaur fossils, the *Quetzalcoatlus* remains were not found in marine strata but in the sand and silt of a large river's flood plain and this has raised questions about how it lived.

Though it is thought that this giant pterosaur became extinct over 65 million years ago, sightings of pterosaurs has continued in Texas right up to this day. As I reported in my book *Lost Cities of North & Central America*,[18] a wave of pterosaur sightings happened around the Rio Grande in the mid 1970s.

One of the first encounters was in the early hours of December 26, 1975 when a rancher named Joe Suárez discovered that a goat he had tied up in a corral in Raymondville, Texas (about 30 miles north of the Rio Grande in southeastern Texas), had been ripped to pieces and partially eaten by some unknown assailant. The goat had been mauled from the right side and was lying in a pool of blood with the heart and lungs missing with the snout bitten away. The blood was still wet and warm when police officers examined the carcass. They could find no footprints around the goat and concluded that a flying creature of unknown origin had caused the death.

Then, in the same town, on January 14, 1976 at about 10:30 in the evening on the north side of Raymondville, a young man named Armando Grimaldo was sitting in the backyard of his mother-in-law's house when he was attacked by a strange winged creature.

"As I was turning to go look over on the other side of the house," said Armando to the Raymondville press, "I felt something grab me, something with big claws. I looked back and saw it and started running. I've never been scared of nothing [sic] before but this time I really was. That was the most scared I've ever been in my whole life."

This strange flying attacker dove out of the sky— and it was something Grimaldo described as being about six feet tall with a wingspread he estimated as being from ten to twelve feet. Its skin was blackish-brown, leathery and featherless. It had huge red eyes.

Grimaldo was terrified. He screamed and tried to run but tripped and fell face first into the dirt. As he struggled up to continue running for his mother-in-law's house, the beast's claws continued to attempt to grasp him securely, tearing his clothes, which were now virtually ripped to shreds. He managed to dive under a bush and the attacking animal, now breathing heavily, flew away into the sky.

Grimaldo then crashed into the house, collapsing on the floor, muttering "pájaro" (Spanish for bird) over and over again. He was taken to the hospital, treated for shock and minor wounds, and released.

Blazing Red Eyes

A short time later, in nearby Brownsville, on the Rio Grande, a similar creature slammed into the mobile home of Alverico Guajardo on the outskirts of town. Alverico went outside his trailer to investigate the crash he had heard. When he noticed a large animal next to the crash site, he got into his station wagon and turned the lights on to see the creature, which he later described as "something from another planet."

As soon as the lights hit it, the thing rose up and glared at him with blazing red eyes. Alverico, paralyzed with fear, could only stare back at the creature whose long, bat-like wings were wrapped around its shoulders. All the while it was making a "horrible-sounding noise in its throat." Finally, after two or three minutes of staring into the headlights of the station wagon, it backed away to a dirt road a few feet behind it and disappeared in the darkness.

These were just the first of a number of bizarre encounters with seemingly prehistoric "birds." Also in January of 1976, two sisters, Libby and Deany Ford, spotted a huge and strange "big black bird" by a pond near Brownsville. The creature was as tall as they were and had a "face like a bat." They later identified it out of a book of prehistoric animals as a pterosaur.

The *San Antonio Light* newspaper reported on February 26, 1976, that three local school teachers were driving to work on a road to the south of the city on February 24 when they saw an enormous bird sweeping low over cars on the road. It had a wingspan of 15-20 feet and leathery wings. It did not so much fly, as glide. They said that it was flying so low that when it swooped over the cars its shadow covered the entire road.

As the three watched this huge flying creature, they saw another flying creature off in the distance circling a herd of cattle. It looked, they thought, like an "oversized seagull." They later scanned encyclopedias at their school, and identified the creature as a pterosaur.

The sightings of flying reptiles over Texas subsided for a while, but then on September 14, 1982, James Thompson, an ambulance technician from Arlingen, saw a "birdlike object" pass over Highway 100 at a distance of 150 feet or more above the pavement. The time was 3:55 in the morning, and this huge flying creature was obviously a night hunter. "I expected him to land like a model airplane," Thompson told the *Valley Morning Star*, the local Rio Grande newspaper. "That's what I thought he was, but he flapped his wings enough to get above the grass. It had a black or grayish rough texture. It wasn't feathers. I'm quite sure it was a hide-type covering. I just watched him fly away." It was as if he were describing the same flying creature as the others: a pterodactyl-like bird.

Paranormal investigator Scott Corrales relates a tale of a similar animal on his web pages, *Mundo Misterioso* (Sept. 23, 2005) about an incident reported in Mexican newspapers. Around 10:30 p.m. on September 22, Jesus Gel Gonzalez of the village of Rancho El Cadillo, Mexico, called police to report six of his goats were found dead with strange, deep wounds on their necks. The bite marks appeared to be the result of some large predatory animal. Corrales says that Gonzalez told the police he had earlier that evening seen a strange creature standing 1.2 meters tall (4 feet), gray in color and with a 4-meter wingspan (12-foot), which he suspected as the culprit in the goat slayings. He added that this is not the first time animals have been killed on his property. Besides livestock, several of his dogs had also disappeared.

Corrales writes that police who investigated the scene of the attack reported finding large prints resembling four-fingered claws. Corrales believes that a Chupacabras was responsible for the incident and says, "Researchers say neither a puma nor coyote could be responsible for the attacks because they rip and tear at their prey. Whatever killed the goats did so by sucking their blood through fang-type wounds in their necks."

Was this a modern attack of a Thunderbird-Pterosaur still living in the remote mountains of northern Mexico? Do the sharp teeth on pterosaurs allow them to rip flesh and drink blood? With stories like these we start to get the idea that the Chupacabras, the Thunderbird and living pterosaurs may all be one and the same animal.

British investigator Ken Gerhard relates the curious testimony of Richard Guzman in his book, *Big Bird!*[27] whom Gerhard met in the fall of 2003. Guzman said that he and a friend named Rudy had witnessed a very strange giant bird in a suburb of Houston around 1983. Guzman recalled that he was in his early 20s and it was a hot and clear day, around six in the evening. He and Rudy were leaning against his car that was parked in front of his house on Lucore Street in southeast Houston.

The two were looking out over a field when suddenly they spotted a strange animal about 40 yards away flying across the field, about 50 feet off the ground. The two watched it for 15 seconds or so while the large, strange "bird" flapped its wings a few times and then glided out of sight to the southeast into some tall trees.

The two men were astounded and looked at each other, wondering if they had both seen the same thing. They confirmed to each other that they had seen what looked like a pterosaur. Guzman told Gerhard that the first thing he noticed was a prominent hump on the back of the creature's head. Even more noticeable, he said, was the two-foot long, snake-like tail that terminated in a fin. Guzman said that the animal was about five feet long, had bat-like wings, appeared to be featherless, with skin that resembled brown—or beige—leather. He also recalled some sort of indentation in the creature's skull. He drew a sketch for Gerhard that looks remarkably like a pterosaur of some sort.[27]

Gerhard also investigated Frank Ramirez in south Texas, who claimed an encounter with a bizarre giant bird in November of 2007. Ramirez, in a local television interview, told Gerhard that he at first thought the noise he heard was a prowler outside his mother's home. Now he says that what he saw on her garage roof is still giving him goosebumps.

Ramirez reportedly said, "Even though it was dark, the thing itself was black. The blackest I'd ever seen. When the thing up there turned toward me, it was in a perched state. It started to move its arms [wings?] and I just ran."

He gave Gerhard a sketch of the creature that was of a large, bird-like animal. Ramirez said the face was the most disturbing thing about the creature. It reminded him of a man's face but with the chin stretched way down. The being was what we might describe as a demon or gargoyle.

Gerhard believes there very likely could be an unidentified flying creature in the region. He bases his assumption on the fact that in south Texas there are still vast areas of land that are uninhabited by humans.

A local Ranger named Stacy Sanchez told Gerhard that she's received numerous reports from witnesses who told her that in the summer of 2007 they saw a raptor-like bird with an 18 to 20 foot wingspan—far larger than any normal bird that is known to exist.

Gerhard and Ramirez did a television interview in which Gerhard said that he's installed cameras in several areas where the huge creature—or creatures—have been sighted in the hope he can get video evidence to convince the skeptics that prehistoric-like birds still fly our skies.

The television interview ends with Ramirez saying that he has installed outdoor lights around his mother's house with the hope it will keep the creature he saw from returning! (Reported by MYSA.com via Kens5Team, TX, Nov. 16, 2007).

Other sightings have been reported in other states, including a well-publicized case in Alaska. "He's huge, he's huge, he's really, really big." So said pilot John Bouker about the gigantic bird the size of a small airplane that he and several others reported seeing flying over southwest Alaska in October 2002. According to the *Anchorage Daily News* on October 15 of that year, Bouker had been skeptical when he heard other reports of giant birds. Then he and his airplane passengers saw one for themselves. Scientists still are not sure what Bouker and the others observed.

I scanned the sky briefly and wondered why Texas had more reports of pterosaurs than other states. Maybe because the "Big Bird of Big Bend" had managed to survive through the millennia, or perhaps Big Bend was a doorway to another world through which they and other strange things from time to time.

A Peek at the Past

We headed north on Texas Highway 385, out of Big Bend National Park toward Marathon. From here we turned west on Texas Highway 90 toward Alpine and Marfa. The sun was starting to get low in the sky; it would be dark in a couple of hours.

I wondered about the ancient world of Texas—had some lost world once existed here among the prairies, rivers and deserts? On April 2, 2006, *The Victoria Advocate* newspaper out of Victoria, Texas (southwest of Houston and north of Corpus Christi) carried an article with the headline: "A Complex People Lived Here 7,000 Years Ago."

The article claimed that an advanced culture had lived in the area and had apparently had contacts with the people of the lower Mississippi Valley and even Florida, something that shocked archeologists (who generally assume ancient man was primitive and had little contact with other communities).

Said the article (available at www.VictoriaAdvocate. com):

> A study of ancient human remains and artifacts found in the Guadalupe River floodplain of south Victoria County shows that a relatively advanced people who had contacts with others living hundreds of miles away populated the area.
>
> "We did not know this culture existed. Period," said Bob Ricklis, the lead archaeologist studying the items. "We didn't know anything about it."
>
> He said not only did it exist, but it apparently did well. He said the people had lifespans comparable to modern-day people and had contacts with others as far away as what later became the Southeast and Midwest United States.
>
> "They are more advanced than we would have expected," Ricklis said.
>
> ... "We're rewriting history because of what's been found out here," he said. "This is of great importance."
>
> He said not only does it rewrite the history of the region, but of the nation.
>
> The excavation produced a large collection of artifacts dating back from 500 to 10,000 years, Ricklis said. A prehistoric cemetery thought to date back at least 7,000 years was also discovered.
>
> "It's one of only three of that magnitude in North America," Ricklis said. He noted that the other known cemeteries older than 5,000

years are Carrier Mills in Southern Illinois and Windover on the east coast of Florida. He also said archaeologists didn't even suspect that people in Texas had major cemeteries 7,000 years ago.

"It's a sizeable cemetery," Ricklis said. "We excavated about 80 burials, but there are a lot more than that in the site."

He estimated there could be as many as 200 burials there that date back 7,000 years. Based on radiocarbon dating, he said, the oldest of the human remains tested dates back 8,500 years.

Ricklis said researchers are confident the site was occupied as far back as 10,000 years ago because of flint points found there that are known to be from that period. "Specifically, we found dart points of the Golondrina, St. Mary's Hall and Wilson types, all known to date to before 9,000 years ago."

Ricklis said he has no idea where the predecessors of these Native Americans originated, but there is nothing to indicate a European connection. He said they could be part of an early population that may have come from northeast Asia.

But he added some in the field question that and believe there may have been immigrants from Europe or the Pacific region who contributed to early American populations.

"Probably the most interesting thing we have regarding the cemetery is a lot of artifacts found with the burials and placed in the graves as offerings," Ricklis said.

He said those artifacts are evidence of links to the Mississippi River Valley, the Southeast United States and possibly even Mexico.

Examples include bannerstones, flint projectile points, beads, shell pendants, and bone and antler tools for working flint. A bannerstone is a piece of stone that was worked by pecking and grinding into an oblong shape. It was typically 4 to 6 inches long, carefully crafted and usually smoothed, sometimes to a polish.

"The bannerstones are not typical of Texas," Ricklis said. "The ones we have are of a certain type much more common in the Mississippi Valley and the Midwest."

Also found were plummets, or teardrop-shaped stones, that have been drilled and are more typical of the Southeast for this time period.

Ricklis said he still doesn't have the final report on the physical anthropology showing the sex and age of the people. But the study showed there were several individuals who lived to be 70 years old and still had their teeth, indicating they led relatively healthy lives.

So, in 5000 BC and even earlier, people in Texas were trading with Mississippi and Florida (and probably Mexico) and living long, happy lives! What happened to these people? Did they simply vanish like so many other civilization of the Southwest?

The Mystery of Rockwall, Texas

As we headed toward Alpine, Texas I wondered about the weird stuff of the Lone Star state. Just north of Dallas is the strange "ruined city" of Rockwall. While geologists claim that it is just a bizarre natural formation that looks like a series of walls and rooms, others think that it is genuinely the remains of some sort of very ancient, man-made structure.

Since the mid-1800s, residents of Rockwall had been digging around what seemed like vertical walls of stacked stone that had been buried in some ancient cataclysm. The first Anglo-American settlers moved into the area in 1851, and established the town in 1854. During the digging of the early wells they discovered the underground rock formations, many of them over 40 feet high, and named the town after what they thought were man-made walls.

Frank Tolbert, a well-known columnist for the *Dallas Morning News*, wrote about the buried city under Rockwall in his November 5, 1967 column. Tolbert mused that the longest-lasting argument in Rockwall County, the smallest county in Texas, was whether or not four of its 147 square miles contained the great stone walls of an ancient fortification or if, as most geologists insisted, the walls were simply "nature's masonry in the shape of sandstone dikes."

Tolbert related that Raymond B. Cameron of Rockwall had once told him that the walls of the mystery city were about eight inches thick, and that the stones had been formed (or placed) on top of each other with the ends breaking near the center of the stone above or below, just as a fine mason would lay bricks in a wall. The stones gave the appearance of having been beveled around their edges, and the walls were too regular in appearance to have been formed by nature. Cameron went on to say that there was a mortar-like substance between the stones.

He then surprised Tolbert by stating, "Four large stones taken from wall segments appear to have been inscribed by some form of writing. This couldn't have been done by erosion, since the stones were underground."

In his column, Tolbert also recalled the visit of a famous archaeologist, Count Byron Kuhn de Prorok, to Dallas and Rockwall in the 1920s: "The count seemed to lean heavily on the theory that these were once the walls of an ancient city. He said the walls looked remarkably like those of buried cities that he had excavated in North Africa and the Middle East."

That there would be writing on some of the stones

seems very curious, and to my knowledge, these stones have disappeared. Count Byron de Prorok was a popular archeologist-adventurer in the 1920s and 30s, very much a pith-helmet-wearing Indiana Jones type who wrote a number of books on lost cities, Atlantis, and King Solomon's Mines among other topics. He was a believer in Atlantis and other ancient civilizations, and had seen many ancient ruins in North Africa, Central America and the Middle East. His belief that the strange walls of Rockwall were indeed the handiwork of ancient man may lend some credibility to that theory of the walls' origin.

Ancient Inlaid Mosaic Tile Floor

Curiously, other buried remains giving evidence of some advanced civilization in the area comes from just north in Oklahoma. Brad Steiger, the well-known syndicated newspaper columnist and author, reported that on June 27, 1969, workmen leveling a rock shelf at 122nd Street and the Broadway extension between Oklahoma City and the suburb of Edmond, uncovered a rock formation that looked just like an inlaid mosaic tile floor.

Oklahoma City geologist Durwood Pate was quoted in the Edmond *Booster* of July 3, 1969, saying: "I am sure this was man-made because the stones are placed in perfect sets of parallel lines which intersect to form a diamond shape all pointing to the east. We found post holes which measure a perfect two rods from the other two. The top of the stone is very smooth, and if you lift one of them, you will find that it is very jagged, which indicates wear on the surface. Everything is too well placed to be a natural formation."

Steiger says that Delbert Smith, a geologist and president of the Oklahoma Seismograph Company, said the formation, which was discovered about three feet beneath the surface, appeared to cover several thousand square feet. On June 29, 1969, Smith told the

71

Tulsa World, "There is no question about it. It has been laid there, but I have no idea by whom."[11]

Steiger also mentions private correspondence from a W. W. McCormick of Abilene, who related his grandfather's account of a strange wall that was found buried in a coalmine:

> In the year 1928, I, A. A. Mathis, was working in coal mine No. 5, located two miles north of Heavener, Oklahoma. This was a shaft mine, and they told us it was two miles deep. The mine was so deep that they let us down into it on an elevator… They pumped air down to us, it was so deep.
>
> One night I shot four shots [referring to the charge to blast the coal loose] in room 24 of this mine, and the next morning there were several concrete blocks laying in the room. These blocks were 12-inch cubes and were so smooth and polished on the outside that all six sides could serve as mirrors. Yet they were full of gravel, because I chipped one of them open with my pick, and it was plain concrete inside.
>
> As I started to timber the room up, it caved in—and I barely escaped. When I came back after the cave-in, a solid wall of these polished blocks was left exposed. About 100 to 150 yards farther down our air core, another miner struck this same wall—or one very similar.
>
> Immediately, [the mining company officers] pulled us out of this wing and forbade us to tell anything we had seen.
>
> The mine was closed in the fall of 1928, and the crew went to Kentucky.
>
> Before I started working on this crew, they had a similar experience in mine 24 at Wilburton, Oklahoma in about the year 1926. They said they dug up two odd things: One was a solid block of

silver in the shape of a barrel, and the other was a bone that was about the size of an elephant's leg bone.

The silver block had the imprints of the staves on it, and the saw that first struck it cut off a chip on the edge of one end. The miners saw the silver dust the saw was pulling out and went back to dig out the block.

What was done with these things, I do not know. In the case of the blocks in my room in No. 5, I don't think any were kept.[11]

According to Steiger an iron pot was found inside some coal that was reported to come from the Wilburton mines where the strange artifacts were supposedly found. Steiger says that Frank J. Kenwood, a fireman in the Municipal Electric Plant in Thomas, Oklahoma, was at work in 1912 when he split a large piece of coal and discovered an iron pot encased within.

"This iron pot fell from the center, leaving the impression or mold of the pot in the piece of coal," Kenwood wrote in a letter to a friend. "I traced the source of the coal, and found that it had come from the Wilburton, Oklahoma, mines."[11]

Certainly, some of the remains found in Texas and Oklahoma were pretty bizarre. Polished concrete blocks? A solid silver replica of a barrel? An iron pot inside a block of coal? What would seem to be impossible artifacts may merely be remnants of the end of the Third World that many Native American cultures say preceded ours—or maybe the end of the Second World, or the First…

You go south from Fort Davis until you come to the place where rainbows wait for rain, and the big river is kept

*in a box and water runs uphill. And
the mountains float in the air, except at
night, when they go away to play with
other mountains.*
—attributed to "an old forgotten cowboy,"
National Geographic, January 1968

The Mystery of the Marfa Lights

As we made our way out of Alpine, it started to rain.
We still had a few more miles to go to Marfa. Before
we reached the town, our headlights hit a highway
sign in the evening drizzle. Jennifer suddenly grabbed
my arm.

"There it is!" she shouted. "Quick, pull over!"

The sign indicated we had reached the "Marfa
Lights Viewing Area" on Texas Highway 90 between
Alpine and Marfa. I quickly signaled and then pulled
off the road. To our surprise, we found ourselves in
an official Texas Highway Rest Area, complete with a
bronze commemorative plaque, restrooms and a large
map of west Texas. I parked next to a white pickup
truck, one of several cars in the parking lot. The drizzle
began to abate, and we got out of the SUV. The night
was chilly, and we knew the moment we stepped
out of the car that we were underdressed. But in our
excitement, we charged on up the walkway past the
plaque and building, on to the official viewing area.
Several people were there, some looking through
the mounted binoculars kindly provided by the
state. Everyone was looking off to the right, toward a
mountain ridge. People were exclaiming things like,
"Oh, there's another one!"; "Can you beat that?!"; "I
wonder what they are?!"

Freezing, knowing we'd need a lot more time at
the site, we hurried back to the car. While we donned
jackets and pulled out blankets, Jennifer confessed

to me that she had not seen the lights. I could hardly believe this, since no one else out there seemed to be missing them. When we returned to the viewing area, I pointed out the big white lights bobbing in front of the mountain ridge to Jennifer. "*Those* are the Marfa Lights?" she asked incredulously, adding, "I was looking for something a lot more ... obscure! I just assumed *those* were headlights of cars on a road over there."

That about sums up the Marfa Lights: they are the most obvious mystery I've ever seen.

The bronze plaque, placed by the State of Texas, gave this description of the lights:

> The Marfa Mystery Lights are visible on many clear nights between Marfa and Paisano Pass as one looks toward the Chinati Mountains. The lights may appear in various colors as they move about, spilt apart, melt together, disappear and reappear.
>
> Robert Reed Ellison, a young cowboy, reported sighting the lights in 1883. He spotted them while tending a herd of cattle and wondered if they were Apache Indian campfires. Apache Indians believed these eerie lights to be stars dropping to the earth.
>
> Many viewers have theories ranging from scientific to science fiction as they describe their ideas of aliens in UFOs, ranch house lights, St. Elmo's Fire, or headlights from vehicles on US 67, the Presidio highway. Some believe the lights are an electrostatic discharge, swamp gasses, moonlight shining on mica or ghosts of Conquistadors searching for gold.
>
> An explanation as to why the lights cannot be located is an unusual phenomenon similar to a mirage, when atmospheric conditions produced by the interaction of cold and warm layers of air

bend light so that it can be seen from afar, but not up close. The mystery of the lights still remains unsolved.

Well, here was the official State of Texas explanation for the strange Marfa Lights. Another notice at the roadside area said that the Marfa Lights were the most consistent anomalous phenomenon in the USA, if not the world. Essentially, the Marfa Lights, as yet unexplained, could be seen almost every night (not just on clear nights as the first plaque seemed to indicate—witness the fact that we were seeing them on a rainy night). This is rather convenient for mystery hunters like myself, as I could essentially pop up at the Marfa Lights Viewing Area any night I wanted, and observe the mysterious lights myself. Indeed, this was very much the case.

After perusing the plaques, I went back to the observation area and looked out into the dark night in the distance. Sure enough, there were several white lights still dancing about out there. Then suddenly they were gone. Then a blue light appeared to one side. Then there were two lights. Then suddenly there were three. They moved about in the distance. Then they were gone. I stared into the darkness. They came back again. There were two lights, one blue, one white. Then only the white light could be seen. Then it was gone, too.

This went on for quite awhile. I looked at the lights through the binoculars. They were bright, fuzzy, and distant. They moved around. They disappeared. They came back. There were different colors: white, blue, yellow, even red.

Jennifer and I got bored with watching the lights after about two hours.

"Well, I've had enough of this anomalous phenomenon," I said. "Let's go back to Alpine and have dinner."

Back in Alpine we ended up at a Mexican restaurant after finding a motel, and began our research into the mysterious Marfa Lights. We found that there were many legends, stories, and explanations for the lights—from the good scientific guess to the utterly wacky.

Marfa My Dear

As mentioned on the official Marfa Lights plaque, sightings of the lights go back to at least 1883 when the young cowboy Robert Reed Ellison reported them. Apaches had noticed the lights before then.

Mrs. W. T. Giddens, who was raised in the Chinati Mountains where the lights are most often seen, told "Off the Beaten Trail" columnist Ed Syers (apparently some time in the 1950s) of a tradition in her family. "I've seen the Ghost Lights all my life and can't remember their causing any harm other than fright. They like to follow you out in the pasture at night, seem to be drawn to people and stock, and animals don't seem to fear them at all." Then Mrs. Giddens told about her father, lost at night in a blizzard miles from home. He thought he would freeze to death when he saw the Marfa Lights flashing almost on him. They "said" to him (he could never explain how) that he was three miles south of Chinati Peak, off his trail, heading in the wrong direction. They "told" him he would die if he didn't follow the lights, which he did. They led him to a small cave, and in that shelter he lived through the night, the largest of the lights staying close beside him. Somehow he was "told" they were spirits from long before that wanted to save him, and that he could sleep now without freezing to death. With morning both the lights and the blizzard were gone. And as anticipated, he saw that he was off the trail, three miles south of the Chinati Peak. Then getting home was no chore at all.[21]

This story may have spawned other legends, such as the one of a cowboy who was lost in a blizzard at night at the foot of the Chinatis. A ghost light appeared and at first he tried to get away from it, but it followed him. Changing his mind, he followed the light for hours, and it made him feel comfortable somehow. When the light suddenly disappeared, the cowboy was happy to find that it had led him to one of the Presidio County Airport gates. Then he followed the road home to Marfa.

The Marfa Lights are friendly in other tales as well, such as the one that says the lights are the ghost of a rancher who once owned the land, and they always shine brighter on his birthday. Another tradition says that early settlers used the Marfa Lights as a guide across Mitchell Flat to avoid encounters with hostile Indians.

Some legends say the lights are the ghosts of Indians. According to one of these legends, Apaches were camped on the flat, on their way to plunder in Mexico. Soldiers from Fort Davis attacked and annihilated most of them. Seeking vengeance, survivors stole lanterns from the settlers and moved around at night, hoping to lure the soldiers into a trap. Their ghosts are still waving their deceptive lanterns to this day. Another version of the legend says that all these Indians were killed in camp, except their scout, and he still wanders with his Ghost Light trying to find his people. In another tale the Indians were not killed but captured when their chief was absent; they were carted off to a reservation in Florida and their chief continues his ghostly search for them to this day.

Another legend says that Spaniards rounded up Indians into slavery and then cut off the chief's head. To their astonishment, the chief picked up his head and walked away with a lantern to find his tribesmen. He got other chiefs to join him, and all those lights are the Indian chiefs searching for their captive fellows.

Some of the legends about the ghost of an Indian chief are tied in with a real Chisos Apache chief named

Alsate. History says that he and his tribe were betrayed at San Carlos, Mexico, and enslaved; legend says that after be escaped, he returned to the Chisos Mountains to live with his wife. An alternate legend holds that he was camped with his Apaches in the Chinati Mountains and that the Spaniards were determined to massacre the lot. They invited Alsate and his tribe to their camp to talk peace, only to ambush them. Alsate escaped to the Chinatis, and his spirit is still lighting fires to summon his dead warriors back to his camp.

A legend apparently designed to entertain children is one of an Indian Princess and a Brave who were in love. Each evening they brought separate herds of sheep down from the Chinatis. Once while she was waiting for him, she saw a flash of light. When he did not join her, she searched for him but found only his belt around the neck of one of his sheep. Where the light had appeared, the ground was disturbed. Though she had many suitors, she vowed never to marry but to continue to search for her beloved. Finally only one suitor was left. Every week on the day her Brave disappeared, the light would appear, and one day, when she approached too close, she was blinded by the light. At this bad omen the tribe moved away, leaving only the Princess and her lone suitor. Though blind, she went again to find her lover. Her suitor found her dead the next day at the bottom of a cliff. Her loyal suitor lived on at that place and believed that the light dancing around was the spirit of the blind Princess still searching for her handsome Brave.

The chief Alsate shows up in a similar legend, according to which he fell in love with an Indian girl and a jealous suitor plotted to kill him. When the jealous suitor followed Alsate and the girl to their trysting place, he accidentally killed the girl instead of Alsate. Then he stole her body and hid it in the mountains. The lights, then, are Alsate and the girl searching for each other. In some versions of this legend, the Indian

79

chief "set himself on fire because he was so upset." And such is one of the explanations of the Marfa Lights.

Another legend claims that in the 1800s a Ranger and his wife lived in the hills between Marfa and Alpine. Being a lawman, he usually was away from home at night. His wife had a lover, and she would signal her friend that the coast was clear by climbing a mountain and starting a fire. The lover also would start a fire, to let her know he was on his way to join her. One night, after about a year, the woman's lover did not respond; for the next two weeks she saw no answering blaze. Then she learned that her husband had killed her amorous friend. After that, in her lover's honor, she would go up the mountain every night and start her fire. Her ghost is still making the Marfa Lights.

Another story told by Mrs. Conaly Brooks to Elton Miles, who grew up in Marfa, is that when there was a terrible famine, an Indian woman gave birth to twins. Worried about their survival, she summoned the devil, pleaded for his help, and agreed to turn her children over to him when they were older. According to the contract, the devil provided them always with food, good health, shelter and clothing. Now the lights are this old Indian woman "searching and signaling for her twins to come back to her from the devil."[26]

A similar story of a ghostly woman accompanying the lights is from Jesus Jacquez (told to Ysrael Valencia and reported by Elton Miles), who was a trapper in the Marfa and Chinati area. When returning at night from working their traps, he and his companions claimed they would see lights flashing against the cliffs. "Then we would see a woman up ahead of us," he said, "signaling for us to follow her into the mountains, where the lights had been flashing. The first time we saw her, we thought she needed help. We tried to call her, but she always started walking back and would wave for us to follow her. Of course no one had the nerve to do that. Every time we made those trapping trips, we always saw the same lights and the same woman."

Some of the old stories relate the lights to outlaws, rustlers, and lawmen. In pioneer days an outlaw killed a woman, who was the sheriff's wife. The sheriff and a posse went hunting for the murderer, and when they reached the mountains, the food ran out. The posse gave up and went home, but the sheriff stayed at it and is still wandering the Chinati Mountains with his ghost light, seeking revenge.

Another story is of a cowboy who turned bad and was rustling cattle from his own boss' outfit. One night he saw the lights flashing about, took them to be a warning from God, and went straight from that day onward. Elton Miles relates that a local Mexican-American father put the Marfa Lights to disciplinary use. When his son grew curious about the lights, he told the boy they were campfires of smugglers and rustlers who would kill him if he started snooping around. We can see here that many of the explanations for the Marfa Lights may well have come out of children wanting to know what they were, and the local adults having to invent some sort of story.

Other pioneer stories abound. A wagon train was camped and destroyed by Indians. The Marfa Lights are the wagon train's ghost campfires. Once an old man went through west Texas cutting down all the trees. Near Marfa he chopped down a huge oak that fell on him and killed him. When he was found, his arms and legs were missing. The Marfa Lights are this old axeman's arms and legs seeking to rejoin his body.

Ghostly Treasure Lights

Elton Miles reports a rather grisly tale, told by the grandfather of Marfa resident Beau White, of a successful rancher who lived in the Davis Mountains. One day while he was working on the range, Mexican

81

bandits plundered and burned his house and barns. They raped the man's wife and 20-year-old daughter, forcing his two younger sons to watch. Then the bandits bound the whole family with wet rawhide around their throats and wrists and left them to die—burning down the buildings as they left. When the rancher returned, he was driven insane by the cruel tragedy. Taking the lantern the Mexicans used to set fire to his property, he mounted his horse and went in pursuit. The bandits had escaped south to the Chinati Mountains and buried their loot on Mitchell Flat. That night, as they headed for Mexico, they hid out in a cave and were sleeping when the rancher found them. The rancher built a fire at the cave entrance, and when the bandits came out, he shot them in the legs. Then he dragged them back into the cave and burned them alive. The Marfa Lights are therefore the Mexican bandits coming back in search of their hidden loot, or alternatively, the rancher (who was never heard of again) looking for his money with the lantern.

That the Marfa Lights are connected with buried treasure is a popular Mexican-American oral tradition. Throughout Latin America, especially in Mexico and Peru, it is believed that all gold treasure troves are guarded by mysterious lights. These lights are often called "La Luz de Dinero" or "The Money Light." In the Andes there is the tradition that if one is walking down a path or road at night and a light is suddenly seen, it is probably floating over a treasure. The person will then drive a stake into the ground where the light has been spotted and come back during daylight and dig in that spot—hopefully finding treasure. Elton Miles relates that in the days of Spanish occupation of Texas, there was a gold mine near San Carlos, Mexico. The Spaniards, after forcing the Indians to carry gold to the Marfa area and dig, killed the Indians and buried them with the gold. Those Indian spirits rise and dance above the treasure, and they say, "If you can find the exact spot of the light, dig and you will find the gold."

Mrs. Olga Parraz of Marfa related a family tradition to Elton Miles of an attempt by her husband's father, brother, and two uncles to find a treasure that was hidden by Indians to keep it from the Spaniards. In their car the men followed the light over rough country, and when they got close, they started digging. Then, suddenly—out of nowhere—a very old car supernaturally appeared beside them. Frightened, they ran back to their own car and gave up the treasure hunt forever.

In another tale two men were digging for gold and were about to dig up a treasure of Indian coins. Their blood ran cold when they heard a voice say, "I am the chief of the Indians and I am supposed to take care of the gold." This indicates to believers that the Marfa Lights are the souls of Indians protecting the gold so that nobody will take it.

A similar treasure tale says that on one of the mountains is a red handprint, which can be seen but is impossible to reach. The hand points to a grove of cottonwood trees planted in the shape of a horseshoe, though this pattern is obliterated by later growth. The Indians hid their gold in the center of the horseshoe, and the Marfa Lights are Indian spirits guarding that gold.[19]

❧ ❧ ❧

Satan's Minions and Teenage Terror

More modern stories of the Marfa Lights tend to stray away from treasure lights and Indian ghosts. The lights have been brought into more modern myths including UFOs and possession by the Devil. Recent legends say that the lights are responsible for fatal car wrecks—shooting out in front of cars, blinding the driver, and thus causing several head-on collisions. One story relates that some out-of-state travelers on Highway 90 saw what seemed to be reflectors on the side of the road. When their car was found, the interior was burned to ashes, and the only remains were nonflammable objects such as coins, keys, and jewelry. According to this myth, the outside of the car was unharmed, but the lights had destroyed the interior and everyone in it.

Many of the modern legends involve cars and jeeps full of young people trying to impress each other with hair-raising tales. In one, a boy and a girl were parked on the old airbase when they saw the lights. The girl began to scream with fright and the boy started the car. As they were leaving, the lights gained on them and the back of the car got hot. The back tires blew out and the couple ran to safety. The next day the car was melted and still smoking hot. In another version of this same story, the girl died of shock. About a week later the boy went back to the scene of the accident and was never seen again.

A similar legend relates how some local high school students went out in a jeep to see the lights and did not return. Searchers followed the tire tracks to where they abruptly stopped in an arroyo, but no further trace was ever found. The lights are those vanished young people signaling with ghost-jeep headlights, still hoping to be rescued.

Other stories mention how cars are scorched by the lights. For example: a driver going west on Highway 90 was pursued by a light ten feet tall. At 100 miles per hour, he could not outrun it, but finally it disappeared. When he reached the bridge on the edge of Marfa, he found that the right back-side of his car was burned black.

Local Alpine historian Judith Brueske interviewed an old-timer named Jack Read who had lived for years at the tiny town of Shafter, who thinks that the lights that he sees there may be UFOs or even agents of Satan. His first view of the lights in the Chinati Mountains that surround Shafter came when he was but a boy. He was born and raised in Marfa, but he had relatives living at the railroad section house of Aragon, about 10 miles west of Marfa (a little settlement that no longer exists). It was while he was visiting there that his cousin showed him the lights on the Chinatis.

"This was at age about eleven or twelve," says Reed. "We were sitting on the porch... and you could see the lights... And we discussed that maybe the lights were where a road goes down there." But his cousin said that they had already asked about that possibility and concluded that "It's not lights on the road because, more or less, they go up rather than sideways."

Since moving to Shafter, however, Reed says that he has seen the lights "all over the place," but mostly rising up the mountainside behind his house known as "Three Sisters Mountain."

Said Read, "When I first got [to Shafter] it was kind of exciting to me, you know, and I started watching them. They walk up the side of the mountain, here and there and I've seen them around close to homes, standing around."[21]

His description of how the lights look is a little different from other accounts. He describes them as capsule-shaped, and about six feet tall. Mostly they emit a bright white light, but he reports having seen a yellow one in 1988. "I woke up sometime in the night. I didn't pay any attention to the clock. But I woke up and walked over to the window and just happened to look out. And lo and behold, right in front of the house... there was a yellow one, real yellow. And I thought maybe this was a UFO..." He says it appeared to be about half a mile away, against the mountain. He furthermore believes that the lights rise from and return to a hole in the mountain, but when asked if he meant to an old mine shaft, he said "no."

Reed's account differs from those of others interviewed also in that he attaches a religious interpretation to the lights. "The Bible says that Satan made himself a light and that his ministers are also light," said Reed. "And in the Bible they're supposed to form a false Christ and bring him back in the sky, and I think this is what they're working on, these kinds of things." Nevertheless, he does not seem to feel that he is personally in any danger from the lights.

When asked by Brueske if he knew the lights to be associated with the performance of the radio or of electrical lights, he said he did not know of any association. (His house did not have electricity.) But he knows that they can stop a car, since the lights have stopped his car on several occasions.

Does Reed consider the lights that he sees to be the same ones that are called the Marfa lights? "Oh yes, the same ones. You see, they're looking at Shafter when they're looking at them. That's where they're coming from."

Brueske relates another story from south of Shafter, between the Chinati Mountains and Presidio, where there is a long flat stretch of highway with a scrub desert on both sides. Most of it is fenced fairly close to the highway except for a short stretch that is unfenced. A Presidio resident, who remains anonymous, had the following experience in 1987, on a clear night, on Highway 67:

"I was driving along in my Chevy, and I had seen a light swerve over in front of me... It was one light and it was about this big [hand gesture indicates about a one foot diameter]. It came in front of me and I thought, 'Oh no, a motorcycle, and I'm going to hit it! Why is anybody coming right in front of me?' Just before I got to it—it was just at the side of the road—it disappeared like that [snaps his fingers]. Whew! I thought the

86

motorcycle went down the far ditch, but then it started bouncing across the desert.

"By bouncing I mean that it was not like a motorcycle... It's one of those things where I tell myself it's a motorcycle for my own sanity. But my experience wasn't right for a motorcycle."

He never fully stopped his car, although he slowed down when the light first came toward him along the side of the road. "After it disappeared, then it bounced out there in the desert for a while, parallel to the direction I was going." His impression is that the light had got on the other side of the fence along the road, something that a motorcycle could not have done.

This person found the experience rather unnerving and professes no interest in finding an explanation. He's not sure that what he saw was a "Marfa Light." "I don't want to know anything about [the lights]. I really don't. I'm afraid of meeting a UFO or anything like that... Over and over again I keep telling myself that it must have been a motorcycle, even though the facts don't quite fit it. I don't want to accept the fact that I'm seeing some kind of strange phenomenon... I think normal reality's fine."[21]

This same person told Brueske of another experience he had had in New Mexico, again while driving in his car. "Something used to get in the car with me and ride [along]. It wasn't bad, but I didn't want it.... it was just a presence that I felt. I had one friend that felt it along with me." No strange lights were seen in association with this experience, but his description can be compared to others who claim to have "visitors" associated with the lights.[21]

UFOs from a Stargate Portal

Finally, there are the super-science and UFO stories

of quite recent date, though some perhaps go back to World War II. Elton Miles says one curious story, told by Ray Fuller of Marfa to Ellis Villalobos, relates that between 1942 and 1945, the United States government built experiment stations throughout the Southwest to develop secret weapons. These were at Los Alamos, White Sands, and the Chinati Mountains Research Center, all secret and in remote desert areas. To work in these places, the government brought in the best of the world's scientists. The atomic bomb was developed at Los Alamos and missiles at White Sands, but at the Chinati Center, the most secret project of all proved a failure.

An M.I.T. nuclear physicist, originally from Israel, was working on a nuclear laser fusion device. The project failed because it was years ahead of its time and created extremely dangerous risks. When a test in the field ran into trouble, the light generated by the laser interfered with the foreign fringes of matter. This caused the laser-fusion light to be locked or lost in space and time. A gigantic explosion followed, which destroyed the research center and left a seven-mile-wide scorch area. The accident was kept secret, but the government sent special investigative teams to study the strange flashes known as the Marfa Lights, apparently to determine whether they had any role in the fiasco. After their investigation, they considered the matter closed and refused to give any information.[26]

Another recently proposed scenario maintains that the area is a "Stargate" or space portal where UFOs from other dimensions enter our reality. In this legend, in pre-colonial times a flying saucer from outer space landed on Mitchell Flat. The ship and its occupants were invisible except for their lights. Similarly, some believe that on the old airbase there is an invisible barrier to that other dimension which keeps opening in spots, and that is what makes the lights. People who have disappeared out there are still in limbo in the fourth dimension. It is said that a well-informed science writer once camped for many weeks to study the lights. He formed a theory based on interdimensional "Stargates," apparently based on the movie and television show, and, says Elton Miles, "his recorded theory was so controversial that the government confiscated it."

Elton Miles tells another modern "legend" of a young Jesus Freak who went out to the old airbase with other students. Whenever he would say anything about Jesus, the lights would appear; when the subject changed, they would fade out.

The myth-making goes on, aided especially by students at the local Sul Ross State University and at the high schools in Marfa and Alpine. Boys like to drive their girls out to the old airbase and get as much scare effect out of the lights as possible. It is all in fun, and they sometimes take along a bottle of cheap wine or a wastebasket full of iced beer. At about third hand, Joan Davis, a Sul Ross student, heard in 1970 that a girl and her date, having gone out to see the lights, were chased by them and knocked down. They hastened home to their dormitories, and next day both discovered they were "sunburned" by the lights. Another student, Buck Reynolds, to intrigue his dates, would start flashing the headlights of his car about a mile before he reached the old airport, as though to call up the lights. When they appeared, he would tell his girl how the lights were orbs of energy from another planet sent to monitor the "goings-on" on earth. He would also tell her how his engine once was cut off by the lights. "He would relate these theories," said his interviewer, "with such seeming sincerity that some of his more gullible listeners would be lulled into a nervous shock."

A number of authors believe that the airbase was closed because of the deadly lights. During World War II, when the airbase served to train pilots, sometimes the lights would line up like runway lights, and several inexperienced student pilots were killed when these fake guides led them straight into the face of the Chinati Mountain cliffs. According to this legend, airport officials sent up a helicopter to locate the lights, but they could not be seen from the helicopter. When the men landed where a light was supposed to be, the copter promptly exploded, leaving no trace of the men.

The legend continues that because of these dubious disasters the U.S. Army seriously set about trying to learn the nature of the Marfa Lights. The most common story, which has several outcomes, tells how during World War II the military organized itself to locate their source. Several jeeps and planes were equipped with intercommunication devices, and the search was on. One jeep was designated to drive directly into a Marfa Light (in the stories the number of men in the jeep is usually given as either two or four). Reports of the outcome of this venture vary:

(1) The jeep reported reaching the light, then suddenly contact with the base went dead. The jeep was located, but of its passengers nothing was found except one sock. It was found at a spot where the rocks drew heat from the sun, radiated it as light at night, and this burned up the men.

(2) When told they were right on the light, two of the jeep passengers said they saw no light. Then communications broke off. Next day the men were found thrown from the jeep and burned to death. The equipment in the jeep was burned beyond repair.

(3) Two scientists, assigned to help the army, were in the jeep, which was found somewhat melted. The scientists were never found.

An alternate story says that two scientists in two trucks were found beside their burning vehicles in a state of hysterical shock; both men were idiots from that day on. One person interviewed in 1973 said,

90

"They sent the two men to a sanitarium in Big Spring. They are supposed to be there up to this date."

Elton Miles thinks that all the burned-up jeep stories have sprung from what local resident C. W. Davis told Charles Nichols in 1972. "One of the people involved was a personal friend of mine. He told me that him and two of his buddies were sort of drunk and decided to look for the lights. They stole a jeep, which they wrecked. They were afraid of getting caught, so they set fire to the jeep and sneaked back to the airbase." Indeed, it seems unlikely that the Marfa Lights have actually set fire to anything, particularly any vehicles. But it is a fact that the army abandoned the airbase after WWII.

Flying into the Marfa Lights

Most people who have seen the Marfa Lights have done so from the ground. But there are plenty of aviators in west Texas, and some of them have spotted what they are sure were the Marfa Lights from an airplane. One man who actually flew in hope of finding the nature of the light was Fritz Kahl of Marfa. He ran a flying service at the old airbase and some years ago organized the International Soaring Contest there. He told an interviewer, "What I have to tell you, I could say in five minutes. I chased them in an airplane, not once but several times, and this was in 1943 and early 1944. My God, there I was, a World War II aviator. Hell, I was twenty-one years old and didn't have any sense, flying airplanes at night out in the hills, right down on the ground. You got to be young. You got to be crazy. But we tried it. Only thing is, you know, you leave the airbase and you get out on that Presidio highway a ways, and you run into the hills right quick." Fritz Kahl could find nothing.

One moonless, clear night in February 1988 a local businessman and pilot, Robert Weidig, and another man were returning to Alpine from Fort Stockton. Weidig told Judith Brueske that the lights of the town of Alpine are visible quite soon after taking off from Fort Stockton. He was looking at the three red tower lights on "A" Mountain in Alpine when he noticed another more distant red light behind them. He recognized it as the beacon atop a phone company microwave tower between Marfa and Presidio, known to him as Alamito tower. "And that's when I noticed the Marfa Lights," he says. As he watched that far off red light, he started seeing moving white lights around it.

They were flying at about 8,000 feet of altitude and still about twenty miles from Alpine, Weidig told Brueske, when they first spotted the lights and were able to observe them for about ten minutes. "We noticed white lights coming up... I don't know how high, but it seemed like several hundred feet. Then the lights would just dissipate... They moved around that tower for some reason. They'd get on the right-hand side of it, the left-hand side of it, and go just straight up."

An even closer sighting is described by Eddie Halsell, interviewed by Brueske in June 1988. The event itself took place some twenty years before. Halsell was a passenger in the plane and they were apparently flying in the direction of the Chinati Mountains. They thought that they saw some lights over there.

Suddenly a bright light came toward them rapidly, seemingly from a great distance. "It came straight at us 'til it got to the hood of the plane... It was engulfing us, larger than the plane." He says that it seemed as though they were inside the light. "We couldn't see to fly. It scared us."

According to Halsell, as they tried to turn away

from the light, it seemed to move in front of them. "Always it moved around us... We made right turns and left turns and it stayed right with us, like it was playing a game."

The light was very bright, but "It was kind of fuzzy, like a halo or aura, a ball of light without an obvious center." The light was white in color, was constant rather than pulsating or flickering, and there was no unusual sound. In the end, and for no apparent reason, the light left them, and the pilot was able to land the plane.

Lights Elsewhere Around Big Bend

While the unexplained lights incidents have occurred mainly in the Mitchell Flat and Chinati Mountains area, they have also been reported further east and slightly south in the Cienaga Mountains and even further east in the Dead Horse Mountains near the center of Big Bend National Park. Hallie Stillwell, longtime resident of the southern Big Bend area, reported to Judith Brueske that she had seen mysterious lights in a variety of places over the years. "We didn't call them Marfa lights, we called them either ghost lights or weird lights. I had seen them in the Chinati Mountains when I was teaching school in Presidio." She was commuting between Presidio and Marfa at that time, and by the time she left school it would be dark. "When we came through Shafter... we saw the lights quite often in the Chinatis."

Between Marfa and Alpine she says that she saw them in the Cienegas, which lie to the east of the Chinatis. "But the most lights that I saw were in the Dead Horses, and that's on this ranch that's just below here." The Stillwell ranch is on Road 2627 that runs from Highway 385, past the Stillwell Store, and through the Black Gap wildlife management area to La Linda. The Dead Horse Mountains are northeast of the Chisos Mountains of Big Bend National Park. When her husband was alive, he and their sons would see the lights quite frequently. "Of course, they'd see them more than I did because I wasn't out at night very much." The lights weren't visible from the house, and she says "we had to go out on the sand pile" in order to see them.

Although Stillwell hasn't seen the lights for a number of years, she recalls their appearance vividly. Seen from a distance and below the horizon, "they look kind of red and orange, and they flickered. They would kind of die down and then come up again, brighter... They looked like flames." She says that she never saw them moving up and down, but only horizontally. "They kind of ran along across the mountains."

However, one time, with her sister, she saw the lights at a much closer range. They "...were so close, they were really kind of scary." The two women were approaching the ranch gate in their car when they saw what at first seemed to be another car in front of them, because the lights were "like taillights." But there wasn't any car there. They knew that one of them had to get out to open the gate, but Stillwell's sister refused. So Stillwell opened the gate.

She didn't commit herself to just how close the lights were on that occasion, since, as she says, "You know how it is out here. Sometimes the atmosphere is clear and things look very close. Other times the atmosphere is hazy and they look far away."

Stillwell says she has never had the experience of lights following her. "The ones I saw were very stationary." Nor has she ever associated any sound with an appearance of the lights. She told Judith Brueske that she is not surprised that no one has been able to physically locate any of the lights. "The country's just too big, that's all."

A Pandora's Box of Explanations

Right from the first pioneers noticing the strange lights there came a host of explanations for the phenomenon. One of the oldest is that they are *sotol* sagebrush burned by cowboys to light their camp or to mark their trail. One old explanation was that hundreds of years ago, Mitchell Flat was an ocean bed, and there was a lighthouse that is still signaling to ghost ships. Or, the ghosts of the sailors are out there signaling with the lights for the ships to pick them up.

Numerous "scientific" explanations have been advanced (some with possible credulity, others silly):

• Moonlight shining on exposed deposits of mica (but the hills have been searched for such deposits and they haven't been found)
• Unknown luminous gases escaping from underground being lit by ambient light
• Uranium glowing in the dark (but uranium is not known to be present)
• Mercury vapor lamps on ranches (which is hardly likely since the lights were seen before such lamps existed)
• Bat guano in caves (does bat guano glow in the dark and does it move about?)
• Little volcanoes (small volcanic eruptions on the prairie?)
• Reflection of the stars and moon off rocks (the lights appear on moonless nights, however)
• Swamp gas (the area is actually a desert, but some swamps exist around Big Bend)
• Phosphorus in the rocks (similar to the uranium explanation)
• Chemicals left by the army at the old airport (however, the lights were seen long before the army airport was built)

•Reflections from silver left in the abandoned Shafter mines (similar to the moonlight reflection explanation)

•Coal deposits (this explanation apparently depends on the coal deposits being on fire)

•Bones in the earth (perhaps an explanation that is teamed with ghosts as an explanation)

•Static electricity (the dry air may be creating excessive amounts of static electricity)

•Irregular "pockets" in the air that collect light, analogous to the telephoto lens (similar to the effect that creates the common water-on-the-road mirage)

•Reflections from a comet or meteor (one would think that this would not be a nightly phenomenon)

•Water flowing between two different ores, which gives off static electricity (similar to the static electricity above)

•Gas formed into large balls, which are somehow ignited (similar to the swamp gas theory)

•A negative charge, which if it ever met a positive charge would blow up the earth (is Marfa the site of some kind of anti-matter creation?)

•Jack rabbits, whose fur glows because they have run through luminescent brush or have picked up glowworms (at least this theory includes the fact that the lights move about)

This last amusing theory was given a brief boost when the January 2005 issue of *Fortean Times* reported the case of a rabbit on fire in Wiltshire, England. Groundsmen at Devizes Cricket Club were startled when just after they lit a kerosene-soaked bonfire on the field a rabbit shot out with its tail on fire. The rabbit tore off towards some sheds, one of which burst into flames about 30 minutes later. The shed contained mowers, wheelbarrows, weed-whippers and other items, including, presumably, gasoline and kerosene. The cricket club claimed £60,000 in damages (about $100,000). There was no sign of the rabbit's remains, suggesting that the blazing critter may have gotten away. The Marfa Lights, however, are probably not connected with flaming jackrabbits.

Japanese Scientists Investigate the Marfa Lights

While, over the years, the Marfa Lights have gotten the attention of scientists of various kinds, it is the Japanese that seem the most interested in them. Yoshi Ohtsuki, head of the Department of Physics at Tokyo's Waseda University, has a life-long interest in ball lightning and similar phenomena. He became fascinated with ball lightning and mysterious light phenomena at the age of 13, when he watched a great, white ball of light drift over a forest in northern Japan.

Professor Ohtsuki accompanied a Japanese television crew to Marfa in 1989 to document the famous lights on film. The crew's nightly vigilance was rewarded by the capture of a very unusual light on the video tape. It was long and thin like a piece of string which shortened very quickly into a ball. Ohtsuki suspected, but was far from certain, that the illumination might be an electrostatic phenomenon caused by changes in daytime and nighttime temperatures and humidity.

In 1992 Ohtsuki returned to Marfa, this time with a very impressive international scientific team. State-of-the-art atmospheric equipment, cameras with telephoto lenses, and various recording devices were flown in and the team set up at a base camp near the official viewing site. The team also brought along a Buddhist priest, in case there was something spiritual about the lights, in which case the priest would try to communicate with them.

97

For three evenings in a row, at sundown, the Buddhist priest performed a ritual to summon up the lights. On the third night after the priest finished chanting, a very bright light appeared on the horizon. The camera crew began taking photos and video footage through telephoto lenses.

Just before the light made its debut, Edson Hendricks, a San Diego expert in the science of spherics who was part of the team, by using a sophisticated sound detection device to listen to the atmosphere, was able to hear a long, descending pitch signal; moments later, the light came on. During the nights that followed, Hendricks heard and recorded the faint, whistle-like sound that seemed to precede the appearance of a Marfa Light on many occasions.

Edson Hendricks was especially fascinated by some very curious images that appeared on several photographs he shot while at the base camp. Using infrared film, Hendricks had photographed the sky at times when no aerial lights were visible. Yet after the film was developed, strange spots could be seen in the photos. Were these infrared flashes of light, or just some imperfection in the film quality?

The most recent book to be written about the Marfa Lights is *Night Orbs*, by James Bunnel of Cedar Creek, Texas. Bunnel has clearly studied the phenomenon at great depth, and spends much of the back of the book showing photos of all of his cameras and other equipment. He managed to get some good photos of the lights, and gives a good rundown of the various scientific theories, including UFOs, mirages and piezoelectrical explanations. None of these solutions hold much water, Bunnel claims. He does however offer his own explanation which is that the lights are connected with the Van Allen Radiation Belt around the earth and the Northern Lights phenomenon. He believes that metallic crystal nodules called Zeolites, which can be found on Mitchell Flat (or just south of there) somehow attract an Aurora Borealis-type light display that moves along the ground where the Zeolite deposits are to be found. Bunnel also relates the Marfa Lights to the Min Min Lights of Australia's northern Queensland, a similar light phenomenon.

Bunnel's theory is an interesting one, but it doesn't seem likely to explain the other lights seen in the Dead Horse Mountains. As we drove past the Marfa Lights Viewing Area the next day in the bright morning light, Mitchell Flats and the Chinati Mountains beyond looked quite ordinary—boring in fact. But the night before we had seen the lights ourselves, dancing in the distance in the lonely Texas desert. Some mysteries may be eventually solved— others may endure. As we left Marfa and the Big Bend area behind, I had the distinct feeling that the ghost lights would continue to baffle tourists and investigators for many years to come.

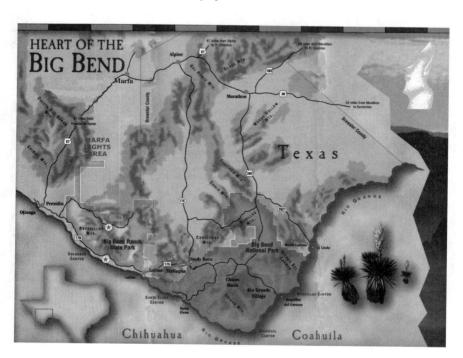

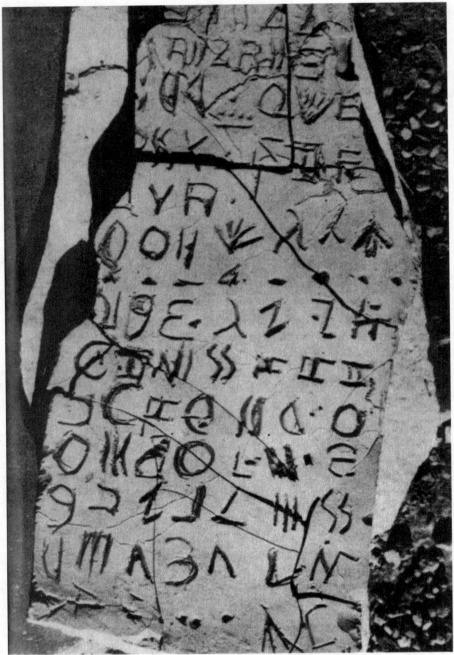

The Big Bend Mystery Tablet discovered in a remote cave in 1962.

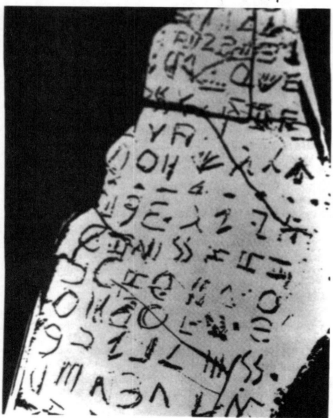

Above: An artist's conception of Roman, Egyptian and Hebrew traders bargaining with Indians along the Rio Grande. Left: Another rare photo of the Big Bend Mystery Tablet.

A drawing of the *Quetzalcoatlus Northrupti*, the largest pterosaurs known to exist. Their fossils have been found around Big Bend. Could living pterosaurs still be flying the skies of northern Mexico and the Southwest?

Top: A time exposure of the Marfa Lights made by Carl Appel. Bottom: The official roadside plaque about the Marfa Lights installed by the state of Texas.

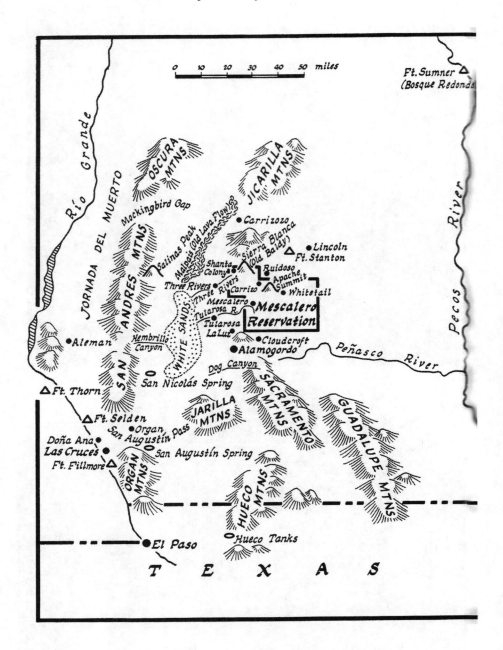

3.

SOUTHERN NEW MEXICO

VICTORIO PEAK AND THE CAVERNS OF GOLD

I've been kicked by the wind,
Robbed by the sleet,
Had my head stoved in,
But I'm still on my feet.
—Little Feat, *Willin'*

When the going gets weird,
the weird turn pro.
—Hunter S. Thompson

I knew I needed to find that lost highway that was somewhere past this rolling blacktop in the distant hills. Jennifer was reading a guidebook to Texas, but we were about to leave that state and head into New Mexico. We were driving north on Texas Highway 54 toward the only town on that road, Pine Springs. Pine Springs is on the eastern boundary of Guadalupe Mountains National Park, and we could see the range in the distance with Guadelupe Mountain itself, the highest peak in Texas at 8749 feet.

We stopped briefly to hike in the Guadalupes. Granite cliffs and rugged trails frame the main peak. Deep inside those mountains is Rattlesnake Springs, a hidden watering spot in the rocky terrain.

It was at Rattlesnake Springs that the renegade Apache chief Victorio fought a battle with United States Army troopers of the Ninth Cavalry and Tenth Cavalry, which were both African-American "Buffalo Soldier" units stationed at Fort Concho, near the site of present-day San Angelo. On August 6, 1880, the Buffalo Soldiers confronted Victorio's troops at Rattlesnake Springs and a three-hour shootout began. Victorio and his men were able to flee westward into the Carrizo Mountains, and from there to Mexico, but it was this skirmish that convinced him to give up trying to take control of the region.

Strangely, Victorio had been coming from a bizarre hollow mountain in the desolate land on the east side of the Rio Grande. But we are getting ahead of our story...

We had left Marfa early in the morning and headed north on Highway 90 to Van Horn on Interstate 10; that major artery traverses the south of the country, in these parts passing through El Paso, Tucson and Phoenix on the way to Los Angeles. But, rather than turn onto the Interstate, we picked up Highway 54, going directly north to New Mexico. The Guadalupes lie just on the state line, and after our stop there, we veered east toward the border. Just over the state border in New Mexico was Carlsbad Caverns, and we made a detour to the Park Headquarters.

It was at Carlsbad Caverns and the area around Carlsbad and Ruidoso that the 1957 movie *The Lone*

Ranger and the Lost City of Gold was filmed. This final film in the Lone Ranger saga, the episodes of which largely took place in southern New Mexico, west Texas and eastern Arizona, concerned a gold mine and cliff dwelling city that was inside a huge cavern system, which is why they filmed at Carlsbad Caverns.

We spent the afternoon hiking around inside the vast Caverns, a tour that doesn't have to be done in guided groups, unlike tours offered at most caverns. At the end of the afternoon, we returned to the elevator that took us back to the surface of the desert, and the visitor's center and parking lot.

We spent the night in Carlsbad, relaxing from several busy days. I wondered about all the intriguing stories I had heard about this area: the UFO crash at Roswell, the first atomic tests at Alamogordo and White Sands, the strange egg-shaped UFO reported at Socorro, plus some of the strangest lost treasure tales in the Southwest.

Browsing some of the books I had with me at the hotel, one of the first things I came across was that mankind had apparently been around the area for a very long time, and strange human footprints had been found in the ancient alabaster of White Sands National Monument near Alamogordo.

The White Sands National Monument contains some 176,000 acres of white alabaster. Geologists theorize that this gypsum was precipitated as winds dried up an inland sea. Somewhere in the great expanse of gypsum are what appear to be the sandal prints of some prehistoric human giant, who could only have made such impressions when the muddy sediment of the primeval sea was beginning to harden.

In the 1970s, the White Sands National Monument distributed a small booklet entitled "Story of the Great White Sands." In this little booklet was told the story concerning the discovery of the gigantic human tracks:

> In the fall of 1932, Ellis Wright, a government trapper, reported that he had found human tracks of unbelievable size imprinted in the gypsum rock on the west side of White Sands...
>
> As Mr. Wright reported, there were thirteen human tracks... each [one] approximately 22 inches long and from eight-to-ten inches wide. It was the consensus [of the investigating group] that the tracks were made by a human being, for the print was perfect, and even the instep plainly marked. However, there was no one in the group who cared to venture a guess as to when the tracks were made, or how they came to be of their tremendous size. It is one of the great unsolved mysteries of the Great White Sands.

Mary Wright, a columnist for the *Silver City Enterprise,* wrote in the April 1, 1971 "Happenings—Past and Present" that a local group of people had contacted a national monument ranger for a tour of the area in which Ellis Wright (apparently no relation) had found the ancient tracks of prehistoric humans. She reported that the group had discovered additional imprints in the gypsum. "Since these tracks, which were in hardened *caliche,* were twice the size of [contemporary humans], who were these early day travelers and what could they have been seeking in the San Andreas Mountains? They were wearing some type of sandal or moccasin. They crossed these lakes when the caliche was soft, as their tracks show."[11]

The Strange Tunnels of New Mexico

We stopped the next day in Roswell. It seemed as if aliens had taken over the entire town! Even the lamps of the streetlights were in the form of alien heads. Roswell became an instant legend when a discoid aircraft—or flying saucer—was reported to have crashed near to the town and the Roswell Army Air Field issued a statement on July 8, 1947 that they had recovered a crashed "flying disc." This was followed by the usual denials by the Air Force, and reports that it was only a top secret weather balloon. Now, with various books having been written on the subject, peoples' claims of seeing aliens and even the surfacing of "alien autopsy" footage, the legend is still very much alive in Roswell.

We visited the UFO Museum in the old downtown movie theater (what was its original name—the Bijou—the Majestic—the Rocket?) and then visited the many alien T-shirt shops and various other stores. Fortunately, there were a few books to buy in some of the shops, and I left with a happy assortment of videos, books, T-shirts, shot glasses and other goodies.

Having stimulated the local Roswell alien economy, we headed west out of town for Hondo, Lincoln and Ruidoso—Billy the Kid country. Along the way, we passed the old dirt road that was supposed to go out to the Roswell flying saucer crash site, the Foster Ranch to the north of New Mexico Highway 380.

We passed through Hondo and stopped briefly at Lincoln. This tiny town was a major cattle town during the Lincoln County War of 1876-1879, in which Billy the Kid, whose real name was Henry McCarty, made one of his most spectacular escapes. After Billy the Kid's employer, an English cattleman named John Tunstall was murdered by a rival cattle gang, all hell broke loose in Lincoln County and a real range war in the lawless West went on for several years. At one point, McCarty "the Kid" and his friends, were part of law-abiding bunch called "The Regulators" who tried to serve arrest warrants for the cowboys who had shot Tunstall and others. Trapped in a blazing house in Lincoln on July 19, 1878, Billy and the remaining "Regulators" shot their way out into the street against overwhelming odds, and many of them escaped alive, including the Kid. This incident was to become one of most famous in the history of the West, immortalized in Sheriff Pat Garrett's 1882 book *The Authentic Life of Billy, the Kid*.

Farther down the road is Capitan, a small town with a ranger station where, yes, really, Smokey Bear hails from (he is often wrongly referred to as Smokey "the" Bear). He was just a small cub when discovered after a forest fire near Capitan in 1950. Originally called Hotfoot Teddy, he became famous as Smokey Bear, the iconic figure in the campaign for forest fire prevention. He died of old age at the National Zoo in Washington D.C. in 1975.

We dropped into Ruidoso for a late lunch and then were headed west again toward the White Sands Missile Range and what is known as the Jornada del Muerto, a desolate area along the east side of the Rio Grande that holds the great lost treasure of the Apache chief Victorio. This amazing story involves Aztec and Spanish treasure, and a hollow mountain with cut-stone stairs going down to a beach on an underground river. The staircase even included a booby-trap, and the whole story would seem like some adventure fantasy were it not for the involvement of Presidential candidate and New Mexico Governor Bill Richardson, President Lyndon Baines Johnson, the famous lawyer F. Lee Bailey, President Richard Nixon and even some

Watergate burglars. A lawsuit stood for many years, and was famous in New Mexico, against the U.S. Army and the White Sands Missile Base for its appropriation of the vast treasure.

But before we get into that story, let us look briefly at the reality of ancient tunnels and underground works. These sometimes go for considerable distances. Because of my years of travel in South America, I was familiar with the legends of tunnels beneath the Andes. As I reported in my book *Lost Cities & Ancient Mysteries of South America*,[46] the gold-clad mummies of the ancient Inca Kings, and much of the treasure from the fabulous Sun Temple, are believed to still be hidden in the tunnels that run under Cuzco and the ruins of a megalithic fortress called Sacsayhuaman above the city.

There are many stories of these tunnels, including one that tells of a treasure hunter who went into the tunnels and wandered through the labyrinth for several days. One morning, about a week after the adventurer had vanished, a priest was conducting mass in the church of Santo Domingo, built on the ruins of the Incan Temple of the Sun. The priest and his congregation were amazed to hear sharp rapping coming from beneath the church's stone floor. Several worshipers crossed themselves and murmured about the devil. The priest quieted his congregation and then directed the removal of a large stone slab from the floor. The assembled group was astonished to see the treasure hunter emerge with a bar of gold in each hand.[46]

The Peruvian government got into the act of exploring these Cuzco tunnels, ostensibly for scientific purposes. The Peruvian *Seria Documental del Peru* describes an expedition undertaken by staff from Lima University in 1923. Accompanied by an experienced speleologist, the party penetrated the trapezoid-shaped tunnels starting from an entrance

111

at Cuzco.

They took measurements of the subterranean aperture and advanced in the direction of the coast. After a few days, members of the expedition at the entrance of the tunnel lost contact with the explorers inside, and no communication came for twelve days. Then a solitary, starving explorer returned to the entrance. His reports of an underground labyrinth of tunnels and deadly obstacles were like an Indiana Jones movie. His tale was so incredible that his colleagues declared him mad. To prevent further loss of life in the tunnels, the police dynamited the entrance.[43, 46]

Many researchers believe that these tunnels run for hundreds of miles through the mountains, as far south as Chile, as far north as Ecuador or Colombia, and as far to the east as the Amazon jungles! They may have been ancient mines, escape tunnels, or a type of highway system. These tunnels do indeed exist; their extent is what remains in question.

As for North America, some historians believe that a similar set of tunnels exists in Arizona and New Mexico, if not Utah, Nevada and California. At the turn of the last century, while the American army was pursuing Geronimo around Arizona, he and his braves would ride into box canyons with the Cavalry in hot pursuit. The Indians would literally vanish, leaving the U.S. Army totally mystified. A day or two later, it would be reported that Geronimo and his troops had suddenly turned up in Mexico, hundreds of miles distant.[18, 46]

This happened not once, but several times. Is it possible that Geronimo was using a system of ancient tunnels that exist in the American southwest? This tunnel system, if it exists, would very likely be centered in the Chiracahua Mountains.

Other tunnels have been reported in the Superstition Mountains and elsewhere in Arizona, but one of the most curious of all is the tunnel and lost treasure reported at Victorio Peak in the Jornada del Muerto of New Mexico. It is one of the great treasure stories of the Southwest—a story of Aztec-Toltec gold, murder, sinister government involvement, and booby-trapped tunnels beneath western New Mexico.

A Treasure Deep Inside a Hollow Mountain

After leaving Ruidoso we drove through Alamogordo, famous for the first atomic bomb testing in the United States during WWII. Then we headed southwest on scenic Highway 70 to Las Cruces, where we stopped for the night.

The next day, we took Interstate 25 north to the town of Hatch, along the southern Rio Grande. We stopped at a local café and had a snack—green chilies are a culinary staple in New Mexico and the vast majority (and best quality) of them come from Hatch.

It was near Hatch that in 1937 a half-Indian podiatrist (originally from Oklahoma) named Milton Ernest "Doc" Noss discovered an astonishing cache of lost treasure on what is now the White Sands Missile Range. Much of the gold may have been Aztec, while other portions were purportedly from the lost La Rue mine that the Spanish had worked a hundred years before. Much of the treasure was in the form of stacked gold bars—hundreds of them— but there were other artifacts as well, such as swords, goblets, crowns, statues and other trinkets.

We continued on to the town of Truth or Consequences, which was known as Hot Springs until native son Bob Barker, who became a famous television host in the 1960s, offered the town money to change the name to that of his show. To the east were the San Andreas Mountains and Victorio Peak, the hollow mountain of gold. It was largely a desert

113

wasteland out there and my mind wandered on to the strange case of Victorio Peak.

Victorio Peak is a craggy outcropping of rock, only about 500 feet high, a minor peak of the San Andreas Range. The mountain sits in the center of a dry desert lake known as Hembrillo Basin. The peak was named after the Apache chief Victorio, who used the Hembrillo Basin as his stronghold.

Originally, ancient hunters many thousands of years ago must have stumbled upon the mountain and discovered the fissures and caves in the worn granite cliffs that make up the top of the peak. Inside this catacomb of volcanic caves was a natural shaft that led steeply down to an underground river.

Eventually, with veins of gold inside the caves, and placer gold along the banks of the underground river, the site must have become an active mine. Perhaps it was mined by the Olmecs as early as 1300 BC and later mined by the Toltecs, Hohokam and Aztecs. Olmec artifacts, such as the Granby Idol, have been found as far north as Colorado.

As Spanish explorers, settlers and missionaries arrived in Mexico and headed into the mineral rich mountains in the north, mines of all types were shown to them by the indigenous people. The Spanish carried samples of gold, silver, copper and other items to show villagers that they encountered, hoping to prompt the revelation of local treasure. And so some ancient mines became Spanish mines, often run by Jesuit Priests who had befriended the local population, and were popular for their ventures in farming and small industries.

The mountain called Victorio Peak would hold many secrets, making some people millionaires; others would die penniless while still others spent their entire lives trying to regain the lost treasure that they felt was within their grasp.

Padre La Rue and his Lost Mine

In the Socorro-Hot Springs-Hatch area there is a local legend about the Casa del Cueva de Oro, or the "House of the Golden Cave." Could this have been Victorio Peak?

This House of the Golden Cave may go back to Toltec and Aztec times. Perhaps this was one of the places of the Seven Gold Cities of Cibola. Some historians theorized that it was the lost mine and treasure trove of the man who founded New Mexico as a Spanish colony in 1598, Don Juan de Onate. He had been seeking the Seven Cities of Gold, but became the governor of New Mexico instead. He was thought to have amassed a large treasure while governor until he was ordered back to Mexico City in 1607.

This may have been the early origin of some of the treasure—a vein of high grade gold inside an extinct volcano. It even had an underground river to boot. These underground rivers, known throughout the west from Texas to Nevada and California, were often said to have glittering beaches of gold sand.

We may not ever know if the underground river at Victorio Peak had beaches of gold sand, but it is quite possible. Gold would naturally build up at bends in underground rivers, and be deposited on the beaches that are sometimes created where these underground rivers go through large caverns.

In the case of Victorio Peak, the large underground cavern could be reached from the shafts and tunnels near the top of the peak. The underground river would have had to be at least 500 feet down the shafts, as it must have been beneath the valley floor which the peak stood above. Doc Noss, whose stories of Victorio Peak are the best documented, was more interested in the already-existing gold bars and other artifacts that he found in the caverns than the sand along the underground river, so he

115

is not known to have mentioned it. This, however, may have been the source of much of the gold.

Another theory on the source of the gold and use of the caverns holds that it was a secret mine that had been rumored in the area for over a hundred years—the Padre La Rue Mine.

David Leon Chandler tells what little is known of Padre La Rue in his 1979 book *100 Tons of Gold*. Padre La Rue was one of 10 young priests from France who arrived in Mexico City in 1797. Allegedly from a French noble family (as were many of the Knights Templar), Father La Rue was sent north and took up work in small haciendas near Paso del Norte (now El Paso). Father La Rue was a kind man who tenderly helped the poor people, Indians and Spaniards alike. He became very popular with his people and one day an old Spanish soldier who had been to many far-flung areas of Mexico, and spent quite a bit of time in New Mexico, told the Padre one day of a mountain two days north of Paso del Norte that had a spring, called Spirit Spring. This was in the mountains of the Sierra Organos, and near the spring was a very high rock, or cliff, and here would be found veins of gold, as well as placer gold.

Shortly afterward, a drought hit the area and crops were meager and a famine was threatening the Padre's small mission. He drew his flock together and told them the story of the old soldier. They then set out to find the fabulous cache of gold which the old soldier had described. Legend says that they arrived in the described area and after a few days' search one of the men brought back some nuggets of gold. Satisfied that they had found the cliff of gold, they moved their camp to the mountain.

Padre La Rue was said to have had the men carve him a room inside a high chalk cliff near the springs. Houses of adobe were made of rocks and mortar for the workers. They then worked the placer gold deposits and also tunneled into the mountain following a very rich vein of gold. Padre La Rue acted as the treasurer and soon they amassed a fortune in gold. They bought provisions and tools with their gold, and became a prosperous small mining community. They were secretive, however, and stored large amounts of gold in the caverns they had found to be abundant in the cliff.

Chandler says that a high stone wall was built about the mountain settlement, and no strangers were admitted. Smelters were built inside the mountain and the camp was alive with activity. As the years passed into early 1800s, Padre La Rue and his followers amassed ever more gold, releasing just enough of it to buy supplies. The Padre did not want the small mission and mining colony to show any great wealth or attract unwanted attention.

Unfortunately, good things like this weren't meant to last, and the church in Mexico City sent a priest named Maximo Milliano to search for the missing Padre La Rue and his flock. Milliano and his expedition spent a year in the Las Cruces region and then finally located the walled colony in the Sierra Organos. It seems that the Sierra Organos are now known as the San Andreas Range, the southern end of which is known as the San Augustin Mountains. The northern section is called the Hard Scrabble Mountains.

Father Milliano demanded that La Rue deliver the gold already extracted from the mine to the Church in Mexico City, and allow the Church to take over the mine, as well. La Rue refused and said that the mine belonged to the people, and was not his to turn over to the Catholic Church. La Rue had been informed of Milliano's arrival some days before and had ordered the mine entrance concealed. He was murdered by one of the soldiers one night after

117

the Milliano expedition arrived at the mine. Some of the colonists were later tortured for the location of the mine, but they refused to talk. With this, the Padre La Rue mine became lost. The year was circa 1830.

Chief Victorio's Secret Torture Chamber

Some 30 years passed when in 1862 a young Chiracahua Apache with the Spanish name of Victorio joined up with the Apache leader Mangas Coloradas and went on raiding parties with him. After Mangas died in 1863, Victorio slowly emerged as a tribal leader, forming a group of Eastern Chiricahuas and Mescaleros into a band of about 300 warriors. United States Army officers who fought against Victorio regarded him as a sound tactician and a leader of men. In 1869 he and his band settled near Fort Craig, New Mexico, to await the completion of a new reservation near Ojo Caliente, New Mexico.

A treaty between Victorio and the Federal Government was reached in the early 1870s, but was broken in 1878 when gold was found in the area and Victorio's band was ordered to San Carlos in Arizona. Victorio went on the warpath for several years, raiding white settlements and robbing traveling parties and stagecoaches. He was said to have amassed something of a treasure, including boxes of gold coins from Wells Fargo. Skeletons were said to have been found inside Victorio Peak, and it was said that Victorio would take prisoners back to the hollow mountain where he would torture them before killing them.

Later Doc Noss would indeed find skeletons, presumably victims of Victorio, tied to stakes in the lower cavern where they would die of starvation and thirst after being tortured.

As a note to researchers who might try to pick up strains of this story, Victorio Peak is frequently misspelled as Victoria Peak, and Phil Koury's 1986 book *Treasure of Victoria Peak* uses the wrong word throughout, including the title. I have seen a number of articles that begin by using the correct name, Victorio Peak, but then lapse later into the incorrect Victoria Peak.

Victorio and his raiders disappeared from the area around 1880. In August 1880, they fought the Buffalo Soldiers at Rattlesnake Springs. They were forced to flee into Mexico with Texas Rangers hot on their heels, fighting small skirmishes with them along the way. The Rangers chased them into the rugged mountains of northern Chihuahua, an area that even today is wild and largely uncontrolled by the central government.

The Mexican army was also chasing Victorio by this time and the Mexican Colonel Joaquin Terrazas met with the Texas Rangers. Terrazas ordered the Rangers back across the border into Texas, and their pursuit ended there. Terrazas later surrounded Victorio at a place called Tres Castillas and killed him and all his warriors, who were now less than 200. The women and children who survived were taken to Chihuahua City where they were imprisoned for several years. One of Victorio's comrades, Chief Nana, escaped with some of his men, and made it to Arizona to join Geronimo and his warriors.

This was the end of Victorio's control of the hollow mountain that he had somehow been shown sometime in the 1860s or 1870s. Maybe the old Apache chief Mangas Coloradas had shown it to him. How Victorio came to use the hollow mountain that bears his name, we will probably never know.

Doc Noss and the 100 Tons of Gold

For over 50 years people forgot about Victorio, and the mountain named after him, until Milton "Doc" Noss, the podiatrist from Oklahoma, stumbled on a hidden shaft beneath a flat stone at the top of the mountain during a hunting party in 1937.

Noss, who was a tall, handsome and energetic man, took shelter from a rainstorm under a rocky overhang near the summit of the mountain, which had a big rocky notch at the top. While waiting for the rain to subside, Noss said he noticed a stone on the floor that looked as if it had been "worked" in some fashion. Reaching down, he was unable to budge it, but after digging around the rock, was able to get his hands under it. After lifting the rock, he found a hole that led straight down inside the mountain!

Peering into the Stygian darkness of this hole in the peak, Doc could see an old man-made shaft with a thick, wooden pole attached at one side. Doc thought that he had discovered an old abandoned mineshaft. When the rain finally stopped, Doc returned to camp, telling his wife, Ova "Babe" Noss of his finds. The two decided to keep the discovery between themselves and return to inspect the mysterious shaft later.

With what little money they had, the Nosses bought flashlights, batteries, ropes and other exploration gear. They returned to the peak and Doc Noss quickly rejected the idea of going down into the shaft using the long, ancient pole that was notched with footholds. He decided to go down using the ropes, while Ova stayed on top.

Doc moved slowly down the rope in the narrow passageway, nearly 60 feet, until he came to a boulder that almost blocked the passage. He maneuvered around the boulder and then found himself at the bottom of the shaft. Walking forward into a passage he then entered a small room. There were some chiseled rock-art faces and paintings on the walls. At one end of the room was another shaft, going steeply down into the mountain. Doc descended down this passage, apparently not needing a rope, and after about 125 feet the shaft leveled off into a natural cavern that held several rooms. Some small rooms had been chiseled into one wall and the cavern stretched off into other larger rooms in the eerie darkness.

Suddenly Noss saw the skeleton of a man whose hands had been tied behind his back. He was in a kneeling position with his neck tied to a stake driven into the ground—a prisoner tortured and left to die. Then, as the glare from his flashlight fell farther back into the cavern, Noss saw more skeletons, each bound to stakes with their hands tied behind their backs. He later found even more skeletons stacked in a pile in one of the chambers, and counted 27 in total.

He continued to explore the caverns and began to find treasure. He found chests, some saying Wells Fargo on them, of coins, jewels, saddles, and priceless artifacts, such as gold crucifixes and a statue of Mary. There were also old letters, the most recent dated 1880, the year Victorio fled to Mexico.

Doc came to an underground stream that was flowing westward—it was dark and wide. He did not want to cross the stream—it was too wide to jump across, and he could not tell how deep it was. In the dark recesses of the caverns, it was quite frightening—a River Styx heading to the underworld. He could see other rooms on the far side, and eventually, with a staff to help him, he carefully crossed the stream, wading through it one step at a time. It was not too deep to wade across.

After crossing the underground stream, Doc

entered the main treasure area of the cavern which comprised an altar room, living room, bedroom and finally a room with stacked gold bars. At first Doc Noss thought that these dark-colored bars stacked against the wall, each weighing 40 pounds or more, were only made of iron or lead. There were thousands of these bars, he estimated.

He filled his pockets with gold coins and grabbed a few jeweled swords and then made his way back to the top of the mountain. When he got to the top he showed everything he had brought, and told Ova the story of the amazing cavern and ancient "mine."

When he told her about the stacks of iron bars, she insisted that he go back and get one of them. He struggled back down the shafts and tunnels and took the smallest of the heavy metal bars he could find and brought it back to the surface. As Ova looked the bar over, she noticed where the gravel had scratched off the black grime that covered the bar when Doc shoved it up onto the ground as he came out of the shaft. She could see gleaming gold shining in the scratches—it was a gold bar, not worthless iron! It has now been estimated that there were a hundred tons of gold, calculated at a worth over two billion dollars, inside the last room in the hollow mountain. In fact, as we mentioned above, David Leon Chandler named his important 1979 book about the Victorio Peak treasure *100 Tons of Gold*.[29]

Now, thrilled that they had found a lost treasure beyond their dreams, Doc and Babe Noss sold some of the gold coins to a pawn shop and then literally camped at the base of the peak in a tent and explored the tunnels inside the mountain. Ova apparently always stayed on top while Doc went inside to retrieve treasure. On each trip he would bring back two gold bars, plus all the other small artifacts, coins, or even documents he could carry.

🌀 🌀 🌀

Doc Noss and the Devil of a Mountain

Doc was thought to have brought over 88 gold bars out of the mountain, and in some accounts, hundreds of bars, plus plenty of other treasure, including a gold and silver crown with 243 diamonds and a large ruby.

But gold fever was taking its toll on Doc, and he trusted no one, not even Ova. He would disappear into the desert around Hembrillo Basin and bury bits of the treasure, including gold bars, where only he knew.

Among the many artifacts that Doc reportedly recovered were documents dated 1797, and he buried these with other documents in the Wells Fargo chests with other items from caves. Originals of these documents have never been recovered, though copies were made of a few of them, and one of the copied documents was allegedly from Pope Pius VI.

Doc was unable to sell the gold bars on the open market because of the Gold Act of 1933, an important act to treasure hunters—and finders— that made the private ownership of large amounts of gold illegal. This law stayed on the books until the early 1970s when President Nixon repealed the statute. Meanwhile, Doc Noss continued to take treasure out of the cave and hide it in the desert. He cared little for the historical value of any of the treasure, but was greedy for the gold. Gold that could either make him rich or land him in prison, or even get him killed. He began to get paranoid. One of his tricks was to saw lumps of gold off of his gold bars, and create small nuggets that he could sell by melting them and dropping them in a barrel of water.

He and Ova went to Sante Fe in 1938 and filed a lease with the state to prospect the entire section of land surrounding Victorio Peak. Shortly after that, he filed several mining claims for Victorio Peak, and even, reportedly, a treasure trove claim. Now he and Ova were the rightful owners of the claim, and he could work the claim openly. He still continued to hide gold bars in the desert and his paranoia of everyone grew, including suspicion of his wife.

Doc and Ova's story began to break in the newspapers, and they talked, to a limited degree, about the treasure they found. Owning and selling gold was still illegal. Local historians and curious folk began to wonder if Doc Noss had found the Casa del Cueva de Oro that was the subject of local legend.

Late in 1939, Doc Noss wanted to enlarge the passageway into the hollow mountain so that the treasures and heavy gold bars could be more easily removed. He hired a mining engineer named S.E. Montgomery. Doc took him to the mountain where he was supposed to blast out the shaft, mainly getting rid of the big boulder near the bottom before the first small room. Montgomery suggested 80 sticks of dynamite. Doc argued with him—it was too many sticks as the mountain was too unstable. Unfortunately, the "expert" won the argument. The blast was too powerful and caused a cave-in, collapsing the fragile shafts down to the first small room and beyond. Effectively, Doc Noss was shut out of his own mine.

It was a famous story told by Ova of Doc, mad as hell, chasing Montgomery down the mountain with one of his boots in his hand to beat the living crap out of his "expert." Montgomery ran for his old pickup truck as fast as he could, and Doc never caught up because the foot without the boot gathered too many cuts and cactus spines for Doc to continue after that no good #!%#![42]

After that, Doc and Ova tried several times to regain entry into the mine, but the shaft was now sealed with tons of debris that had caved in from above. With volunteers, and some paid workers, they began to excavate the main entrance and get the debris out. They built mining-style cages and pulley bars to bring out rocks and clear the shaft.

Although Doc had hidden away millions of dollars in gold bars already, he was obsessed with gaining entrance to the mine again. Also, he was frustrated with the difficulty of selling his gold. He was becoming a bitter, frustrated and angry man, and this caused problems in his marriage. He was secretive around his wife, and began having affairs. Doc Noss then left Ova and they got divorced in November 1945. He married Violet Lena Boles two years later, and that would complicate ownership of the treasure rights for years to come because Ova Noss would soon file counter-ownership claims against her ex-husband. After all, how many divorce settlements have to decide the ownership of a mountain that held a hundred tons of gold?!

Doc Noss teamed up with a man named Joseph Andregg, and they transported some of the treasure, including gold bars, to Arizona, where they sold them at some border town black market. It was not illegal to own gold in Mexico, and that would seem the likely way to get rid of it—by taking it over the border and ultimately to Mexico City. Still, reportedly it was not easy for them to find buyers, and it was a difficult—and suspiciously paranoid—time for everyone. It was proving very troublesome trying to sell illegal gold for a high price—a price that had to be paid because the bars of gold were quite large and valuable, as they weighed from 40 to 80 pounds apiece.

The end came for Doc when he met an oil explorer named Charlie Ryan in 1948. Ryan had the large amounts of cash that Noss needed to effectively sell his gold, and the technology to possibly open up the hollow mountain. They made an agreement that Noss would turn over some of the gold bars for $25,000 in cash from Ryan. This was quite a sum of money at the time, and Noss wanted to use it to buy digging equipment to reopen the mine.

However, Ova had filed a counter-claim to the Victorio Peak mining claim, and for the time being, Doc Noss was denied access to his precious hollow mountain with the hundred tons of gold. The ownership of the mine was now in question and Doc feared that Ryan would back out of his deal, and take the gold without paying him the $25,000. These deals were hard to set up and went bad too easily!

Noss and Ryan had agreed on an amount of the gold bars and they had buried them together in a place they both knew. But now, Doc Noss went out and reburied the gold, fearing that Ryan was going to double-cross him. Noss moved the gold to a place known only to him!

Ryan was supposed to secure in a private plane, load up the gold bars that Noss had shown him, pay the $25,000 in cash and fly to an undisclosed airstrip in Mexico. Strangely, there had been an airplane crash at Victorio Peak just the day before Noss met with Ryan for the last time. A bulldozer that had been working near Victorio Peak had broken down and needed a part. The part was being flown in from El Paso by the bulldozer owner and his cousin when a downdraft suddenly pushed the small plane to the ground as it was beginning to land. The plane broke up as it hit the ground. The pilot was instantly killed and the bulldozer operator was badly hurt but still alive. Doc Noss drove the injured bulldozer operator to Hot Springs where he could get treatment. Ironically, the bulldozer that had broken down was working on building a private airstrip.

Ryan had arranged for a private plane to land near Victorio Peak on this airstrip, but now the whole deal was falling apart. Ryan's plane, could however, still land on the partially constructed airstrip.

As we cruised up Interstate 25 heading for Socorro, I thought about the whole fantastic story. It was like one of the serials 1930s or 40s—*Rocket Men, Spy Smasher, The Shadow* and other cliffhangers of the era. There was the incredible lost treasure from centuries before, the secret meetings and double-crosses, explorers versus the government and local crime bosses. It was a pulp fiction tale taken from the real goings on of a small New Mexico town.

Ryan was furious when he found out that Noss had now moved the gold bars. Ryan knew the treasure existed, and that the gold bars were real, but Doc Noss was suspicious of everyone. Ryan would not show Doc the money before the deal went down. Did he have it? Doc figured he wanted to pay after he got the gold, but that was not good enough for Doc. Was Ryan real? Perhaps he was some sort of agent who was setting Doc up in the first place. Everything was clandestine.

The now-familiar drug deals featuring small airplanes landing in a remote spot where the occupants exchange cash and merchandise had not happened yet; they were ultimately to fine tune the art of private airstrip commodity exchanges. Plenty of gunplay and disastrous deals have occurred since then, but Doc Noss' big sale may have been the first

127

such deal gone bad.

On March 5, 1949, the day after the airplane crash, Doc Noss arrived at Charlie Ryan's place in Hatch. Ryan was sitting at his kitchen table with a pistol in his hand. He demanded that Noss tell him where he had moved the gold, while Noss insisted on seeing the $25,000 in cash. They argued and Ryan threatened Noss, saying he would not live to enjoy his gold if he did not tell him where he had hidden the gold bars they were to exchange.

In the intense argument that ensued Ryan flaunted his pistol. Noss suddenly ran for his car. Ryan later testified that he was afraid Noss was going after a pistol that was in his car, parked out in front of Ryan's house. Ryan fired a warning shot with the pistol he had been brandishing at Noss. He demanded that Noss get away from his vehicle where he was attempting to retrieve the gun. Noss did not stop and Ryan shot his gun a second time, hitting Noss in the head and killing him instantly.

Charlie Ryan stood trial for murder and was acquitted. He never paid out $25,000. He never got any gold. Doc Noss died with $2.16 in his pocket. The gold he buried in the desert around Hembrillo Basin was never found (or at least acknowledged to be found).

Ova Noss, who was to now deem herself the owner of the mountain, hired various men from time to time to try to clear the rubble out of the central shaft. The military then stepped in, and starting in 1955, the White Sands Missile Range began expanding their operations to encompass the Hembrillo Basin. Ova Noss began a regular correspondence with the military, requesting permission to go to Victorio Peak and work her claim, but she was always denied. From then on, every attempt of Babe's to clear the rubble from the plugged shaft met with a military escort out of the

128

area.

This was the beginning of long legal battles over the ownership of the claim. The military claim stemmed from a statement made by New Mexico officials on November 14, 1951 which withdrew prospecting, entry, location and purchase rights under the mining laws, reserving the land for military use only. However, disputing the military claim, New Mexico officials later stated that they leased only the surface of the land to the military. Further, they stated that underground wealth, in whatever form it took, belonged to the state or to any legal license holders.

The American Army had just won two majors wars, and it needed to expand. Huge areas of the United States were ceded to the U.S. Military in the 1940s and 50s. The military snapped up the entire southwest corner of Arizona along the Mexican border—a huge area—that is now the Barry Goldwater "Bombing Range." Victorio Peak, and its fantastic secret, were to fall victims to America's military buildup. The White Sands Missile Base, home of the Atomic Squadron, needed more land. They didn't care about Victorio, or Padre La Rue, or Doc Noss or for a hundred tons of gold. Or did they?

"Operation Goldfinger" and Ova Noss

Ova Noss continued to ask the military for permission to prospect on her claim, but she was continually denied. Meanwhile it was discovered that the real owner of the land was a rancher named Roy Henderson, who had leased the land to the Army. A settlement was reached in court that gave the Army the right to use the surface of the land, but it was not to do any "mining." However, they could prohibit entry to the land without special permission.

This of course they did, and Ova was effectively shut out off from the mountain. However, Army personnel were not shut off from the mountain, and two airmen from nearby Holloman Air Force Base would later say that they had found the gold cavern in 1958, entering the cave from another natural opening in the side of the peak. The soldiers, Airman First Class Thomas Berlett and Captain Leonard V. Fiege, claimed that they had found approximately one hundred gold bars weighing between 40 and 80 pounds each in a small cavern in Victorio Peak. It is generally thought that this cache of gold bars was Doc's big stash, which he had stowed in the small cave on the peak. Fiege supposedly told several people that he had caved in the roof of the newly-found entrance to try to make it look as if the tunnel ended.

Berlett and Fiege formed a corporation and made a formal application to enter White Sands for a search and retrieval of the gold. However, White Sands issued an edict expressly forbidding them to return to the base.

During the summer of 1961, on the advice of the Director of the Mint, Major General John Shinkle of White Sands allowed Captain Fiege, Captain Orby Swanner, Major Kelly and Colonel Gorman to "work" the claim.

On August 5, Fiege and his party returned to Victorio Peak, accompanied by the commander of the Missile Range, a secret service agent, and 14 military police. Fiege attempted to tunnel into the opening he had used three years earlier, but every attempt he made failed. General Shinkle finally had enough and ordered everyone out.

Apparently, Fiege then took a lie detector test and convinced the Army that he had indeed discovered the gold bars in the small cave. Now the Army actually believed him and began, in something of a secret operation, with Fiege as part of the deal, a full-scale mining operation at the Peak. The Army, with its heavy equipment resources, was going to open up that mountain!

But now Ova became suspicious of the Army's maneuvers in the area, and hired four men to spy on activities around the peak. These men were caught trespassing, and after being escorted from the area, they reported to Ova that they saw a military jeep, a weapons carrier, a number of poles about the width of telephone poles, and other timbers that were cut and notched, like the old ladders of Mexico and the Southwest.

It was at this time that the military moved in to retrieve the treasure. This may have been the original "Operation Goldfinger" (the name used for Ova Noss' later attempt to regain control of the mountain and the gold) says Chandler in *100 Tons of Gold*. He claims that a man named Fred Drolte was the CIA operative who facilitated the removal of the gold. Drolte was a one-armed pilot (presumably having lost his limb in WWII or the Korean War) who would fly daring missions into remote landing strips—one arm and all.

Little is known of Drolte, other than he was later arrested for gun running with an airplane and arraigned at the U.S. District Court in El Paso on March 16, 1966, where a newsman took a photo of him. This is the only known photo of Fred Drolte. Apparently, over the course of a number of flights, he flew the 100 tons of gold out of the Victorio Peak area.

During this time, a New Mexican Judge named Moreland reported the Army activity on Victorio Peak to Ova Noss. She told Oscar Jordan with the New Mexico State Land Office, who then contacted the Judge Advocate's Office at White Sands Missile Range. By December 1961, General Shinkle was forced to shut down the recovery operation and excluded everyone from the range who was not engaged in missile tests.

Thirty days later, under cover of darkness, Moreland and some friends returned to the Peak. It was totally deserted. Moreland saw the remains of extensive excavations, apparently carried out by the government. Judge Moreland and the others saw that there were roads and scaffolds and tunnels, even a metal door, on the peak. The Army, however, denied that they had found anything in the mountain.

In 1963, thinking that somehow the Army hadn't recovered the gold and other treasure, the Gaddis Mining Company out of Denver, Colorado, with a contract from the Denver Mint and the Museum of New Mexico, obtained permission to work the site. Starting on June 20, 1963, for three months the group used a variety of techniques to search the area; however, they failed to turn up anything. Apparently the Army (and Secret Service) had already taken the treasure, down to the last little piece, and then sealed off the mountain.

Did they create a nice military tunnel into the mountain, and clear out the debris down to the underground river? There did they reinforce the walls and begin to bring out the contents of those caverns? Surely, all the caverns hadn't caved in with the explosion of 80 sticks of dynamite? It seems that the Army did indeed recover the gold bars, probably worth at least a billion dollars, despite the fact that much had already been lost or sold.

But who actually got this gold? When the CIA and military fly gold bars out an Army Missile Range, where does it go? It would be something of a secret operation, one that would include the higher generals and, one would think, the President. Indeed, there is evidence that President Nixon was aware of the gold and that certain operatives within his administration carried these raw gold bars to trade in certain deals that they made in far-flung areas of the world.

As word of the incredible story and treasure leaked out, the famous lawyer F. Lee Bailey became involved in the dispute. In 1972, he litigated for some 50 clients including Ova Noss, the Captain Fiege group, Violet Noss Yancy (Doc's second wife), Expeditions Unlimited (a Florida based treasure hunting group), and a number of others who had invested or had some interest in the billion dollars of gold.

Reaching a compromise with Bailey and his clients, the military allowed Expeditions Unlimited, representing all of the claimants, to investigate and excavate the peak in 1977. This became known among the group as "Operation Goldfinger," named after the James Bond movie and novel, and referring to their belief that a secret government operation had already removed some of the treasure. However, the Army placed a two-week time limit on the group and they had hardly started before they were forced to leave, without finding much. Apparently they walked through steel doors, opened by the Army, to view part of a tunnel that had collapsed. With nothing to really show, the Army then shut down all operations stating that no additional searches would be allowed.

This was all big news at the time, especially in New Mexico, and everyone was interested in the story.

Lots of good publicity came from the 1977 investigation of Victorio Peak, but no fortune. If nothing else, it showed that fantastic treasures could actually exist—and that they could be grabbed and covered up by the government. It remains a good story. But it is not over yet!

Every mystery solved,
Brings us to the threshold of
A greater one.
—Rachel Carson

Harvey Snow and the Tunnel at Hard Scrabble Peak

Ova "Babe" Noss died in 1979. Her grandson Terry Delonas continues to try to gain access to the caves inside Victorio Peak. Even the Governor of New Mexico, Bill Richardson, has been part of legal proceedings involving Victorio Peak, and is fully aware of the astonishing story that I have just told.

Because of an article published in the November, 1968 issue of *True Treasure* magazine there was renewed interest in the fabulous cache, and a prospector named Harvey Snow was approached by three ranchers who lived in the area west of the Victorio Peak site. Snow had spent 25 years exploring the entire White Sands region, and the ranchers felt that Snow could lead them into the treasure area, bypassing the Army patrols that guarded the missile range.

Snow believed that the treasure of Doc Noss was not at Victorio Peak, but on another mountain (also on government property) named Hard Scrabble Peak. A cowboy that Snow had met many years before had once told him of how he had seen Doc Noss disappear into a secret cave on Hard Scrabble Peak and later emerge with pack mules loaded with (presumably) gold. The cowboy had gone into the nearly invisible cave, found cut stairs going down underground and began to follow the stairs. They went deep underground, but the cowboy did not follow them to the bottom. He was very much afraid that Doc Noss would kill him, and he never returned to the cave. Here was a different mountain with a different cave!

Harvey Snow took the ranchers to Hard Scrabble Peak in late November of 1968. They searched the mountain for two days before running out of supplies. They then returned to the mountain with new supplies and Snow was left there to search the southern face of the mountain. It was arranged that the ranchers would come back and get him in three days.

In his book *100 Tons of Gold*,[29] Chandler tells the incredible story of Snow's discovery on Hard Scrabble Peak. Snow told Chandler, "On the second day, I found the cave with the sloping steps. I went down the steps; down and down. I don't know how far. I estimated maybe thirteen hundred or fourteen hundred steps. The bottom step, the last one, was rounded at the bottom so that when you stepped on it, it would roll. It was tied to a bow and arrow with rawhide, but the rawhide had rotted away long before I got there."

Snow is describing an ingenious booby trap, apparently rigged by the Apaches, but possibly from some earlier culture. As someone stepped on the last stone of the stairway, he would trigger an arrow that was aimed at the step, thereby causing his own death. This may have been set up in 1880 shortly before the Apache chief Victorio's death.

Snow continues his story, "At the bottom you are in a big room. There is a stream of water running through. Now Noss described a cold stream, but this stream is hot. It has a copper and sulfur taste. It ran from east to west, toward the Jornada, and along what I assumed to be an old earthquake fault."

The Jornada that Snow speaks of is the Jornada del Muerto, Spanish for "the dead man's route." The Jornada is a wide plain to the west of the White Sands Missile Range and is named for a German trader who was imprisoned by the Spanish in Sante Fe in 1670 on the charges of being a heretic and a necromancer. He escaped jail but died on the trail as he fled south, hence, "the dead man's route."

Snow, now at the bottom of the stairs was in a tunnel with a stream flowing through it. "I followed it, going from room to room. In many places I had to get down on my hands and knees, and in a few places on my belly. After that first room, where the steps come down, I came into another room. Here I found some things. I found small stacks—one of gold, one of copper, and one of silver.

"I figured I would come back for that and went on. I next came to a big room. Here there were a bunch of side tunnels running north and south. They were all natural, nothing man-made. Here where they intersected, they made a big W. I did not go down those north-south tunnels. I stayed with the stream, going west.

"At the far end of the main room I found some things I cannot tell you about. But I will tell you what happened next. I kept going west, kneeling, crawling, and walking, hauling my little pack of food. I kept going through there for two days and two nights. I eventually followed that tunnel for fourteen miles.

"Where I was coming out was under the Jornada. That tunnel must not be far below the surface, because I could hear jets flying overhead, and when the train was traveling it sounded so near you thought it was in the tunnel with you.

"Finally, I felt some fresh air on my face and then I saw some light. The tunnel had been getting narrower and narrower all this time, and I figured I

136

was about to the end of it. I came to the hole where the light was coming from and stuck my head through. I was standing in a hole covered by bushes and I was smack in the middle of the Jornada."

Snow would not tell Chandler what was in the main room. He did tell Chandler that he had subsequently made a "few trips" to the room where he found the small stacks and removed some of the metal bars.

Snow's story is fascinating and virtually unbelievable to most people. He walked for 14 miles in an underground tunnel. The 1,400 steps or so that he walked down to the subterranean river must have taken him a good 700 or 800 feet below the entrance. The tunnel was crossed in at least one spot by another tunnel running at a right angle to the one he was following. The tunnel, which continued on past the spot where Snow exited into the dry plain, had an underground river flowing through it.

And what was in the main room that Snow would not describe? Was he sworn to secrecy or was it something that was indescribable? It may have been bodies, including a recently murdered treasure hunter, or could it have been something that was from some ancient, forgotten civilization? Perhaps Harvey Snow could not tell what he had seen because he was afraid that no one would believe his story if he did mention it. His story is fantastic enough without embellishing it with further details that would strain his credibility.

So, what of New Mexico's hollow mountain of gold? Father La Rue used it to help the people. Chief Victorio hoarded the gold and added to the cursed treasure. Doc Noss got some of it, but he greedily blew up the entrance and it killed him in the end. Ova Noss and others knew it was there, if only they could get to it. Ultimately, it seems, the U.S. Army

137

got the treasure. But we will revisit this in a bit.

What Happened to the Gold from Victorio Peak?

As we pulled into a gas station in Socorro, I looked out toward Hembrillo Basin to the east. Filling up the SUV with gas, I washed the windows and noticed a penny on the ground. Picking it up, I wondered what had happened to the gold taken from Victorio Peak? Had the Army spent it on new tanks and cannons?

In my previous book in which I wrote on Victorio Peak, *Lost Cities of North & Central America*, I said that the U.S. Government had gotten the gold, along with the Army and the CIA. Now it looks like the U.S. Government did not really get the gold, but elements within the CIA got their hands on some of the gold bars.

The Army was known to have bulldozed the peak out, and even placed a steel door over the entrance to the mountain. The state of New Mexico was particularly interested in the treasure claims, because under State Law, the treasure belonged to them. The Army assured the state that there was no gold in Victorio Peak and never had been.

Chandler gives good evidence in his book that a top secret operation took place at White Sands Missile Range in late 1961. On that date, the Secret Service, with the help of certain Army personnel at the Range, recovered the gold, and moved it to various locations for various purposes.

Chandler also shows that former White House counsel John Dean told of CIA operatives dealing with bars of gold in his book *Blind Ambition* (1976, Simon & Schuster, p.155): "Egil Krogh had described to me how, when he was bored with his deskwork, he had carried bars of gold bullion through Asia's

'Golden Triangle' in CIA planes and bargained with drug chieftains." The gold bars used in these illegal, clandestine operations allegedly came from the tunnel system inside of Victorio Peak.

A few years ago, I got a letter from a man who said he was Dr. Oren Swearingen. He told a strange story that dovetailed nicely with John Dean's story of gold bars, apparently from Victorio Peak being used by the CIA in Indochina. Dr. Swearingen said in his letter to me:

> Dear Mr. Childress,
> I have just today acquired a copy of one of your books, namely *Lost Cities of North & Central America*.
> I have not yet read it, but I browsed through it before buying it, and noticed several interesting things—which I would like to bring to your attention—Your book certainly covers a wide range of areas! Chiefly, I was very interested in your comments about Victorio Peak, and the Noss treasure—This happens to be a subject I know a great deal about...
> [A] big error is the big lie told by Harvey Snow about his "Cave of Steps" in Hardscrabble Mountain-—In the first place, Harvey was never inside the Cave of Steps, and he never knew where it was! In the second place, it is NOT on Hardscrabble, but is in Domijohn Canyon!
> Harvey got the story of the cave from a friend, who never told him where it was, because he didn't trust him—I have been to the cave with that man—Harvey finally admitted to me that he did not know where the cave was, and he told me who did know! I contacted him, and he drove from Oklahoma

139

to show me the cave—As for the number of steps in the cave, nobody knows how many, because nobody has gone all the way to the bottom! In that regard, nobody knows what (if anything) is at the bottom!

You are correct when you say that the gold in the peak was taken out by the army! Some of it ended up on the LBJ ranch in Johnson City—the fiancé of Linda Bird, on the occasion of a visit with her at the ranch, was pressed into service, helping them bury a shipment of 2000 bars—He didn't marry her, but he now lives in Amarillo and owns cattle ranches and a radio (and / or a TV) station! His name is Joe Batson—In the early stages of the recent ONFP (Ova Noss Family Partnership) project on the peak, we were contacted by a group of men, one of whom was LBJ's nephew, who wanted us to buy 79 tons of gold which they had stored in a New Jersey warehouse—offering it to us for 50 cents on the dollar—The family refused, not wanting to negotiate with crooks! They indicated to us that the JFK assassination was connected to LBJ's acquiring of the gold, which had been discovered while JFK was still in office—and as a result of his death, it went to LBJ instead of him!

So LBJ profited in TWO ways by the death of JFK! And curiously, it was LBJ who altered the parade route, sending it under the book depository!

Isn't that strange??

I look forward to reading the rest of your book!

Best Regards,

Dr. Oren Swearingen, College Station, Texas

I thought of that letter, and its accusation that LBJ had somehow ended up with most of the gold. It seemed fantastic, but something like that must have happened. Army Intelligence and the CIA must have gotten their share—probably thousands of bars of gold in all were removed from the cave. It could have bought entire governments! Maybe it did.

My head was spinning as we pulled out of the gas station. Was there really another cave with a "bottomless" staircase in Domijohn Canyon? Where was that? All of these areas are on military land where trespassers could be shot! Wherever it was, it would have to wait for another adventure.

Out where the desert meets the sky
Is where I go when I wanna hide,
Oh, Peyote,
She tried to show me,
You know there ain't no cause to weep
At Bitter Creek.
—Eagles, *Bitter Creek*

With Socorro in the rear view mirror, we headed north to Albuquerque. We had just enough time to stop at Los Lunas, about 35 miles south of Albuquerque. Here, on Hidden Mountain, we could view the mysterious Los Lunas Stone, which supposedly has a version of the Ten Commandments, or Decalogue, chiseled into it.

The Los Lunas Inscription is carved into the flat face of a large boulder resting on the side of Hidden Mountain. A trail leads from the road to the inscription. The language is Hebrew, and the script is the Old Hebrew alphabet, with a few Greek letters mixed in. Maps refer to it as "Phoenician

141

Inscription Rock," but it also has been called the Mystery Stone, the Ten Commandments Rock and the Decalogue Stone.

The inscription was apparently known to locals for many years. It got the attention of Cyrus Gordon,[158] Barry Fell[35] and others, who felt it was a genuine ancient inscription by trans-Atlantic voyagers.

In 1996, Prof. James D. Tabor of the Dept. of Religious Studies, University of North Carolina, interviewed Professor Frank Hibben (1910-2002) who was a retired archeologist for the University of New Mexico (we'll learn more about Hibben later). Tabor said that Hibben was "convinced that the inscription is ancient and thus authentic. He reports that he first saw the text in 1933. At the time it was covered with lichen and patination and was hardly visible. He was taken to the site by a guide who had seen it as a boy, back in the 1880s."[35, 36, 129]

According to specialized epigraphers like Barry Fell and Cyrus Gordon, the inscription uses Greek *tau, zeta, delta, eta,* and *kappa* (reversed) in place of their Hebrew counterparts *taw, zayin, daleth, heth,* and *caph,* indicating a Greek influence, as well as a post-Alexandrian date, despite the archaic form of aleph used. The letters *yodh, qoph,* and the flat-bottomed *shin* have a distinctively Samaritan form, suggesting that the inscription may be Samaritan in origin.

In 1949, Professor Robert Pheiffer of the Harvard Semitic Museum, translated the writing on the stone and concluded that the text is Paleo-Hebrew and is based on *Exodus* 20:2-17.[35, 36, 129]

Line one of the stone reads: "I am Yahweh thy God who brought thee out of the land…"

Line two contains text that seems to have been added to the original passage: "There shall not be unto them other gods before me."

142

In lines three through eight, the well-known text continues: "...of Egypt, out of the house of bondage. Thou shall not make unto thee a graven image.

"Thou shall not take the name of Yahweh in vain.

"Remember the day of the Sabbath to sanctify it.

"Honor thy father and mother that thy days be long on the soil which Yahweh thy God (hath) given thee.

"Thou shalt not kill.

"Thou shalt not commit adultery.

"Thou shalt not testify falsely against thy neighbor.

"Thou shall not covet thy neighbor's wife."

We climbed up to the top of the mountain and viewed the stone. Writing could clearly be seen on it. The sun was casting shadows over the stone and it would be getting dark soon.

Was this part of the legacy left by Phoenicians, Romans, Hebrews, Greeks, Egyptians and others who came up the river valleys, looking for gold and the Seven Cities of Cibola? If ancient Hebrews were coming to North America circa 100 AD, possibly with Romans, were they looking for a new Zion—a new Jerusalem? The Tribe of Dan—one of the "12 Tribes of Israel"—were also a branch of the Phoenicians. They were the ocean-going tribe of the Israelites.

Also, at the end of the Punic Wars, Rome had the largest navy in the world with over 2,000 ships by 32 BC. The newly defeated Phoenician-Carthaginian navy was estimated at 1,500 ships, while the Spanish armada of 1588 that attempted to defeat England had only 120 ships.

With such a huge navy, had Rome sent an armada of several hundred ships on probably several trips across the Atlantic? Such expeditions would have had a very international crew, as is typical among sailors in the Mediterranean. Roman ships of the time would have had Hebrews, Greeks, Anatolians, Libyans, Berbers, defeated Phoenicians as well as Roman citizens themselves. In Roman times the Roman citizen was of extremely high rank within the empire—they were the Free-Man who could pass without hindrance throughout the land. He was subject to no man's will, except the Roman Senate. Every ship would have been captained by a Roman Admiral with a loyal staff of well-trained Centurians. The crew would have been the mishmash of sailors with limited writing ability and a mix of alphabets, just as Barry Fell asserts.[35]

That night as we pulled into a motel in Albuquerque the waxing moon was just coming up over the Sandia Mountains to the east of the city. We had dinner in the central plaza of the old town, and walked along the sidewalks of the old city. Now the largest city in New Mexico, it still only had only a million people.

But, it had the quick pace of any big city. The ghosts of the early visitors—the Spanish explorers, the Apache raiders and the pilgrims who had come out west to meet an uncertain fate—they all walked these streets on that breezy evening.

The City of Rocks near Silver City, in an old print from 1854. Early travelers mistook the bizarre natural formation for an ancient city.

Another old print from 1854, this one showing a dust devil or prairie tornado.

The Mescalero Apache chief Victorio.

Above: American Army units attempt to ambush chief Victorio. Left: A 1951 comic about chief Victorio.

Milton Ernest "Doc" Noss.

"Doc" Noss on his horse with his faithful dog Buster.

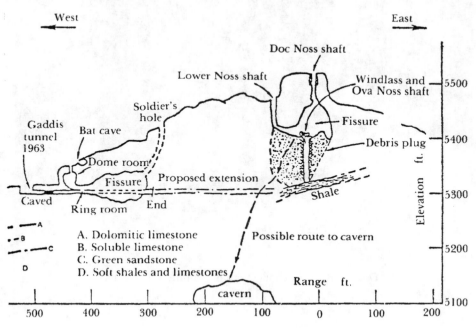

Top: Victorio Peak, seen from a distance. Bottom: A diagram of the various fissures, caves and tunnels that made up the core of Victorio Peak.

150

Milton Ernest "Doc" Noss standing in front of the cave at the top of Victorio Peak, circa 1938.

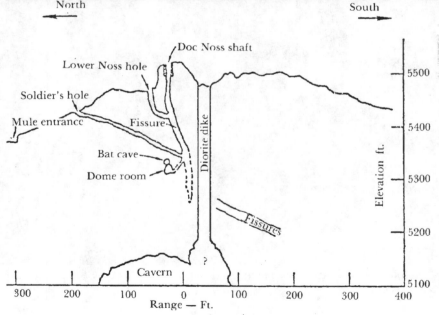

Above: A photo of Victorio Peak showing the roads built by the Army to reach the summit where the main shaft was located. Botttom: A diagram of the shafts inside Victorio Peak.

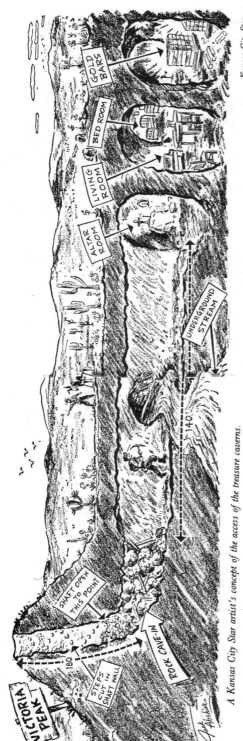

Kansas City Star

GOLD BARS

BED ROOM

LIVING ROOM

ALTAR ROOM

UNDERGROUND STREAM

140

SHAFT OPEN TO THIS POINT

ROCK CAVE-IN

STEPS CUT IN SHAFT WALL

180

VICTORIA PEAK

A Kansas City Star artist's concept of the access of the treasure caverns.

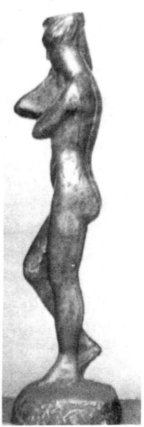

Left: A drawing of the tunnels inside Victorio Peak from the *Kansas City Star*. Above: A gold statue that reportedly came from the Victorio Peak treasure.

153

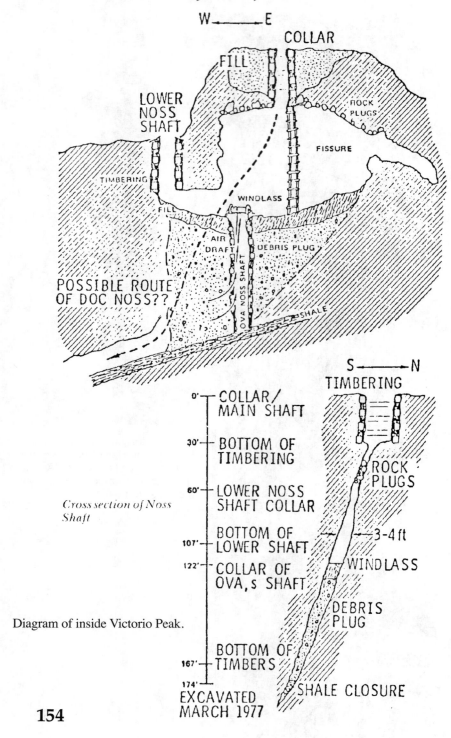

W ← → E

COLLAR

FILL

LOWER
NOSS
SHAFT

ROCK
PLUGS

FISSURE

TIMBERING

FILL

WINDLASS

AIR
DRAFT

DEBRIS PLUG

POSSIBLE ROUTE
OF DOC NOSS??

OVA NOSS SHAFT

SHALE

Cross section of Noss Shaft

S ← → N

TIMBERING

Depth	Label
0'	COLLAR / MAIN SHAFT
30'	BOTTOM OF TIMBERING
60'	LOWER NOSS SHAFT COLLAR
107'	BOTTOM OF LOWER SHAFT
122'	COLLAR OF OVA'S SHAFT
167'	BOTTOM OF TIMBERS
174'	EXCAVATED MARCH 1977

ROCK
PLUGS

3-4 ft

WINDLASS

DEBRIS
PLUG

SHALE CLOSURE

Diagram of inside Victorio Peak.

154

"Doc" Noss shot to death in Hatch, 1948.

Ova Noss holding up some gold slag for photographers, circa 1965.

155

Above: Victorio Peak in 1977 showing the granite cliffs of the very top. Left: An Army private helps Ova Noss at Victorio Peak in 1977.

Top: Several of the gold bars recovered by Noss inside the hollow mountain.
Bottom: Only known photo of the mysterious pilot Fred Drolte.

157

Top: Barry Fell at the Los Lunas inscription in 1865. Photo by Ida Gallager. Bottom: Photo from the 1950s of the Los Lunas stone and its Hebrew inscription that is apparently the Ten Commandments.

A Coptic Greek memorial stele from Cripple Creek, Colorado. Deciphered by Barry Fell, the stone reads: "Herein is the last resting place of Palladis, the servant of God." From Fell's book, *Saga America*.

159

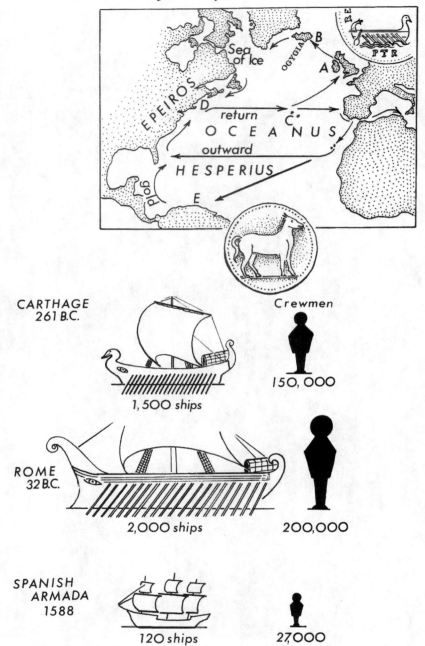

CARTHAGE
261 B.C.

Crewmen

1,500 ships

150,000

ROME
32 B.C.

2,000 ships

200,000

SPANISH
ARMADA
1588

120 ships

27,000

Top: Barry Fell's map of transoceanic traffic in the Atlantic. Center: A Roman coin found at E (Venezuela) and D (Massachusetts). Below: The relative size of the Phoenician, Roman and Spanish navies at their height. It has been said: "Who ever has the largest navy, rules the world."

160

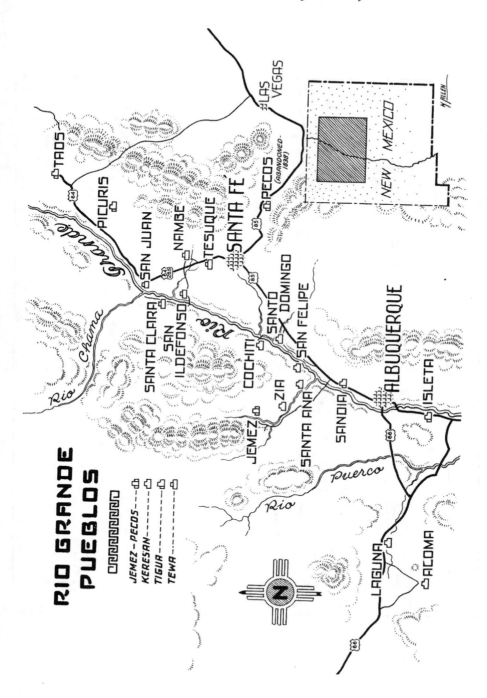

RIO GRANDE PUEBLOS

JEMEZ-PECOS-----
KERESAN-------
TIGUA--------
TEWA-------

NEW MEXICO

PECOS
(ABANDONED-
1838)

LAS VEGAS

TAOS

PICURIS

SAN JUAN

NAMBE

TESUQUE

SANTA FE

SANTA CLARA

SAN ILDEFONSO

COCHITI

SANTO DOMINGO

SAN FELIPE

ZIA

SANTA ANA

JEMEZ

SANDIA

ALBUQUERQUE

ISLETA

Rio Grande

Rio Chama

Rio

Rio Puerco

LAGUNA

ACOMA

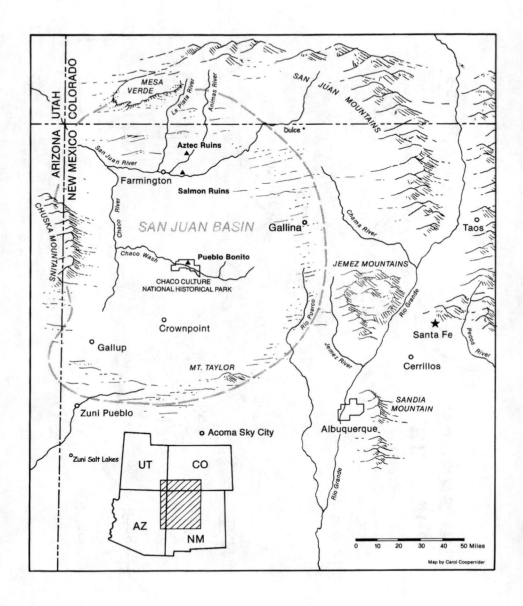

A map showing the San Juan Basin region with labels including MESA VERDE, SAN JUAN MOUNTAINS, Aztec Ruins, Salmon Ruins, Farmington, SAN JUAN BASIN, Gallina, Taos, Pueblo Bonito, CHACO CULTURE NATIONAL HISTORICAL PARK, JEMEZ MOUNTAINS, Crownpoint, Gallup, MT. TAYLOR, Santa Fe, Cerrillos, SANDIA MOUNTAIN, Zuni Pueblo, Acoma Sky City, Albuquerque, Zuni Salt Lakes. State boundaries for ARIZONA, UTAH, COLORADO, NEW MEXICO, CHUSKA MOUNTAINS, rivers San Juan River, La Plata River, Animas River, Chaco River, Chaco Wash, Chama River, Rio Puerco, Jemez River, Rio Grande, Pecos River, and Dulce. Inset map of UT, CO, AZ, NM. Scale bar 0 10 20 30 40 50 Miles. Map by Carol Cooperrider

4.
NORTHERN
NEW MEXICO

GHOST RANCH,
CHACO CANYON
AND THE ZUNI WARS

Well, they say, that Santa Fe
Is less than 90 miles a way.
...Oh, Albuquerque.
So I'll stop when I can,
Find some fried eggs and country ham,
I'll find somewhere,
Where they don't care,
Who I am.
—Neil Young, *Albuquerque*

The next morning we returned to the plaza in the old town of Albuquerque for breakfast, and I looked around at the various shoppers on the street. This crossroads of the Interstate system is now New Mexico's largest city. The Kirtland Air Force Base at the Sandia Military Reservation is nearby, occupying the southeast corner of Albuquerque. Rumor has it that the Air Force has a number of flying saucers stationed in Albuquerque and they can occasionally be seen coming out of the Sandia Mountains to the

163

east.

In 1980, an engineer named Paul Bennewitz who operated a small electronics company, Thunder Scientific Laboratory near the Sandia Military Reservation, became involved in observing and filming objects which he had sighted on the ground and in the air near Kirtland AFB and the Manzano range. The lights seemed to appear almost every evening and to fly towards Coyote Canyon, also a part of the Kirtland Air Force Base.

Subsequently he contacted Earnest Edwards of the Kirtland Security Police who, over the period of the next few months, became concerned and requested that the guards on the Manzano Weapons Storage Area report to him any sightings of unusual aerial lights.

At the beginning of August 1980 three guards reported sighting an aerial light that descended on the Sandia Military Reservation. Edwards reported the sighting to an Air Force Intelligence (AFOSI) agent named Richard Doty. Edwards was unaware that Doty had already heard from Russ Curtis (Sandia Security Chief) that a Sandia security guard sighted a disc-shaped object near a structure just minutes after the sighting by the three Manzano guards. Doty included these incidents and several others in his official report and forwarded the documentation to AFOSI Headquarters in Washington.

Bennewitz was called down to a meeting at Kirtland AFB at which several major Air Force officers and Sandia personnel were present, including a Brigadier General. Bennewitz presented his "evidence" that flying saucers or other UFOs were buzzing the base.

In that same year, Bennewitz and a psychologist/ UFOlogist named Dr. Leo Sprinkle investigated the story of a deeply troubled woman named Myrna Hansen who claimed that she and her young son had seen a UFO while driving on a rural road near Cimarron, in northeastern New Mexico. With the patient's permission, Dr. Sprinkle began hypnotizing her, and over a three-month period, Bennewitz and Sprinkle heard a very unusual story.

Under hypnosis, Hansen said that not only had she seen several UFOs that day, but she had also seen cattle being abducted—beamed up into the craft by some sort a "ray." She also said that she and her son had been abducted by aliens and taken to a secret underground base where they saw cattle being mutilated and drained of their blood and saw vats containing human body parts. She further said that some sort of devices were implanted in their bodies and that the aliens could control their minds through these devices.

Bennewitz believed Hansen's story, and he believed that it was connected somehow to the lights he was seeing over the Sandia Military Reservation. He began filming the lights, amassing over 2,600 feet of film. He also came to believe that he could receive signals from the craft that he observed. He built antennas and receivers to receive low-frequency electromagnetic transmissions that he believed came from the alien craft. Bennewitz called his "mission" *Project Beta*.

Bennewitz also came to believe that an underground alien base lay in the vicinity of the small town of Dulce in northern New Mexico, near the Colorado border. He came to believe that this is where Hansen had been taken by the aliens, and flew his private plane over Archuletta Mesa several times, looking for possible entrances into the supposed underground base.

UFO researcher Bill Moore met several times with Bennewitz and later claimed that he was recruited to lead Paul Bennewitz astray by giving him false information. Moore claimed that he was given his orders by an AFOSI Agent (probably Richard Doty) and that for four years he was asked to feed disinformation to Bennewitz. This disinformation included "verification" of Bennewitz' beliefs about the gray aliens and that there was an underground base near Dulce.

Bennewitz told Moore that the alien transmissions he had received indicated that two types of aliens had invaded the U.S.: The peaceful "whites" and the evil "grays." The grays, who he said were responsible for cattle mutilations and the abductions of humans, had a treaty with the U.S. government that allowed them to build a secret underground base beneath Archuleta Peak on the Jicarillo Indian Reservation where Dulce is the main town.

Unfortunately, Bennewitz gradually became more and more paranoid, claiming aliens came through the walls of his house at night and injected him with chemicals. He began keeping guns, knives and other weapons in various places around his house. Finally he had to be hospitalized for "exhaustion."

Paul Bennewitz never really recovered from his bizarre adventures into UFOdom, and he died on June 23, 2003, probably never knowing what had happened to him. Perhaps no one really knows.

Paranoia strikes deep.
Into your life it will creep.
It starts when you're always afraid.
Step out of line— the man come to take you away.
— Buffalo Springfield, For What Its Worth

Airships Over the Wild West

Finishing my coffee and leaving a tip for the waitress, I said to Jennifer, "Well, if Paul Bennewitz thought there was an alien base in Dulce, New Mexico I guess we'll have to go there and check it out."

"Well, we need to stop in Santa Fe on our way," she said. "We can look for aliens there first."

"Okay," I agreed, and we headed out of Albuquerque, going east to Tijeras and then turning north on Highway 14. This was the Turquoise Highway, going past Sandia Peak, through ghost towns and ancient turquoise mines. We stopped in the old coal-mining town of Madrid, where the movie *Wild Hogs* was filmed.

Today, Madrid is tourist town, with craft shops, art galleries, and other tourist offerings. We checked out the old saloon, and I bought a crystal skull, a few inches high, at a jewelry and gemstone shop.

The next town north is a quasi-ghost town that was once a mining boom-town that serviced the workers at various turquoise, gold, silver, lead, zinc and coal mines in the rich Cerrillos Hills north of town. This area is now a state park. It is believed that these were ancient mines used by the mysterious Anasazi and the Pueblo Indians who are their descendents. Historians say that the early Spanish enslaved locals to mine turquoise with crude hand tools prior to the Pueblo Revolt in 1680.

After the Pueblo Revolt the mines were eventually worked again and the town had 21 saloons and 4 hotels during the mining peak of the 1880s. Today there is a saloon and café, plus a gift shop or two.

We continued over the mountains on Highway 14 towards Golden. East of us was the small town of Galisteo on Highway 41. It was in Galisteo that a famous airship incident occurred in 1880.

Like some episode of the 60s television show *The Wild West* with futuristic western-sci-fi stories, the incident near Galisteo makes us wonder if truth is stranger than fiction. Throughout the 1880s and 1890s there were a number of mysterious newspaper reports of airships cruising the American West, including an early report from the March 29, 1880, issue of the *Weekly New Mexican* headlined: "A Mysterious Aerial Phantom."

The newspaper article said that several men had been walking near the railroad tracks at Galisteo Junction the evening of March 26, when they heard voices that seemed to come from the sky. At first, they thought it was an echo from someone talking in the nearby hills, but looking up, they saw a large airship approach from the west. Though not mentioned in the story, the object may have been following the railroad tracks, apparently going east.

As the airship approached, they were able to make out what they said was a gigantic balloon, shaped like a fish. It swooped low enough that the amazed observers could see distinct writing, or characters, on the side of the gondola that carried the passengers. The article mentioned that, "The air machine appeared to be entirely under the control of the occupants, and guided by a large sailing apparatus." They described it as "monstrous in size," and speculated that it could carry eight or ten persons. The unnamed men were amazed by the speed and maneuverability of the "air machine."

Inside the airship, the people were apparently having a great time, as the men could hear music, laughter, and voices in a language they could not understand coming from the vessel. Several objects were suddenly dropped from the balloon. In the darkness, however, the men found only "a magnificent flower, with a slip of exceedingly fine silk like paper," on which there appeared to be some sort of writing that they thought resembled Japanese. Then the vessel "assumed a great height and moved off very rapidly towards the east."

On the very next morning the men returned in search of other objects dropped from the balloon. They uncovered a cup "of very peculiar workmanship," and very different from anything the men had ever seen. Both the cup and the flower they found the night before were reported to be on display at Galisteo Junction, where they could be examined "by anyone who desire[d] to see them."

Then, according to the bizarre article, the following day, a "collector of curiosities" had gone to see the flower and cup. The unnamed collector was quite taken by the objects dropped from the balloon and he offered the men "such a sum of money for them that it could not be refused." The new owner of the airship artifacts then proceeded to express his opinion that the balloon was undoubtedly from Asia, most probably, he said, "from Jedde."[55]

One might have thought that this was all that was to be heard about the mysterious airship, but a few days later the newspaper ran another story which revealed that the individual who bought the flower and cup had been "excavating for ancient curiosities" at the old Pecos Pueblo church, one of the oldest buildings in New Mexico. According to the paper, a group of tourists stopped by to visit him, and among them was a "wealthy young Chinaman" who was touring the Wild West. The group was shown the objects from the airship, and their attention was drawn to the writing on the wrapping of the flower that had been dropped from the balloon.

When the young aristocrat from China saw the writings, he shouted for joy, and exclaimed that he knew who had dropped the objects! He then explained that for some years, the government of China had held "great interest" on the subject of "aerial navigation." The Chinese government had spent quite a bit of money on experimental aircraft shortly before he had left Peking, and "strong hopes were expressed that victory had at last crowned these efforts." The Chinese visitor remarked that the "mysterious aerial phantom" was in fact "the first of a regular line of communication between the Celestial Empire and America."

The article finished by saying that when the young Chinese visitor had left Peking, he had been engaged to marry a young lady from a very wealthy family. His fiancée, who had a sister who lived in New York, was apparently aboard the balloon. Knowing he was in this part of the country, he surmised that she must have written the note, placed it in the cup, and dropped it overboard, hoping, as it did, that the message would find its way to him. The visitor from China was reportedly last seen boarding the train at Galisteo and heading for New York City, confident his fiancée and others from the airship would be awaiting him upon arrival.[55]

Like many newspaper stories of the old frontier, this one seems quite far-fetched. That some mysterious airship had indeed been seen, or even landed along the tracks at Galisteo Junction seems possible, though a Chinese tourist whose fiancée was on board the airship makes the whole story appear to be fabricated, when perhaps only parts of it were. That the airship was of Chinese or Japanese manufacture, or from "Jedde" is a fascinating assumption, perhaps because all things strange and fantastic must come from the Orient or exotic Arabia where Mecca and Jeddah were at the time the major cities.

Perhaps they were ancient masters flying in their *vimanas*, those who followed the teachings of Osiris, they were the Djedi, named after the Djed column of Egyptian iconography. Many Arabian names originally come from ancient India, like Jeddah, Oman, Mohamed, Socorro, and others.

The Giant Snake of the Pecos Ruins

We made it that night to Santa Fe, where we stayed with an old college friend of Jennifer's named Maria. Fortunately she had a guest room that we could stay in for a few days while we explored the area. The next day, Maria accompanied us on a trip to the Pecos Ruins, east of Santa Fe.

The scattered stone ruins of Pecos are the remains of what was once the largest Indian pueblo in the Southwest. Pecos Pueblo dominated a major trading route between the farming Pueblo Indians and Great Plains hunters. This area was the western edge of the grazing area for the huge herds of buffalo that once roamed the Great Plains. Archeologists say that the site is the setting of a continuous story of human habitation covering a 7,000-year period.

Archeologists believe that current pueblo dates back to sometime around 1100 AD, when Pueblo settlers in the Rio Grande Valley moved into the upper Pecos Valley to form scattered hamlets. Over time, the population slowly grew, but around 1200 AD, it dramatically increased, possibly as a result of immigration.

The locals called the city Cicuye, but the Spanish renamed it Pecos. The main pueblo was constructed like a fortress, with high outside walls. From its ramparts, Pecos warriors had a clear view in all directions. A perimeter wall provided a defensive line against attackers.

The name "pecos" may come from the Spanish "pecoso," meaning freckled. Historians are baffled why the Spanish named the pueblo this. It is an interesting thought that the people were genuinely freckled on their skin, much like Vikings and other red-haired people. Did the Pecos people somehow have Viking genes in them? Wherever it came from, the name became permanently established and has been applied to the nearby river and to two towns.

The pueblo contained numerous ceremonial chambers, known as "kivas," and was built around a central plaza on a rocky ridge. What gave Pecos a military advantage was its strategic trading location between the agricultural Pueblo communities of the northern Rio Grande to the west, and the nomadic hunting tribes of the plains.

In 1540, while searching for the lost cities of Cibola, one of Coronado's lieutenants with accompanying soldiers arrived at Cicuye. The arrival did not provoke a furor among the people of the pueblo because some of them had previously seen Coronado and his followers at Zuni Pueblo to the west. A Coronado chronicler described Cicuye as "a strong village, four stories high. The houses do not have doors below, but instead ladders are used which can be lifted up like a drawbridge."

Pecos was left alone until 1590, when the conquistador Castano de Sosa and his men stormed and occupied the pueblo. In 1598, Juan Onate, first governor of New Mexico, assigned a priest to live in the pueblo; he attempted to convert the inhabitants to Christianity. A church was eventually built named "La Mission de Nuestra Senora de Los Angeles."

In 1880, banker turned archaeologist Adolph Bandelier began investigations of southwestern Indian culture by examining the Pecos ruins. He studied the tumbled walls, photographed them, accumulated artifacts and interviewed local residents about their recollections of the village and its former occupants. Bandelier also saw the church gone to ruin because uncaring persons had ripped out beams, scarred the walls with graffiti, and even exposed dead bodies in the cemetery. Later, from 1915 to 1927, Pecos was the subject of one of the first organized excavations of a southwestern ruin.

Mystery surrounds the site, and Willa Cather who immortalized the ruins in her 1927 novel,

Death Comes for the Archbishop[75] says that, "Pecos had more than its fair share of dark legends. ...This tribe was particularly addicted to snake worship, they kept rattlesnakes concealed in their houses and somewhere in the mountains guarded an enormous serpent which they brought to the pueblo for certain feasts. It was said that they sacrificed young babies to the great snake and thus diminished their numbers."

In Willa Cather's novel there is an episode where the main character, Father Latour is caught in a snowstorm with his Indian guide Jacinto. Jacinto leads the priest to a cave somewhere in the vicinity of the Pecos ruins where there is a high ceiling and the charred wood and ashes of a large fire.

Jacinto tells the priest that the cave is a secret place and that he must forget about it after they leave. He then proceeds to a part of the cave where there seems to be a doorway to another part of the cavern and begins to deftly place stones one after the other to seal up the small doorway. After sealing up this section of the cave he builds a fire in the remains of the campfire and the two spend an uneasy night. Father Latour ponders as he lies by the fire in the night what dangerous thing had been sealed up in the other part of the cave.[75]

In his book *More Mysteries & Miracles in New Mexico*,[31] Jack Kutz writes about a giant snake in the Pecos Ruins. Kutz tells the story of an old sheepherder who told stories in the ruins circa 1838 when they were abandoned. Says Kutz:

> In days gone by, the old man said, the people kept a holy fire constantly burning in a mountain cave. They had been commanded to do so by the Lord of the Aztecs himself, Montezuma, for in the depths of that dark cavern dwelt a giant snake—a monstrous

173

reptile so fearsome it could only be kept confined by fire.

When Montezuma left Pecos, he ordered the people to keep the cave fire burning until his return. This the Pecoseños did faithfully, but Montezuma never came back. Eventually there was no one left to feed the flames. The fire had gone out, and now, no one knew for sure what had become of the great snake.

...Josiah Gregg, in his book *Commerce of the Prairies*, wrote that "on one occasion I heard an honest ranchero assert that entering Pecos very early on a winter's morning, he saw a huge trail of a reptile in the snow, as large as that of an ox being dragged."

Equally odd was the tale told to Helen H. Roberts, author of *The Reason for the Departure of the Pecos Indians for Jemez Pueblo*. Roberts had spent a couple of summers during the 1920s collecting pueblo songs and had made close friendships with a number of Indian families. Ignacio Aguilar, a San Idlefonso Indian about 70 years old, told her of an incident his grandfather had witnessed. He said that one day, while his grandfather and some friends were hunting along the Rio Grande, a band of very excited Pecos Indians appeared.

When asked why they were so far from home, the Pecoseños said they were searching for their snake god which had escaped from its den near their pueblo. They showed the San Ildefonsos the trail of flattened brush the creature had left behind. The elderly Aguilar and his companions timorously joined the Pecoseños in following the serpent's track.

Before long, they found the place where the snake had slithered into the river, apparently vanishing forever. According to Ignacio

Aguilar, the serpent's disappearance was a major factor in the Pecos people's decision to abandon their pueblo. With the snake no longer there to grant favors, their hard times grew even harder, forcing them to move on.[31]

Kutz mentions that folklorist Frank Applegate believed that the tale of Montezuma having come to Pecos Pueblo was in reality the story of the Pueblo prophet Pose Ueve, who wandered from pueblo to pueblo as a shaman sometime prior to the Spanish Conquest.

Pose Ueve is thought to have been born at or near the present day Tewa Pueblo of San Juan. As a youth, he supposedly wandered in the forests and talked to animals, including birds, which constantly surrounded him. Eventually, he talked with spirits that others could not see. He became a *cacique*, a high priest who traveled from pueblo to pueblo.

He settled in Pecos and was famous for his ability to bring rain and to warn the people of approaching enemies. Eventually Pose Ueve left Pecos and supposedly told them to keep their sacred fires burning forever—and perhaps started the rumored serpent cult. [31] For hundred of years the fires were kept at Pecos, but they burn no more.

As we headed back to Maria's house in Santa Fe, I wondered about the giant snake of Pecos. Did such huge snakes like this exist in the American Southwest? I had heard rumors of rattlesnakes that were 55 feet in length and as thick as the large branch of a tree. Did the Pecos priests somehow keep a monster rattlesnake like this captive in a cave as the legends claimed? It seemed incredible!

Another curious thing about the Pecos ruins is their supposed use of "light machines." David Chandler mentions that the Hopi had a fascinating generator for making light that was made out of luminescent quartz. It consisted of a rectangular base of pure white-vein quartz with a groove in it and a bolster-shaped upper piece of the same material. Rapid friction by rubbing produced a strong glow in the dark, which was used to light the sacred kivas. These light machines were used in other pueblos, and one was discovered in the ruins at Pecos.

Says Chandler, "The machine still worked perfectly when it was discovered by archaeologist Alfred Kidder in the Pecos ruins, as he reported in 1932. Archaeologist S.H. Ball remarked upon it, 'Here we have a perfected machine perhaps seven hundred years old; the first Indian to observe luminescence of quartz must have done so centuries earlier."[29]

Chandler goes on to say that similar "lightning machines" or "glow stones" have been found at several other localities in north-central New Mexico. Chandler also speaks of emeralds coming from these ancient mines that the Apache so fiercely guarded. Emeralds are not known to exist except in Colombia and Brazil, but were thought to exist in some areas of the Southwest, including New Mexico, Arizona and southern California.

Chandler is quoting from Stuart A. Northrop's *Minerals of New Mexico* (1959, University of New Mexico Press, Albuquerque) on both the existence of emerald mines and the quartz light machine that the ancient Indians used. These machines to generate light may still be being used by Hopi, Zuni or other tribes, in secret ceremonies in their kivas.[29]

The emerald mines were apparently in the vicinity of Santa Fe, according to Northrop, but the location of these ancient mines remains a mystery. The ancient mines around Cerrillos may have also held emeralds in ancient times. Or perhaps these lost mines were closer to the Pecos Pueblo—we may never know.

With the sun setting in an orange glow on the horizon, the lights of Santa Fe began to twinkle in the distance. A cozy restaurant with Mexican food and cold margaritas was waiting for us somewhere downtown. The ancient gem and buffalo skin bazaar that had formerly been in the central plaza of the Pecos Pueblo had now moved to the central plaza of Santa Fe. Perhaps the major difference between then and now is that the modern folks of Santa Fe don't keep rattlesnakes in their houses like they did back in Pecos.

First left my woman,
It was down in Santa Fe.
Headed for Oklahoma, I was ridin' night and day
All my friends are strangers…
I'm an outlaw man.

—Eagles, *Outlaw Man*

Ghost Ranch and Beyond

After another day seeing Taos, and driving through Questa, Red River and Angel Fire in a circle around the Sangre de Cristo Mountains, we headed out of Santa Fe one bright morning and drove west from Espanola on Highway 64 to Abiquiu, and then north to the Ghost Ranch.

The Ghost Ranch was owned by Arthur Pack when the famous painter Georgia O'Keeffe (1887-1986) first came to northern New Mexico in 1917 with her sister. The soon-to-be-famous artist described her instant love for northern New Mexico by later saying, "When I got to New Mexico, that was mine."

O'Keeffe moved from her home in Texas to New York City and became a famous painter. It was 12 years before O'Keeffe returned to New Mexico and even longer before she found her way into the beautiful valley that would eventually become her summer home. Although she never owned Ghost Ranch, O'Keeffe eventually purchased a small home from Arthur Pack and later a home in Abiquiu. She spent many years exploring and painting the Ghost Ranch environs.

The 21,000 acres that comprise Ghost Ranch were part of a land grant to Pedro Martin Serrano from the King of Spain in 1766. The grant was called *Piedra Lumbre* (shining rock). However, the locals preferred to call the area the *Rancho de los Brujos*—meaning Ranch of the Witches (or Warlocks) since the area was said to be haunted by evil spirits. The name "Ghost Ranch," was commonly used in English.

According to the official brochure that they give out at the Ghost Ranch, the area is haunted by several entities. There have been frequent reports of six-foot tall "earth babies" covered with red hair howling at night, and a ghost cow with the ghosts of men killed in battles between sheep and cattle ranchers, and also the spirits of rustlers who once lived in Ghost House.

For many years only a narrow dirt road led up the twisting Chama River Valley northwest from Abiquiu. The turnoff to Ghost Ranch was marked by the sun-bleached skull of a steer years before Arthur Pack bought the ranch in 1936.

There were many bones to be seen in this high desert country and O'Keeffe was entranced by them, painting them, displaying them, and shipping a barrelful back to New York. O'Keeffe made a drawing of the skull of a steer and presented it to Arthur Pack as a gift. He promptly adopted the artwork as the logo for the Ghost Ranch. Ultimately, the Ghost Ranch was given by Arthur Pack and his wife to the Presbyterian Church in 1955. By 1971, partly at O'Keeffe's suggestion, her familiar skull design was firmly established as the official Ghost Ranch logo. She died in Santa Fe on March 6, 1986.

As we walked around the Ghost Ranch, visiting the excellent Paleontology Museum and gift shop, I wondered if the "earth babies" were the Southwest's version of Bigfoot, stinky and making their standard wild screams at night, scaring the crap out of everyone for miles. Bigfoot screams are like the high-pitched wailing of the banshee, and those who have heard it say that it is very frightening and seems to be the awful sound of something supernatural.

The museum had fossils of small raptor-like dinosaurs called *Coelophysis* that had roamed the area in the late Triassic era (said to be 200 million years ago). The *Coelophysis* is now the New Mexico state fossil. The name means "hollow form" and its bones were hollow like bird bones. This carnivore could grow to eight feet tall and it used its forepaws as hands. Parts of over 1,000 dinosaur skeletons have been removed from the Ghost Ranch Quarry.

While paleontologists speculate that these mini-dinos have been extinct for millions of years, they are occasionally reported in northern New Mexico and Navaho territory. Are mini-dinos, like the ones seen at the Ghost Ranch, still running around the remote ravines and river valleys around there?

Maybe it was the ghosts of the dinosaurs that roamed the Ghost Ranch and areas beyond. Bigfoot and the witches flew up and down the canyons on windy nights, or crept under the bushes in the ravines, ready to pounce on travelers, or just howled like banshees under the full moon. In that strange part of northern New Mexico, anything could happen.

The Mystery of the Stone Towers

Jennifer and I continued westward on Highway 96 after visiting the Ghost Ranch. We passed through the red dirt streets of Youngsville and Coyote. Another half an hour along the winding mountain road, we came to Gallina, a tree-shaded town that was originally settled in 1818. Says the *Roadside History of New Mexico,* "The post office was not established until 1890. The most remarkable feature of the area is the nearby ruins of the Gallina towers; they have been called New Mexico's lost cities."[76]

A cowboy named Joe Arellano noticed piles of stone scattered throughout the Rio Gallina area in 1934. The piles of rock, some round, some square, were scattered around the mesas and canyons of the area and Arellano thought that there might be gold or other treasure in these ruins. He did some digging, but all he got were some broken pottery vessels and a fine from the local rangers for digging on government property.

According to Francis and Roberta Fugate, who wrote *Roadside History of New Mexico:*

> Excavations revealed a series of ruins along the Gallina River from Cuba to El Vado. There were subsurface pit houses, single-unit houses, cliff dwellings, and large stone towers. Towers in any form are not common to the Southwest, but there were hundreds of them. They were built with crude blocks of sandstone held in place by adobe mortar, often more than 30 feet high, entered from openings in the roof.
>
> Everywhere there was evidence of violence, death, and destruction wrought by unknown invaders. Every community in the widespread complex had been attacked and burned. Skeletal remains revealed that one middle-aged warrior fell clutching his throat. He had arrows in his neck and arm. A young boy had been in a tower when it was fired. Though struck in the hip by an arrow, he had apparently tried to climb the ventilating shaft.

The lower half of his body was burned; the upper half was preserved by the heat. Ten skeletons were found in one pit house, arrows deeply imbedded in their backs and stomachs. Others had gaping axe wounds in their heads. Even more mystifying, the fingers of some had been sliced off at a peculiar angle, leading to the supposition they were tortured prior to being killed.

The questions—Who did it? When? Why?—remain a mystery. The arrows were similar to those made by the Gallinas themselves.[76]

Frank Hibben and the Mongol Invasion of North America

What great battle had been fought at these mysterious towers? Was it the battle that ended the pre-Pueblo Anasazi peoples? University of New Mexico archaeologist Frank C. Hibben was the first to excavate the 700 year-old archaeological mystery that has yet to be solved. His little-known discoveries at the series of "medieval-looking fortifications" in the remote Gallina River valley were published in the *Saturday Evening Post* for December 9, 1944 under the title "The Mystery of the Stone Towers." Except for Hibben's article, published some years after his expedition, almost nothing is known about this strange and remote valley.

Frank Hibben was born in Lakewood, Ohio in 1910 and first came to New Mexico in the mid-1930s on an expedition to collect small mammals and birds for the Cleveland Museum of Natural History.

A 1933 Princeton University archaeology graduate, Hibben was so fascinated by the Native American cliff dwellings that he decided to attend graduate school at the University of New Mexico and make New Mexico his home. Dr. Hibben received a master's degree in zoology with field studies of the mountain lion from the University

181

of New Mexico in 1936.

He continued his education at Harvard, receiving his Ph.D. in archaeology in just one year, and then returned to New Mexico to begin his teaching career at UNM. During World War II, Hibben served in the Navy as a commissioned officer and aide to Admiral Foy of the Joint Chiefs of Staff in Washington, D.C. His duties were to memorize final battle plans and carry them—only in his mind—to commanding officers in the various war theaters. He was in a plane shot down toward the end of the war by a German submarine, and carried shrapnel until his death.

Some of his books include *The Lost Americans* (1946), *Treasure in the Dust* (1951), *Prehistoric Man in Europe* (1958), *Digging Up America* (1960), *Hunting in Africa* (1962), *Kiva Art of the Anasazi* (1975) and a series of limited editions including the most recent *Under the African Sun* (1999). His articles appeared in the *Saturday Evening Post, Reader's Digest, Field and Stream, Outdoor Life*, the *Denver Post, Empire* and many sporting magazines and professional periodicals.

Hibben was controversial for some of his views and was accused of possible fakery by his conservative peers. The primary source of the controversies was Hibben's claim to have found a deposit with pre-Clovis artifacts (including projectile points, which he termed "Sandia points") in Sandia Cave near Albuquerque. Hibben believed the layers to be about 25,000 years old, much older than the Paleo-Indian cultures previously documented in the U.S. Southwest. Others doubted his claims and "exaggerated" date of 25,000 BP. Hibben writes briefly about the find in his book *The Lost Americans*.[77]

Hibben was fascinated by the towers of Gallina and found evidence of a mass slaughter in the valley from a fierce battle. Inside the stone towers were the skeletal remains of the defenders, many with arrowheads still embedded in their chests and backs, as described above.

182

Hibben described the towers as typically square and from 25 to 35 feet high. Each tower had a parapet at the top for men to stand on and fight. There were no doors or windows in the towers; they could only be entered or exited from the top. Massive slabs of sandstone were perfectly fitted into the floor.

Inside the first tower, where a few defenders had died and had fallen back inside when the roof collapsed, were the well-preserved remains of women-warriors. Says Hibben, "The remarkable dryness of the Southwestern climate, together with the charring action of the fire, had perfectly preserved the bodies and the evidence with them. They were better preserved than many Egyptian mummies. Here was the body of a woman sprawled backward over one of the storage bins. She had been crushed by falling stones from the top of the wall, but her body was remarkably preserved even to a look of intense agony on her somewhat flattened face. Studded in her breast and stomach were the charred ends of 16 arrows of cane with flint heads. She still clutched in her left hand a bow, even with a part of the string still on one end. It was a short bow, powerful looking, of oak wood, and yet the body was undoubtedly that of a woman."

Hibben calls the attack on the Gallina towers, "vengefulness without any quarter." Through tree-ring dating, Hibben said the dates for the construction of the towers was from the year 1143 AD to the year 1248 AD. Apparently, in one century, the towers were built and "equally apparent is the fact that some people swept through the country and destroyed them all."

Hibben says, "It seems obvious that the Gallina people were not ordinary Pueblo Indians. The physical make-up of the skeletons in the towers was slightly different. Many of the their utensils and weapons were radically different. For instance, their

183

typical cooking pots with the pointed bottoms are absolutely un-Pueblo-like. The fact that they used elk antlers for axes and adzes is unlike the Pueblos. The very fact that they built stone towers in itself distinguishes them from any of the pueblo peoples that we now know. In one of the towers we found a handful of pieces of pottery of a type which is not indigenous to the Southwest at all. This is a variety of pottery known in Nebraska, and even farther to the east in the Mississippi Valley."

Concludes Hibben, "They came from the plains, possibly as far eastward as the Mississippi Valley itself, and brought with them a number of their characteristics." Hibben, after analyzing the arrows used in the attack, decided that the Pueblo Indians were responsible for the total decimation of these mysterious people.

Were the strange people who had been killed in the towers some sort of early wave of the Apaches, the Dene and Na-Dene speakers, who originated in Siberia and Canada?

Jennifer and I were discussing the massacre on the tailgate of the SUV where we were having a snack. I carried cardboard boxes of various things in the back of the SUV. One box was full of tools and automotive things. Another box held camping and survival stuff, including ready to eat soups, candles, first aid, cutlery and other items, while still another box held guide books, atlases, histories and other works on ghost towns, haunting spots, power places and ancient sites.

"Yet, there is other evidence as to who these people might have been," I suggested. I pulled out an unusual book published by the Institute for the Study of American Cultures (ISAC) in Columbus, Georgia. The book was *The Dene and Na-Dene Indian Migration 1233 A.D.—Escape from Genghis Khan to America* by Ethel G. Stewart. The book is a thick hardback that is

184

authoritatively researched and presents a strong case that the Dene and Na-Dene Indian tribes, known commonly as Athapaskan (also spelled Athabaskan) Indians, came into America as late as the 13th century, but had been arriving centuries earlier as well.[177]

Who were the Dene and Na-Dene? Na-Dene was the Asiatic-Alaskan language spoken by Athapaskan Indians who migrated into North America from Siberia. Says the *Smithsonian Book of North American Indians*[178]:

> ...about AD 750, some Athapaskan dispersed to settle the coasts of Alaska, British Columbia and California, giving rise to the ancestors of Pacific Northwest tribes such as the Haida, Tlingit and Hupa. Others moved east across central Canada north of the Great Plains. About the fifteenth century AD, some Na-Dene appeared in the Southwest...their arrival caused some disruption among well-established south-western cultures about the time of the first European contact. ...The bow and arrow probably came to the Plains dwellers via the Na-Dene, Athapaskan speakers who migrated south out of the Asia-Alaska region into western Canada and the Plains. The people of Wyoming's High Plains adopted the bow quickly, because it has important advantages over the atlatl and spear.[178]

Kingsley Craig, a historical researcher and an epigrapher from Oregon working with the Epigraphic Society, formulated a theory using Hibben's information on the Gallina battle and Stewart's book on the Dene and Na-Dene migrations. He said that the Mound Builders of the Midwest and the Pueblo Indians of the Southwest were destroyed at approximately the same time, about 1250 AD, by a roving army of 20,000 Mongol

185

men and women, who, in the years around 1233 AD, had escaped from the ruling Khans in Mongolia and traveled in a mass migration into Canada and down into the Midwest. According to Craig, these Mongols, because the men had long hair, and because their women fought with them, became known historically in North America as *Amazons.* His belief is that many of the legends of Amazons in Europe and Asia refer to the fierce Mongols.

According to Craig, these marauding Mongols brought destruction in much the same manner as had the Mongol invasions of western Asia and Europe. They laid siege to Aztalan, a fortified mound city in southern Wisconsin, and destroyed it. They then moved down the Mississippi Valley destroying the cities and temple areas as they went. The Mound Builders' cities had wooden fortifications that were burned during the sieges, on a repeated basis. According to Craig, this was the destruction of the Mound Builders along the Mississippi River and its tributaries. He says that the Dene-Mongols headed west along the Arkansas River, destroying the ancient city at Spiro Mound, Oklahoma and then traveled along the river into southern Colorado and northern New Mexico.

Craig's theory is that the Mongols eventually arrived in the Gallina River area of northern New Mexico, near the small town of Cuba. Here, they encountered the towers previously built as defensive works by the Anasazi. They occupied these towers, but were then decimated by a coordinated attack on them by the Pueblo Indians. While the Pueblo Indians may have won this early battle, successive waves of Dene and Na-Dene overwhelmed the area and Pueblo Indians had to retreat to their remote Pueblos at Zuni, Acoma and other areas. Today, the Apaches, traditional enemies of the Zunis and other Pueblo Indians, live just to the east of the Zuni Reservation, in an area that is known to have been occupied by the Zunis before their arrival. Apache, the modern word for the Dene people, means "enemy" in the Zuni language.

So the question remains: who were these Gallina River Valley people and where did they come from? Had they built the towers, or merely occupied them for the big final battle? Hibben thought that they had migrated to New Mexico from the Mississippi Valley, but wasn't sure who they were. Kingsley Craig surmises that these people were the first wave of the Dene invaders, who would ultimately conquer most of New Mexico, Arizona and western Texas.

As Jennifer and I drove out of Gallina, having driven down some of the local dirt roads searching for the remains of one or two of the towers, I wondered about the legendary battle that took place in this remote valley of northern New Mexico. Chaco Canyon was directly to the west—did the abandonment of Chaco Canyon have something to do with the battle that took place along the Gallina River?

The history of North America was one of continual invasion and displacement, a history much more interesting than the one normally told of a few Ice Age hunters following game into Alaska and eventually populating two huge continents.

North America was experiencing some major cutural shifts around 1200 AD. Aztalan was destroyed about this time. 1250 AD is when the Hopewell people came to an end. The Gallina culture in New Mexico also came to an end at this time. The Toltec Empire of Mexico and Arizona was in decline by the end of the 12th century and it was during this time that the Aztecs migrated into the Valley of Mexico.

187

Could the Dene-Apache invasion of the Southwest have triggered the Aztecs to migrate further south to the Central Valley of Mexico? It was an interesting speculation.

The Strange Elephant Stones of Aztec

We stopped briefly for gasoline in Cuba, the main town on Highway 550. From here we continued north to Aztec, along the Animas River. We checked into a local motel and discovered that the Aztec Library was having its annual library benefit UFO conference. This conference is held every March to commemorate the supposed crash of a flying saucer on a mesa east of town. In fact, that direction was the way to the town of Dulce and the Jacarilla Apache Reservation that is supposed to have an underground UFO base.

The modern town of Aztec was founded in 1880 on the opposite side of the Animas River from the ancient ruins that early settlers had believed had been built by the Aztecs of central Mexico. The first modern explorer to see the ruins was the geologist Dr. John S. Newberry who visited them in 1859. He found walls 25-feet high and the remains of many-storied buildings gathered in clusters up and down the river. The anthropologist Lewis H. Morgan arrived in 1879, but by then nearly a quarter of the stones had been carted away by newly arrived settlers who needed building materials. The ruins became a national monument in 1923.

Self-guided trails wind through the lower story of the immense West Ruin. Here are precision-aligned rooms and doorways of shaped stone, a compelling testament to the engineering skills of the Anasazi. In some rooms, original ceilings of pine and juniper logs, lashed together with yucca strands, are as solid as the day they were built 900 years ago.

Two dozen small kivas, probably used by individual clans, dot the ruins, while in the main courtyard is the Great Kiva, a community ceremonial chamber, 43 feet in diameter. In 1934 an archaeological team carried out a two-year project to restore the kiva to appear as it did in the 12th century. It is the only fully restored kiva in the Southwest.

Walking around the extensive ruins, I marveled at the fine walls, masonry that is similar to that found at Chaco Canyon—alternating courses of large rectangular sandstone blocks with bands of smaller stones. The Great Kiva is especially impressive with its reconstructed huge pine poles to hold the roof, and three large stone disks as the base. The four large columns support a massive roof of latticed wooden beams, logs and earth weighing an estimated 90 tons.

In the museum it was interesting to see boomerangs plus exotic trade and shamanic items like quartz crystals and feathers from Central America. Rubber balls for the ball courts have also been found. Archeologists believe that the early part of the extensive city was built between 1106 and 1124 AD. They think that it was abandoned shortly afterwards, in 1175 or 1200 AD, "perhaps because of drought or area-wide misfortune. There is no evidence the residents were driven away."[76]

Curiously, archeologists think that the city was reoccupied in 1225 AD when people of the Mesa Verde culture arrived and took up residence with their distinct pottery, textiles and beadwork. They further abandoned the ruins by about 1290 AD. Who were these people and where did they go? Did they migrate to Mexico and become the Aztecs? Were they decimated in the Zuni-Apache wars of 1250 AD? Was Aztec the remains of a Toltec-Phoenician-Hohokam culture that farmed and mined in the rich river valleys of northern New Mexico and the Four

189

Corners region? Perhaps the mysterious Elephant Slabs found near Aztec are evidence of this lost civilization.

About 1910 a small boy playing in Flora Vista, New Mexico, a tiny settlement along the Animas River just north of the Aztec ruins, dug up two slabs of carved rock inscribed with what appeared to be some sort of ancient writing.

The young boy presented the slabs to local archeologists and a controversy raged. First of all, the slabs contained a number of symbols of an ancient language that no one could decipher, and secondly, the slabs contained petroglyphs (rock drawings) of easily recognizable local indigenous animals— and animals that were obviously elephants, drawn complete with trunks, floppy ears and tusks![11]

While at first no one suspected a hoax, the fact that elephants were carved on the slabs presented some serious problems. While mammoths had once roamed the area, they had become extinct, supposedly, over 10,000 years ago.

Similarly, while elephants still live in parts of Southeast Asia and Africa, official history maintains that North American communities were isolated from the rest of the world and would have been totally unaware of what an elephant looked like.

In his book *Ancient Man: A Handbook of Puzzling Artifacts*,[17] William Corliss has one brief page on the elephant slabs including an illustration of the inscriptions. They appear to be early Shang Chinese script, which was in use circa 1100 BC. Dating of the slabs by local archeologists, who thought they were authentic, was circa 1200 AD. They based this date on potsherds that were found at the site. However, the slab may have been an ancient relic, kept in a safe place for hundreds of years at a time, while the potsherds could be of much more recent manufacture and come from the time of the destruction of Aztec,

Flora Vista and the nearby Salmon Ruins, which was 1200 AD.

Said the archeologist Charles Avery Amsden, who purchased the elephant slabs from the boy in 1910, "I can see no reason to doubt the authenticity of these specimens, but how to explain them I would not say. In all my experience I have seen nothing similar."[17]

The smaller, principal slab measures six inches wide and 6 inches long with a deep groove on the left-hand side which shows where it was probably broken off from a larger stone. The unknown carver meticulously chiseled 55 signs and pictures into exceedingly hard stone and left no obvious traces of tool slippage or over-crossed lines.

The second slab is longer at 6 inches wide and 14 inches long. It bears only ten faintly incised signs including the outlines of an elephant as well as a bird and a mountain lion. So, three elephants were apparently carved on the elephant slabs, two on the smaller slab with more symbols, and one on the larger slab. Both were said to be similar to stone hoes used throughout the Southwest, and may have been used as such for hundreds of years as important ritual objects.[17]

In the book *Montezuma's Serpent*,[11] Brad Steiger and his wife Sherry Hansen Steiger ask, "Is it possible for someone to draw a picture of an elephant without ever having seen one? And, more specifically, was it possible for an ancient Native American to have sat on a bank of the Animas and accidentally, by chance, have etched the image of an elephant on stone?"

They provide some alternative explanations for the find, such as the petroglyphs being artistic representations of African elephants that found their way to ancient New Mexico via the trade ships of Phoenicians between 900 and 200 BC; or that the memory of the great woolly mammoths had been preserved by the Indians' oral tradition or by representations of the great beasts made by even more ancient artists.

A third possible answer is that an Asiatic potentate launched an invasion fleet, complete with war elephants, to colonize the New World: "Many scholarly researchers have suggested that the ancient Chinese could well have reached the west coasts of the Americas. If such an invasion did take place in historical times, the native dwellers would certainly have been impressed by the giant mammals and would have surely captured the beasts' likeness for posterity."[11]

Another candidate for bringing elephants to North America is the ancient Cham, or Kam, of Vietnam and other areas of Southeast Asia. These Egyptian-Asians were seafaring Hindus who later became Buddhists, and ranged far out into the Pacific, perhaps to areas that are now California and Mexico. Could these Buddhist Sea Kings have brought some war elephants with them to some port on the Colorado River and then brought them to the Colorado Plateau on an important visit to the Grand Canyon, Chaco Canyon and Aztec? It seems incredible!

Another similar artifact is the Granby Idol, found in Granby, Colorado in 1920. A rancher named Bud Chalmers was removing rocks from an excavation he was planning for a reservoir. Though he was pitching heavy granite blocks, one rock seemed heavier than the others and he paused to look at it. It was 18 inches long by 12 inches wide, the black basalt had been carved into a smiling, primitive face by some ancient artist who could carve very hard stone.

The Granby Idol has three-fingered hands and unintelligible symbols carved around him. On the backside of the stone two figures were carved, one a prehistoric hairy mammoth and the other a long-necked dinosaur, similar to a brontosaurus.

The Granby Idol was featured in an article in *Old West* magazine in 1969, and diffusionist authorities such as Cyclone Covey took interest in the curious stone. Covey believed that the idol had ancient Chinese symbols on it and was proof of trans-Pacific voyages from China in ancient times. The idol has now disappeared and the area where it was found is now the flooded site of Granby Lake.

Modern Chinese scholars now claim that early Olmec script is identical to ancient Shang Chinese script, and believe that Asian voyagers reached Mesoamerica by 1300 BC, helping to jumpstart the Olmec civilization, which ultimately led to the great Mayan culture.[9]

Other authors support the idea of continual trans-Pacific traffic from ancient India, Egypt and Southeast Asia, such as W. J. Perry (*Children of the Sun*[173]) and Igor Witkowski (*Axis of the World*[174]), both of whom present considerable evidence for ancient civilizations having crossed the Pacific and interacted with American cultures.

Perhaps Bud Chalmers and the young boy in Flora Vista had somehow hoaxed the strange items they presented. But, other elephants have popped up in the Americas from time to time, including an elephant effigy mound in northeastern Iowa and the famous statue at the ancient Mayan city of Copan in Honduras, which apparently shows an elephant complete with a "mahout" or elephant driver.

Even today, elephants are widely used for logging and other tasks in Southeast Asia, and any Chinese-Buddhist-Hindu expedition to the Americas would include people who certainly were familiar with elephants. It is conceivable that such an expedition may have actually brought trained elephants with them, is a similar manner that horses and cattle were transported in ships. War elephants were popular in Southeast Asia and used up until relatively modern

193

times.

The Phoenicians were known to use the small Atlas elephants that once inhabited Morocco and are now extinct. These were the war elephants that were used by the Phoenicians in the Punic Wars against Rome. Hannibal was able to walk some of these elephants over the Alps to assist in his campaign against Rome in 217 BC.

Clearly, the Phoenicians traveled with elephants by ship, having to take them across the Mediterranean to Spain. Could several Atlas elephants have made it to the New World with the Phoenicians? Like many of the mysteries of the Southwest, the mystery of the New Mexican elephants may never be solved.

From Aztec we were off to the mysterious town of Dulce, to find out what we could about the underground UFO base that was allegedly located beneath Archuleta Mesa just north of the town. We drove east on the winding mountain highway (New Mexico 64), going past Navaho Reservoir and then down into the pine forest valley of Dulce—which means "Sweet" in Spanish, named for the clear, pure water of the valley.

Dulce was established in 1883 as a school and trading center for the Jicarilla Apaches (a branch of the southern Mescaleros) who lived around Dulce and in the mountains to the south. This million-square-mile reservation consists of some of the most pristine mountain wilderness left in the United States today, teeming with wild animals. It is known as an unspoiled hunting ground for sportsmen—and as an active area for both UFOs and Bigfoot.

We stopped at the local casino where the desk clerk, after a bit of conversation about UFOs and other strange things in the area, told us that there was security camera footage from some ten years ago of small, furry man-like critters jumping up and down on the hoods of some of the cars in the casino parking lot.

"Hmm," I thought. "That is a curious incident, all right," I said to the clerk. "Perhaps they were young Sasquatch who were unhappy with the building of a casino in their mountain wilderness."

The clerk nodded and answered the telephone that inconveniently rang just then. I wondered if these hairy mini-men were related to the ones that are reported around the Ghost Ranch?

Jennifer and I had lunch at the restaurant and looked around town a bit. The large supermarket next door to the casino had lots of good stuff, so we bought some drinks, snacks and other camping supplies to stock up the SUV. Back at the casino, we met up with old friends Greg Bishop and his wife Sigrid. Greg was there to speak at a UFO conference similar to the one at Aztec, and he and Sigrid were staying at the casino for several nights. We walked back to the supermarket and chatted with other folks who were attending the conference next door.

The local folks were friendly, and told us about the many different stories and events that had occurred in the area. This included cattle mutilations, literally dozens of them, on the Archuleta Ranch to the north of town in the 1980s. UFOs had been seen around Archuleta Mesa north of town, and many acknowledged that they had heard that there was a UFO base somewhere north of Dulce—which would actually be in Colorado.

We even met a local Jicarilla Apache policeman named Hoyt who had a fascinating encounter while riding fences at his ranch. Greg and I went with him in his 4x4 pickup down a remote dirt road to the spot where he told us he had come face-to-face with Bigfoot.

Hoyt was a great guy, getting on in years, but still with lots of energy and enthusiasm for his many past adventures, and obviously had many more still to come. He showed us where he was inspecting an electric fence that ran along the northern part of his property. The fence was turned off at the time, and suddenly as he came up the hill along the fence, partially hidden behind a pine tree was a Bigfoot crouched down and inspecting the wires of the electric fence to see if they were alive.

"Suddenly," said Hoyt, "The Bigfoot saw me and stood up in surprise. He was taller than the highest wire on the electric fence, which is 8-feet high. We were both shocked and scared. He dove through the fence, which had wide gaps between the loose wires, and then was gone. I suddenly saw him up the hill behind a pine tree looking back at me. I was shocked in the beginning, and ran toward him. But then I ran back to my ATV that I had parked back a bit when I began inspecting the fence, and drove out into the middle of that field out there."

He pointed out back towards the muddy ranch road back to the south. "I parked my little ATV and just sat on it in the middle of that open spot and caught my breath. Once I calmed down, I went back to the cabin over there." He waved toward the cabins and old barns that had been there since the early 1900s.

Greg and I looked at each other and acknowledged Hoyt's amazing story. "Wow, that's a really interesting story, Hoyt," I said. "Have there been other bigfoot encounters around here?"

He told us of a few other incidents: rocks being thrown at them by a hidden entity, banshee-like screaming at night and even a huge party of nearly 20 Bigfoot researchers camped there for five nights a few years ago.

On the way back into Dulce, Hoyt took us up on a ridge to see a good view of the panorama to

196

the north. We got high up on a mesa to the south of Dulce and we jumped out of the truck to look at the mountains that spread low across the horizon.

"You see," Hoyt said, "there are three areas: Archuleta Peak, Archuleta Mesa and Archuleta Mountain." He pointed to the sheer mesa of Archuleta Mesa that was at the far right of the panorama. "Archuleta Mesa goes from east to west. There is a road that goes up there. I've been on it a few times. There was some hippies up there in the late 60s living on the mesa. The government eventually chased them off. I had to go up there later and check out their former camp. There was some old campers, cars and other stuff left up there."

It was getting windy and we headed back to Hoyt's pickup truck. "Thanks for pointing out the difference between the various mountains," said Greg. Greg was the author of the book *Project Beta*, which is the story of Paul Bennewitz and his strange pursuit of the alien base somewhere around Dulce.

On the way back to the casino, I asked Greg what he thought of the story of an underground base somewhere around Dulce. He said that he doubted the existence of the base because he knew that the secret operations against Bennewitz were meant to have him believe that there was something going on at Dulce when actually things were really going on elsewhere. Something like a magician saying "look over here," when he really doesn't want you to look over there.

We returned to the casino in Dulce where Jennifer and Sigrid were waiting for us. We said our good-byes and shortly, Jennifer and I left town and drove back to Aztec. Our next destination would be Chaco Canyon: the mysterious ruins deep in lost canyons of northwest New Mexico.

The full moon was rising over a dark mesa in the east. Jennifer and I were camped along Highway 57 for the night, off the side of the dirt road, under some trees. There was an old campfire spot with some large rocks that held a blackened and warped iron grill.

We got the fire going and grilled some turkey sausages for dinner. Jennifer poured us each a shot of tequila. Cutting up a lemon she tossed her hair back and told me to "get ready."

"Ready for what?" I asked, looking her in the eye.

She tossed the shot of tequila back in a fluid motion and just as easily took a bite of a lemon slice. I instinctively did the same.

"Ready or not!" she said, putting her arms around me and kissing me hard. The stars twinkled in the distance, and with blurry eyes I looked up through the screen of the tent at the clear skies above, scanning for possible UFOs. The hills were lit up by the Eye in the Sky, the big full moon that is Earth's mysterious satellite. Would the UFOs and Sasquatch be out tonight? As shadows crept over the camp late that night, I looked out beyond the SUV to the mesas in the distance. Reality was what you make it.

I like the way your sparkling earrings lay,
Against your skin, it's so brown.
And I wanna' sleep with you in the desert tonight,
With a billion stars all around.
—Eagles, *Peaceful Easy Feeling*

We woke up the next morning with sun pouring down on the tent and the high desert of northwest New Mexico starting to heat up. I dragged myself out of my sleeping bag and took a piss near the SUV. I grabbed a mango juice out of our cooler and opened it up to break my fast.

I started up the SUV and got Jennifer groggily

into the passenger's seat. Moments later we were bouncing down the dirt road that was Highway 57 to the Chaco Culture National Historical Park.

According to the park brochures, the cultural flowering of the Chacoan people began in the mid 800s and lasted more than 300 years to about 1200 AD. Using masonry techniques unique for their time in the area, they constructed massive stone buildings (Great Houses) of multiple stories containing hundreds of rooms much larger than any they had previously built. The buildings were planned from the start, in contrast to the usual practice of adding rooms to existing structures as needed. Constructions on some of these buildings spanned decades and even centuries. Although each is unique, all great houses share architectural features that make them recognizable as Chacoan.

Says the brochure for the park:

> During the middle and late 800s, the great houses of Pueblo Bonito, Una Vida, and Peñasco Blanco were constructed, followed by Hungo Pavi, Chetro Ketl, Pueblo Alto, and others. These structures were often oriented to solar, lunar, and cardinal directions. Lines of sight between the great houses allowed communication. Sophisticated astronomical markers, communication features, water control devices, and formal earthen mounds surrounded them. The buildings were placed within a landscape surrounded by sacred mountains, mesas, and shrines that still have deep spiritual meaning for their descendants.
>
> By 1050, Chaco had become the ceremonial, administrative, and economic center of the San Juan Basin. Its sphere of influence was extensive. Dozens of great houses in Chaco Canyon were connected by roads to more

199

than 150 great houses throughout the region. It is thought that the great houses were not traditional farming villages occupied by large populations. They may instead have been impressive examples of "public architecture" that were used periodically during times of ceremony, commerce, and trading when temporary populations came to the canyon for these events.

What was at the heart of this great social experiment? Pueblo descendants say that Chaco was a special gathering place where many peoples and clans converged to share their ceremonies, traditions, and knowledge. Chaco is central to the origins of several Navajo clans and ceremonies. Chaco is also an enduring enigma for researchers. Was Chaco the hub of a turquoise-trading network established to acquire macaws, copper bells, shells, and other commodities from distant lands? Did Chaco distribute food and resources to growing populations when the climate failed them? Was Chaco "the center place," binding a region together by a shared vision? We may never fully understand Chaco.

In the 1100s and 1200s, change came to Chaco as new construction slowed and Chaco's role as a regional center shifted. Chaco's influence continued at Aztec, Mesa Verde, the Chuska Mountains, and other centers to the north, south, and west. In time, the people shifted away from Chacoan ways, migrated to new areas, reorganized their world, and eventually interacted with foreign cultures. Their descendants are the modern Southwest Indians. Many Southwest Indian people look upon Chaco as an important stop along their clans' sacred migration paths—a spiritual place to be honored and respected.

What puzzles archeologists is why such a sophisticated structure was built in the remote canyons of the Chaco River, a tributary of the San Juan River, thereby flowing to the north. It is about halfway between the San Juan River and Zuni.

Also, there are no burials around Chaco Canyon. For such a large city, it puzzles archeologists that there is no large cemetery in the vicinity that they have found. While archeologists wonder why there are no burial grounds, it is the custom of many cultures, especially Hindus, Buddhists (and early Christians) to be cremated. While wood for cremation would have to have been largely imported—almost everything in Chaco Canyon was probably imported! Was Chaco Canyon some sort of cremation ceremonial center? It would explain some of the baffling discoveries made there.

We drove up to the Visitor's Center at Chaco Canyon and showed our National Park pass. The gift shop and museum were fascinating, and soon we drove to Pueblo Bonito and began to walk among the ancient trails and alleys. I had been to Chaco Canyon several times before, but it had been some years since I had been here and it was an exciting and fresh place to visit.

The construction of the various structures associated with Chaco Canyon is massive in scale and the work was extremely well executed. It was as if master craftsmen from somewhere else, presumably to the south, had come and built the network of buildings in what seems to be the middle of nowhere.

Consider this: The nearly flawless piecing together of the different layers of rock to form walls, and the engineering and planning to make such large structures, even against cliffs, was of builders who were clearly experienced.

It is estimated that 50 million pieces of sandstone were fitted together to create the building complex known as Chetro Ketl. It has 18 kivas and other subterranean areas, which means that tons of earth had to be removed. These kivas had massive ponderosa pine posts in their center to hold up the roof, and some of these rested on sandstone disks that weighed half a ton. Typically there were three such stones on top of each other that were used as shifting foundations that could spin on each other during earthquakes.

It is interesting to note the use by the Anasazi of large stone disks; as a curious aside, gigantic stone disks are used as money on Yap Island in Micronesia—albeit they are not a very convenient form of currency.

Archeologists believe that at least 200,000 pine tree poles were needed to build the main pueblos around Chaco Canyon. Each one had to be brought from no less than 35 miles away, where the closest pine forest can be found. Perhaps a pine forest had existed at a closer distance to Chaco Canyon but was completely devastated in some sort of ancient version of clearcutting.

Supposedly the ancient people of Chaco did not know of writing or the wheel. Yet, they used huge stone disks as the foundations for their kiva poles, and other wheeled objects, such as spinning whorls and even toys were known. The Anasazi, like the present-day Hopi and Zuni hunted with boomerangs and throwing sticks.

How did they move the great Ponderosa pine poles 35 miles to the Chaco Canyon structures? Perhaps a hundred men each grabbed a part of the pole, and they all heave-hoed their way down the many roads to Chaco Canyon.

With their large stone disks, they might have been able to make some sort of a cart with an axle and wheels that could have helped moved the cumbersome and heavy pine poles. Many of the poles were not so large as the great kiva poles, but considering the fine building technique, the builders spared no expense in their grand scheme of things at the time.

Jennifer and I pulled up to the largest of the structures, Pueblo Bonito. It had four stories, 800 rooms and covered three acres. Walking along the path below the ancient walls, I was amazed at how the thin and high walls had stood the test of time over the 850 years that they had been abandoned.

The roads around Chaco Canyon are in pretty bad shape for a good portion of the year. We drove over the high edges of the muddy ruts left by previous trucks that had dug deep channels in the red Chaco clay that makes up much of the area.

"This would make good material for ceramics, all this clay around here," I said, avoiding a sudden deep cut of cracked earth across the road. A dry ravine was coming up ahead.

"Yes," said Jennifer, holding on to a handle above her door. We bounced up and down momentarily, as I virtually came to a halt. We lurched forward again and gained speed going uphill for a short bit. "Pottery-making is a very famous skill of all these people, including the Hohokam. This area would make some fine clay pots. Maybe that's one reason it was an ancient trading center."

It is interesting to think of Chaco Canyon as a regional center for many things: it is on the Continental Divide, as is the Zuni Pueblo, and is in a sense the "Center of the World" insofar as this portion of North America is concerned.

It is often said that the ancient highways of a continent are the waterways—the many rivers and often interlocked systems of rivers, lakes, rivers and more rivers and lakes. Much of the American

Southwest was like this with its "basin and range" style geography that tends to be oriented on a north-south axis in North America, except for some areas like the Grand Canyon or the Columbia Gorge in the Pacific Northwest that go east-west.

Chaco and Contact with Mesoamerica

One of the mysteries of Chaco culture surrounds some curious ceramic jars found in the various ruins around Chaco Canyon that were unlike any of the other ceramics that had been found there. *The New York Times* reported on February 3, 2009, in an article entitled "Mystery of Ancient Pueblo Jars is Solved," that University of New Mexico anthropologist Patricia Crown, for years, had "puzzled over the cylindrical clay jars found in the ruins at Chaco Canyon, the great complex of multistory masonry dwellings set amid the arid mesas of northwestern New Mexico. They were utterly unlike other pots and pitchers she had seen."

Said the article:

> Some scholars believed that Chaco's inhabitants, ancestors of the modern Pueblo people of the Southwest, had stretched skins across the cylinders and used them for drums, while others thought they held sacred objects.
>
> But the answer is simpler, though no less intriguing, Ms. Crown asserts in a paper published Tuesday in *The Proceedings of the National Academy of Sciences*: the jars were used for drinking liquid chocolate. Her findings offer the first proof of chocolate use in North America north of the Mexican border.
>
> How did the ancient Pueblos come to have cacao beans in the desert, more than 1,200 miles from the nearest cacao trees? Ms. Crown, a University of New Mexico anthropologist,

noted that maize, beans and corn spread to the Southwest after being domesticated in southern Mexico. Earlier excavations at Pueblo Bonito, the largest structure in the Chaco complex, had found scarlet macaws and other imported items.

Dorie Reents-Budet, a curator at the Museum of Fine Arts in Boston and a Smithsonian Institution research associate specializing in Mayan cylinder vases, said that a sophisticated Mesoamerican trade network extended to Chaco in the north and as far south as Ecuador and Colombia.

The Mayan vessels, decorated with court scenes and hieroglyphics, were used to ceremonially consume chocolate at sumptuous feasts, Ms. Reents-Budet said. An expensive luxury, the cacao beans were fermented, roasted and ground up, then mixed with water and flavorings before being whipped into froth. It made sense to present the beverage in a special vessel, she said.

"It's as if you were having a dinner party and serving Champagne," said Ms. Reents-Budet. "You serve Champagne in really nice glasses."

After an exchange with Ms. Reents-Budet in October 2007 about the resemblances between the Chacoan and Mayan earthenware, Ms. Crown said she thought about having the Chacoan cylinders checked for cacao residue.

Ms. Crown turned to W. Jeffrey Hurst, a senior bioanalytical chemist for the Hershey Company, the giant chocolate maker, whose bosses have been allowing him to test Mesoamerican ceramics for cacao for two decades. In 2002, he co-published a paper in *Nature* showing that early Maya were using cacao by 600 B.C., pushing back the earliest chemical evidence for their cacao use by 1,000 years.

Ms. Crown submitted five fragmentary shards to Mr. Hurst's laboratory, which subjected the samples to high performance liquid chromatography and mass spectrometry testing, which confirmed the presence of *theobromine*—a bio marker for cacao—in three shards.

"The results were unequivocal," said Mr. Hurst, who wrote the new paper with Ms. Crown.

The shards were among 200,000 artifacts excavated from trash heaps next to the 800-room Pueblo Bonito. They date from 1000 to 1125, when Chaco civilization was at its height.

An earlier expedition had uncovered 111 cylinder jars beneath a room in Pueblo Bonito. The jars, of native clay, are about 10 inches high with black geometric designs over a white background, said Ms. Crown, an expert on Pueblo ceramics. Ms. Crown speculated that the Chacoans might well have followed Mayan ritualized chocolate drinking practices, given the similarity of the drinking vessels.

"It's likely that this was not something everybody consumed," she said. "It's likely it was intended for only this one segment of society."

As we drove out of Chaco Canyon, heading south on Highway 14, I chuckled at how amazed modern archeologists are that the Chacoans were in contact with Central America and had consumed chocolate, probably in large quantities. Montezuma was known to drink 50 cups a day, according to legend.

It seems that archeology in the Southwest has come full circle in many ways. The early explorers, settlers and anthropologists were convinced of the following things about the Southwest: it was the area of the Seven Cities of Cibola; it was where the Aztecs had originated; the Hohokam, Anazasi, Sinagua and Chaco People had wide trading networks that went far into the eastern plains and far south to the Aztec, Zapotec and Mayan areas; the Zuni, Hopi, Acoma, Taos and other Pueblo tribes were the descendants of these "vanished" people.

In the last 100 years, however, archeologists and historians have painted a different picture. They believe the following things about the ancient Southwest: it was an area where explorers sought the "mythical" Seven Gold Cities of Cibola; the origin of the Aztecs is completely unknown; the Hohokam and Chaco People did not travel or trade extensively and were largely isolated communities; for unknown reasons the large cities of the ancient peoples were mysteriously abandoned and smaller communities of new people just sprang up in the pueblos at the Hopi Mesas, Zuni, Acoma, and Taos, among others.

Now anthropologists like Patricia Crown are showing how wrong long-held assumptions have been. Frank Hibben likewise had to battle myopic scholars who could not believe that man had been in the Americas before 13,000 BP. The great archeologist Harold Gladwin parodied the myopic scholars in his 1947 book *Men Out of Asia*.[128] It was this book that coined the term "Phuddy Duddy," which was used to characterize some esteemed and learned experts as folks who couldn't see past their own textbooks.

It has been slow going, changing those textbooks. Every year a few textbooks get incinerated and a few slightly changed versions are printed. But still, most universities teach the longstanding mainstream dogma of communities in North America being

207

isolated from each other, as well as the dogma that no significant ocean-going trade was happening in North or South America.

Journey to the Sky City of Acoma

We spent that night in Grants, on Interstate 40 and the next day we drove south on Highway 38 to the Acoma Pueblo, sometimes called Sky City.

The Sky City of Acoma is situated on top of a mesa 357 feet high, and access to the pueblo is difficult as the faces of the mesa are sheer. The top of the mesa is accessible via a vertiginous staircase cut into the rock, or by a sand dune filling a large fissure. Today there is a paved trail that goes along the fissure that can be walked to the top of the mesa. Guided tours are now generally required.

The Pueblo was established in the 12th century or even earlier, and its location was clearly chosen in part because of its defensive position against raiders. Acoma is regarded by some historians as the oldest continuously inhabited community in the United States, along with the Hopi Pueblos. Archeologists confirm that it has been inhabited since 1075 AD.

There are several interpretations of the origin of the name "Acoma." Some believe that the name comes from the *Keresan* words for 'People of the White Rock'; *ako* meaning 'white rock' and *ma* meaning 'people.' Others believe that the word *aa'ku* actually comes from the word *haaku* meaning 'to prepare'; a description that would accurately reflect the defensive position of the mesa's inhabitants. It is worth mentioning here that, during our visit, we were instructed in the proper pronunciation of Acoma: the emphasis goes on the first syllable ('ACK-oma), as the people are *not* in "a coma."

According to legend, one night very long ago the

forebears of the Acoma people crawled from a hole in the earth, creeping like freshly hatched grasshoppers, their vulnerable bodies naked and soft, their eyes sightless. Iatik, the mother, lined these helpless creatures up in a row facing east. Then she caused the sun to rise above the horizon. When its light shone on the babies' eyes they opened. From that time on, the Acomas practiced a form of sungazing with newborn babies, who are taken outside by a shaman, who sits on a sand painting of a tortoise and conducts the sun-child naming ceremony. This ceremony goes on to this day.

In ancient times access to the sky city was gained only by means of the hand-cut staircase carved into the sandstone. Acoma Pueblo was first "discovered" in the fall of 1540 by Hernando de Alvarado, one of Coronado's soldiers. Coronado's men could not scale the cliffs to attack the pueblo and deemed it impregnable. Then in 1598, Spanish conquistador Don Juan de Onate, under orders from the king of Spain, invaded New Mexico, and began staging raids on Native American pueblos in the area, taking anything of value. Upon reaching San Juan Pueblo, Onate had all the Native Americans who were living there removed from their homes, and used it as a base to stage more raids on other Native American pueblos in the area. In response, the Acoma fought back, and several Spaniards were killed in the battle to re-take the San Juan Pueblo from the invaders. During the battle, the Spaniards brought a small cannon up the back of Acoma Mesa, and began firing into the village.

The capture of Acoma was a siege lasting from January 21 to 23, 1599, and is reported by Gaspar Perez de Villagra in his *History of New Mexico* (1610). Villagra says that during this siege a Lt. Zaldivan and 14 soldiers were killed while trying to extort grain. In retaliation, the brother of the slain Lt. Zaldivan,

209

with about 30 men, climbed the rock and defeated the Acomas in hand-to-hand battle. During and after this battle, over 600 Acoma Indians lost their lives; many leapt from the high cliffs rather than surrender to the Spaniards. In further retaliation, the Spanish command ordered a foot to be chopped off of 200 warriors over the age of 20.

At that time, several thousand Indians may have lived in the village. Today only a few members of the tribe remain, the others having settled in a community nearer the highway or in the valley below. Today they run the large Sky City Casino near the Interstate.

The mission at Acoma was established in 1629, and is dedicated to St. Stephen. It is the largest of the early New Mexico churches, but during the Pueblo Revolts of 1680 and 1692, the mission was destroyed and the resident priest was slain. Acoma and the mission were rebuilt after the re-conquest.

The place is impressive today, especially with the strange spire of Katzimo Mesa to the east. Jack Kutz, in his book *Mysteries and Miracles of New Mexico*,[30] calls this 400-foot tall sheer tower of sandstone the Enchanted Mesa. Kutz says that Acoma legend maintains that there was a pueblo on top of this tower of rock, that could be reached by a natural rock ladder and staircase cut into the rock. Then a great storm lashed the area one night and a great downpour came over the cliffs of Katzimo and undermined the fragile sandstone fractures. Suddenly, a huge section of the mesa came crashing down as sections of the cliffs collapsed.

Kutz says that the early archeologist Adolph Bandelier viewed Katzimo and declared it "one of the most imposing cliffs of the imposing cliffs of the Southwest" and noted that its summit was "utterly beyond reach." Still a climber named Charles Lummis claimed that he scampered up the mesa in 1883 but found nothing at all on top. In 1885 an F.W. Hodge of the Bureau of Ethnology in Washington

D.C. failed in an attempt to climb the mesa, but did discover some ancient foot and hand holds that had been carved into a promising area for ascending the cliffs to the summit.

Finally, in 1897, Hodge made it to the top, by bringing his own ladder. He discovered some hidden sticks on this trip, that were the secret of ascending the trickiest part of the cliff: there were holes drilled in the rock, and sticks, strong enough to hold a small person, were stuck into these holes and protruded like the spokes of a ladder. Hodge and his party spent the night on the mesa, and later discovered potshards, a prayer stick, a shell bracelet, an axe blade and even a crude stone monument made of rock slabs.

Was there ever a "lost city" on top of Katzimo Mesa? As Acoma Mesa and Katzimo loomed in the rearview mirror, I thought it seemed like a good place for flying saucers to land, should they have the inclination…

For my part, I travel not to go anywhere, but to go.
I travel for travel's sake. The great affair is to move.
—Robert Louis Stevenson (1850-1894)

El Morro and the Lost City of Great Kivas

We drove back to the Interstate and headed west to Grants. We then headed south and west on Highway 53. We were now in the El Malpais area—the badlands of hardened lava flows and caves. We stopped briefly at the ice caves, a private tourist attraction, and took to the highway again, occasionally inspecting the weird lava rocks along the road. Soon we were entering the Ramah Navaho reservation.

As we continued west on Highway 53 we

suddenly saw the massive sandstone mesa called El Morro rising over 200 feet above the valley floor in front of us.

On March 11, 1583, a Spanish expedition rested by the base of the massive bluff. El Morro was called by the early Spanish travelers *El Estanque del Penol* ("the waterhole of the rock") but later travelers called the rock *Questa el Morro*, which is Spanish for "the headland' or "the bluff." Subsequent American travelers referred to El Morro as "Inscription Rock," but when it came to naming the National Monument in 1906, the earlier Spanish name persevered.

A waterhole is hidden at the base of the cliffs and has been used for thousands of years. Around 1375 AD two villages on top of the bluff were created. Older settlements may have been around El Morro, but if so, they haven't been discovered. By the 1380 AD, at least 1,500 people occupied the largest village, today called *A'ts'ina*.

In 1598, Don Juan de Oñate established the first Spanish colony in what is now New Mexico. While exploring the vast territory, Oñate stopped at El Morro many times. However, it wasn't until 1605 he changed the sandstone face forever. On the 16th of April, he deeply engraved an announcement of his discovery of the southern sea (Sea of Cortez), recording his success for all to see.

Spaniards continued to carve lengthy messages into the stone as late as 1774. These historic writings, with words running together, and unique abbreviations, are a challenge for today's readers.

In September 1849, U.S. Army lieutenant J.H. Simpson and artist R.H. Kern made their camp at El Morro. The artist spent two days copying the petroglyphs and Spanish messages. The two recorded their visit as well, becoming the first to leave an English inscription on the bluff.

We showed our pass at the Visitor's Center and

then hiked around the cliffs. It is an impressive and historic site, the signatures, calligraphy and petroglyphs a puzzle to look at and wonder about. I pondered the many military expeditions that had camped here, attracted by the reliable waterhole, surrounding grass, and shelter. A bit of the history of the Southwest had been carved into this rock by travelers riding or walking into the great unknown. Today it is forbidden for normal tourists to carve their names and dates into the sandstone walls of El Morro.

I stepped on the gas and we headed for Zuni Pueblo. We would first stop in Nutria. We passed through Ramah, a town first settled in 1876 by Mormon missionaries to the Navajos. Originally, the town was called Navaho, but there was another town in New Mexico Territory that already had that name, so the town was named after the hill in upstate New York where the sacred gold tablets of the Mormons were supposedly discovered and then hidden again.

Ramah was one of the few Mormon towns in New Mexico territory, though there were others, like Reserve, mainly along the New Mexico-Arizona border. When the 1862 polygamy bill hit Congress, Utah and the Mormons came under intense scrutiny. Even the small Mormon community of Ramah was written about in an editorial in *The New Mexican* in 1900 as a place where people were not necessarily abiding by the law.

According to one of the accounts of Billy the Kid, when his "body" was turned over to some Mexican women for burial, they instead substituted the body of a Mexican man who had died the night before. The legend says that Billy the Kid was nursed back to health by these women, and he eventually left them to go to Ramah to live under the alias of John Miller.

Only a few miles past Ramah going west, we came to the turnoff for the small Highway 5 that goes north to Nutria Lakes, Lower Nutria and Upper Nutria. The whole area is a pleasant, green ranching and farming valley and nearby is the canyon known as *Yu'ashah kwi* by the Zunis, meaning "Lonesome Place."

At the end of the valley is an archeological site known as the Village of the Great Kivas. It has a ceremonial room two feet wider in diameter than the largest kiva at Chaco Canyon. The Village of the Great Kivas was once a major Anasazi dwelling, an outlier to Chaco Canyon. Was it once a Zuni city? It is very close to the modern pueblo of Zuni.

Jennifer and I looked around the area of Upper Nutria and saw very few signs of human life. Some very old cabins could be seen down some dirt track roads, and the open remains of the kiva foundations and sunken areas were to the north of where the road ends.

Back on the main Highway 53 heading west, we noticed that it was getting late. "Maybe we should go to Gallup for dinner and get a motel," suggested to Jennifer. Half an hour later we slowed down for the first traffic light in Gallup, a town known as "The Indian Capital."

Gallup started out as a way station in the 1860s, with a tavern named the Blue Goose Saloon, built next to an adobe house that was a station for the Overland Mail. In 1881 the railroad came through Gallup and the town by then had 22 saloons and two dancehalls.

Today, Gallup is a noisy town with some of those saloons still in full gear, and with trains rumbling through town all night long, often keeping weary travelers from getting a good night's sleep. I hoped that wouldn't be a problem as I lay back on the pillow in the motel. My stomach was full of enchiladas, rice and beans from a local Mexican restaurant. My head was full of tequila from that same restaurant, and a faint noise in the distance sounded like the drums and rattles of Zuni dancers, but perhaps it was just the wind in the bushes.

The Mystery of the Zuni

We drove into Zuni the next morning and stopped at one of the local craft shops. This one had a huge selection of Zuni fetishes plus many raw stones for the local craftsmen themselves to buy.

Zuni is said to be the largest inhabited Pueblo in the United States. It was built upon the ruins of the ancient site of Halona, thought to be one of the fabled Seven Cities of Cibola sought by the Spanish conquistador Francisco Coronado in 1540 AD, among others. Ruins of other "cities" may be found along the Zuni River watershed.

Archaeological evidence from the nearby site of Hawikuh demonstrates that the Zuni people (who call themselves *A:shiwi* in their language) have lived in the area since at least 1300 AD. Although the Zunis were forced to move around, and did not always occupy the same "cities," there is an unbroken continuity of settlement in the area from at least 650 AD.

The Zunis themselves say they have lived there for thousands of years. Their traditional history states that they emerged from the underworld somewhere west of their present location (the Grand Canyon and the Mojave Desert have been suggested) and wandered until they found Itawanna (the "Center Place," the center of the world), which is their present home.

Like the Hopi and Acoma, the Zuni believe that they came from inside the earth. Legends say that there "were four caves, one over the other. Men first

215

lived in the lowest cave. It was dark. There was no light, and the cave was crowded. All men were full of sorrow." We have already pointed out that similar stories are told in the creation legends of the Maya, Zapotec and presumably, the Olmecs.

The search for the "gold" cities of Cibola had brought the early explorers into the area. The Spanish had heard tales of seven cities that were paved with gold far to the north. Arriving in the area, Coronado found, not streets paved with gold, but a community rich in tradition and living a highly adjusted, organized existence. The Zunis were an agrarian people with irrigated farms of corn, beans, squash and cotton. Above all, strict religious beliefs of high moral standards and peace toward peoples, combined with their daily routines, made their society an exceptional one.

The Spanish had little trouble in conquering the peaceful Zuni people. But, in spite of Spanish occupation and a decree from the King of Spain to force Zuni acceptance of Roman Catholicism, the people continued to perform their ceremonies in hidden kivas or ceremonial rooms.

According to Zuni beliefs, the Cibola cities, their own Halona among them, were destroyed when Apaches, Navajos and other nomadic tribes overran the area during the 13th and 14th centuries, or before. Those Zunis who had escaped returned to the site of Halona, now called Zuni, to reestablish their homes in 1699.

The Zuni people first encountered Europeans in 1539 when Fray Marcos de Niza set out from Mexico with the former Black slave Esteban hoping to discover the fabled Seven Cities of Cibola, which Esteban had been repeatedly told about as he wandered in the area now known as Texas.

You may remember that Esteban had been shipwrecked with the Narváez expedition the Gulf

Coast in 1528 and had, with Alvar Nuñez Cabeza de Vaca, wandered for seven years across Texas and the Southwest (possibly as far as southern Arizona), before returning to Mexico City. Their tales of the fabled Cibola excited everyone in Mexico City as well as in Spain, and this led to the Niza expedition.

Marcos de Niza was a Franciscan friar who led Spain's first big expedition across the northern deserts. In northern Mexico, Niza sent Esteban ahead, but when Esteban reached Zuni, he was regarded with suspicion and is said to have been imprisoned and ultimately executed. When he returned to Mexico City, Niza claimed that Esteban was killed and that he had come within sight of large towns rich in precious stones, gold and silver.

The legend of Cibola was thus further promoted by Niza, which led to the 1540 expedition of Francisco Vásquez de Coronado. Coronado found the Zunis living in six villages, including Hawikuh and Halona. The Zunis attempted to stop Coronado, but after a brief battle they retreated due to the military superiority of the Spaniards who had rifles, armor and horses. Coronado was disappointed to find that Zuni was not the fabled Cibola; no riches were to be found. What had made Zuni wealthy were the salt mines that they controlled.

Salt mines have been important in the economies of countries all over the world. While salt is widely common today, in ancient times, it and herbal spices were exotic and quite valuable. The Hopi of Arizona also control a salt mine, which is in the canyon of the Little Colorado River. The Incas had an important salt mine near Cuzco, and it was one of the sources of their wealth.

We have seen that certain cultures were accomplished jewelers and metalworkers in ancient times, and that they were working with gold, silver, copper and other metals that were coming from ancient mines in northern Mexico and the whole

217

Four Corners region.

But, at the time of the Conquest, the Zuni were not working metals too much, although they had copper beads that they used with turquoise and other material in jewelry making.

Silversmithing was introduced to the Zuni in the 1870s, and since that time, the tribe has made the craft its own. Most of the turquoise used by the excellent Zuni jewelers comes from around the mountains just east of Sante Fe, on the "Turquoise Trail."

Typically, Zuni work is done within families. A husband may do the silver work, a wife the inlay, and another family member may help with buffing.

In general, particular designs will "belong" to particular families and these designs and their adaptations will be passed from older family members to the young. There is probably no village in North America which has a higher concentration of skilled craftsmen than the Pueblo of Zuni.

The Spanish continued to send expeditions into New Mexico and two other Spanish expeditions reached Zuni in the late 1500s with little impact on the people, but in 1598 Juan de Oñate launched his colonizing expedition to New Mexico. He reached Zuni in November and duly obtained their formal submission to the Spanish crown, as he had with most of the other Pueblos, but no Spanish settlement was made at Zuni by Oñate due to its distance from Santa Fe.

Zuni was virtually left alone by the Spaniards until 1629 when the first churches were built at Halona, Hawikuh and two other settlements. But only three years later, in 1632, the Zunis killed two of the resident friars at Hawikuh, Fray Francisco Letrado and Fray Martin de Arvide. Little or no missionary work was done at Zuni until after 1660. Because of its remote location Zuni was vulnerable and subject to nomadic Indian raids. In 1673 the Apaches attacked Hawikuh, burned down the church, and killed many Zunis and the resident friar, Fray Pedro de Avila y Ayala.

After this, the Zunis took part in the Pueblo Rebellion of 1680. They burned the churches at Hawikuh and Halona and killed Fray Juan de Bal. Another friar at Hawikuh was said to have escaped death, and according to Zuni traditional history he was adopted into the tribe. In 1692 Diego de Vargas began the Reconquest of New Mexico. At Zuni he found all the residents had taken refuge on nearby *Dowa Yalanne* (Corn Mountain).

When Spanish control was reestablished, the Zuni consolidated into one community at *Itiwanna*, the true middle, which was also called Halona. In 1699 they finally returned to the Pueblo from their mountain refuge, and abandoned all the villages except Halona because the population had been greatly reduced both by the hardships of living in exile from the Pueblo and by the ravages of European diseases introduced by the foreigners. The disruption caused by years of refuge on *Dowa Yalanne* and the consolidation of six villages into one produced a major re-organization of Zuni. They had been especially resistant to Spanish efforts at Christianization and kept their religion viable throughout this tumultuous period.

Because Zuni was so remote, on the virtual edge of the Spanish territory of New Mexico, to serve there was considered a form of exile for the Franciscan monks in the eighteenth century. Indeed, given the fate of several friars of the seventeenth century, an appointment to Zuni would seem dicey as best. It was also a form of punishment for criminals who were drafted as soldiers and then sent to Zuni to protect the pueblo against frequent Apache and Navajo raids. Three of these unruly Hispanic soldiers who were stationed there in 1703 came into conflict with the Zunis because of their bad behavior, and were promptly killed.

After consolidation of the population at Halona in 1699, the Zunis soon enlarged this settlement to encompass both sides of the river that ran through it. They also established nearby summer farming villages near their peach orchards where they planted crops and grazed cattle. These villages also served as places to conduct their own religious ceremonies without interference from the resident friars. In the nineteenth century the Zunis established three more outlying farming villages, Ojo Caliente, Nutria, and Pescado, all of which are still in use today.

Frank Hamilton Cushing and the End of the Zuni Wars

Through the eighteenth century the Zunis continued to suffer from sporadic raiding by the Apaches and in the nineteenth century by the Navajos. Zuni warriors occasionally joined with Spanish troops in retaliatory expeditions, and after 1846 they frequently assisted United States troops in their campaigns against the Navajos. In July and August 1850, Navajos attacked Halona in two successive raids, killing the Lieutenant Governor of the Pueblo in the second one.

The Zunis counter-attacked in September of that year, killing 30 Navajos. In October, while many men were away from the Pueblo, a large group of Navajos laid siege to Halona for sixteen days and stole much of the corn crop. Periodic raids by the Navajos continued until the establishment of Fort Wingate in the 1870s. In spite of this record of conflict with the Navajos, many of the Navajos maintained friendly relations with the Zunis as the Zuni Pueblos had always been important trading places.

After the American occupation of New Mexico in 1846, Zuni Pueblo had occasional visits from American authorities and surveying expeditions, but it was still very difficult to travel there until

220

the Atlantic and Pacific Railroad was finished at Gallup in 1881. Two kinds of American visitors soon came to Zuni: anthropologists studying the Indians, and land sharks trying to take their lands. Early ethnographic studies at Zuni were done by the James and Matilda Stevenson expedition beginning in 1879. Its personnel included the young ethnologist named Frank Hamilton Cushing.

Cushing lived for several years at Zuni, learned the language, and was admitted into the Bow Society, one of the Zuni peoples' various ceremonial clans. In addition to recording and translating (often inaccurately it has been said) many myths and stories and much ethnographic information, he helped the Zunis in their dealings both with the United States government and with the land sharks.

In 1882 Cushing learned of a land grab by two Army officers from Fort Wingate who tried to take Zuni land at Nutria for their cattle ranch, and he aided the Zunis in regaining ownership of the disputed land. One of the officers, however, was the son-in-law of Senator John A. Logan of Illinois. Logan was angered by Cushing's interference and pressured the Smithsonian to order him to leave Zuni and return to Washington in April 1884. The Zunis were not always so fortunate in maintaining their lands. Most of the large area which was traditionally recognized by neighboring tribes and Hispanic settlers as Zuni territory was lost to them in the late 1800s, including all their lands in today's Arizona, but through the twentieth century they gradually regained some portions of their lands, increasing the reservation to its present size of ca. 450,000 acres.

Over the years, the Zunis, along with other Pueblos, gradually changed from the traditional theocratic form of government—in which spiritual leaders made decisions—to the secular tribal council form of government. The Zuni government is now

221

modern in every respect and takes care of all the normal functions of any municipal government: water and sewage systems, law enforcement, schools, new housing, road maintenance, etc. In 1970 the Indian Service of the federal government formally gave control of the Zuni reservation to the tribal council.

Frank Hamilton Cushing Tried for Sorcery in Zuni

Cushing gives us an interesting insight into the workings of the Zuni, and their strong beliefs in witchcraft and sorcery. Cushing was at one point accused of being a sorcerer and forced to stand trial in a secret kiva ceremony. Cushing related the strange story in a lecture, "Life in Zuni," delivered in Buffalo, New York, December 10, 1890. (Envelope 214, Hodge-Cushing Collection, Southwest Museum, Los Angeles.):

> The day of my greatest ordeal came after more than two years of life among the Zunis. Unknown to myself and because of enmity here and there, and whispered slanders from the outside world, from amongst Mormons, Mexicans, and even Americans who never liked my Indian experiment, I had been accused of sorcery, the most heinous crime this people knew of.
>
> I was peacefully sleeping in my little room one night; late it was, the fire on the hearth had burned low. I had not noticed that those who gathered around as usual to talk, and listen, as they were always ready to do, to my stories of old world history, were somewhat more solemn than usual. Finally I felt a tapping at my feet and awoke. The room was nearly dark. Some one was bending over the fire and stirring up the embers to make light. As the glow became brighter I saw standing beside

the doorway two men, ceremonial war clubs in their hands, badges of the war priesthood over their breasts. The one who was tapping me on the feet (their way of waking a sleeper, in order that his soul, if absent in dreams, will not be rudely shocked), as well as the one who was stirring the fire, was thus attired also.

One who lives the daily life of Indians becomes marvelously trained to take in details in an instant. Before I was fairly awake, I knew that I was suspected of sorcery. I thought I was doomed when the one at my foot said, "Come, Little Brother." Very gravely, but kindly, he said it. "Come, take your smoke." For it is customary when the priesthood is about to try a man for crime to bid him smoke, meaning his last smoke.

To gain time, I pretended ignorance. "You are pretty fellows," I said, "to be joking in this way, and pulling a fellow out of dreams from as far away as Washington." But I reached for my tobacco, and at the same time slipped an extra bag and some corn shucks and my pistol under my blanket, which I drew up around me, arose, and said suddenly, "So it is serious, is it? Then let us go, since go we must. Whither?"

One before me, one behind me, one on either side, they proceeded through the dark narrow ways of the pueblo to the other end, and led me deep down through a turning, tunnel-like entrance into a great low chamber, where a bright fire was burning, and where nearly a hundred members of the esoteric societies were gathered, row behind row. Down in the middle of the floor was a stool-block, a blanket already spread over it. My adopted father, my poor brother (Pa-lo-wah-ti-wa) and his father were sitting near it on the right hand side,

223

the only defenders of the accused, who was quickly singled out, as they motioned me to sit down on the empty stool-block.

"Smoke," said I, joking again, as I threw the tobacco on the floor. "You must be sleepy, for you are not owls."

"You ought to know," said a voice gravely from their midst. He was alluding to the practice of sorcerers, who deal with owls' feathers and charms of the night.

But I kept on joking, talking out whatever came into my head, for I was endeavoring to gain time, when my old adopted father extended his hand, and said, "Son, pray do not joke; this is a grave matter."

"Grave, said I, changing again in a minute. "Come then," I said, sitting down, "let us hear what it is."

A man arose from the ranks on the other side, came forward and sat down. He accused me of practicing sorcery. Alas! that I had entered the meeting of the Fire Order when newly come to Zuni, for the man before me was one of its chief priests. He alluded to that. He told the others how I had transgressed; how also I had stolen with brilliant colors the shadows of the sacred dance, and thereby disturbed the souls of the gods; how I had, not long before, put up a magic string, with tin cans at the ends of it, which extended farther than the steps of three arrows, yet which spoke at one end whatever had gone into the other; how I had brought strange medicines into the tribe, and predicted the deaths of children whom I would not cure, which predictions had invariably come true; had refused to treat their children when they were dying of the "red rash," as they called the measles; how the children had not died until those strange medicines were brought with which I had pretended to paint my doorway (they were merely boiled oil and turpentine, such as these people had never seen before, much less smelled). Then he said,

"We have referred the matter to the Mexicans, and they say he is an *ichesero,* or witch."

They had also referred to the Mormons, who shook their heads and did not dare to deny it; and they had referred even to other Americans, who had proven no less non-committal.

I listened to the long harangue, gathering my forces together. I had then been for more than a year a leading chief in the tribe, and had learned much of their ways. When he had finished speaking,

"Speak, my son," said my father.

"Yes, speak," echoed my brother.

"It seems, then," said I suddenly, "that you have all, men, as well as women and children, been such fools as not to see this long ago. Everything you have said is true. Why did I come here? Did you not notice that I left my weapons at your doorways when I entered your houses? You ought to have seen that was not for politeness but because I was a magician and fearless. Suppose that I did wear your dress and consent to call you brothers and fathers? Suppose that I did eat from one bowl with each one of you, as though born of the same mother?" My father and brother looked aghast. "No man who loved you," I continued, "would do such things as these."

Here, suddenly, my old father lifted his head and shouted: "Listen, fools, listen."

"Why did I counsel that the Mormons should not share your lands? Why did I lead

225

your parties of young men to drive away the Mexicans from your pastures? No man who loved you would do such things as these. For the Mormons, who wear stems of red canvas for breeches (the Zuni description for the poorest and most worthless of Americans), are, as you all know, the wisest and greatest of the Americans. They never lie. They love you so much that they long to live with you, and even to build their homes on your land."

"Listen, fools, listen," said my old father and my brother together now. Several of the men opposite raised their hands and cried,

"Enough! Shame is soiling the blankets that cover us."

"Go on," said my brother, with a flaming eye, and I continued:

"As for the Mexicans, you ought to have known that I was a sorcerer when I tried to drive them away; for they loved you so much that they came here to your pasture-grounds and brought thousands of their sheep, not to feed them on your grass but in order that they need not have to leave you. You have a proverb that the Mexican lies even when he prays,—But not to you, oh no! "

"Enough! Enough!" said one and all. "We are even as women in cold weather, and as weeping children."

"Yes, rise, Little Brother," said the old priest who had spoken against me, stepping over to where I was sitting and lifting me by the hand. He was trembling violently, but he solemnly embraced me and pronounced a prayer over me, as did every other one, except my brother and the two fathers, who accompanied me home and sat explaining and joking until the coming of dawn; and that was the last of my difficulties and dangers from superstitious causes among the Zunis.

Zunis share many Pueblo traits with other Southwestern people, including strong beliefs about witchcraft; but their language is unique and cannot be linked to any other Native American language. The language of the Zuni is called by linguists a "language isolate" because no connections with other languages have been found. Attempts to connect it with some California Indian languages have not been convincing. The uniqueness of the Zuni language adds support to the idea that they have lived in the present location for millennia.

Nancy Yaw Davis, in her book *The Zuni Enigma*,[83] says that she has found evidence for the Zunis speaking a form of ancient Japanese. Davis thinks that the Zunis are connected to ancient Japanese Buddhists who were searching for the "Middle of the World." Asks Davis on the back cover of her book: "Did a group of thirteenth-century Japanese journey to the American Southwest, there to merge with the people, language, and religion of the Zuni tribe?"

Davis acknowledges that for many years, anthropologists have understood the Zuni in the American Southwest to occupy a special place in Native American culture and ethnography. Their language, religion, and blood type are startlingly different from all other tribes. Most puzzling, she says, is the Zuni appear to have much in common with the people of Japan. She goes on to describe the circumstances that may have led Japanese on a religious quest—searching for the legendary "middle world" of Buddhism—across the Pacific and to the American Southwest more than seven hundred years ago.

I had the book in the SUV and had a quick look at it. The Zuni were an interesting bunch. Were they a group of Buddhists who had come to the west coast of America, either in California or Baja, and then come to the Continental Divide that is the "Middle of the World" for the North American continent? Indeed, this is the area around Zuni, Chaco Canyon, Acoma and other nearby pueblos or Anasazi ruins.

We drove out to the ruins of the early pueblo known as Hawikah, where we parked and found bits of pottery, stones and a mound of dirt. South of us were the salt lakes of Zuni, source of an important trading item. To the west was the sacred mountain of the Zuni, where all their spirits go after death. This mountain is west of Zuni and actually in Arizona. This is an area known as the Witch Wells.

Nearby was the strange Scalp House, a photograph of which is in some of the old books about the Zuni. It is a strange stone and mud structure that is built like a cone. Some of the rocks in the Scalp House look to be quite large, and it has the look of a man-made building, possibly combined with a natural formation.

The sun was starting to set so we got back on Highway 53 west out of Zuni—the rebuilt ancient pueblo of Halona. It was a desolate road, going just north of the Zuni River. The sun was a red ball of fire hanging low in the sky. No other cars were ever seen as we crossed the Arizona State Line and the Highway became Arizona Highway 61.

I thought about the Zuni Wars, and the idea that the Chaco culture and the Anasazi peoples were also the Zuni. Did the many roads that led to Chaco Canyon mean that—beyond the normal trading—people from all over the Southwest met at that sacred place for special ceremonies? Perhaps they later met at a secret spot somewhere in the southern Zuni areas? This area was "the Great Middle" according to the Zuni, and it was indeed the Continental Divide with North America's rivers flowing from here both east and west. The Zuni River in fact, flows westward to the Pacific. And, as a British friend of mine who knew the Zunis well, and knew their fear of witches and warlocks, would like to say to his Zuni friends as they drank beer and broke bottles around their house to keep witches at a safe distance, "What about the witches?"

And indeed, as we came to the crossroads of Highway 61 and Highway 191 we found a strange crossroads bar called "The Witch Well." We stopped for a quick drink and headed toward the Interstate on Highway 191. The World Explorers Club in Cottonwood was only a few hours away. The sun had now set over the mountains, turning the western sky various shades of pink, orange and purple. Perhaps we would be coming back this way again.

A stone statue once in the temple at Pecos Pueblo, now in the Pecos Museum.

Top: Coronado arrives at Pecos Pueblo, complete with attack dogs. Bottom: The remaining walls of the old Spanish Mission at Pecos.

Top: Frank Hibben examining Ice Age bison skulls in 1969. Middle: The logo for Ghost Ranch. Bottom: Frank Hibben on safari in Africa, circa 1995

232

In 1915 archeologist Earl Morris discovered the towers in the Gobernador region near Gallina, in northwest New Mexico.

Inside the recreation of the Great Kiva at Aztec, New Mexico.

Top: An aerial photo of the Aztec Ruins, circa 1934. Bottom: Aztec ruins in 1918.

DETAIL OF SLAB B

Top: The strange inscriptions on the two slabs discovered at Flora Vista near Aztec, New Mexico in 1910. Both of the slabs appeared to depict elephants. Bottom: A drawing of a possible elephant with his mahoot, or driver, depicted on a stele at the Mayan city of Copan in Honduras.

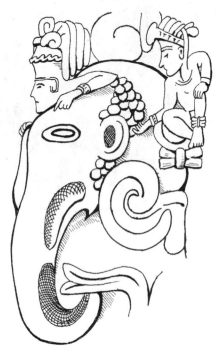

The Granby Idol, carved on a basalt boulder. Thumbs up!

Top: Sandstone formations in the vicinity of Chaco Canyon become carved walls of rock in this fanciful drawing from 1876. Bottom: The pueblo of Acoma depicted on top of a sheer mesa in another fanciful 1876 drawing.

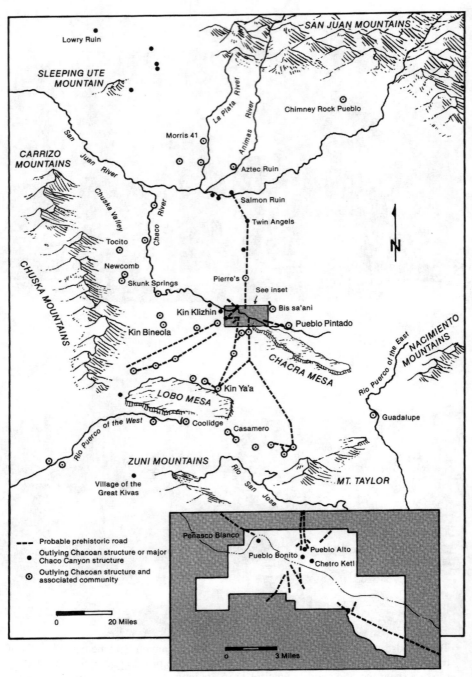

A map of the Chaco Canyon roads.

Map by Carol Cooperrider

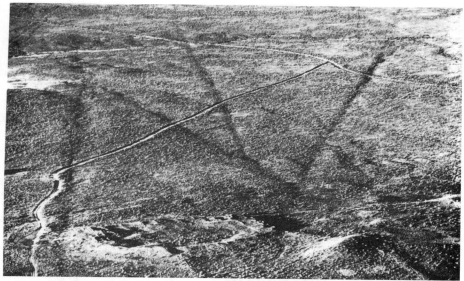

An aerial photo of Chaco Canyon showing the various roads radiating out from Pueblo Bonito (see map on opposite page).

An aerial photo of Chaco Canyon showing the convergence of rivers.

An old print of the entrance to Acoma with the natural sandstone walls made to look a bit like megalithic blocks of stone.

240

An aerial photo of the Sky City of Acoma.

Top: An old photo of the entrance to Acoma. Below: An 1860 print of the bluff known as El Morro and its fascinating inscriptions.

EL MORRO
Locations of some of the inscriptions

The locations of the many inscriptions at El Morro.

A map of the Zuni Region.

An aerial photo of the mysterious complex of buildings and kivas in the Nutria Valley near Zuni called the Village of the Great Kivas.

An 1853 drawing of "a curious Zuni altar" that may be the ruins at El Morro, or possibly the Village of the Great Kivas.

245

PUEBLO OF ZUÑI.

Top: Zuni in 1850. Bottom: A drawing of the main street in Zuni around 1870, called the Road of the Red Door.

Frank Hamilton Cushing dressed in full Zuni regalia.

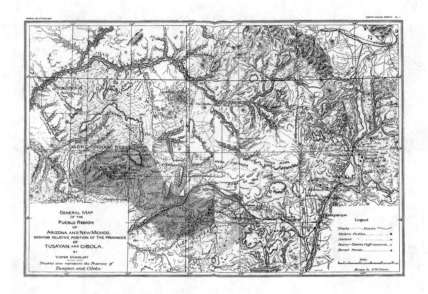

SCALP HOUSE

Top: An old map of the Zuni and Tusayan (Hopi) area. Bottom: The rare photo of a Zuni Scalp House.

5.
SOUTHERN ARIZONA

CRUISING THE DEVIL'S HIGHWAY FOR LOST CITIES

I ran into the Devil and he lent me twenty bills.
I spent the night in Utah in a cave up in the hills
I set out runnin' but I take my time.
A friend of the Devil is a friend of mine.
If I get home before daylight,
Just might get some sleep tonight.
—Friend of the Devil, Grateful Dead

Cruising the Devil's Highway
Ahead of me was a vast, rugged desert. My foot was on the gas pedal and I was leaning slightly on the driver's door. Seated next to me with her long blond hair blowing from the open window was Jennifer, looking out at the desert around us. Jagged mountains virtually devoid of vegetation surrounded us. In the dry sandy plain leading up to the rocky peaks I could see saguaro and organ pipe cactus liberally dotting the landscape. Except for the familiar cactus species, it would seem like a foreign planet.

Jennifer and I had stayed at the World Explorers Club in Cottonwood for a few weeks, and then had driven south to Yuma on Arizona Highway 95. After a

249

night in a motel in Yuma we crossed the border to the small Mexican town of San Luis Rio Colorado. This was a good starting point to explore the "Devil's Highway" and we began the drive east on Mexican Highway 2, which parallels the ancient road called "Camino del Diablo" at this point. After going only a few miles out of town we came to a military roadblock.

"Where are you going?" asked the green-uniformed soldier, in English.

"We are going to Sonoyta," I said.

He glanced in the back of the SUV. "Okay," he said, "you can go."

We were off again, through the barren wasteland of the northwest corner of Mexico's Sonora State. Highway 2 runs along the northern border of Mexico from Tijuana all the way to Ciudad Juarez, on the border opposite El Paso; we were going to drive only a small part of it. Our destination, the Mexican town of Sonoyta, was over 200 kilometers ahead across the drifting sands. There are no towns along this section of the road, nor on the old Camino del Diablo that lay just over the border to the north. In fact, that part of the old road is now located in the Cabeza Prieta National Wildlife Refuge and the Barry M. Goldwater Air Force Range, and access is strictly regulated. The old road dipped south as it neared Sonoyta—in fact, we would actually travel the ancient route for a short time coming into town, as Highway 2 was built on its foundations in that area. After Sonoyta, the Devil's Highway runs north to Ajo, Arizona.

For over a hundred miles in front of us stretched a road of burning tar and hot cement. Not another car was in sight. I felt satisfied—this was a land of lost cities and ancient mysteries. While most of the Southwest boasts tales of lost mines and buried treasure, the vast Sonoran Desert that covers northern Mexico and southwest Arizona (from Casa Grande

250

west to Ajo and eventually the Colorado River) seems too barren a wasteland to have ever supported cities and mines—but I thought I might find a few choice tales of treasure.

The ancient civilizations of the Sonoran region mined precious metals in this mountainous terrain, and over the last several hundred years, further gold and silver veins were found by immigrants and prospectors who came into this forbidding and dangerous country in search of their fortunes. Sometimes they stumbled upon ancient mines that had been abandoned; other times they discovered brand new deposits of placer gold, or a gold reef within the strata of a mountain. Sometimes they were lucky enough to come upon hidden treasure!

In the Ajo area there are curious legends of Montezuma's treasure, an ancient gold mine and a mysterious energy vortex. And we were headed there, following the ancient and treacherous road through the desert known as the "Camino del Diablo."

The History of the Camino del Diablo

The east-west portion of the Camino del Diablo stretches from Sonoyta, Mexico to the Colorado River. The road would appear to be very ancient, and was probably used by the early Hohokam, and various other unknown travelers, going from the Hohokam settlements to the Sea of Cortez. There, shellfish, salt and other items were easily found.

In places, this part of the Camino del Diablo zigzags across the current Mexican-American border, starting at Sonoyta in Mexico and soon crossing over into Arizona. During its use, however, the Camino del Diablo was entirely in Mexican territory. The road is approximately 115 leagues long, or about 250 miles. It was traveled extensively for hundreds of years, but had almost no water.

From its beginning at Sonoyta, the only water

251

available for 150 miles was found in *tinajas*, or mountain water tanks, often cut into solid rock and meant to hold rainwater for a week or two. Some tinajas were natural, others were man-made. The Camino del Diablo had two major tinajas on it as one left Sonoyta, the first being Tinaja del Tule, also called the Agua de la Luna. Some 25 miles after this was Tinaja Altos, which was also called Agua Escondida. As one got closer to the Gila River, there was another mountain water tank called simply La Tinaja. Today this tinaja is apparently known as Carrizo Spring. After this, one came to the Gila River at a small Mexican settlement called San Pedro, near present-day Wellton, Arizona.

These tinajas were often dry, as it may not have rained for many months. Even recent rains may not have provided enough water to last more than a day or two in the blistering heat. With such little water to be had, many early travelers perished on the Camino del Diablo. Animals were usually the first to go, and a coach might suddenly have to be abandoned, and the traveler would be on foot. Soon, he could become the stereotypical man crawling across the desert looking for a drink. The Camino del Diablo can be found on certain old maps, often with the tinajas featured as important stopping points.

Treasure hunter Charles Kenworthy, in his book *Unfound Treasures of Mexico*,[34] claims that the Camino del Diablo is a wealth of lost treasure. Says Kenworthy, "Along this trail today can be found many thousands of treasure artifacts in the form of wagon wheels, trunks, weapons, items buried to ease the load when horses and mules died, with the thought to return one day and recover. Gold coins and full jewelry boxes have been found near the trail. Take water, a metal detector, and a big truck to bring back your treasures. Remember, artifacts *are* treasures and many times worth more than gold.

252

This trail is a coin-shooters paradise."

In the last few hundred years, approximately 1,000 people have lost their lives along that parched and thirsty road. History records tell that the first European to travel the Camino del Diablo (and its first known victim) was the Spanish Conquistador Melchior Diaz. As part of the Coronado expedition of 1540, Diaz was the commander of a troop of lancers. Using local guides, probably from the Tohono O'odham tribe (formerly known as the Papagos or Pimas), they began at the Sonoyta River and rode through the organ pipe cactus all the way to the Yuma Indian lands on the Colorado River.

On the return trip, Diaz was mortally wounded by his own spear while chasing a coyote on horseback. As he galloped along, his lance point accidentally dug into the ground, and the momentum sent the wooden spear shaft through Diaz' middle. Carried on a litter, he lived until the group of lancers again reached the Sonoyta River. For their own safety the troopers buried Diaz in an unmarked grave—the Indians considered him a god-like person who could not die. If the Indians became aware of his mortality, it might not go well for his underlings. Diaz Peak, on the southern edge of the Ajo Mountain Range, was named for him.

Diaz was third in command to the famous conquistador Francisco Vasquez de Coronado. The Coronado expedition had been sent to find one—or all—of the legendary Seven Gold Cities of Cibola. Diaz had visited the Colorado Delta region at the northern end of the Sea of Cortez a few years before. Historical evidence indicates that Diaz traveled on the Colorado River as far north as the present location of Blythe, California. This curious location is home to the Blythe Intaglios, giant figures etched into the desert sands that can only really be appreciated from the air, much like the Nazca Lines in Peru.

Little is known of the history of the area for the 153 years between 1540 and 1693, when Father Kino, a Jesuit priest, arrived and founded the famous California Missions and established pearl fishing on the Sea of Cortez. We do know that Father Kino traveled the Camino del Diablo and made seven trips to California from Tucson. Father Kino established a large cattle ranch in the Sonoyta area and taught the Indians ranching and farming until his death in 1711.

Looking out at the road rushing under my wheels.
I don't know how to tell you all just how crazy this life feels.
I look around for the friends that I used to turn to,
to pull me through.
Looking into their eyes I see them running too.
—Jackson Browne, *Running On Empty*

Cruising to the Devil's Town

As we neared Sonoyta, Mexico Highway 2 followed the course of the ancient Devil's Highway. I looked down at the speedometer and then at the fuel gauge on the SUV. It showed that we were on empty. There were no reserve tanks. The devil had struck! I had not filled up the tank as we left Yuma.

"Don't panic," I said to Jennifer, "but we're running out of gas!"

"We can't run out of gas out here!" said Jennifer, panicking.

"Sonoyta is just up ahead," I said. "I think I can see some buildings."

Out in the distance, we could just make out some shacks and a few trees. As we progressed, we began to pass the small roadside shacks—all empty and abandoned. Soon more sturdy concrete buildings began to appear and, finally, like some sort of desert oasis or cantina for the thirsty, a Pemex gas station came into view. The SUV sputtered on the last fumes from the gas tank as I coasted into the station.

Once I had the car fueled up, a bottle of good tequila seemed in order. One didn't travel the Camino del Diablo without lots of water and a bottle of good tequila. And, we weren't finished with the Devil's Highway yet. We were headed to Ajo on the spur that continued north, through equally hostile desert. After purchasing some tequila and visiting the site of an old Father Kino mission, we headed for the border. The U.S.-Mexican border had essentially been drawn to put Sonoyta in Mexico. The American border is immediately north of town, and Sonoyta's one main street ran right up to the American border post.

There was only one car ahead of us as we pulled up to the immigration and customs booth. I handed over our passports as the officer asked me if we had bought anything in Mexico. I told him about the bottle of tequila, and he seemed satisfied.

"Okay, you can go," he said as he motioned us forward with a big sweep of his arm.

"Thanks, officer," I said as I put the SUV in drive and pulled away slowly. Now we were in the good ol' USA. However, the border is always a dicey area.

Lukeville is a very small town with a post office, a gas station, a grocery store and a few houses, mainly for border patrol and park service employees. We got some ice at the gas station just inside the border and prepared to head north to the Devil's town, Ajo.

Legend of the Maze and the Giant Snake

The gas station and border post receded in the distance as I stared at the empty desert in front of us. We were now entering, within a mile from the border, Organ Pipe Cactus National Monument. Jennifer took out our map and unfolded it. The desert was whizzing by as I looked at her. Her hair was still blowing in the wind and the sun was catching her tanned cheeks with a strong orange tinge.

"We're heading for Why," said Jennifer, reaching for some limes on the back seat, and her Swiss Army knife.

"What?" I responded.

"Not what, Why," she said, grabbing the bottle of tequila.

"Why?" I said.

"Why's coming up," she said, putting some slices of lime on the dashboard.

"When is Why?" I asked in desperation.

"Here, take a shot of this," she finally said.

I did as I was told, and then had a bottle of water. Park rangers and border patrol police roamed the park at will in four-wheel drive vehicles. Such had become the Devil's Highway.

As we cruised toward the crossroads at Why, I thought about a curious story of the area. Legend has it that there is a maze of tunnels somewhere in the region, possibly around a mountain called Montezuma's Head. The maze was an important symbol for the Tohono O'odham and Hohokam, and is often pictured on their baskets and pottery. A man must choose his path carefully to find his way to peace and harmony. This is represented in the maze design by many paths leading to its center. Many paths do not go to the center, however, and reach dead ends, much like modern mazes.

A story is sung in the Tohono O'odham legends. It goes back to "the beginning of time":

> After battling the forces of evil with no victory, Ee-Ea-Toy returned to where he lived in the sacred mountains. To confuse his evil enemies, he built his home in the center of a maze, a cave with many offshoots and dead

ends. To enter the maze, a large opening was provided. His evil enemies would enter the opening and try to find the true path to the home of Ee-Ea-Toy.

This entrance resembled the mouth of a fierce monster. The evil enemy would enter with awe, fear and wonder. Only one could enter at a time. They would get lost in the tunnels, gasp for air and die, not being able to find their way out. None could reach the center of the maze.

Ee-Ea-Toy was safe in his home, knowing that his enemies could not find him, and survived.

According to the Tohono O'odham, years ago a large snake emerged from the underworld and started eating everyone. Elder Brother Ee-Ea-Toy came to the rescue from the center of the maze. He fought the snake with four stakes, propping open the snake's large mouth. With the snake not being able to close his mouth, Elder Brother slid down its throat and cut out its green heart. He returned to the center of the maze, taking the green heart with him. The Indians believe that he still lives at the center of the maze. He protects his people from the giant snake, who is still searching for his lost green heart.

This curious legend may be nothing but myth, but is there some basis for this story of a maze of tunnels and a giant snake? Why is the giant snake searching for his lost green heart? Could this green heart be made of jade, which was a very valuable green stone? Was there a lost jade mine somewhere in the area? Mines are built with a series of interconnected tunnels, much like a maze. It is a mystery where all the jade used in Mesoamerica came from. One jade mine has been located near Quirigua in Guatemala, but it is thought that some jade mines were further north. Jade can be found in Nevada and at Jade Cove on the California coast south of Monterey. But no jade mines have been found in Arizona—yet.

Also, where are these "sacred mountains" where the maze is located? They may be in the Montezuma's Head area of the Ajo Mountains, or perhaps the "sacred mountains" are the Superstition Mountains where tunnels are also said to exist.

I glanced up at the sign on the roof of a building off to the right of the highway that said "Why Cafe & Gas." We had come to the crossroads at the small town of Why. We pulled into the café to have a quick bite to eat. Soon, we were back in the car and headed north out of town. To the east was Arizona Highway 86 going through the Tohono O'odham reservation. As we headed north from Why toward Ajo, I mulled over these curious legends of treasure, a dangerous maze of tunnels, and tales of lost mines.

The Treasure of Montezuma's Head

Looking out at the rugged, barren mountains and organ pipe cactus around me, I tried to identify the peak known as Montezuma's Head. For a hundred miles in every direction from the Ajo Mountains this lofty peak resembling the head and shoulders of a large Indian can be seen clearly outlined against the sky as he sits majestically on top of the mountain. According to legend, hidden away for more than four centuries in the secret recesses of the barren Ajo Mountains is a great treasure of such wonderful richness that it was guarded night and day for three hundred years. The legend says that the ancestors of the Tohono O'odham Indians helped bury a great Aztec treasure in a mountain cave beneath Montezuma's Head—and that it is guarded by none other than Montezuma himself.

When the Spanish conquered Mexico in 1521, the Aztecs sent as much of their treasure as possible north to their ancestral homelands. According to some legends, seven caravans of Aztec treasure left Tenochtitlan in that year and all of them marched far to the north. Each was buried in a separate and secret place, each location somehow connected to the Aztecs. These treasure troves are thought to range from northern Mexico to as far north as Colorado and Utah.

The great store of gold (running into millions of dollars in value) that found its way to the land of the Tohono O'odham was taken from the placer mines in Mexico a short distance to the south. These ancient mines were of such great richness that many tons of pure gold were picked up from the surface of the ground and the creek beds where it had been exposed by erosion.

The Tohono O'odham say that after the treasure had been safely stored away in the cave, Montezuma climbed up to the mountaintop and turned to stone. Today this stone god sits on his mountain throne overlooking the peaceful valleys. There was a village near the base of the mountain but the ancient dwellings have long since fallen into decay. Their rooms are deserted now and the happy voices of the Indians have passed into silence. Corn grinders, pieces of broken pottery and some ancient graves are all that is left.

Those who would search for the treasure, as many have done before, should bear in mind that the treasure must be very close to the original village. The story the old Tohono O'odham handed down from father to son says, "When the Indians were engaged in storing the gold away in the cave they were so close that they could, on a still night, hear the tom-toms beat and the dogs bark in the village below."

The Ajo Mountains are the home of the storm gods and in the rainy season dark clouds hang over Montezuma's Head, flashes of lightning chase each other up the ridges, and thunder rumbles through the canyon walls. Torrents of rain descend from the mountainsides into the valley below.

Old legends say that on these stormy days the descendents in the nearby villages sit around the campfires and in hushed tones talk about the great treasure stored away in the mountain cave. They believe that someday the spirit of Montezuma will come out of the East and he will climb down from the mountaintop and open the secret cave—then all the wealth that it contains will be given to the Indians to whom it rightfully belongs.

Dust Devil Wars & the Lost Gold Mine at Ajo

It is said that the Tohono O'odham Indians found placer gold in the gullies around the site of the present day Ajo mine pit. This seems probable as the great ore bodies at the present time carry about 20 cents per ton in gold. Erosion over untold centuries carried this gold down from the hillsides and concentrated it as placer on the bottom of the arroyos.

The Tohono O'odham established a village near the mines (probably previously occupied by their ancestors, the Hohokam) and made their living by panning gold and killing the wild game that roamed over the boundless plains below the mines. The country at that time belonged to Mexico, so every year the Tohono O'odham chief led his people down to Caborea, in the Altar district, to barter their gold for supplies.

One year, while the Indians were at the market, the Spanish authorities discovered the source of the gold and quickly sent an expedition of about 500 men to Ajo to work the mines. The Spanish brought provisions and supplies sufficient to enable them to work the mines for a year before returning to Caborea to market their gold. Upon returning to the mines the Indians were forced to abandon the workings. Being a gentle people toward the Spanish, they left the mines without a fight. The Spanish established their camp in the vicinity and took out a large amount of ore. This mine became known as the *Planchas de la Plata* (Plata means silver, which was also present, was well as copper).

Suddenly, after the Spanish had worked the placers for six or eight months, a large band of Apache Indians on their way from the Sea of Cortez to their stronghold in the Superstition Mountains, swooped down upon them from the nearby mountains. Apache men were fierce warriors controlling much of the mountain country of eastern Arizona; they often rode in bands that would raid villages, rob and kill the occupants, then disappear into the desert like phantoms. They had already taken control of the Turquoise Mountains in eastern Arizona and were pushing steadily westward, into the Tohono O'odham territory. The surprised Spanish put up a stiff fight but, being outnumbered, they were finally defeated and fled, leaving their supplies and a large bucket of gold nuggets buried somewhere around the camp.

Watching the attack from the safety of the surrounding hills, the Tohono O'odham decided that it was time to fight. The Apaches were heavily armed, each carrying a long bow and a quiver of arrows and most of them had large tomahawks in their belts. The Tohono O'odham were outnumbered and had fewer weapons than the Apache, but they had confidence in their medicine man. The magical medicine he prescribed was a strange powder, carried in a small buckskin pouch.

When this powder was thrown into the air, it would start a whirlwind that would destroy everything in its path. The chief held up his right hand as a signal for silence. Every warrior stopped and remained motionless. The medicine man untied the buckskin

261

sack, took out a large handful of powder, and threw it high into the air just as the warriors let out a blood-curdling war whoop that shook the very hills as it echoed back and forth across the canyons.

Almost immediately, as if by magic, a great funnel-shaped whirlwind was seen to drop out of the eastern sky and come rushing into the west, headed straight for the Apache camp. Nearer and nearer came the great whirlwind, tearing up trees by the roots and bending the greasewoods and sagebrush to the ground like grass.

The Tohono O'odham warriors began leaping down the hillsides toward their ancient enemies. The Apaches were mounted on horses and ponies in a long line, plainly outlined against the deep blue sky. A large number of squaws and papooses that had accompanied the bucks on the trip to the Sea of Cortez were along. Frightened by the hideous yelling of the Tohono O'odham warriors and the terrible noise of the whirlwind that was now kicking up large clouds of dust, the ponies stampeded and headed for the tall bushes, bucking the squaws and papooses off as they went.

The Apache warriors, now thunderstruck with superstitious fear, were having a hard time controlling their own horses that were trying frantically to join the others rushing down toward the flats below. The Tohono O'odham warriors were racing down upon them from the south and west, yelling like demons, and the great whirlwind was coming out of the east directly toward them: the Apaches were justifiably frightened.

Apache warriors were greatly feared by the Tohono O'odham, but this time the Tohono O'odham had the Apaches on the run. The Apaches decided to flee and, as the women and children picked up and got back on their ponies, the Tohono O'odham followed in hot pursuit. Furthermore, another whirlwind, even bigger than the first, was headed across the flats kicking up great clouds of dust and roaring like the devil himself—a true Dust Devil. The Apaches rode out as fast as they could for their stronghold in the Superstition Mountains—several days away.

Having chased off the Apaches with bravado and their medicine man's Dust Devils, the Tohono O'odham returned to the mining camp, claiming the supplies and equipment left behind by the fleeing Apaches. They found a small amount of gold, but nothing like that supposedly buried by the Spanish. They helped themselves to the provisions and supplies and occupied the site for another year. According to the local historical society in Ajo, no part of the treasure has ever been found. There remains out in those hills a lost pot of gold nuggets, now Ajo's most famous treasure story. This legend was probably the origin of the Lost Bean Pot Mine fable—another tale of a lost treasure yet to be found.

Still to this day, at the same time every year, the Tohono O'odham congregate at the village of Moivavi ("Many Wells") for a great fiesta where they celebrate with eating and dancing the victory they won over the Spanish and Apaches. When the fiesta is over and the stars come out, the medicine man gets out a buckskin pouch from its secret place and ties it up again with a strong string to keep it safe and ready for use in case the Apaches ever come back again.

Ajo in Ancient Times

The sun was setting over the gigantic Ajo mine as Jennifer and I saw the first lights of the city in the distance. We drove slowly through the town square and then stopped for the night at one of the motels on the northern edge of town. The next morning we checked out and drove into the downtown plaza, a large square with a park in the center and business entrances under a broad covered sidewalk. We had breakfast in a spacious diner and read about Ajo's strange geology and the unusual phenomena in the area.

The local mountains around Ajo range in age from the Precambrian basement Sneiss in the Little Ajo Mountains to the late Tertiary lava north, east and south of Ajo. Many features in the area were formed by the lava and are thought to be approximately six million years old. Black Mountain, located to the south of Ajo is part of the same lava flow.

Gastropods, brachiopods, corals and other fossils of the Cenozoic era have been found in alluvial deposits south of the mine. The area around Ajo was an ocean before more recent volcanic activity and erosion filled in the land.

The Coffee Pot Mountain area, eighteen miles east of Ajo, is approximately nine million years old, according to geologists. It is the core of an ancient volcano with its alluvial sides eroded away. This area is well known to rock hounds, where bacon agate, quartz, chalcedony, jasper, geodes, rhyolite marbles and obsidian can be found.

Human presence in the Ajo area dates back eleven thousand years. The climate may have been different then, with more rain and standing water. Today, it is one of driest areas in the world. Ventana Cave, where archeologists have uncovered evidence of human habitation, is located east of Ajo on the Tohono O'odham Reservation; Indians believe that the Devil Wind God lived in this cave. Broken bits of pottery, arrowheads, spear points, axe heads and other artifacts have been found in all directions from Ajo, indicating humans existed for a very long time in the area.

The Hohokam Indians, "the people that went

away," inhabited most of Arizona, including Ajo and the Devil's Highway area. Local archeologists estimate that the Hohokam inhabited Arizona from 200 BC to AD 1475, when they suddenly collapsed. The Hohokam made regular trips from their irrigated towns around the area of Phoenix and Casa Grande to the Sea of Cortez to collect seashells for tools, ornaments and food.

They would naturally have passed through the Ajo area, but, because of its extremely hostile environment it is unlikely that there were any large Hohokam settlements, such as those found around Casa Grande and Phoenix. On the other hand, the Ajo area may have been a copper and gold mining area for the Hohokam, and the area was a source of obsidian, quartz and other important stones. This may very well have necessitated the building of roads to link the mines with well-watered agricultural areas.

It seems likely that Ajo was an outlying Hohokam town connected by roads to the east and north. The Devil's Highway went to the west, through the worst of the desert. The Hohokam had turquoise mines farther to the east in the remote Turquoise Mountains directly east of Tombstone.

With the collapse of the Hohokam cities around the Gila and Salt Rivers, and the invasion of hostile Apaches from the eastern mountains, what was left of the Hohokam moved into the more remote desert areas of southern Arizona and northern Sonora State where the Tohono O'odham are found today. At this time, Ajo may have become a larger permanent settlement.

There are some ancient ruins, known as the Lost City of Growler Valley, some twenty miles west of Ajo, where semi-permanent villages were located. They were inhabited in the spring and in the fall when the Tohono O'odham, like the Hohokam before them, made their semi-annual trips to the Sea of Cortez. Even today there are piles of oyster shells there.

After the Apache takeover of northern and eastern Arizona, that land of hostile elements and tribes was called *Terra Incognita* ("Unknown Land") by the early Spanish, who controlled New Mexico from Sante Fe. Indeed, northern Arizona was never claimed by the Spanish. The Spanish did lay claim to the southern parts of Arizona in 1693, however, and Ajo was part of the claim. After the Mexican War of 1846-48, Mexico claimed all the land to the south of Gila Bend and this included Ajo.

In 1853, U.S. politician James Gadsden negotiated the purchase that bore his name with General Santa Ana, who was president of Mexico during that time. The purchase consisted of land stretching from the Colorado River eastward across southern Arizona all the way into New Mexico. The United States government paid Mexico ten million dollars. The area consisted of 45,535 square miles, land that was unsuitable for agriculture, therefore of little value to the Mexicans. For the Americans, however, it provided a route for the Southern Pacific Railroad that would take goods to and from southern California. It also ended the boundary disputes with Mexico. Ajo, virtually the only town in this western area, had now become a part of the United States.

Today, about twelve miles east of Ajo begins the Tohono O'odham reservation, which consists of approximately 2,500,000 acres and stretches east most of the way across the desert toward Tucson. In the 17th century, Spanish conquistadors used a corruption of an Indian word for bean to name the Tohono O'odham the "Papagos" or "Bean Eaters." Josiah Moore, the tribal chairman, lobbied the U.S. government for a name change, which took place in 1984.

The early Ajo district was called *Tinaja de Mui*

Vavi (meaning "contained much water") because of a natural rock water tank. This tank was held in much reverence. A Cuprite red copper oxide was also found in the area, and was used for body paint. The Tohono O'odham word for the copper body paint was Au-Auho. The Spanish shortened the word to Auho, which was close to the Spanish word ajo, meaning garlic. Because of this similarity, there was some confusion as to the origin of the name. The Mexican invaders named the area *Minas de Cobre de Ajo*, (Copper Mines of Garlic), and the settlement has been known as Ajo since 1854.

Ajo Museum's Mysterious Egyptian Head

After breakfast in the town plaza, we drove up a steep paved road going directly out of the middle of town and up to the edge of the massive open pit mine. Here we stopped the car and got out to look over the huge orange hole dug out of the earth. The museum was just a bit farther up the road and was apparently once one of the mine's buildings.

Inside the museum was a hodgepodge of different paraphernalia: old mining tools, pioneer items, old news clippings and oddball exhibits. There were some old maps and clippings about the Devil's Highway and one curious cabinet held some strange rock items that had been found out in the desert and along the Devil's Highway.

One of the old newspaper articles on the Devil's Highway mentioned that a curious rock construction was discovered at a remote spot along the road. Large stones were stacked up to form a dam in a dry gulley. It was speculated that it had been built at a time when there was more water (and more traffic) along the treacherous road. This ancient dam was apparently many hundreds of years old. If the dam had been working and there had been more rain than currently falls, then there would have been a sizable man-made reservoir at an important stop along the road. Today there is only parched desert.

One of the items on display was a carved stone head that appeared to wear an Egyptian headdress. The stone head was about five inches high and had no plaque explaining it. The volunteers at the museum could only say that it had been found out in the desert and had been given to the museum. They apparently felt it was an authentic ancient artifact.

I showed it to Jennifer and took a photo of it with my digital camera. "Doesn't this look Egyptian?" I asked her.

"Yes, it does," she replied. "Did the Egyptians come to the Southwest?"

"Well, there are the stories of Egyptian catacombs in the Grand Canyon," I said. "Plus there are many theories of the Egyptians sailing across both the Atlantic and the Pacific. Perhaps they arrived in the American Southwest by crossing the Pacific. It is known that the ancient Chinese and Japanese voyaged to California. The easiest way to reach the Hohokam cities would have been to come by ship to the northern coast of the Sea of Cortez and then march north to Ajo."

"Well, it seems incredible that the Egyptians came through here. It seems so barren!" said Jennifer. She wandered off through the rest of the museum and I checked out some of the pamphlets and booklets that the museum and its volunteers had published over the years. Among this material I found some pretty interesting stories and legends.

Modern Mining at Ajo

Looking around the museum I was able to glean some of the history of the town. It is thought that the population of Ajo in 1850 was less than 50 people. It was in 1854 that Peter K. Brady remembered the abandoned diggings at Ajo. He helped form the

Arizona Mining & Trading Company to explore the possibilities of finding more wealth. They outfitted in San Diego and Los Angeles and crossed the desert to Fort Yuma. Traveling east along the treacherous Devil's Highway they came to Ajo, taking over the mine in 1854. The Ajo mine contained quite a bit of native copper, with copper ore as rich as 50% being exposed. There is little doubt a great deal of copper, and some gold, in nearly pure form, came out of the Ajo diggings in ancient times.

The modern mining was mostly confined to small bodies of native copper and Cuprite ores. With the invention of dynamite, numerous explosions blew out part of the Ajo diggings. A wagon road was cut across the Ajo Valley and went through present day Wellton to Fort Yuma. The first ore shipped went in wagons pulled by oxen, horses and mule teams. They labored all the way to the Colorado River at Fort Yuma. The ore was then loaded aboard steamboats and transported 109 miles down the river to the Mexican port of Puerto Isabel. There it was loaded aboard ships that sailed down along the coast of South America, around the Horn and up the Atlantic Ocean to smelters at Swansea, Wales. That first shipment of thirty tons netted the company the good sum of five thousand dollars.

The second shipment met disaster when it was caught in a storm and sank while trying to make it around the Horn. This great loss, along with high production costs and lack of water, brought an end to the Arizona Mining & Trading Company's operation in 1859. Ajo's isolation played a great part in the company's downfall. The mine was sold that year at a Sheriff's sale to satisfy a $5,000 claim by a watchman for his services.

1860 to 1890 were years that saw a few attempts to establish mining in the area, but no real success was made. The isolation, lack of water and transportation problems hindered every attempt. By the late 1890s, Tom Childs and Reuben Daniels had acquired many mining claims.

The Southern Pacific Railroad was built shortly after the Civil War. It ran within 44 miles of Ajo through the Gila Bend area. It followed the Old Spanish Trail from Tucson to Gila Bend, and then went along the Gila River to the Colorado. Eventually the New Cornelia Mine was established at the turn of the 20th century and Ajo began to develop into the important, though remote, town that it is today. The Ajo mine today covers an oval shape about one and one quarter miles long and one mile wide and is about 1,000 feet deep.

The Energy Vortex of Crater Range

"This is curious," I thought as I flipped through the museum literature. "Ajo has its own phantom hitchhiker, as well an energy vortex."

Arizona State Highway 85 traverses an area 12 miles north of Ajo called Crater Range. Compass readings are sometimes erratic within the Range. It was thought for many years that the crater had been formed by a meteorite striking the earth, much like the famous meteorite crater in northern Arizona. But geologists now think that the Range was formed by a horizontal lava flow of basaltic andesite and tuffs from the Batamote Volcano located in the Batamote Mountains northeast of Ajo. It may have a magnetized basalt core with a great deal of iron in it.

Old stories claim the area to be the caldera of an ancient volcano. The area is a rounded basin from Tertiary time. Over the years erosion has taken its toll. This has left a circular basin with sheer walls and odd-shaped columns.

The local Tohono O'odham tell of strange happenings in this forbidding place. As Ajo grew and the population acquired radios and such, it was noticed that some of the old crystal type radios, and even some of the new radios, would play north and south of the crater area, but not in Crater Range itself. Was there some sort of energy field at work blocking out radio transmissions?

The width of Crater Range is only two miles from south to north, but over the years, many people have been killed on this two-mile stretch of Highway 85. It is said that ghosts and other unnatural things have appeared to motorists traveling through this area late at night. Sometimes, a friendly driver would pick up a hitchhiker, only to have him disappear from the seat when the vehicle left Crater Range!

This mysterious area has generated lore similar to that of the Bermuda Triangle or the Zone of Silence in Mexico. A writer for the Ajo Museum claimed that in 1947, he was flying a light aircraft over the area at about 4,000 feet when a very strange thing happened: "Without warning, a down draft forced the craft to fall. It felt as if a giant had placed his foot on the airplane, trying to push it to the ground. By going into a dive with full throttle, I was able to control the aircraft a few hundred feet above the ground. From then on I detoured around the area when I was flying."

UFOs have been sighted in the area and the Ajo museum publications say that in 1950, before the radar station was built on top of Childs Mountain, a group of people having a picnic south of the crater witnessed a UFO that appeared a few hundred feet above the range. For a while it was floating without motion, and they watched as it then moved across the sky like a streak of light.

As we left the museum and looked out over the vast open pit mine, I wondered about this curious oasis in middle of one the hottest and emptiest deserts in the world. We had Egyptian heads, UFOs, phantom hitchhikers, Aztec treasure, radio-killing

271

vortices, killer Dust Devils and a lost pot of gold. Not bad.

We wanted to head east, so the best thing was to drive back to Why and east on Highway 85. With the bright desert sun beating down on the cactus, scrub and rocky hills that surrounded us, it all seemed painfully normal. Perhaps it was when the sun went down and the moon was rising that the area became another world—a world where the Devil cruised the dusty back roads of Ajo, Sonoyta and Why.

We went to war with Mexico to get Arizona.
Now we should go to war to make her take it back.
—General William Tecumseh Sherman

Casa Grande and the Mystery of the Hohokam

Coming out of the Tohono O'odham Reservation, we stopped at Casa Grande, the large ruins near Coolidge, Arizona. The main portion of the ancient city is a huge, square ruin that was once an astronomical observatory, archaeologists now believe.

The sun was bright as we drove down the back roads toward the main entrance to the National Monument. In the distance I could see a very large square building that was a deep orange-red against the blue sky. A huge metal roof was suspended above it on poles to shield the ancient structure from the occasional rains.

Here was the central site of the mysterious Hohokam, a civilization that tamed the desert over a thousand years ago much as the Egyptians had done in Egypt in 3000 BC. Who were these peaceful people? How had they come into this dry land with powerful rivers? How advanced was their civilization? Could they have been as advanced as the Toltecs and Maya? Did the fleeing Hohokam become the Aztecs? Did

Montezuma send his treasure back north to Aztlan/ Casa Grande?

Also, were the Hohokam in contact with trans-Pacific cultures such as ancient India, China and Japan? There is reason to think that this is possible. Some scholars now think that the Zuni (who live further east from the Hohokam settlements) speak a dialect of Japanese. Chinese historians claim there are records of Chinese visits to the Grand Canyon.

There is evidence the Romans and Greeks had been in the Tucson area and it is likely the Egyptians and Hittites came before them. Olmec, Mayan and Toltec ships would have made the journey up the Rio Grande as well. A road system passing the Turquoise Mountains and into the El Paso area would have existed at this time.

I wondered if the "Kam" in "Ho-Ho-Kam" referred to the Cham or Champa people of Vietnam and Southeast Asia? Kam or Khamet is also the ancient Egyptian word for their country: Egypt. Often where the word Kam/Cham/Kham is used it has something to do with ancient Egypt. This may—or may not be—the case with Kam in Hohokam.

The Hohokam may have been at the crossroads of the North American continent where rivers from the Atlantic and Pacific Oceans came near to each other. The New Mexico pueblos like Chaco Canyon, Zuni, Acoma and Taos were all on the Atlantic watershed, while the Hopi, Sinagua and Hohokam were on the Pacific watershed. Was this the legendary lost worlds called variously Cibola, Quivera, and Aztlan?

We parked the car and then stared at the impressive four-story structure which gives the site its name (Casa Grande means Big House in Spanish). According to the tourist literature, the site, like much of the Phoenix area, was built and occupied by the Hohokam culture. It is thought the Hohokam culture began around 200 BC, but the Big House is thought to have come late in this long-lived civilization. Early archaeologists' conservative estimates placed the building of the large structure at about AD 1350 and figured it was in use to about AD 1450. Archeologists now think that the Big House was probably in use from AD 900 to 1100.

Coronado was probably the first European to see Casa Grande and the other Hohokam structures, but the site was named by Father Kino in 1694, who was quite impressed by the large buildings. He reported later that while he had not found the fabled Seven Gold Cities of Cibola, he had found ruined cities and canals.

As pioneers, soldiers and prospectors came out to Arizona, settling originally around Prescott and Camp Verde, they marveled at the thick walls of the many-storied building. Eventually the Smithsonian and several universities became interested in the ruins and sent archeologists to study them. The purpose of the Big House evaded archeologists for over a hundred years.

Says the conservative archeologist Folsom in his book *America's Ancient Treasures*[160] about Casa Grande: "It may have been a ceremonial center or fortress or both. Its massive walls, made from a special kind of clay, are not typical of Hohokam. The building is much more like those seen farther south, in Mexico. The usual Hohokam dwellings were separate, single-room houses, made of brush and mud.

"Throughout the semiarid Gila River Valley, the Hohokam managed to raise crops by irrigation. They built more than 250 miles of canals, which were between two and four feet wide and about two feet deep. Some can still be seen today."

The special kind of clay that they are referring to is a cement-like material called caliche. The builders shaped the mud by hand in a layer about two feet thick, let it dry and then added another layer.

The Hohokam's Rare Astronomical Observatory

Archeologists didn't understand what the Big House was built for until the mid-1970s, when Dr. John Molloy of the University of Arizona suggested that ancient Mayas may have used the Caracol Tower at Chichén Itza as an astronomical observatory. Furthermore, he theorized that the astronomers of Caracol could have established a network of pre-Conquest observatories that may have extended throughout significant sites in Central and North America. In pursuit of his theory, Molloy also searched for astronomically significant alignments at the Big House.

In the June 1976 issue of *Sky and Telescope*, Robert D. Hicks III considers Molloy's research and writes that the Big House "is a three-story rectangular building of caliche and adobe, set upon a one-story platform substructure. The symmetrical plan contains five contiguous room tiers, four of which rise two stories and surround a central three-story tier. Astronomically significant alignments are found for windows and holes in the second-story west wall and for the third-story walls."

Molloy's theory holds that the various alignment holes all have lines of sight to the horizon and give the appearance of having been placed with great care. Of the fourteen openings investigated, eight were found to be celestially aligned, basically to the Sun and Moon, with the solstices and equinoxes indicated.

"Two sets of openings, Holes 6 and 7, are located directly above 8 and 9, all giving eastern horizon positions," Hicks states in his article. "This redundancy provided for 'fine tuning.'"

Molloy's research appears to have demonstrated numerous affinities between the Big House in Arizona and the Caracol Tower "observatory" in

Yucatan, Mexico. Such study, Hicks points out, will undoubtedly provide "new insights into the ancient American past" and demonstrate the establishment of pre-Columbian astronomy.

Around this same time, Jonathan Reyman of Illinois State University investigated astronomical alignments at various sites in the area of Chaco Canyon, New Mexico. A number of solstitial markers were tentatively identified by this astro-archaeologist.

Warren L. Wittry has described an astronomical observing station at Cahokia Mounds built circa A.D. 1000, a large Indian settlement near what is now St. Louis, Missouri, called the "American Woodhenge" because of its superficial resemblance to the European henge stone monuments.

Conservative archeologists, and even the Park Rangers at Casa Grande, have expressed skepticism about the Hohokam having astronomical observatories, but there seems little doubt, even to mainstream archeologists. Indeed, as we shall see, the connections between the Hohokam and the Yucatan go deeper than just having astronomical observatories.

Civilization begins with order,
grows with liberty,
and dies with chaos.
—Will Durant

The Canal Cities of the Hohokam

What is not usually mentioned by most authors is that the Hohokam not only built an extensive canal system, but it was lined with caliche-cement, which is much harder than adobe. This huge, ingenious canal system was used to irrigate the entire Gila River and

Salt River drainage basin. The central desert, where Phoenix stands today, was once the center of a great civilization that turned the desert into an agricultural paradise in which the desert literally bloomed with corn, beans, flowers and other plants. Naturally, fish, waterfowl and other animals would be attracted to such an artificial paradise.

The early settlers in Arizona believed that the land had never been occupied by anyone except Apache Indians and a few Pueblo Indians in the north. Zuni Indians lived in seven pueblos to the east in New Mexico. Then, in the late 1800s, the ancient canal system was discovered. A fascinating map of the canals was published by the Phoenix Free Museum in June of 1903, and this map has been expanded on since.

Hohokam civilization is fascinating, though little is actually known about it. The heartland of this ancient culture is the Phoenix area, where the Gila and Salt Rivers meet. The large area of their culture stretched as far south as the Tucson area, as far north as Prescott and probably as far to the east as the headwaters of the White and Black Rivers flowing from the Mogollon Rim.

Like many ancient cultures, a map of the river systems gives a pretty good map of the civilization itself. In this case, the Gila and Salt Rivers flow into the Colorado delta and out into the Sea of Cortez, or Baja California Sea. While it is never discussed in archaeological literature of this area, it can be assumed that some sort of naval traffic occurred at times along the west coast of Mexico up into the Hohokam area, which apparently extended to the coast.

Present day anthropologists generally consider the natives of the American Southwest as so primitive however, that they did not use large boats. Thus, we are left with the contrary evidence of a sophisticated canal building culture that was ignorant of sophisticated boatbuilding.

Contrary to Folsom's statement quoted above, the Hohokam did not live in mud and stick houses, but in large pueblo buildings, probably the forerunners to the Zuni and Hopi pueblos. At the time of the American colonization of Arizona, the Tohono O'odham Indians who lived around Phoenix did in fact live in small mud and stick huts.

While the Hopis, Zunis, and other Pueblo Indians still lived in adobe buildings farther north, southern Arizona was without any large well-built cities at the time of European expansion. They had fallen into ruins. Why had the cities been abandoned? Was there an invasion that collapsed their civilization? Did some drought, famine or epidemic wipe them out? Like the mysterious abandonment of the Mayan cities in the Yucatan and Peten jungles of Guatemala, the Hohokam vanished, leaving behind large buildings and unused canals.

In a December 2005 article by journalist Heather Whipps released to newswires it was claimed that recently-discovered Peruvian canals were the most ancient in New World. Whipps was reporting on anthropologist Tom Dillehay of Vanderbilt University and his team's work in Peru's northern Zana Valley which exposed four canals almost certainly used for irrigation agriculture. Dillehay said that there was solid evidence of canals confirmed to be at least 5,400 years old. The find is the oldest of its kind anywhere in South America.

The news release said that the canals range in size from 0.6 to 2.5 miles (1 to 4 kilometers) in length and were designed to slope downwards, relying on gravity to send water from an upper stream to the crop fields below. The layout essentially created artificial garden plots with fertile earth suitable for intensive agriculture.

One has to wonder, if the ancient Peruvians were making sophisticated canals 5,400 BP, is it not possible that canals around the Gila and Salt Rivers are also extremely old? They could be many thousands of years old, and used continually for hundreds of years at a time and then finally abandoned just prior to the Spanish Exploration because of a prolonged drought and the invasion of the Apaches into Southern Arizona. In short, it was a civilization in long decline, much like the Mayans, that was put over the edge by extreme drought, civil unrest and the sudden appearance of fierce invaders.

The Ballcourts of the Hohokam and Toltecs
Other evidence of the high state of civilization and intercity trade of the Hohokam is the various artifacts found in the area. The people did not dress in a buckskin loincloth as the typical museum display in the west has most natives dressing, but in colorful cotton clothes and ponchos. They made beautiful pottery and artifacts out of sea shells (evidencing contact with the Pacific Ocean) and most importantly, they played the same ball game as was played by the Toltecs, Mayas, Zapotecs and other cultures much farther south in Central Mexico, Yucatan and Central America. In view of the extensive ball courts throughout Arizona, it would seem impossible that the Hohokam had no contact with the ancient civilizations such as the Toltecs, Mixtecs, Aztecs and even the Maya.

Many scholars argued there could have been no contact with other civilizations further south and therefore, the Hohokam could not have ball courts like those in Mexico. They claimed the ball courts were ceremonial dancing platforms.[162] American Indians never went anywhere, they believe. When the "experts" cannot even see inter-American contact among cultures, it is easy to see why they likewise

279

take a dim view of intercontinental contacts.

Then a rubber ball, obviously coming from southern Mexico, was found at the Hohokam site near the appropriately named Toltec, Arizona. The rubber ball proves the relationship between Arizona and the Valley of Mexico and the jungles of Central. Indeed, as the early settlers guessed, there was evidence to suggest that the Toltecs, or some offshoot of their civilization had lived in Arizona. The ball was dated as having been manufactured between AD 900 and 1200. The rubber game ball is now at the Arizona State Museum in Phoenix.

More than a hundred Hohokam ball courts have now been identified. Apparently the Hohokam were very enthusiastic ball players, and probably imported thousands of rubber balls from southern Mexico. While the balls could be—and were—made of all sorts of materials, the preferred material for any ball would be the highly prized chicle-gum that comes from the Chicle rubber tree found in the Yucatan, Guatemala and Chiapas. These bouncy and all natural balls must have been highly prized as trade items.

The Hohokam must have been a wealthy culture with extra leisure time to play ball games. Probably they paid for the rubber, spices and exotic feathers with turquoise, jade, gold, silver and copper.

They may have also played a number of different ball games, some of them derived from the Egyptians. It was reported from Cairo in July 2007 that Egyptian archeologists had discovered a literal "bowling alley" from the second or third century AD, at recent excavations some 56 miles south of Cairo.

The game, they said, was a mixture of bowling, billiards and bowls, which was played by two players positioned at the two ends of a lane that had a hole in its center. One would throw a smaller ball, the other a bigger one.

According to Edda Bresciani, an Egyptologist at Pisa University, Italy, "They would throw the balls at the same time. Most likely, the bigger ball was thrown along the lane to prevent the smaller ball from entering the hole at the centre. When this happened, the smaller ball could be easily recovered from the sand-filled terracotta vase below."

According to her, scoring with the smaller ball, thrown alternately by each player, determined the winner of the game. "Obviously, the winner was the player who was able to place the ball into the hole more times," Bresciani said.

The great ball game, in its many forms, was played from South America, throughout Central America and as far north as Utah, Colorado, Iowa, Wisconsin and Michigan. Canadians will no doubt want to claim ancient ball courts up there—and I am pretty sure they will be found! Today our games of bowling, cricket, basketball, football, baseball and soccer are all derived from the ancient games played around the world by the Egyptians, Babylonians, Harappans, Chinese, Olmecs and Mayans. Other games played by the ancients were chess and Parchesi and the many other games derived from them.

So here again we have a sophisticated culture with long links of trade emerging in the Southwest. These people irrigated the desert with cement-lined canals, but archaeologists still want them to live in primitive mud and stick huts, living off prickly pear cactus fruits. How unfortunate for present-day historians that the past refuses to cooperate with their theories!

Looking out at the ancient canals and ball courts of Casa Grande, I envisioned an Egyptian-like desert-water city with green and blue canals teeming with fish, mussels, crayfish and water plants. Add to that an abundance of ducks and other waterfowl, plus the sophisticated irrigation to grow maize, beans,

281

squash and other garden plants, and you have a literal paradise in central Arizona.

The Southwest's Most Sophisticated Culture

The sophistication of the Hohokam, with their many ball courts, use of cement, astronomical knowledge and extensive canals has amazed archeologists. Given the sophistication of the Hohokam culture, one has to wonder if they built bridges across some of these rivers and canals? A good example of the bridges built in southern Mexico is the Mayan bridge at Yaxchilan. This excellent suspension bridge over the Usamacinta River may have served as an example for Toltec bridges that were built farther north. Several such bridges may have been built in the Hohokam area, giving the cities of Cibola a very sophisticated look.

Ancient hydrological engineering works like those of the Hohokam take a great deal of planning and organization to construct. It is interesting to note that some of these ancient canals were incorporated into the present-day canal system in use around Phoenix. Phoenix is named after the mythological bird that dies and then rises from its own ashes to another life, an ancient symbol of the cycle of life, death and reincarnation.

Richard Petersen, a Phoenix resident, wrote that ancient Phoenix and the whole Hohokam area was the Cibola of legend in his 1985 book *The Lost Cities of Cibola*.[161] Petersen argues convincingly in his book that the extensive canals of the Hohokam are the remains of this advanced and extensive civilization. Some remaining buildings, like Casa Grande, and ball courts are also the silent evidence for Cibola, maintains Petersen.

Petersen also promotes a controversial thesis that both Easter Island and Cibola were destroyed by a catastrophe involving a comet whose trajectory took it across parts of the South Pacific, starting south of Easter Island and heading north toward the tip of the Baja California peninsula and eventually crossing southern Arizona. Petersen thinks that chunks of the comet grazed the Earth, causing catastrophes and massive destruction. Thus, says Petersen, was "Cibola" destroyed. Petersen's ideas are fascinating, and even if his comet catastrophe is a bit fanciful, he is certainly right about the sophistication of the Hohokam, and the possible identification of them as the great lost civilization of Cibola.

Modern-day Phoenix is aptly named, as it is indeed a city which has risen from the ashes of an earlier metropolis, a city whose name we do not know. The name may have been Cibola. As I have noted, the look of this city would have been one of almost Egyptian-like splendor. In a dry land of bright sun was a lush canal-ridden oasis that spread between the Phoenix area south to the Casa Grande area and westward including all the land in between. There would have been thousands of houses, made of caliche, with many large buildings and ballcourts. There may have been elegant suspension bridges across special sites on the rivers and smaller bridges over the canals. Some of these bridges may have served as customs posts.

Metals and turquoise, plus other valuable items, would have been commonplace. The people probably dressed in fine cotton clothes that were elaborately embroidered and adorned with jewelry and feathers.

Were the Hohokam peoples the northern Toltecs, as some have called them? Rather than there being just tenuous connections with southern Mexico, it seems that there were deep connections with the Toltecs, Zapotecs and Maya. The Aztecs arose, coincidently, around the time that the Hohokam disappeared. Was there a connection here? Many historians think there

283

was. Even more incredibly, the Hohokam, and the Sinagua around Tuzigoot in northern Arizona, may have also been allied with the Romans and Hebrews who came to Mexico, and up the Rio Grande, shortly after the Punic Wars between Carthage and Rome.

A Roman Kiln in Arizona

We spent that night in a motel in Casa Grande and headed south to Tucson the next morning. We had lunch in the old town of Tucson, and I scanned a strange story of some Roman artifacts found in the western part of the now sprawling city.

On September 13, 1924 Charles Manier found artifacts on Silverbell Road northwest of Tucson that included an array of ancient Roman objects, mostly made of lead. The trove, discovered in a lime kiln, included more than 30 items, including a 62-pound cross, spears, daggers, batons and swords. The objects were encrusted in caliche—a sheet of hard, crusty material formed by the reaction of chemicals and water in desert soils over many years. This encrustation was proof to the excavators that the objects were hundreds of years old.[109]

The University of Tucson apparently became involved briefly, and authenticated the find, which included a heavy broadsword with a depiction of a dinosaur on it. Many of the artifacts bore both Hebrew lettering and a form of Latin used between AD 560 and 900. As one might expect, controversy rages over their authenticity.

Dr. Cyclone Covey, a former history professor at Wake Forest University in North Carolina, wrote about his theory of a Roman Jewish colony in the Southwest in his book *Calalus*.[109] Like Barry Fell and others, Covey wrote that there had been constant trans-Atlantic traffic in Phoenician and Roman times.

When the Punic Wars ended and Rome became the dominant naval power in 146 BC, Rome began to send ships across the Atlantic.

Covey and Fell believed that the Romans encouraged various groups within the vast Roman realm to settle in newly created Roman ports in Florida and other areas around the Gulf of Mexico.[35, 36, 37, 109]

Covey theorizes that a group of Roman Jews had sailed from the Portuguese port of Porto Cale and founded a city in Florida, naming it Cale. This city is now modern day Ocala in north-central Florida.

The Latin form of Porto Cale was Calalus, and this was known by the Roman-sponsored colonists as their "Mother City." Covey thinks that the success of the new Roman city in Florida, called Cale, encouraged further expansion of Roman trading cities and they began to penetrate the major rivers like the Mississippi, Arkansas, Ohio and Rio Grande. This culminated in the Romans and Jews reaching the Tucson area in 775 AD. Covey says that the city they founded on the site situated where modern Tucson lies today was named Rhoda. One of the leaders, or the captain of one of the ships, Covey believes, was born on the island of Rhodes.[109]

Covey, like Fell, surmises that the Punic Wars, in a sense, continued across the Atlantic. According to him the Phoenicians and Carthaginians fled overseas with their fleets after their decisive defeat in 146 BC The Romans, having taken over the Carthaginian ports in the Mediterranean and Atlantic, began to follow the escapees across the ocean. The hated Romans, plus Jews and other Roman subjects, arrived to explore and colonize the New Lands across the Atlantic.[35, 109]

Covey thinks that the Toltecs were the remains of the Phoenician-Carthaginian military that survived along the northern coast of Mexico, with their capital in the nearby mountains at Tula. They consolidated their power in the region for several hundred years, and were powerful enough to attack the Jewish-Roman colony at Rhoda by around 900 AD. Covey believes that 100 years after the Toltecs had finally defeated the Jews and Romans at Rhoda, they turned their attention south, capturing Chichén Itza in the Yucatan. There they built the so-called Temple of Warriors. Covey says that they had a Caucasian king with a thick beard.[109] It is true that many Toltec warriors sported thick mustaches and beards as is seen in the many statues of them.

So the idea that there would be Roman artifacts around Tucson may not be as curious as it first seems, but one of them, bizarrely, depicts what appears to be a brontosaurus! One of the swords is quite clearly etched with a picture of a large animal with a long neck and a long tail that is an excellent sketch of a dinosaur known as a diplodicus. With details like this we can see why mainstream archeologists refuse to consider such finds.

Did the Romans come across a dinosaur skeleton somewhere in the Southwest? It is certainly possible, and they occur in large numbers around the Petrified Forest and the Painted Desert area between the Hopi and Zuni Pueblos. Had a legion of Roman soldiers visited the Petrified Forest? If so they may have seen a complete skeleton of a diplodicus. Another area rich in dinosaur fossils is around Big Bend in Texas, not very far away. Fossils were also powerful medicine and sought after by shamans.

Perhaps the crew of the Roman ship had seen a sea serpent on their voyage, with a large body and long neck. Or maybe, as some cryptozoologists claim, certain dinosaurs survived mass extinction to exist in remote swamps until only a few thousand years ago. We have already recounted the curious tales of living pterosaurs. Could larger animals have survived extinction as well?

On the Trail of Father Kino

After dinner I investigated the antiquity of Tucson on the Internet, and discovered that in 2005 the local Channel 13 News in Tucson, KOLD, had reported that city archeologists had located a 2,800 year-old settlement just northwest of Tucson.

The archeologists discovered, about seven feet below the current ground level, stored food in large pits, including the oldest corn found in southern Arizona, as well as spear tips, figurines, burnt antlers and other artifacts. Archeologists said that water coming off of the slopes of the Tortolita and Tucson Mountains, at a place where the Rio Santa Cruz spreads out, was a really prime place for agriculture. The area was wiped out in a huge flood, archeologists believed, similar to the giant Tucson flood in 1983. The time frame of around 800 BC is the mysterious period of the Olmecs in Central America, a time of great sophistication and technological achievement, at least in that region.

We drove out of Tucson to visit the old mission of Tumacacori. It was directly south on Interstate 19 and has been a National Historical Park since 1908. Today the Tumacacori National Historical Park preserves the ruins of three early Spanish colonial missions on 47 acres of southern Arizona.

This was one of the early missions of the amazing Father Kino, who used Tumacacori and San Xavier (which became Tucson) as his main missions in the area. Father Kino knew that the missions that he was establishing were in the area of the legendary lost cities of gold—often said to be seven lost cities—usually called Cibola. One of the seven lost cities was said to be Quivera, or Gran Quivera. Quivera may have been the ancient city of Baboquivari, which was first visited by Father Kino in 1691.

Father Kino was one of the earliest Spaniards to

venture into the American Southwest, and he succeeded in establishing a number of missions, including the mission at Sonoyta, at the beginning of the Devil's Highway. Kino was born on August 10, 1645 in Tirol, which at the time was an independent country, though now it is part of Italy. He distinguished himself in the study of mathematics, cartography and astronomy in Germany, and taught mathematics for a time at the University of Ingolstadt. He became a member of the Society of Jesus (Jesuits) in 1665.

In 1681 he arrived in Mexico City, and after an abortive mission to Baja California in 1683, began his longtime mission to the Tohono O'Odham Indians in the dangerous and unexplored province of Pimeria Alta. The province of Pimeria Alta comprised the northern portion of Sonora State in Mexico, and the southern portion of Arizona up to the Gila River. Phoenix, just north of the Gila was not part of the Pimeria Alta, but was in what was known as *Apacheria*, or sometimes just plain *Terra Incognita*. The Hopi area further north had the separate name of Tusayan, which is what Major John Wesley Powell called it in his various books and pamphlets.

Father Kino made about 40 expeditions into Arizona. In 1694, he was the first European to visit the Hohokam ruins of Casa Grande. He is also said to have explored the sources of the Rio Grande, the Colorado and Gila rivers. His explorations of the area around the mouth of the Colorado River in 1701 convinced him that Baja California was a peninsula, not an island. Because large remnants of the inland sea in California still existed, including the Salton Sea and the huge Tulare Lake around Fresno, the early Spanish explorers into the region—traveling by horse and by ship—had somehow come to believe that California was a huge island. We will discuss this in great detail in Chapter 8.

In 1687, Father Kino established his first mission

among the rural Indians of Sonora at Nuestra Senora de los Dolores. It became the headquarters for his explorations, as well as for the founding of other missions, including San Xavier del Bac (1700) near Tucson, Guevavi and Tumacacori. Father Kino was also the first to visit the area that is now the southeastern part of Arizona. The capital city of this place was known as Quiburi or Baboquivari.

Father Kino typically set out from his base at Dolores in northern Sonora, directly south of Tumacacori and Tucson, and traveled north to Bacoancos. Sometimes he took a different road that headed northwest and took him to Magdalena, Uquitoa, Pitiquin, Caborca and then directly north to Sonoyta.

Father Kino's 1705 map of this whole area became the standard reference for the southwestern desert region for more than a century. Father Kino was warmly welcomed by the Tohono O'odham peoples, and he helped them diversify their agriculture and aided them in their constant wars with the Apaches.

Father Kino also opposed Indian enslavement in the silver mines of northern Mexico where mining was—and still is—a major concern. Mines located in the Pimeria Alta, and even farther north, are the subject of countless old treasure books of the American Southwest.

Father Kino had his autobiography published in Mexico City in 1708 entitled *Favores celestiales* which was translated into English as the two-volume *Kino's Historical Memoir of Pimería Alta* in 1919 (reissued 1948). He died at Mission Magdalena in Sonora on March 15, 1711.

"Arizona" Derived from Ancient Hohokam

At the time of Father Kino's early explorations into the Southwest he learned of an old pueblo that had been the capital of an ancient empire. This city was called Baboquivari. On one of his earliest sojourns, Father Kino headed north from Mexico City and stopped in Magdalena, San Ignacio and Bacoancos; he then headed to Guevavi and further east into the area of Baboquivari.

Here he founded a small settlement called Santa Cruz de Gaybanipitea. Apparently, the once glorious city of Baboquivari was now in ruins. Father Kino, having seen such large buildings as the one at Casa Grande, realized that he was observing the remnants of some great lost civilization. He was fascinated by the scattered bits of this lost civilization, and sought out those pueblos or ruins that were associated with it. This is what brought him to such places as Baboquivari.

In 1751, the Pima Rebellion was brought on by sudden activity in the Pimeria Alta caused by the revelation of a rich silver vein in an arroyo west of the Santa Cruz Mountains. This was in the vicinity of Arizonac, just south of the current border, only a short distance east of Nogales, almost directly south of Baboquivari.

Arizonac was a former Tohono O'odham rancheria situated between Guevavi and Saric, in Sonora, Mexico. The Tohono O'odham are generally considered to be the descendents of the Hohokam. Arizonac was a *visita* of the mission of Saric very close to Nogales on the upper waters of Rio Altar. In 1736 a Yaqui Indian named Antonio showed the local Jesuit priest and other authorities a massive concentration of virgin silver ore in huge slabs of silver. One giant nugget of silver was said to weigh nearly 2,500 pounds.

In 1736-41 the finding of these balls of native silver of fabulous size caused a sudden influx of treasure seekers from Mexico City, and through the fame that the place thus temporarily acquired, its

290

name, in the form "Arizona," was later applied to the entire country thereabouts. When the New Mexico Territory was divided, Arizona was adopted as the name of the new Territory.

Apparently, as Charles Polzer mentions in his book *A Kino Guide: His Missions — His Monuments,*[71] the mine at Arizonac was actually an ancient Aztec mine, and what was supposedly "virgin silver" was actually slag from a far more ancient mining operation.

This area, basically along the current U.S.-Mexico border east of Nogales, was an ancient mining district used by the Baboquivari people and contains many of the early Hohokam place names that derive from the same roots as Arizonac. Aside from the rancheria-silver mine called Arizonac, other names of Tohono O'odham-Hohokam origin are: Apozolco, Arivechi, Ariziochic, and Arizpe.

The Ouster of the Jesuits

The Jesuit missionaries had learned over 150 years of working with the Indians that the presence of mining camps and the "dregs of humanity" that came with them often led to unrest among the native populations. They therefore declared that the discovery of silver nuggets or a rich mine would be considered a "treasure trove," so that the wealth would belong only to the Spanish crown. They hoped this would block the immigration of opportunistic locals. Indeed, the normally ordered society of the pueblos in northern Mexico, New Mexico and Arizona were severely disrupted by the crass, violent, anarchical chaos that pervaded all of the Wild West mining camps and other towns. Literature and movies about the Old West are filled with the many day-to-day dramas that happened when Spanish culture clashed with the cultures of the Aztecs and the remnants of the Toltecs in northern Mexico, and those civilizations north of the border.

291

Ultimately, things turned nasty when the erratic Spanish governor, against the strong protests of the Jesuit missionaries, appointed a Tohono O'odham half-caste named Luis Oacpicagigua (called Luis of Saric) as the captain general of the Pima auxiliaries. The main mission of the Pima auxiliaries was to attack the Apaches, with the tacit approval of the Spanish, to try to reclaim the land taken from them by this enemy. Luis had a reputation for cruelty, however, and the Jesuits considered him dangerous. Luis dutifully fulfilled his post for a short time, but ultimately turned against the Spanish and led the Pima Uprising. The mining towns were besieged; many of the miners and priests were killed. The rebellion was quickly suppressed but the effects lasted for many years, and it became more dangerous to travel widely in the remote parts of the Pimeria Alta. With the first line of defense—friendly natives—gone, the Apaches began to penetrate deeper into Sonora becoming more of a problem for the Spanish authorities.

After the rebellion, mines and missions were gradually being built up again, but it all came to a sudden halt in 1767 when the Society of Jesus—the Jesuits—were expelled from the Spanish realm by decree of King Charles III. No area of the world was exempt from this order, and the unusual penalty of death for failure to arrest Jesuits was issued. Dragoons arrested Jesuits in even the remotest parts of the frontier. Many Jesuits were marched to concentration camps at ports and then put on ships to be taken to Acapulco or Vera Cruz.

This expulsion drew a curtain on Jesuit missionary activity in northwestern Mexico, and in some cases, Franciscans filled in at the missions. But many of the ancient mines were permanently closed. Some of these rich mines are still lost today, and have become the lore of treasure books.

In her book *Canyon of Gold,*[72] Barbara Marriot

discusses much of the history and mystery of the Santa Catalina Mountains east of Tucson. Marriot claims that this area has a lost city, and was one of the most dangerous places in all of Arizona. Says Marriot:

> Throughout the Santa Catalinas are canyons that earthquakes, wind and water have cut. One of them is called the Canada del Oro. Leaving its origin deep in the mountain, it meanders towards Tucson going north to west to east to south. It varies in size from a squeeze between two ridges to the width of a four-lane highway. There is no asphalt, no concrete, just sand and brush, but in the past a walk in the Canada del Oro could very well mean death.
>
> Through part of the canyon there is an arroyo, but these days, it is mostly dry as the water seldom comes down from the mountains, and then only after a heavy rain. They say once water ran steadily for nine months a year. Now it is considered a fortunate day if it runs for nine hours. Mostly the creek is dry. Not a drop glistens; not a mud patch shows itself as a dark splat.
>
> The lack of water in its creek is not the only thing that makes this canyon incongruous. Its name is the major confusing factor. It is called the Canada del Oro, a canyon of gold. But gold has not been found here for a long time, and even then, it was mostly placer gold that some believed was washed down from a major vein high in the mountains.
>
> There are rumors, talk and mythical beliefs that Jesuits worked a rich lode here and the mine was so productive a city was built nearby for the workers. The city was called Nueva Xia Ciudad and was anchored on a plateau. In this city was a huge church with golden bells that summoned

293

the laborers from the fields and mines.

In 1767, the King of Spain, Charles III, issued an edict expelling the Jesuit Order from Spain and her possessions. When the Franciscans acquired supremacy in the church, the Jesuits fled these mountains. However, before the Jesuits and workers left the Santa Catalina Mountains, an iron door was placed over the mine and secured in a way that would take a considerable amount of time to open.[72]

Marriott also mentions a spook light, similar to the one at Marfa, but not as consistent. Her mentioning that the climate in this area was once much wetter is important. The entire American Southwest, including California and Nevada, has been in a drought that has been going on for hundreds of years. Archeologists have now concluded that extended droughts were part of the collapse of the Mayan civilization, as well as those of some of the pueblo tribes of Arizona and New Mexico. The old lakes of California and Nevada have been drying up for many hundreds of years, and even within the last few hundred, lakes in central and southeastern California have completely disappeared. More of that will be discussed in Chapter 8.

Marriott mentions the curious story of another lost city in the Santa Catalina mountains. The Romero family was a long established one in Spanish Tucson and one of the family, Francisco, was to work as a surveyor during the Gadsden Purchase. He then began ranching with his wife Victoriana in the Canada del Oro. Says Marriott of his establishing a homestead:

Francisco thought he had found the ideal spot, on a ridge with a nice mound for foundation, near water and fertile fields. It didn't bother Francisco that the mound was the ruin of an ancient town. He built his ranch walls upon the stubby foundations of the Hohokam walls, and then built his five buildings within these walls. The "main house" had two rooms and a corner fireplace. The other buildings were single-room structures.

This land had been considered a mystery by townsfolk for years. There was a rumor that it was the site of the fabled Mission of Ciru and its rich gold mine. Francisco called his ranch Pueblo Viejo in honor of this prehistoric site.

Marriott goes on to say that a Tucson columnist named George Hand had claimed that a fortune in gold bullion was buried under a church in the Santa Catalina Mountains.

The *Arizona Citizen* reported on March 6, 1875 that, "Romero and Zeckendorf have within ten days discovered and located what presents all the superficial proofs of a most valuable gold and silver vein on the eastern slope of Santa Catalina mountains only about 12 miles northeast of Tucson... within 2 miles of the ruins of a town once of considerable size."

However, as Marriott says, this must have actually been on the western side of the mountains, not the eastern side as stated in the article. One has to wonder if Romero actually found the lost mine with the iron door and then kept it secret for the rest of his life. This ancient mine and lost city has yet to be found.

The Giants of Crittenden

Jennifer and I stopped for some hours in Nogales, going across the border and shopping on the Mexican side. After the obligatory shot of tequila at one of the many bars in Mexico, we returned to the U.S., showing our identification to the border agents as we walked through the fencing and controls.

We then drove north out of Nogales and turned northeast on Highway 82 toward Tombstone and Patagonia. We stopped for some ice cream in Patagonia, and then checked the map for the lost city of Baboquivari and the ghost town of Crittenden.

I had with me a book by Gene D. Matlock with the odd title of *From Khyber (Kheeber) Pass to Gran Quivira (Kheevira), NM and Baboquivaria, AZ,*[73] and as its title stated, it was about the ancient Hindus from the Indus Valley and the Khyber Pass and their activity in what is today the American Southwest.

Matlock's basic premise in this book, and another one from the year before entitled *The Last Atlantis Book You'll Ever Read,*[74] is that the ancient Phoenicians and Hebrews were known as the Kyber, Khaiber, Kheeveri, Kubernetees, Kubernan and other such names. Matlock says that the word "cyber" comes from these ancient peoples who were omnipresent sailors, miners, metallurgists, engineers, and jacks of many trades of ancient times. He also says that they were the Hyperboreans of ancient Greek texts.

Says Matlock:

> Perhaps the most shocking and amazing evidence I can give, proving the Kheeberis (Phoenicians and Jews) once covered and dominated every single inch of this earth is the prefix Cyber to such words as Cybernetics, Cyberspace, Cyber-communications, etc. Predictably, our English language habits have changed this so-called "Greek-derived word," Kheeber, to be pronounced as "Sigh-bur." Cybernetics derives from the Greek Kubernetes (meaning "Governor"), and Kubernan ("to govern"). But it is not even a Greek word. The Greeks derived it from Khyber (pronounced Kheeber), a dialectical representation of the Sanskrit Kuber/Kubera, the Hindu god of

riches and good fortune and the name of the first civilized human beings and imperialists: the Phoenicians and the Jews. Cyber (Kheeber) refers to anything that is spread everywhere; that which is in control everywhere. This linguistic evidence alone should hold us in awe of an ancient people from India, known as "twins," mentioned in our Bible as Heber, who once colonized, inhabited, and controlled every region in the world! The historians either do not themselves know this—or they refuse to tell us. The only way we can find out is through the way this word is used in our respective languages.

Matlock makes the provocative statement that, from 2000 BC to 500 BC, the Phoenicians controlled the world with their vast maritime empire. They were in South America, Mexico, the Southwest, Pacific Islands, the Caribbean, southern Africa, Southeast Asia, and all over Europe and the Mediterranean. They were the Phoenicians, the Hebrew, the Kyber, and the Baboquivari, he says.

As Jennifer and I looked around the earthen mound and various walls that were the ruins of Baboquivari, I wondered at Matlock's assertions. In ancient times these men of the sea and of the mountains—experts in metallurgy—had ruled much of the world (Matlock claims all of it) with their swift and large boats loaded with warriors armed with all sorts of iron, bronze and copper weapons. Had they actually made it to Mexico and southern Arizona?

If they had, they would be part of a long line of Egyptians, Phoenicians, Africans, Chinese, Hindus and Buddhists to come to the Americas. We can also throw in Vikings, Basque, Irish, Welsh and many others. It seemed that ancient America, much like modern America, was a melting pot of many races, creeds and colors.

A curious story is told about the discovery of a sarcophagus of a giant that was unearthed by workmen in Fort Crittenden, just north of Patagonia and just west of the ancient city of Baboquivari.

Originally known as Casa Blanca, Fort Crittenden, also called just Crittenden, was a town that had its origin in the 1860s. There was a rail depot and much mining activity from the mid- to late 1800s. Currently it is a ghost town listed on maps as Fort Crittenden Ruin, and the only standing building is a hotel built in 1885. In 1887, an earthquake damaged the hotel and the second story was removed and that is how it stands today. By 1900, most residents had moved elsewhere as the mines played out. An abandoned railroad line runs just south of the ghost town and the San Ignacio del Babocomari reservation is just to the east.

In 1891 workmen were digging the foundation of a house when they unearthed a stone coffin that once held the body of a man approximately 12 feet tall. A carving on the granite case indicated that he had twelve toes.[52]
[70]

According to Brad Steiger, *The New York Times* on December 2, 1930 carried an item that told of the discovery of the remains of an apparent race of giants who once lived at Sayopa, Sonora. Sayopa is a mining town three hundred miles south of the Mexican border, south of Crittenden and Baboquivari. Steiger says that J. E. Coker, a mining engineer, stated that laborers clearing ranchland near the Yazui River had dug into a very old cemetery and had found "bodies of men, averaging eight feet in height, buried tier by tier."[11]

Was the ancient mining center of Baboquivari a land of giants from some forgotten empire? One has to wonder: are there undiscovered graveyards of giants throughout northern Mexico and the American Southwest? One would think so—some have been found!

I didn't attend the funeral,
but I sent a nice letter saying I approved of it.
—Mark Twain

Ghosts of Old Tombstone & the Turquoise Mountains

We spent that night in Tombstone, the old mining town that was the site of one of the most famous shootouts in the Old West—the Gunfight at the OK Corral. Many of the buildings from the 1800s still line the streets, and the sidewalks are still the old-fashioned "boardwalks." After getting into our cowboy duds, including boots and hats, we headed down the boardwalk into town. Our first stop was Big Nose Kate's Saloon, where we ordered up shots of tequila followed by beer chasers.

After a few fights broke out, we proceeded to a restaurant. Heading back to our motel later that night, the only sound being the steady clop of our bootheels along the boardwalk, I thought I caught a glimpse of one of the ghosts of Tombstone in the moonlight.

The next morning we headed east from Tombstone, along Ghost Town Road. We stopped briefly at a shop that sold everything rattlesnake, down a deserted side road. No one was there, but the shop was open anyway. A sign on a wooden box said to list any items purchased in the notebook provided, and put the money in the box. We bought some rattlesnake earrings, bookmarks, pens and coin purses and scrambled to come up with the correct change.

Just up the road were the Turquoise Mountains and the ghost towns of Gleeson and Courtland. Both had sprung up when people came to the area hoping to exploit the ancient turquoise mines along the northern part of the mini-range. These ancient mines were apparently worked by the Hohokam, and that means possibly by the Toltecs, Phoenicians and Romans.

The Apaches had taken control of this eastern portion of Arizona from the Tohono O'odham, and this area was very close to the stronghold of the famous Apache Chief Cochise. Until Cochise's death in 1872, the Turquoise Mountains and the nearby Dragoon Mountains were very dangerous places to wander around. The highest mountain in the Dragoon Mountains is called Cochise Peak, in honor of the brave warrior who resisted Manifest Destiny with great determination. It is possible to drive there in a four-wheel drive vehicle today.

After the death of Cochise, prospectors who had heard that there was turquoise in the mountains began to settle Gleeson and Courtland. Henry Durant made official mining claims by around 1890, and a considerable amount of turquoise was produced. Copper was also discovered in the area, turning Gleeson into a boomtown.

The area abounds with lost treasure and ancient buildings crumbling to dirt. Gleeson's most mysterious resident was Yee Wee, who had a run a restaurant in Gleeson until the copper mine suddenly closed in 1929. People began moving out of Gleeson in droves, and then a fire swept through town. Yee Wee was the only resident until he died in 1968. Upon searching his belongings in his cluttered house, they found a bank draft for $605,200 payable to anyone.

It was wondered how so much money, uncollected even, was in the possession of the mysterious old Chinaman. Had he been an opium dealer? Had there been unknown visitors to him in the lonely years he lived in Gleeson from 1930 to 1968? It was thought that a treasure was buried in Gleeson—or nearby—by the mysterious Yee Wee.

Encounter with "The Thing"

From Gleeson we continued north through the ghost town of Courtland, and then to Pearce. At a desert intersection, we got on Interstate 10 heading east. The sun was setting behind us as we sped along the interstate near Wilcox.

A billboard on the highway asked with big red letters: "What is The Thing?"

"The Thing?" asked Jennifer, looking up from a book. "What *is* The Thing?"

"I don't know, but Things happen," I said. This was met by silence.

Then the exit for The Thing appeared. It was a gas station and tourist trap on the highway. We needed gas and, of course, we had to see The Thing. Eagerly I parked the truck and bounded into the large gas station gift shop.

"Where's The Thing?" I asked breathlessly.

"You want to see The Thing?" they asked in a reserved sort of way.

"Well, yeah," I said, starting to prepare to be disappointed.

"Only one dollar," said the old man behind the cashier.

"Mister, you got a deal," I said, pulling a well-worn dollar bill out of my wallet. Heck, a dollar to see The Thing, whatever it was, was a good deal as far as I was concerned.

After viewing some old cars and pioneer artifacts, I turned a corner in the "museum" hallway and suddenly there it was—The Thing!

I stared at it for a few minutes as it lay in its glass case. What is The Thing? It is a mummy of a woman, holding a mummified child. The woman is well preserved, but not especially tall. She still had long black hair and fairly good teeth. Mummies are a controversial topic in the Southwest, as we will see in upcoming chapters.

As I mentioned our visit to this roadside attraction in conversation, I started to hear stories that this curious double mummy had come from catacombs inside the Grand Canyon—catacombs that contain mummies plus Egyptian and Hindu-Buddhist artifacts. That story will be told in a following chapter.

After filling up our gasoline tank, we continued east and then south on Highway 80 to the Chiricahua Mountains and the small town of Portal. This area had also been an Apache stronghold, where Geronimo eventually surrendered to General Nelson Miles. Around Portal are the old ghost towns of Paradise and Galeyville, best known as the hideout of the famous outlaw Curly Bill.

In July of 1881 Curly Bill and his buddies, Zwing Hunt and Billy Grounds, are said to have robbed a very wealthy Mexican wagon train just south of the border and taken the treasure in a wagon to Skeleton Canyon just south of Portal. The bandits were all later killed, but were reported to have claimed on their deathbeds that there were 39 bars of solid gold, 90,000 in minted Mexican dollars, two gold statues and a cigar box full of diamonds. The treasure is said to still be in Skeleton Canyon, though there are stories that in the 1890s a mysterious German built a little hut at the mouth of the canyon and spent several years digging holes all over the place. One day he just disappeared and was never seen again.[12]

We stayed that night in the small winter cabin that my father kept in Portal. As we dozed away on a sofa bed on a cool spring night, I thought of the ghosts of Geronimo, Curly Bill, Cochise and all the others. No doubt on nights like this they roamed the cactus-covered hills with their rifles and knives— only the howl of the occasional coyote to disturb their nocturnal wanderings.

NORTH

Scale in Miles

0   50   100 miles

💀 THE DEVIL'S HIGHWAY

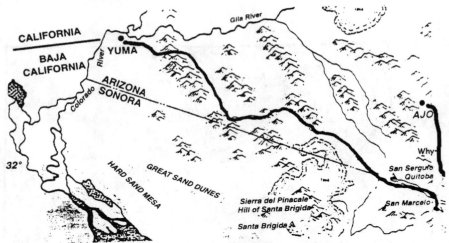

The Devil's Highway in southwestern Arizona.

**Interior Provinces
of New Spain 1776-1821**

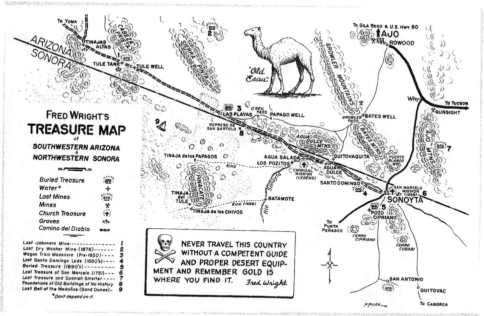

Fred Wright's 1966 map of the Devil's Highway.

An old print of a Pima Villge in 1864.

Faces of the Hohokam found at Snaketown.

The Ajo Museum Egyptian-like carved stone.

Father Kino's 1710 map of northwestern Mexico.

An old print of Casa Grande from 1864.

Aerial photo from 1967 of the Hohokam canals around Phoenix.

An old photo of Casa Grande from 1892.

A 1934 photo of the Hohokam ball court found at Snaketown.

A Hohokam pottery motif.

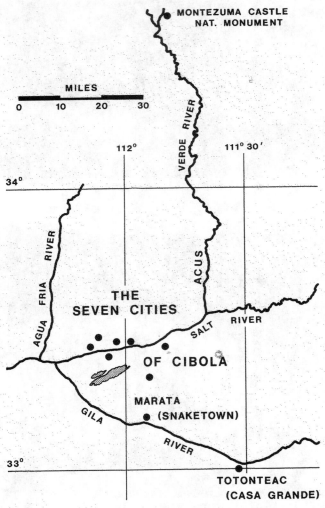

Petersen's map of the Seven Cities of Cibola, which curiously includes 10 points. In general, I think Petersen is correct in identifying the land of Cibola with the Hohokam.

310

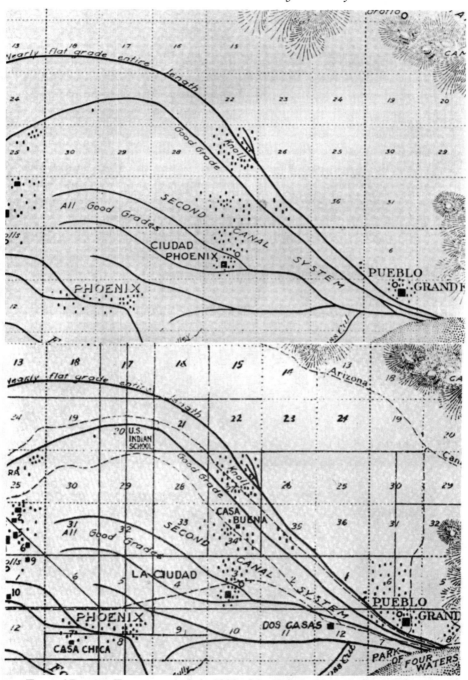

Top and Bottom: Two maps made in 1922 of the Hohokam canals around Phoenix.

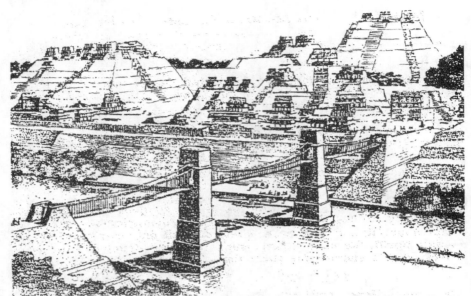

A drawing of the Mayan bridge at Yaxchilan. Did the Hohokam build similar bridges?

Hohokam ink pallets for grinding ink sticks and mixing with water, as used in China.

312

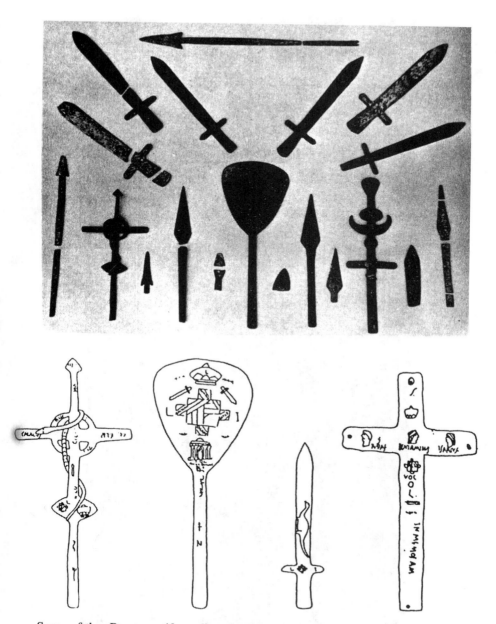

Some of the Roman artifacts discovered in 1924 in Tucson, including the cross with a snake coiled around it and the broadsword with the dinosaur etching.

313

The Roman cross with a snake coiled around it from the Tucson discovery in 1924.

The Roman broadsword with a dinosaur carved on it.

The Roman cross with Latin writing and etchings on it from the Tucson find.

Two different Roman crosses with Latin writing from the 1924 Tucson find.

An old postcard for the roadside attraction known as "The Thing."

317

"The Thing" is the mummy of a woman cradling the mummy of a small child. Some say that these mummies come from the catacombs of the Grand Canyon.

6.

CENTRAL ARIZONA

THE SUPERSTITION MOUNTAINS AND THE LOST DUTCHMAN MINE

It's hard to say to say for sure
Whether what I hear is music or the wind
Through an open door.
There's a fire high in the empty sky
Where the sound meets the shore
There's a long-distance loneliness
Rolling out over the desert floor.
—Jackson Browne, *The Fuse*

Ahead of me was a vertical wall of rock. Saguaro and organ pipe cactus liberally dotted the flat desert plain in front of the mountains. Relatively new homes were slowly crawling up the hillside toward the western wall of the Superstition Mountains.

The ever-spreading metropolis of Phoenix now reaches nearly to the foothills of the Superstitions, towering granite mountains of 3,000 foot-high sheer cliffs and rugged spires of rock.

I had picked up an old friend of mine, British author John Michell, at a hotel in Phoenix where

319

he had been speaking at a conference. John had his first book published in the 1960s, *The Flying Saucer Revelation*, and was well known for other books such as *The View Over Atlantis* and *The Dimensions of Paradise*. He was something of a lost mine buff, so I invited him out to have a look at the Superstitions with me.

I grabbed John during a lunch break at the conference and dragged him out to the parking lot. Soon I had him stepping up into my 4x4 Chevy Tahoe SUV.

"Where are we going, David?" he asked me.

"We're going to search for the Lost Dutchman Mine," I said.

"Oh, great! It's good to get away from that conference for a bit," John said, fastening his seat belt. "Phantom mines, like many elusive treasures, have always interested me."

I told him that we were headed east to the mysterious Superstition Mountains—the greatest sight in the Phoenix metro area! John rolled a cigarette as we drove east out of the city and headed for Apache Junction, the town on the eastern edge of the metropolitan sprawl. Indeed, only a few decades ago, this area was a few lonely stores and a couple of houses.

Soon enough, the divided highway ended and we were sitting at that proverbial stop sign in the desert. I signaled left and we skimmed along the tarmac of the Apache Trail, the highway that goes around the Superstition Mountains, past Tortilla Flat to Roosevelt Dam, and on to Globe.

John looked out into the desert haze and was suitably amazed by the towering granite cliffs that make up the western edge of the Superstitions. We drove past saguaros with their arms held up like travelers being robbed by bandits. We skirted past a few biker bars and Mexican restaurants and then turned left into Goldfield, the old gold and silver mine that is now a "tourist trap."

I loved Goldfield, a mini-ghost town with a saloon, blacksmith, church, gift stores, and authentic mining train. At the saloon, on the spacious back veranda, were industrial binoculars that took a quarter and allowed you to view the western massif of the Superstition Mountains very closely.

John went up to the bar and got each of us a mug of lager, while I fished around in my pockets for some quarters. I found a few and put them in the binoculars.

"Come here, John. Check out the Superstitions. See if you can find the Lost Dutchman Gold Mine." He viewed the red granite cliffs while I proceeded to tell him about my research.

The Thunder God's Gold

The Superstition mountain range probably holds more legend, lore and fascinating fact than any other similar area in the world.

Originally, the area was part of the Hohokam empire, today it is a Wilderness Area in the Tonto National Forest. It is the gateway to the ponderosa pine forests of eastern Arizona, and would have been the source of some of the mining that went on in the area in ancient times. As described in the previous chapter, the mysterious Hohokam peoples occupied a large area of what is now Arizona during a period thought to have begun about 300 BC and ending about 1450 AD. They were famous for their sophisticated irrigation networks, and their known archeological sites include the ruins at Casa Grande, Snaketown, Catalina State Park, the Hoh-Hardy Site, Painted Rocks Park, the Sabino Canyon Recreation Area, and other places.

The Hohokam territory certainly abutted the Superstition Mountains, and probably included the range and the important Salt River that was extensively used in the irrigation of the flat plains around Phoenix. Any ancient mines in the Superstition Mountains would have probably been worked by the Hohokam, if not by some even earlier people.

Indeed, it is the ancient connection with metallurgy, silversmithing, veins of gold and turquoise deposits of this southern extension of the Rocky Mountains that makes the entire Southwest an area of tremendous history—one of ancient mining, lost cities and treasure to be found.

Many men have perished in the Superstitions, the deaths we know of starting with the early Spanish explorers and continuing right up to modern times.

The Spanish Conquistador Francisco Vasquez de Coronado arrived in the Phoenix area from northern Mexico in 1540. His expedition had come north to look for the legendary Seven Gold Cities of Cibola. What he found was a stark desert with the ruined cities of the Hohokam lying in crumbling decay. The Apaches had newly arrived in eastern Arizona, New Mexico and west Texas and were controlling the eastern mountain areas of Arizona. Apache raiding parties would occasionally descend into the lower desert areas inhabited by the Papago (now called Tohono O'odham). Coronado's party was using Tohono O'odham guides, but the Apaches controlled the Superstitions with small bands of warriors. The Superstitions are like a natural fortress of rock, especially at the western end of the range, so this was an ideal citadel from which to watch the area below.

Native Americans believed this land was a sacred place. They called it the home of the Thunder God and his people. They knew that in this mountainous area the Thunder God owned a great treasure. One of the most influential books written on the Lost Dutchman Mine and the Superstition Mountains was Barry Storm's 1945 book entitled *Thunder God's Gold*.[65]

While some have explained the association with

the Thundergod as coming from the occasional violent thunderstorms that occur in the Superstitions, often causing floods on the valley floor, others have a different explanation. John Wilburn, a mining engineer from Phoenix who wrote a small booklet on the Superstitions and the Lost Dutchman Mine, says that the Superstitions make a noisy rumbling sound about once a year or so, because of earthquake tremors that are centered under Peter's Mesa. According to Wilburn, windows rattle and the mountains rumble for an hour or more. He surmises that hot magma is stirring deep inside the earth, moving rock along faults. The heat builds up pressure, creating stress, and then subsides, and the rumblings stop. He thinks that there may be a "hot spot" beneath the Superstitions, which has a past history of violent volcanic activity.

Coronado wanted the friendly Tohono O'odhams to guide him and his men in a search for the fabled treasure of the mountains—possibly a rich vein of gold—but the Tohono O'odham guides refused. They said that all who trespassed on the sacred land of the Thunder God would be punished. Coronado and his men started exploring the mountains on their own. Strange things were said to have happened: some of the men fell off cliffs, some broke bones, others are said to have simply disappeared.

In July, August and September, the Arizona monsoon can create spectacular—and deadly—storms with accompanying flash floods and terrific lightning. Coronado and his men thought it was eerie the way the storm clouds gathered around the mountains. They began calling the place Monte Superstition after witnessing a number of violent thunderstorms, and recalling the accidents and fatalities suffered in their early exploration attempts. Other names were given to the mountains, but it was "Superstition" that has lasted through the centuries.

For the next three hundred years the area of central

Arizona was largely unexplored, as we have noted. The country north of Tucson and west of Santa Fe and Socorro in New Mexico was known on maps as *Terra Incognita*—the unknown land, or sometimes as *Apacheria*, Land of the fearsome Apaches. While the Spanish controlled California and New Mexico, plus the most southern parts of Arizona, the huge area in the middle was an un-colonized no-man's-land. This area included most of Arizona, Colorado, Utah and Nevada plus much of the mountainous western portion of New Mexico.

It was 1832 when the first American explorer, Pauline Weaver, began to penetrate the rocky terrain of the Superstitions, bordered on the north side by the Salt River.

Pauline (Paulino) Weaver was a famous mountain man, guide, prospector and early Arizona pioneer. Weaver first visited Arizona in 1825 when the region was still part of Mexico. Weaver returned to the Superstitions again in 1853. In that year Arizona went from being part of New Mexico to being a separate territory. It was during this historic trip into the spooky mountains that the great spire of rock in the middle of the mountains became known as Weaver's Needle. When Weaver first saw the 1,000-foot tall granite needle, he was the scout and guide for a party chasing a group of Apaches who were accused of stealing horses. This towering needle of rock would feature prominently in many of the stories of the Superstitions and the Lost Dutchman Mine. Weaver's Needle, sometimes called Sombrero Butte, appeared on military maps as early as 1853, making it one of the oldest Anglo-American named landmarks in the Southwest.

Don Miguel Peralta and the Superstitions

"You know, John," I said to my friend as we drank our beers and looked out over the Superstitions. "Your name and the name of a famous lost treasure writer are nearly the same."

"Oh, really," he said, putting down his mug of foamy beer. "Who would that be?"

"That would be John D. Mitchell, the old west author."

"Oh, yes," said John, adjusting his scarf. "I know who you mean."

John D. Mitchell was a wealthy American mining engineer who wrote a 1933 book entitled *Lost Mines of the Great Southwest*.[40] Like any writer on lost treasure, including myself, he had to sift through a lot of vague and sometimes contradictory accounts to get to what seemed to be the truth of the matter in any given case. Dates are often fluid, and even names can vary in spelling, especially for immigrants or the illiterate. In the case of the Lost Peralta Mine in the Superstitions, Mitchell had the advantage of interviewing someone who had actually taken part in the story. He met Jose Ballesteros de Madrid in Mexico in 1910. Using Mitchell's information and other accounts, it seems the Peralta story is roughly as follows.

Don Miguel Peralta was a wealthy Sonoran cattle rancher in the mid-1800s. In the 1840s, he and his father worked some mining claims around Prescott. When these petered out, he went to the Superstitions, where he found a rich gold mine and starting working it.

The main camp for processing the ore was on a bend in the Rio Salado known later as Mormon Flat, an area now covered by the waters of Canyon Lake. The ore itself came from an 18-inch vein some distance away, around which the miners built a tunnel and shaft. According to Mitchell, "The ore from the vein averaged several thousand dollars to the ton."[40]

Don Miguel went back to the mine every year with his sons. Because the surrounding area contained much high-grade gold concentrate, they made several other mining shafts besides the primary one. Don Miguel was always able to remember exactly where the mine was located by a landmark, an unusual peak that looked to him like the pointed top of a sombrero hat. Don Miguel was thought to have taken millions of pesos worth of pure gold concentrate from the mining shafts of his Sombrero Mine.

Carving Hieroglyphics Onto Stones to Mark the Mine

During the period of Don Miguel's mining in the Superstitions, Mexico signed in 1848 the Treaty of Guadalupe Hidalgo that gave the land north of the Gila River to the United States. This included the Superstitions and the Phoenix area. The Peralta Sombrero Mine was now a part of the United States.

Supposedly, Don Miguel decided to make one final trip to his Sombrero Mine in 1848, leaving his sons behind to manage the ranch in Sonora. On this final expedition he took a mini-army of 400 men and as many mules and burros. He told people that he planned to bring back many more millions of pesos of gold.[62]

For many months in 1847-48 the well-armed Peralta mini-army worked the Sombrero Mine, refining a great deal of gold that was apparently in the form of nuggets and gold dust. This ancient mine must have had a large vein of gold that was practically inexhaustible. Hundreds of years earlier it was probably used by the Hohokam, but it was now in an area control by the Apache invaders. The Apaches had also taken control of the turquoise mines near Tombstone from the Tohono O'odham.

Aware of the Peralta mini-army in the Superstitions, the Apache leaders Cochise and Mangas Coloradas joined forces and gathered together a large contingent of warriors, with the intent of attacking the miners.

Don Miguel Peralta, upon learning of their plan,

suddenly stopped operating the mine. His men covered and hid the shaft openings as best they could and made preparations to depart. They knew that the Apaches knew about the mine, but they wanted to keep it hidden from other prospectors in case they were ever able to return. As this story goes, Don Miguel drew a map of the mine's location and carved out hieroglyphics on some rocks as a key to the map.[61]

Having hidden the mine and made the signs on certain rocks, Don Miguel withdrew his miners and equipment to a mesa, high in the Superstitions. There he planned to load the burros and mules with all the gold concentrate that they could carry. During the night they would steal away from the 3,000-foot mesa and make it back to the larger camp commanded by Peralta's friend, Jose Ballesteros, which was on the river far below and to the west. From there the entire group of 400 would head back to the ranch in Sonora.[66]

The Apaches were carefully watching the miners from high up in the Superstitions and quietly placed their warriors along the canyon and cliffs of the escape route. The main group of Mexicans was camped at the processing center on the Rio Salado, but the gold was with a smaller group now high on the mesa.

As Peralta and his men with their gold-laden mules and burros tried to move from the mine through the narrow rock canyons of the Superstitions, going from the north side to the south side, they were suddenly ambushed by arrows raining onto them from the rocks above. The pack animals stampeded, frightening the horses of Don Miguel's guards.

The fierce attack continued for an hour with Don Miguel's men firing their pistols at the Apaches on the cliffs, and the pack animals, many of them wounded, dashing headlong up and down ravines. In the end, the Apaches killed Don Miguel and all the miners except for three who managed to hide in the thick underbrush.

327

These three men eventually made it back to Ballesteros at the river camp and reported the massacre of all their companions. Ballesteros thought it would be too dangerous to go back to try to recover the gold, and decided to abandon the mine entirely until it could be worked more safely. The men decamped immediately and headed south for the Peralta ranch on the Sonora coast.

Ballesteros decided to join the pirates working around the Isthmus of Panama waylaying miners and ships traveling from the gold fields of California, and was himself a rich rancher when he met with Mitchell later in his life.

Several years after the Apache raid, a squad from the United States Army came across the bloody scene in the Superstitions and gathered up what was left of the bodies and gave them a burial in a large common grave. Don Miguel's body was never found. The journal records do not indicate whether the army ever found any of the gold concentrate.[63]

But the legend of a lost gold mine in the Superstitions was born. The story was told all over Sonora and southern Arizona. The lure of millions of dollars in gold nuggets, plus a workable vein of pure gold, was to stimulate many a treasure hunter over the next 150 years. To find this ancient mine would instantly transform one's impoverished life—for better or for worse. Ultimately, the Sombrero Mine would become the most famous lost gold mine of all time, in that it later became known as the Lost Dutchman Mine!

I put down my empty mug and looked at John, who was staring out at the mountains.

"So, what do you think of the Superstition Mountains now?" I asked.

"It seems that these mines are some sort of phantom reality," he said.

"How so?" I asked.

"Well," he said, "it's like the stuff in Charles Fort's books or other phantom realities. Like various phantom things—large black dogs, coyotes, werewolves and others—they only exist for a brief period of time."

"You mean these legendary gold mines also pop in and out of various dimensions?" I asked, filling our mugs with the last of the beer in the pitcher we had ordered after the first pints of lager went down so well.

"Yes," he said, taking a swig, "It seems likely that some of these mines are phantom mines—interdimensional in nature. Do you see what I mean?"

"Yeah, I see what you mean," I nodded. Indeed, as my research into the Lost Dutchman Mine was to later show me, there was some sort of interdimensional nature to this legendary treasure, one that had consumed the lives of a number of people, often in great tragedy.

The Search for the Lost Peralta Mine

I continued telling John about the Lost Dutchman Mine. All of Arizona became part of the United States with the Gadsden Purchase in 1853 and the territory saw a wave of pioneers, prospectors and explorers coming into the largely unknown terrain. As forts, depots and saloons were set up around Camp Verde, Prescott and eventually Phoenix, adventurers in search of lost treasure turned their eyes to the towering Superstitions. It was a hard life in Arizona in those days, with few towns and hostile Apaches in the mountains, but the lure of millions of dollars in gold was powerful enough to make men mount expeditions into the Superstitions in search of the lost Peralta Mine and the saddlebags of gold.

Sometime around 1850-51, after the end of the Mexican-American War, two army veterans, down on their luck, came to the Superstitions to look for the Peralta gold. Sean O'Connor and Aloysious Hurley were prospecting near the Superstitions when they found the skeleton of a burro and part of a disintegrated packsaddle. The saddlebag contained some of the gold concentrate from the Peralta Mine. Camping in the mountains and searching for weeks, they found the decayed remains of several other mules. In each instance, a dusty saddlebag lay nearby filled with gold. They apparently could not find the Peralta Mine.[63]

These two Irish fortune seekers eventually made it to San Francisco and sold the contents of the bags to the mint. Gold at the time was worth approximately $13 an ounce and the two men received a total of $37,000 for their find, a massive sum for the time. The two had become rich men by finding some of the Peralta gold. They believed that there was more to find.

Hurley and O'Connor returned to the Superstitions and stayed for several years. They supposedly continued to find an occasional skeleton and a decaying saddlebag filled with its precious ore. Although the men tried to keep their finds a secret, somehow the information leaked out.

Not only did they have to deal with the treacherous and rugged terrain of the mountains, they soon began to meet up with robbers and riffraff determined to follow and kill them for their gold. Not finding any more gold (or so they said), and realizing that their lives were in danger, they moved to Idaho where they lived in comfort and told many a tale of the Superstitions over drinks at a saloon.

By 1860 the legend of the lost Peralta Mine had gone from campfire legend to proven fact. But where was it? Some argued that the mine was located deep in the Superstition Mountains; others believed it was in the Goldfield Hill area against the west side of the Superstitions. Still others claimed that Peralta's mine was in Yavapai County near Bumble Bee. The remote mining town of Crown King is up a steep canyon beyond Bumble Bee, and it is probably this site that was being referenced in these claims, but I think it is too far afield to have been the Peralta Mine.

The first big thing to happen to Arizona after it became a territory was five years later when the first Arizona Gold Rush occurred in 1858. In that year, rich placer deposits were discovered near Gila City, in Yuma County. These placer (river gold) deposits were later known as the Dome placers, and Gila City became Arizona's first true boomtown. The town lasted only a few short years and was destroyed in a flood in 1862. At that time it had over 1,200 residents and was probably the largest town in Arizona. Today, nothing remains of Gila City—a ghost town of ghost towns.

❧ ❧ ❧

Dr. Abraham Thorne Sees an Ancient Gold Mine

In 1865, a young army doctor named Abraham Thorne received his first appointment to the newly established Fort McDowell, near Phoenix. Thorne's responsibility was to provide the settlers with medical aid. The military was needed in this area because of continuing harassment from hostile Indians. Fort McDowell also gave sanctuary to those peaceful Indians who detested the constant fighting. These Indians lived in a nearby area and were provided with some means for survival.

Originally from Illinois, the young doctor was completely fascinated by everything he saw in Arizona. Once he had seen to the immediate medical needs of the settlers and soldiers, he decided to use his spare time to give what medical help he could to the peaceful Indians living nearby.

Determined to help in whatever way he could, he began to teach himself their language and to slowly win their trust. Both the Apaches and Tohono O'odham were amazed by his abilities, and his quick mastery of their different languages. They grew to like and respect him and called him their brother.[61]

One day, the famous Apache chief Cochise came to meet Thorne. Cochise's youngest bride was experiencing a difficult pregnancy and would soon give birth. Would the great friend of the Indians come and see his wife?

Dr. Thorne helped Cochise's young wife give birth and the chief was grateful. Shortly afterwards, Dr. Thorne was given orders to be transferred to New Mexico. Learning this, Geronimo and Cochise summoned Thorne to come to their camp, where the doctor was told that because he had helped their people, it was their wish to give him a gift. He would have to wait for a day and a night and then they would take him—blindfolded—to a place where there was much gold. He could take as much as he could carry as payment for his services. Dr. Thorne had heard of the lost Peralta gold and, trusting the Apache chiefs to protect him, he agreed to their gift.

Dr. Thorne was blindfolded and taken over a long and circuitous route, apparently into the Superstition Mountains. When the group finally stopped, and the doctor's blindfold was taken off, he looked around and saw that they were in a narrow canyon. The Indians waved to a large pile of rocks directly in front of him. The rocks were gold-bearing ore of very high grade. He was told to fill his saddlebags with the ore.

Thorne was blindfolded again for the trip out, so he was never certain where the Indians had taken him. At one point on the return trip the Indians took off the blindfold to allow Thorne the opportunity to have a drink of water. He immediately saw that he was in a much larger canyon. When he looked into the distance, he saw an immense spire of rock that he recognized as Weaver's Needle.

Thorne went to San Francisco to visit family before going to his new post in New Mexico. There he sold the ore to the mint for an undisclosed sum of money. The amount paid off a loan his father owed on a business venture and gave his two brothers sufficient funds for each to build a substantial home. Dr. Thorne eventually retired, still a wealthy man— and part of his wealth had come from the lost gold mine of the Superstitions.

Tales of gold in the Superstitions sparked the so-called Miner Expedition in May of 1871. It was undertaken as a consequence of stories told by a man named Miner, who acted as guide. He claimed that while prospecting in the Superstitions, one of the men with him panned out seventeen ounces of gold from a single shovel full of earth, and that he could lead the party to the place.

The Miner Expedition numbered about 267 men who had assembled at Prescott and divided into five companies; they failed to find any gold diggings, and Miner's story was believed to be false. This group was the largest expedition ever formed in Arizona to search for the precious metal but ultimately came to nothing. Ironically, the expedition passed over wealthy areas of gold, such as Goldfield and the other mines in the area, including what was probably the Peralta Mine.[61]

This expedition gave name to the small sharp peak located on the south side of the Superstitions and to the north of Bark's Ranch known as "Miner's Needle." Miner had depended on spotting a lone sharp peak to identify the placer ground. This peak is different from "Weaver's Needle," which is higher up in the Superstitions.

Enter the Dutchman

It was getting late and John had to get back to his hotel. I paid the saloon bill and we jumped into the SUV and drove back to Phoenix while I told him the end of the tale. The lights of Phoenix began to twinkle in the distance, and a dull orange glow covered the metropolis.

The story of the Old Dutchman—actually a German—Jacob Walz, and his Lost Dutchman Mine has become the most famous lost mine story in the world. The real name of the "Dutchman" has been disputed, and he is variously called Walz, Waltz and Walzer. According to the early Superstition historian Barney Barnard, his real last name was Walzer. While many authors have called him Jacob Waltz, for the reader's sake, I will use the more common Walz, which is probably what he called himself.

Jacob Walz was a large man, over six feet tall. He was a physically imposing man who had been educated as a mining engineer. He heard about the California gold rush of 1849 and came to the United States with dreams of striking it rich.

Walz arrived in California about 1850. His name appears on several California census records. He prospected and worked as a miner in California for eleven years. It was on July 19, 1861, in the Los Angeles County Courthouse, that Jacob Walz became a naturalized citizen of the United States of America. Walz worked as a miner on the San Gabriel River for a man named Ruben Blakney. It was probably here that he met Elisha M. Reavis, who was later to become known as the "Hermit of Superstition Mountain."[67]

Reavis, something of a wild mountain man,

became famous around Phoenix in the late 1800s as a hermit who lived around the Superstition Mountains. He may have been the source of Walz's early interest in the Superstitions and perhaps planted the thought of a lost gold mine such as the Peralta Mine, in the Dutchman's psyche.

The 1849 gold rush sparked an army of '49ers, as they were called, to invade California looking for the "mother lode." To early prospectors, a "lode" was originally a stream of water, but because a lot of the early gold was found in riverbeds, the term came to mean a vein of metal ore—and the particularly rich vein of ore was the mother lode. Walz, however, did not find his mother lode in California in the 1850s and, after becoming an American citizen, Jacob moved to Arizona as a prospector. Prescott was the main center of activity in those days and there is a recorded mining claim of Walz's filed in the Walker Mining District near the town. Like those of so many others who sought after the elusive dream of gold, Jacob's claim brought little reward. Gold and other precious metals were found around Prescott and Crown King, but not by him.

In 1863, Walz abandoned his claim and worked as an ordinary miner at one of the most famous gold mines in Arizona, the Vulture Mine, located near Wickenburg. While employed at the mine, Jacob saw others' dreams of striking it rich come to fruition, as millions of dollars in gold ore were extracted for the benefit of the owners.

The Vulture Mine was very rich and became famous for the practice of workers "high-grading" (hiding) ore in their lunch pails, in the cuffs of their trousers and pockets. This term for stealing from the mine apparently originated at the Vulture Mine and Walz, along with other miners, was accused of being a "high-grader"—essentially stealing from the mine by keeping choice nuggets of high-grade gold ore for themselves. These would then be sold in Wickenburg, Phoenix, Prescott or elsewhere.

With little proof, charges were dropped and Walz and the other miners were told to get out of Wickenburg. Walz had fallen in love with a beautiful young Apache woman named Ken-Tee and they moved to the Phoenix-Mesa area, only 13 miles from the Superstition Mountains.

In 1864, while living in Mesa, Walz met another German prospector, Jacob Weiser (also known as Wiser). The two men soon became good friends and often would go into the mountains prospecting for gold. On one occasion, the two men were prospecting in the mountains near Nogales, Mexico. They heard about a fiesta that was taking place in the neighboring town of Arizpa. Intrigued with the bustle and activities of the festival, the two Jacobs decided to go for a drink in the local saloon. There they watched a card game that was in progress. One of the players was the son of Don Miguel Peralta.[61]

In a scene out of a Spaghetti Western, Walz and Weiser soon noticed that the card dealer was cheating and informed the young Miguel Peralta. Miguel, angry that the card game was rigged, accused the dealer, who vehemently denied everything. The argument escalated—Peralta and the dealer drew their revolvers and began firing at each other. In fact, in true Old West shootout fashion, the entire card table drew their guns and began shooting, and so did Walz and Weiser. The gunfight left the card dealer dead, young Miguel shot in the chest, and Weiser wounded with a bullet in his arm. Walz escaped unharmed.

Walz and Weiser immediately found medical help for Miguel, thereby saving his life. In order to repay the two men, young Miguel invited them to the Peralta hacienda in Sonora and during their visit told them about his father's Sombrero Mine, which had now become a part of the United States. He then offered them the proposition that they become his partners, and he would show them where the mine was located. As Americans, Walz and Weiser could lay claim to it and then all three of them could share in the profits.

A party was outfitted and they traveled north through Tucson to the Superstitions. Using his father's map and the hieroglyphic signs carved on the rocks, Peralta, Walz, Weiser and their companions were able to find the mine. They set up camp and began to work the ancient mine again. It is said that the gold ore they extracted earned them $30,000.[61]

Apaches Attack the Lost Dutchman Mine

The young Don Miguel Peralta and his companions returned to Mexico with their share of the gold. Walz and Weiser now bought houses in Florence with their newfound wealth. It was not long before they returned to the Superstitions to get more gold ore from the mine. They continued to work the mine for many months, one of them returning to town for supplies every once in a while.

The year was now 1881, and one day Walz returned to town and told everyone in Florence that Weiser had been killed by Apaches.

In the standard version of the story told by Walz, he returned to the mine with supplies to see the shocking sight of Weiser's dead body—pierced by a dozen arrows. Walz hurriedly buried his partner and returned to Florence, fearful of another Apache attack.

The Apaches were watching and followed Walz back to Florence. When they saw that he was living with Ken-Tee, the Apaches became convinced that it was she who had shown him the location of the mine.

Planning revenge on Ken-Tee they raided Walz's house in the early morning hours and kidnapped the woman.[61, 62]

Walz and a group of neighbors quickly followed in pursuit as the Apaches fled on horseback towards the Superstitions. Walz and his companions caught up with the Apaches and began firing at them. During the fight the Indians released Ken-Tee. Walz leaped off his horse, rushed to the fallen Ken-Tee and cradled her in his arms. She had been stabbed in the back and had her tongue cut out—she died in Walz's arms.

Walz left Florence and moved to Phoenix where he befriended a number of people.

I had to brake suddenly, and exit the Interstate near the airport to get John back to his hotel and conference. As usual, Phoenix was jam-packed with traffic, and it seemed like an endless freeway of intersecting on and off ramps.

"How about that," I said. "This was all remote desert a hundred years ago, full of lost treasure. Now it seems like they've paved over the veins of gold. It's all vanished."

"Well," said John, giving the passenger door a good shove, "we may never know the truth of these fabulous gold mines of legend. They may not exist at this time and place. Where it had been before, its not there now."

"Ha, ha," I laughed as he passed near the door. "I'll keep looking for my lost cities anyway. I think they are still out there—and I will find them! See you later!"

With that I drove off into the night, taillights fading in the distance. As I got back onto the freeway with the night closing in, I thought about the lure of those desolate places, where rocky trail met the occasional creek or spring—a hard land with a heart of gold. Gold is where you find it, and find it the old prospectors did! The Old Dutchman had lived his dream, but it was a bitter success.

The End of the Dutchman

That night I ended up meeting Jennifer at the home of her sister and brother-in-law in Cave Creek, an eastern suburb of Phoenix. The next morning, after breakfast, we put on our hiking shoes and headed for one of the trailheads for a good morning hike in the Superstition Mountains. Maybe by examining the heart of the Superstitions ourselves, we could come to some conclusions about the Lost Dutchman Mine.

We could see the great granite walls of the Superstitions in front of us, and continued driving past Apache Junction on Arizona Route 60 toward Florence Junction, and then turned north onto Peralta Road and slowly headed into the foothills of the mountains. We parked at the trailhead of the Peralta Ranch and got ready for our hike.

Soon we were hiking up the winding, and sometimes steep, trail that went into the heart of the Superstitions toward Weaver's Needle. Cactus and occasional clumps of grass clung to the crevasses and flash flood areas of the mountains. We passed a number of hikers coming down from the trail already, having started early in the morning. Eventually we came to a high point for this part of the Superstitions, and we took a much-needed rest. Around us were granite walls and awesome vistas of desert and sky.

On our way around the south edge of the mountains, we talked about the life of the Dutchman. By the end of the year 1881, Walz's world had been destroyed. His beloved wife was dead. His partner was also dead. He bought a house in Phoenix, near Buckeye Road and Seventh Street.

Walz returned to the Superstitions every once in a while after moving to Phoenix. From time to time he would disappear for several weeks and come back with large quantities of gold ore. Walz would then take his ore to the local Wells Fargo office. From there he would ship it to the United States Mint in San Francisco. Eventually he would receive thousands of dollars in return.

When the money would come in to Wells Fargo, the Old Dutchman would spend some of it in the local saloons and become roaring drunk. Sometimes he would brag about knowing where there was enough gold to pave every street in Phoenix.[63]

The Old Dutchman became a figure of speculation and fascination in Phoenix. Attempting to discover the source of his treasure, some people tried to befriend him. Others took to spying on him, following him wherever he went. As he was viewed as an eccentric local celebrity, reporters and writers tried to interview him.

Walz was suspicious of everyone, and he remained aloof. He did however participate in shooting contests. Perhaps he believed that his sharpshooting skills would discourage those who might want to kidnap him or try to follow him to the mine. Meanwhile his reputation continued to grow.

One famous story says Walz made a trip to the mine in 1882, and took two burro loads of ore to Tucson and sold it for $1600. Three famous locals, Colonel Poston, George McClarty and Charlie Brown, were witnesses to the transaction and asked the Old Dutchman some questions. They figured out that Walz did not have the mine properly staked and recorded; the three men attempted to follow the Dutchman to claim the mine. The crafty Walz, who apparently had good reason to be paranoid, knew he was being followed. The three men kept up with him to Whitlow's Ranch on Queen Creek, but after that, Walz eluded them in the backcountry of the Superstitions, probably crossing over to the north side and the Goldfield area. When the three men returned to Tucson, they told the tale over and over again, where it became a familiar anecdote in saloons.

Walz continued to visit the mine occasionally, but by now was a very old man. In February of 1891, a disastrous super-flood struck Phoenix, completely devastating it. His house was situated near the north bank of the Salt River, and was suddenly caught in a torrent of water. He was forced to climb a tall cottonwood tree that stood near his home. He was now 83 years old, but he was determined to survive. He lashed himself to the tree, knowing that lack of sleep or fatigue would cause him to lose his grip, and he would plunge into the swirling waters below.

For two days he lay lashed to the tree, exhausted, until he was rescued and taken to the home of Mrs. Julia Thomas. Thomas was a black woman who owned a boarding house and confectionery store, and was one of Walz' better friends. The Old Dutchman had contracted pneumonia from exposure and managed to live with Thomas for several months on the edge of death. He eventually passed away at her boarding house on October 25, 1891.

Grateful to Thomas for her hospitality, on his deathbed Walz told her the location of the secret mine. A short time later, with no explanation to anyone, Thomas sold her store and, with a 17-year-old boarder named Rhinehart Petrasch, she set out for the Superstition Mountains. After some months of searching, she appealed to Rhinehart's father and brother, who were experienced prospectors, to join them. The search continued for another year before it was abandoned at the end of 1892. Thomas apparently returned to her business of running a boarding house.

Ironically, Julia Thomas and the Petrasches probably walked over the rich gold deposits at

Goldfield on their way back to Phoenix without discovering them. Indeed, as we will see later, this group, like many others, passed by the very gold mine they were searching for when they went high into the Superstitions to the vicinity of Weaver's Needle. Gold mines on the northern edge of the Superstitions were claimed and filed when the rich Black Queen was discovered in November of 1892, and the rich Mammoth Mine was discovered on April 13, 1893. Both these mines produced large amounts of gold, with the Mammoth Mine producing about three million dollars worth of gold bullion in four years—a huge amount for the time.

Many Arizona pioneer historians believe Julia Thomas gave an interview to Pierpont C. Bicknell, a freelance writer and lost mine hunter, shortly after her return from the Superstition Mountains in September of 1892. He probably paid her a token fee for the story.

Bicknell, maybe more than any other journalist or tale-teller, is responsible for the enduring legend of the Lost Dutchman Mine. Bicknell was the earliest writer to associate Weaver's Needle, the Peraltas and Jacob Walz with the mine in his oft-repeated newspaper articles. Bicknell's first major article on the "Dutchman's Lost Mine" appeared in the *San Francisco Chronicle* on January 13, 1895, and revealed several details as to the location of the mine. The story was eventually circulated all over the world, and Europeans became just as familiar with the Lost Dutchman Mine as were Americans.

Bicknell used a variety of names for Weaver's Needle, confusing early treasure hunters. He called the it Needle Rock, Sombrero Peak and El Sombrero in different articles he wrote about the Dutchman's Lost Mine. Many years later, Julia Thomas revealed to Jim Bark, a prominent Arizona rancher, the information Jacob Walz had told her. "Walz told me," she said, "that the mouth of the mine could be found on a spot upon which the shadow of the tip of Weaver's Needle, that well known peak, rests at exactly four in the afternoon."[62, 63]

However, Julia told Bark, "The directions seemed simple enough, until you realize that the sun's shadow moves every single day throughout the year. But, we followed that shadow and we carefully searched the surrounding area. The only thing we found was a trench dug on a claim near Goldfield, but never a mine. I believed him," said Mrs. Thomas. "It sounded so real. He said that the mine had a ledge of rose quartz with an additional few inches of crystal hematite. How could he have made this description up?," she muttered to herself. "One-third of those few inches was gold, and the rose quartz was generously sprinkled with pinhead-size lumps of gold. He told me that it was a king's treasure waiting, waiting for someone to discover."

Julia Thomas laughed bitterly. She had given up her store believing the Old Dutchman's story. "I think now he made it all up because he couldn't pay me at the end. But he had gold. We all knew he had some gold—he lived on it for years. All I know is that he made it sound so very, very real."[61, 62]

Goldfield, Charles Hall and the Lost Dutchman

One possible solution to the mystery of the whereabouts of the Lost Dutchman Mine is the rich gold dike in the area of Goldfield. About 1890, a mining prospector from Denver named Charles Hall came to the mines around Prescott to work. Hall decided that while he was in Arizona he would look around for other mining possibilities, and check out the Superstition area. He was particularly interested in Goldfield Hill on the western edge of the Superstitions, which was not far from the site of the Peralta massacre.

Closely examining the type of rock on Goldfield—which had small specks of gold in it—he began to suspect that Peralta had in fact mined that area, and then taken the ore elsewhere for processing. If he was right, this would mean the gold mine was not in the Superstitions per se, but along the northwest side just beneath the great walls of rock. In fact, it seems that previous treasure hunters had been misled by the fact the massacre occurred in the mountains, and the remnants of the pack animals were found in ravines deep within the stony walls. We have already seen that the probable explanation for this is that Peralta had removed his men from the mine, and they were killed while in transit from the camp on the Rio Salado.

Hall bought the mining claims to Goldfield Hill from some Mormon owners who apparently didn't realize that they might own the rights to the Lost Dutchman Mine, and put together a mining operation. He called it the Mammoth Mine.

Hall decided to sink his first shaft directly down the center of the hill. What he found was high-grade gold concentrate. During the next few years, Charles Hall took out millions of dollars of gold from his bounteous mine. It now appeared that this man had finally found the elusive gold of Don Miguel Peralta and Jacob Walz. Hall felt that he had solved the mystery of the location of the Lost Dutchman Mine. Other claims were made in the vicinity, and soon the Mammoth Mine had other smaller operations around it.[61, 68]

If Hall had indeed found the Lost Dutchman Mine, the great Thunder God of the Superstitions was to take it away from him. One day, after several years of successful mining, black thunderclouds began to build up, and lightning flashed ominously over the mountains, as it would from time to time. At first Hall was not alarmed, but then the rains came like a river of water pouring off the mountains, joining together in an ever-increasing force. Flash floods had happened before, but this time the rains did not diminish; instead they became worse. As water poured off the Superstitions, an awesome flood of torrential waters crashed over the Mammoth Mine's site smashing machinery and tossing equipment. Thousands of tons of sand, debris and earth completely filled the shafts, burying the mine entirely.

Hall, who was quite old, had made millions already on the mine, and he decided not to try to reopen it. Eventually his daughters sold the rights to a former mayor of Phoenix, George Young, who sank a test shaft at the site and found that a powerful underground river now flowed through the mine. Young attempted to pump the water out but his efforts failed. The Mammoth Mine was never reopened. Today it is the popular ghost town of Goldfield, where I took John Michell for drinks.

Not everyone was satisfied that the Mammoth Mine fully fit Jacob Walz's description to Julia Walker. These people wondered if there was yet another mine still undiscovered. They continued to look into the mountains for the lost mine, and some still do today.

We had made it to the top of the trail and were catching our breath on some large rocks just off the path. Weaver's Needle was rising up from the other folds of rock in front of us. It was great spot for some snacks and a rest. As I munched on a granola bar, I stared at Weaver's Needle: so much had happened around it, including a number of deaths. In the blue sky of that day, it seemed majestic. Yet, there was a certain menacing aspect to the Superstitions, I could feel it.

What was the secret of the mysterious Superstition

treasure, I asked myself, looking around. Some say that the Goldfield Hill Mine, at the western foot of the Superstitions is the ancient mine that was so long sought—and found—by many. Millions of dollars in gold ore were taken from the mine.

Others believe that the still-unfound mine is high on a plateau of the mountains, above the towering cliffs that one sees from Goldfield Hill. Weavers Needle is thought to be the key to uncovering the now buried diggings. Perhaps some old miner, even Walz, had blown up the mouth of the mine with dynamite.

The story of the Lost Dutchman Mine continues to be repeated throughout the U.S.A. and Europe. But the whole story actually creates more questions than it answers. Was there an ancient mine with tunnels going deep into the Superstitions? Or was it more of an outcropping of gold like around Goldfield? Why did Jacob Walz never exploit his mine by filing a claim? Was it because he had found something so astonishing that he needed to keep it a secret? Many theories have been offered.

I am an outlaw, I was born an outlaw's son
The highway is my legacy
On the highway I will run.
In one hand I've a Bible,
In the other I've got a gun.
—Eagles, *Outlaw Man*

Strange Men Living Inside the Superstitions

Hiking up the trail to Weaver's Needle from the Peralta Trailhead on the south side of the Superstitions, I mulled over some odd beliefs and tales about the Superstitions. Supposedly, there were secret granite doors in the mountains that led to tunnels deep within the mountain and its volcanic corridors. There were "stone men" that are seen on the western side of the Superstitions, and presumably live inside the mountain. The rocky crags could hold many secrets.

Indeed, this was sort of the popular vision of the Lost Dutchman Mine: a hidden entrance in the rock face that led down a granite crevice to a vein of glittering gold! Many times I had looked through binoculars at Goldfield and scrutinized the great vertical wall of rock that is the western edge of the range. I would scan the rock face looking for caves and "windows" into this supposed inner world of the Superstitions.

The most famous of the stories of a hollow world inside the Superstitions came from a woman named Maria Jones. She arrived in Phoenix in the late 1950s to look for the Lost Dutchman and eventually came to believe that strange men were living inside the mountains, and that a secret cave entrance lay high up on Weaver's Needle.

Jones, a black woman, claimed that she was related to Julia Thomas, in whose boardinghouse the Dutchman had died. The newcomer said she had been a singer and claimed she had studied music at Juilliard College. She was fond of showing visitors a scrapbook that contained photographs of her in her younger days on stage in a nightclub or concert hall.

Maria Jones was a well-known character during the exciting '60s in the Superstitions. Robert Sikorsky tells some interesting tales about her in his book *Quest For the Dutchman's Gold*.[57] Sikorsky came to Arizona in 1959 from Pennsylvania and almost immediately got involved with Maria Jones and her cohorts.

Sikorsky relates how he, Jones, and her helpers Raymond and Louie, would stop by a gypsy fortuneteller on their way out of Phoenix en route to the Superstitions. On one visit heading out of Phoenix the gypsy said, "You will have good luck on this trip, Maria. Fortune is smiling on your group."[57]

Sikorsky spent several years with Jones and her oddball crew of treasure hunters. Like other prospectors and treasure hunters in the Superstitions, they wore a pistol in a holster on one hip and a large, sheathed knife on the other.

Jones must have heard Julia Thomas's quote that "the mouth of the mine could be found on a spot upon which the shadow of the tip of Weaver's Needle, that well known peak, rests at exactly four in the afternoon." However, Jones came to believe after spending much time camped in the mountains, that Weaver's Needle was actually hollow and the Dutchman's Lost Mine was inside the massive spire of rock. Perhaps a rock tunnel went down beneath the spire of rock and connected to other tunnels.

At some point early on, Maria Jones had filed some sort of mining claim on Weaver's Needle and she felt it was her own private property. The band that she formed to explore the peak was known as the Maria Jones Gang; it was a well-armed motley crew of drifters, henchmen, treasure hunters and backcountry boozers. They may have been responsible for some of the many unsolved murders that occurred in the Superstitions in the '60s and '70s.

Another private army was hunting the Superstitions at this time, as well. This was comprised of Ed Piper and his gun-toting friends, Bernie Gheardt, Jim Lori and John Brower. Collectively, they were known as Piper's Army, and they often camped out near Weaver's Needle as well, this being the all-important centerpiece of the Superstitions.

Piper's Army and the Jones Gang even got to shooting at each other from time to time. Sikorsky wrote in his book about one incident when rifle fire filled their camp late one night. They ran for the cover of the many boulders in the Superstitions and hid until morning. After that bizarre incident, Sikorsky decided to give up treasure hunting in those mountains.

Things got worse, and within a few months Ed Piper had shot and killed Robert St. Marie, who was working for Jones at the time. This occurred in the vicinity of Weaver's Needle. At his trial in Phoenix, Piper claimed that it was self-defense. Inconsistencies in Maria Jones' testimony lead to him being acquitted of murder. Piper died of natural causes a few months after his acquittal, and that seemed to bring the whole affair to a close.

With all the unsolved murders and other deaths, the Phoenix public had begun to wonder if some sort of dangerous gold fever had broken out in Apache Junction.

Sikorsky eventually realized that Maria Jones believed that she actually saw people moving about on the Needle, and believed that the entrance was on a ledge, now unreachable, about halfway up the eastern face of the towering rock spire.

Sikorsky describes Maria's vision in one chapter of his book *Quest for the Dutchman's Gold*[57]:

> It was not uncommon for Maria Jones to see people coming in and out of Weaver's Needle. The first time she called my attention to it I was dumbfounded. We were in camp and it was suppertime. The Needle, as always around sunset, was illuminated to a brilliant orange-brown and every crack and crevice on its west face was boldly outlined in shadow.
>
> Maria casually asked me if I could see the people coming in and out of the uppermost portion of the spire. I couldn't believe her question. I looked, straining my eyes for

any type of movement—I saw nothing.

"Look! Up there, Bob, near the top. Don't you see them? They're going into a cave. See them, see them!" she shouted frantically.

I looked at Louie. He sat there expressionless, his eyes fixed on the towering precipice. He said nothing—he had been this route before.

"I don't see anything, Maria," I replied.

"They're gone now. It's too late. But they will be back. You'll get a chance to see them again."

I thought just because I didn't see anything, did not mean she didn't. As I found out in subsequent people-sightings, she really believed that she saw people up there and who was I to argue with her? I recalled a time that a friend of mine had tried and tried to point out a walking stick sitting motionless on a tree branch. Try as I might, I couldn't see it. But it was there nevertheless. Perhaps Maria's people were there, too. I hoped for her sake they were.

Maybe she really did see people and maybe they were really going in and out of the Needle. She knew they were there, she saw them, she believed in them, she sang songs to them. They were carrying treasure from room to room, from opening to opening, moving it about to confuse searchers of the mine. They were the keepers of the treasure, visible proof that the bonanza was inside the Needle itself.

Maria saw people on the Needle at increasingly frequent intervals. Indeed, by the end of my stay with her, daily sightings were common. I never did see them. Louie was noncommittal, shrugging his shoulders when I asked him if he saw them. I knew he was trying hard to see them, trying hard not to disappoint Maria. He didn't want to crush the dream. He didn't want to say definitely that they weren't there, for saying that would be saying that the treasure wasn't there and the dream would collapse and vanish into the still Superstition air.

Sikorsky tells the story of a rock climber from Phoenix named Bill Sewery who had met Maria Jones and her men near Weaver's Needle in the early 1960s. Sewery and friends were interested in technical rock climbing on the Needle and one day asked Jones if she would let them climb the spire. She said okay, but she wanted them to call her Phoenix residence before their attempt. Sewery called several times and Jones always refused permission. According to Sikorsky, "Finally they decided to go anyway—permission or not. Wasn't this public land?"[57]

Says Sikorsky:

From the base of Weavers Needle in East Boulder Canyon they hiked up the west slope into the gully of the Needle. A Jones henchman approached the climbers as they prepared to ascend the Needle. He was armed with a knife and revolver—a grubby sort of fellow and not pleasant. He told them to leave the area, but after much disagreeable discussion the climbers proceeded, ignoring the threats. A little while later rocks came raining down on them. Apparently the Jones men climbed the Needle by the east face route and got above the climbers so they could tumble rocks off the cliff. After the rocks stopped, the climbers continued up the west gully, around the chock stone, and up to the top of Weavers

Needle where they met the Jones men again and eventually found something in common to talk about. The Jones men wanted to know more about their rock climbing techniques. Sewery and the other climbers were happy to show them everything they knew. From that point on, there were no more confrontations with the Jones camp.

Bill Sewery remembers every time they walked by the Jones camp, Maria would give them a look that seemed to say, "There they go again, what can you do?"

Sewery recalls that Jones eventually found a use for them and asked him and some others to come over to her house on Van Buren Street in Phoenix.

Sewery knocked on the door and one of her armed men answered. With arms folded, wearing a revolver and knife, just like in the Superstitions, he nodded them inside with a gesture of his head. They were motioned into the kitchen where they sat down at a table with a human skull. A candle was mounted inside the skull to light the room. It all seemed a bit melodramatic. Jones sat on one side of the table and explained her plan. She wanted Sewery and the others to climb Weavers Needle and rappel off the north face to check out a notch in the rock. The treasure was supposed to be located there.

A mining engineer employed by Jones was also to rappel with them. Sewery said they needed to give the mining engineer some lessons in rappelling or he would be useless out on the cliff and would probably kill himself. The expedition never came off but rock climbers Doug Black and Bill Forrest, at a later date, made an agreement to do the work for Jones. They never got paid. Jones seemed to have a reputation for not paying the climbers. Later, one of the mining engineers that Jones hired fell to his death from the top of Weaver's Needle.[57]

Despite her belief that people were actually living inside of the Superstitions, Sikorsky seemed to believe that Jones was on to something. Sikorsky theorizes that the Needle was damaged in a massive earthquake that hit the Superstitions on May 3, 1887. The small town of Pinal, used by the Peralta family, on the southern side of the Superstitions was destroyed in the quake.

Sikorsky thinks that part of the southeastern face of Weaver's Needle came shearing off at this time. This destroyed the precarious trail up to the ledge and supposed entrance into the lost mine and its vein of pure gold. This earthquake happened after the Dutchman stopped going to the Superstitions, so he never knew that the way to the mine entrance had been lost.[57]

Jennifer and I were sitting on the Peralta Trail, having a drink of water from our canteens and looking at Weaver's Needle. While Weaver's Needle has always featured in the Lost Dutchman Mine mythos, it would seem that Maria Jones and her gang, as well as Sikorsky, were putting too much emphasis on this famous spire of rock. Rather than the lost mine being inside this narrow granite tower, it was actually just an easily seen landmark. Walz had told Julia Thomas, some researchers believe, that he could see Weaver's Needle from his mine. She assumed that the mine was near the rock spire, putting it in the center of the rocky Superstitions, when it could be that Walz was telling her that he could see the Needle from his gold mine east of Goldfield. As I have noted, Julia Thomas, Maria Jones and everyone else had walked across the area around Goldfield many times as they went high into the Superstitions to search around Weaver's Needle. They were walking over the very veins of gold that they were looking for!

The Lost Dutchman is Found Again!

Jennifer and I hiked back down the trail, and soon we were back at the parking lot. It was getting hot as we got back on Highway 60 and headed toward Apache Junction. We stopped at the Goldfield saloon for a quick drink, and I showed Jennifer the binoculars that took a quarter. We searched the walls of the western cliffs for the next few minutes.

It was reported in the 1970s that a man named Alfred Strong Lewis claimed he had found the Lost Dutchman Mine near the Goldfield Hill area, but closer to the Superstitions themselves. Lewis told his friend Ted Sliger about the discovery and Sliger wrote a number of articles for Phoenix newspapers on the intriguing story, as the Lost Dutchman Mine was always of interest.

Lewis told Sliger, "I know it sounds crazy, after all this while, but I think, I just think I've found the old Dutchman's mine. I was exploring in an area just a short way from the northwest part of the Superstitions and no more than a mile from where the Peralta massacre occurred. That's when I saw this large boulder. When I examined the boulder closely, I noticed what looked like a mysterious little entrance right under it. At first I thought I was mistaken.

"Sometimes things look contrived when in fact they are just a natural phenomenon. Anyway, I explored further and I found the remains of a neatly dug passage. I decided to get me a few sticks of dynamite and topple the boulder. I found a shaft made of old timbers of ironwood. The wood was fashioned the way the Spaniards used to work ironwood over one hundred years ago. It looks like it might be an old Peralta mine shaft."[60]

Sliger was fascinated by Lewis' tale and agreed to become his partner. Sliger found two other partners that night, and the four men contacted the owner of the property and bought the mining rights for $20,000, backing the agreement with a $5,000 deposit.

When the men began to explore the shaft, they could see where someone had broken off chunks of ore that contained a high percentage of free gold. Everything seemed to point to this being not only one of the Peralta shafts, but also Jacob Walz's lost mine.

The new mining venture began to take ore out of the shaft and they soon amassed about $42,000 in gold. Then the vein of gold abruptly stopped. They continued to tunnel further and suddenly broke through a wall of rock into another abandoned shaft. This one was of a more modern construction and it appeared to be a branch of the Mammoth Mine works.

Exploring this shaft as far as they could, they discovered that some sort of landslide had cut off the vein. The flooding of the Mammoth Mine seemed to have mixed everything up underground. The vein seemed to be gone—broken up and churned in some cataclysmic episode.

The men brought some large dirt-moving machinery and began scraping and digging the surface around the two shafts. Every foot of the ground contained gold, but only enough to pay for costs, and not enough to make a profit. After moving more earth around the shafts in hopes of hitting the lost vein, they eventually gave up. Had Sliger discovered the Lost Dutchman as he claimed?

Goldfield and the Final Say on the Lost Dutchman

As I looked out at the massive walls of the towering western slope of the Superstitions from the tourist site of Goldfield, I could see why so many people's imaginations were fired up by the fantastic tale of the Lost Dutchman Mine. Here were vertical granite cliffs hundreds of feet high stacked up on top of each other, and somewhere beyond those imposing walls was the Lost Dutchman. That is what the Dutchman had said, right? Walz had told Julia Thomas and Rhinehart Petrasch that his mine was "a short distance back from the western end of the main Superstition Mountain."[63, 68]

But they thought that the old Dutchman had meant back a short distance to the east. That would be behind the majestic cliffs of the western wall of the Superstitions, an area of rocky granite towers like Miner's Needle and Weaver's Needle. It was here that so many prospectors had searched for lost gold—some losing their lives in the process.

Geologist John Wilburn explained why veins of gold were unlikely to be found within the main part of the Superstitions in his self-published 1990 booklet, *Dutchman's Lost Ledge of Gold and the Superstition Gold Mining District*:

> The entire Superstition Wilderness is a vast region of deeply eroded lavas and welded volcanic ash, dacite tuff, at least 25 million years old. Erosion has stripped nearly 3,000 feet of rock, exposing no ore deposits.
>
> Ore is the result of hydrothermal activity intruding favorable rocks along preexisting faults subsequent to igneous intrusions. The intrusions are porphyry dikes and stocks that have intruded older rocks. They are not found in the wilderness, and there is no hydrothermal

alteration associated with ore deposits. This is why after 120 years and a million prospectors, from greenhorns to geologists, no ore has ever been found there.

On the other hand, the ore in Goldfield is typical of rich epithermal veins of mid-Miocene deposition. Here are favorable host rocks, old Precambrian granite and Oligocene indurated arkosic conglomerates containing preexisting faults intruded by porphrytic dikes and subsequent quartz veins bearing gold. The veins typically carry gold and silver (electrum) averaging 36 per cent silver. In all veins and lodes the gold occurs abundantly free as wire, dust and flakes in white to glassy crystalline quartz stained strongly by pyrolusite, hematite and limonite. Some veins carry galena, a lead sulphide, and copper minerals, malachite and chrysocolla. The gold ore is some of the richest in Arizona. The veins are about 16 million years old, reaching 1,500 feet below what was then the surface. They have been exposed to erosion.

So, did everybody get that, then? What Wilburn is saying is simply that the underlying geology of the Superstition Mountains is not conducive to the formation of ores, while the underlying geology at Goldfield makes it primo real estate for the creation of rich veins.

There are many gold mines in this area along the western edge of the Superstitions. We have already mentioned the fabulous Mammoth Mine. Others include the Bull Dog Mine, the Black Queen Mine, the Old Wasp Mine, the Golden Hillside Mine, the Copper Crown Mine, The Bluebird Mine, the Treasure Vault Mine, the Tom Thumb Mine, the Fair Stake Mine, the Highflyer Mine, the Doc Palmer Mine, the Gold

Bond Mine, Gold Strike, Government Well, and the Lazy Doc Claim. All of the claims produced nuggets of high quality gold, some producing millions of dollars in gold.

Government Well, located three miles northeast of Goldfield, was an old well that was an important stop for travelers coming over the old Apache Trail, which in the late 1800s led through some pretty wild territory. Miners and soldiers on the trail were continually under attack by the Apaches who dominated the large forests east of the Superstitions, today the White Mountain Apache Indian Reservation.

Deep inside this mountain forest are the mysterious ruins of Kinishba. This abandoned city may have been a stronghold for Apache raiders. I was determined to head in that direction, along the north side of the Superstition Mountains.

> *In a soldier's stance, I aimed my hand*
> *At the mongrel dogs who teach*
> *Fearing not that I'd become my enemy*
> *In the instant that I preach.*
> *My existence led by confusion boats,*
> *Mutiny from stern to bow.*
> *Ah, but I was so much older then,*
> *I'm younger than that now.*
> —Bob Dylan, *My Back Pages*

An Ancient Cavern in the Superstitions

Jennifer and I paid for our drinks and, after a quick stop at the Lost Dutchman Museum near Goldfield, we headed north on Highway 88, the modern designation of the famous Apache Trail. Ahead of us was a winding road that led through the saguaro-filled desert and eventually to the trading post known as Tortilla Flat. The sun began to set in the rearview mirror. Tortilla Flat, we decided, was our destination for the time being. We had heard there was a restaurant and saloon there.

With the last of the mines around Goldfield behind us, I couldn't help but think that there was still something unusual going on in the Superstition Mountains. The many deaths associated with the mountains were one thing, but there were other oddball items to hold up to the light—such as the strange Tumlinson tablets.

Several authors of books and booklets sold around Phoenix and Apache Junction have told the story of the tablets, supposedly found in the late 1940s by a man from Portland, Oregon named Travis Tumlinson. According to such booklets as Travis Marlowe's *Superstition Treasures* (1965)[68] and Jim D. Hatt's *The Peralta Stone Maps* (2005)[69], Tumlinson was supposedly passing through Arizona and pulled off Highway 60, somewhere west of Florence Junction, to take a break and stretch his legs in the desert. He just happened to stop near the south side of the Superstition Mountains.

Tumlinson, while walking about in the desert beyond his parked car, stumbled over the corner of something hard. He allegedly discovered four slabs of sandstone about 18 inches wide, 12 inches high and just over two inches thick. The slabs appeared to show the way to a secret mine—they were adorned with very nicely carved pictures, signs, letters and wavy lines. One was called the Horse Map, another the Priest Map, a third the Heart Map (there is a heart-shaped peak in the Superstitions) and finally the Trail Map. The latter seemed to indicate the trail to the lost mine, but it proved indecipherable.

Another story about the tablets is that they were actually sold to Tumlinson by a local man named Noble Dwyer for $100. Tumlinson apparently used them to search for the Lost Dutchman Mine, but was not able to find anything. Eventually the stone maps fell into the murky lore of the Lost Dutchman and were largely forgotten. Marlowe's 1965 booklet is a great tourist introduction to the lore of the Superstitions and has good black and white photos of the tablets. Hatt's more recent booklet, *The Peralta Stone Maps*, has recent color photos of the tablets. Hatt appears to be the new owner of these stone maps to a lost treasure.[68, 69]

The Tumlinson tablets, with "clues" that didn't really lead anywhere, have been largely branded a forgery by most authors. Looking at those stones in photos, my first impression was that they are fairly modern, and not typical of old Mexican characters, glyphs or workmanship. They may well be a hoax, possibly pulled off by Dwyer on gullible treasure hunters.

But what of stories of ancient rock-cut vaults in the Superstitions, dating from the Hohokam or before? Of note here is the curious story about a sealed cave with a door cut into the rock that was published in the Phoenix *Herald* in 1892. The article is quoted in a chapter entitled "Royal Treasure?," published in a book entitled *Arizona Cavalcade*[102] by Joseph Miller in 1962. The book is a compilation of old newspaper reports and it contains several very curious articles.

The 1892 article is about a man named Andrew Pauly who claimed to have made a discovery around 1889, while searching for some stolen horses. He saw a "most peculiar appearance of the face of the rock in one of the remote recesses or clefts of the cliff up which I had gone looking for water, which gave me the impression of the work of some human hand. It looked like a small door cut in the rock and again skillfully closed by some dusty material. I was too thirsty to have any curiosity then, so I pulled on for the top of the range."

Andrew Pauly then returned to the place in 1892.

believing that the sealed cave entrance was a door to a treasure chamber. Says the *Phoenix Herald:*

> As was noted last week that he was about to go out in search of what he considered a very peculiar artificial opening in the rocks among the mountain which now prove to be not very remote from the orchard of the upper valley, Pauly started out with a prospector's outfit and succeeded in finding the object of his search, and furthermore, that it was a genuine piece of masonry in a cut opening in the solid rock and of such thickness and consistency that with a prospecting pick, hammer, and other tools, he was five days in making an opening though the cement and rock that packed the opening which is not now much larger than a man can crawl through.
>
> Pauly tells a wonderful story of his discovery in the chamber behind the barricade through which he has worked his way. He found a chamber apparently cut from solid rock not less than twenty by forty feet in dimensions and about ten feet in height. The floor was covered by seven immense skeletons of men who in life must have been not less than seven feet in height, and there was further evidence that they must have been warriors as the remains of what were copper shields, copper spear heads, and battle axes and other artifacts were found with the skeletons.
>
> A most interesting discovery was a small ornament, a crude amulet apparently, of gold, a metal that has never before been found in all the searches that have been made of the ancient Aztec mounds and ruins so plentifully distributed through this region of country. A yet more important and startling

361

discovery was an opening at the farther end of the chamber also closed with what appears to be a sort of rude bronze door. So neatly and accurately filled into the solid rock that barring a jut of the rock over and at the sides of the door it might have grown there, so solid does it appear. It is about two by three feet in dimensions and of unknown thickness, but when struck sounds as though it either lay against solid rock or was of great thickness.

The mystery of this second discovery now occupies Pauly's attention and he provided himself with the necessary means to remove the door or heavy bronze plate set in the side of the cave, or whatever it may be. As we have above indicated, the place may prove the treasure house of the Aztec tribes or it may prove nothing more than has been found, but at any rate the discovery is a startling and interesting one. Pauly, who works entirely alone, so far, traveled to town on foot yesterday, and guards his treasure with the greatest secrecy so far as its location is concerned, though he talked very freely with a *Herald* representative as to what he had found and what he thinks he may find which he believes to be nothing less than the treasure vault of an ancient royalty.[102]

Nothing more was ever heard about this astonishing find. The seven-foot skeletons on the floor are very intriguing. Was this some Hohokam burial ground? Or a remnant of one of the early Hindu-Egyptian-Olmec explorations into the area? Perhaps they had the elongated and deformed skulls of the Egyptians, Olmecs and others.

Whatever else he may have found, Pauly apparently decided to keep it a secret—when large treasures are located, it is not really in the finder's best interest to have the fact publicized. If there is anything unusual about Pauly, it is that he is too talkative to the press, though he was a former newspaperman himself.

I relate a similar story in my book *Lost Cities of North & Central America*.[18] In this book I tell of a conversation I had more than 15 years ago with a friend in Sedona named Richard. Richard told me about some acquaintances who told hin they had discovered a tunnel that goes underground for quite a distance in the Superstition Mountains.

According to him, "After penetrating deep into the cave they came to cut stones and carvings in the rock. The remains of ancient structures and walls made out of well-dressed rock were found. They then discovered at this place a spiral staircase built out of cut stones that descended down, down, down, into the earth."[18]

One person in the group descended the staircase and came to a large room with more cut stones. A gigantic rock-cut throne, big enough for a giant, or two people sitting together, was in the middle of the room. Supposedly there were artifacts on the walls. The team felt that they were in a sacred place that should not be disturbed and so left the tunnel, and decided to keep the entrance a secret.

I seek not to know the answers,
but to understand the questions.
–Caine, *Kung Fu*, 1972

After dinner at the friendly saloon in Tortilla Flat, we camped out for the night. While the bar was basically empty the night we were there—a cold January night—obviously thousands of travelers had passed through this remote establishment. Hundreds, if not thousands, of dollar bills as well as foreign bills, were signed by patrons and glued to the wall. I sipped my beer and took a closer look at some of them as the evening wore on.

We woke up the next morning and had breakfast at the café. I bought some postcards and a book on lost treasure in the area, and we headed back to the 4x4 to make sure we had plenty of water and other desert supplies. From Tortilla Flat we headed farther up the Apache Trail, toward Roosevelt Dam. The winds blew along the south side of the man-made Canyon Lake which is connected to the man-made Apache Lake. Here, were the huge water reservoirs for metropolitan Phoenix, a giant thirsty city on the sprawling desert floor below us.

Plenty of tourists and modern-day treasure hunters had come up this rugged dirt road. We drove slowly around the tortuously narrow and winding road that often had sheer drops on either side. It was clearly a road to be driven carefully and with plenty of time to spare.

We stopped briefly at a dirt-track turn off, and I got out and took a piss in the dust. There was a rusted and faded sign saying it was the turn-off to the Reavis Ranch Trailhead.

Apparently the original desert rat, Elisha Reavis, lived here in the back area of the Superstitions, along what is now Apache Lake and the Salt River. You may recall that Reavis was known as the "Hermit of Superstition Mountain" and there is little else in the steep desert rocks that mark this entire area of the Four Peaks. Little remains of his early homestead. This mysterious man was quiet and known to keep many secrets, as did most desert rats and mountain men of his time. He may have known of many of the secrets around the Superstitions.

Some of these sites may now be under water.

Three artificial lakes have been created along the Salt River; I have already mentioned Apache Lake and Canyon Lake. Farther up on the Mogollon Rim is the massive concrete wall of Roosevelt Dam and then a few miles beyond, the artificially created Roosevelt Lake.

It is unfortunately very possible that certain ancient Hohokam-type sites, including ancient mines and vaults such as the one described by Pauly are now submerged.

As we wound slowly up the dirt road that precariously threaded the cliffs of the Salt River Valley, I wondered about the supernatural entities that were said to lurk in the Superstitions. Was there really an underground world beneath the stone towers of the Superstition cliffs as Maria Jones thought?

Did the people who lived there have something to do with Pauly's ancient treasure vault guarded by the skeletons of seven-foot giants? As we turned a sharp corner at five miles an hour that dropped off into the ravines below, I couldn't help think that the high plateau above held some of the answers to the lost civilization the once ruled central Arizona.

As we crept along the steep dirt road, it boggled my mind that there might actually be secret caves, tunnels or vaults within the rugged granite mountains that make up the area thoroughly searched by many treasure hunters. Were there special burial vaults cut into solid granite like at the Valley of the Kings near Luxor, Egypt? During the Hohokam period, were there special ceremonial areas among the granite walls of the Superstitions?

High up in the eastern part of the Superstitions is a mysterious stone circle. The stone circle is similar to others in the west, such as the famous Wyoming

Medicine Wheel. Like other stone circles, it appears it was used for ceremonial purposes and observation of the stars and planets.

The extreme lack of water in the highlands of the Superstitions makes any form of life there very difficult to sustain. Except for occasional rain pools, there are no streams or other forms of water; there is very little game or anything else to eat. The Superstitions make a good lookout post to the surrounding areas below and little else.

As we came around a sharp bend in the dirt road I could see some of the tall granite spires in the rearview mirror.

I said to Jennifer, "The Superstitions would be good for tunneling into. If someone wanted to tunnel into very hard and stable granite, the Superstitions would be a perfect place with the many spires, cliffs and granite faces."

"Who would be able to do something like that?" she asked, bands of light glinting on her sunglasses.

"Well, the Egyptians cut into solid rock, like at the Valley of Kings. The ancient Peruvians also cut into solid rock to make vaults and tunnels. The Olmecs were able to carve giant blocks of basalt, even harder than granite. The Egyptians and others carved basalt as well," I answered her.

I went on, "Though the Superstitions may be a lousy place for gold mines, it was a good place for tombs, secret tunnels and vaults, and possibly diamond or emerald mines. If advanced ancient cultures like the Olmecs, Zapotecs, Phoenicians, Hindus and Chinese were coming to America and interacting with the Hohokam culture of Arizona, they may have put royal tombs in the Superstitions!"

"I can agree with that," said Jennifer. "In the Old World, kings and queens and other royalty were often interred in very fancy rock-cut tombs."

The Superstitions were originally named for their

lightning, thundering and mysterious phenomena. Not only have people disappeared within the area, as well as been gruesomely murdered, others have reported being followed by invisible entities who made noises and "foot sounds" without being seen at all. We had received a letter from a World Explorers Club member who reported she had experienced just such incidents while hiking.

The Superstitions are a granite wonderland of fractured andesite, caverns and caves. It would be hard to distinguish between artificial caves or natural ones. Tunnel entrances, leading to stone-carved rooms with passageways may well await explorers in some remote part of the Superstition Mountains. Perhaps some of these tunnels led to windows on the sheer cliffs of the western wall of Superstitions.

Does something like a Mount Shasta secret city exist in the Superstitions? Some people think so! Another bizarre tale told of the Superstitions involves a crystal skull that could be seen inside of a fissure of rock inside a cave somewhere in the northeast Superstitions. I had recently met with an acquaintance named Rob Boomer in Phoenix for lunch, and he showed me an old newsletter from the 1990s called *Treasure Hunter Confidential*. In it was a story entitled "Skull Cave" by Chuck Kenworthy. Kenworthy is also the author of the book *Treasure Secrets of the Lost Dutchman* (a self-published book).

Kenworthy claims that in 1984 a group of six men discovered a cave that had room for five men to stand inside. This cave is "120 feet upslope from Labarge Wash." From this cave the men could look through a rock fissure about a foot wide and see a crystal (or glass) skull that is wedged inside the fissure as if it was guarding a room beyond. If fact, the men claimed that they could see a room beyond the skull and in this room they could see seven wooden boxes.

According to Kenworthy, the men attempted

to use dynamite to blast the fissure into a wider passage, but only got two feet into the fissure that they thought was about 50 feet in length. Presuming that there were other entrances to the cave, they threw smoke bombs into the far room in the fissure, hoping to see the smoke come out of a hidden entrance. Unfortunately, they did not block up the entrance to the cave that they already knew about, and all the smoke came back out the entrance where they stood. They claimed that a steady breeze came through the fissure and it was impossible to keep a match lit.

Boomer told me that he was going into the Superstitions with a friend the next day to camp for a few days and look for the cave. I wished him good luck and then heard from him a few days later. He phoned me and told me that they looked for several days but could not find the mysterious cave. Did it ever exist? Why would Kenworthy make it up? The Superstitions, as they say, abound in strange stories.

Our plan after stopping at Roosevelt Lake was to circle around the Superstitions on the Apache Trail—here Arizona Route 88—to Globe. From there, we would normally circle around back to Phoenix by going through Florence Junction on the southern side of the Superstitions, but this time we were heading east on Route 70 to the San Carlos Indian Reservation.

We stopped in Globe, and toured the abandoned city of Besh-Ba-Gowah. These mysterious ruins are attributed to the Salado culture who lived on the southern edge of Globe around 1150 AD. Besh-Ba-Gowah has stone walls that are 30 feet high and well-laid-out streets. As Jennifer and I wandered through the buildings and eventually the museum, I was impressed by the workmanship. Were these people also connected to the Hohokam? Were the Hohokam also connected to the Hopi and Zuni and other pre-Apache groups in the area?

This vast region, which includes such Apache reservations as the San Carlos and White Mountain, has mysterious ruins deep within the forests. This huge area—larger than most Eastern states—also contains the Sitgreaves National Forest, the Tonto National Forest, the Apache National Forest, the Fishhooks Wilderness, the Coronado National Forest and other designated areas. It is possible that there are ancient cities still to be discovered within its bounds.

The one site that we know about is the mysterious Kinishba Ruins, near Fort Apache Junction on the Fort Apache Indian Reservation. These ancient buildings—pre-Apache—are at the base of the mini-range known as the Sawtooth Mountains, south of Show Low and Pinetop.

Kinishba is a 600-room pueblo with high stone walls for many-storied buildings and large patios, much like the Zuni and Hopi pueblos. The name we use for the ruins comes from the Dene (Apache) words that mean "Brown House."

The builders of these ruins, whose name is apparently unknown, would probably be related to the Hopi and Zuni tribes. These tribes are quite different, though peaceful. They speak different languages, but do live relatively near each other.

Kinishba—whatever it was originally called—was thought to have been built by some sort of ancestral Pueblo group about the year 1300. Though it is not commonly thought that they were associated with the Hohokam, it would seem that they probably were.

It was dark as we drove down Arizona Highway 260. We turned south on Highway 373 to Greer. Greer was an old mining town and hunting lodge at the end of a mountain valley. We had dinner at the Molly Butler Lodge, and then after a couple of drinks at the bar, we went to bed. Exhausted and falling asleep, I looked out the window through the pine trees and up at the stars. I wondered about the Superstition Mountains. Had this area contained the burial vaults, and gold mines, of the Hohokam? Did the Hohokam cut—like the ancient Egyptians— secret vaults within the granite rock faces that exist all over the Superstitions? As a waxing moon began to rise over a distant ponderosa pine, anything seemed possible.

An old advert for the Apache Trail.

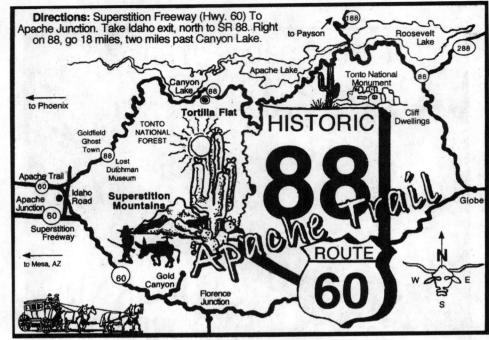

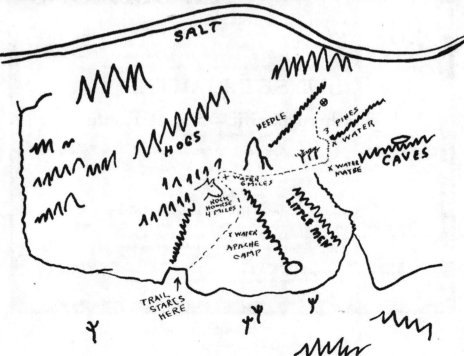

A 1938 map to the Lost Dutchman sold to tourists.

To ROOSEVELT DAM

SALT

RIVER

FISH

Mormon
Flat

Tortilla Flat

Apache
Gap

To PHOENIX

WILLOW SPRS. CR.

LA BARGE

BOULDER CAN.

NEEDLE CAN.

NEW FORK

WHITE FORK

CR.

**Lost Dutchman &
Peralta Locality**

CAN.

SUPERSTITION

MTNS.

SUPERSTITION   MTNS

Weaver's
Needle

Miner's
Needle

RANDOLPH CAN.

FRAZER CAN.

To PHOENIX

60
70

80
89

WHITLOW CAN.

QUEEN

CR.

60
70

To SUPERIOR

N

Florence
Jct.

80
89

To FLORENCE

HORTON ALLEN

An early 1960s map of the Superstitions from *Desert Magazine*.

373

Top: Jacob Walz in New York. Bottom: A general store in Mesa, 1898.

Top: An old photo of Weaver's Needle. Bottom: The Julia Thomas map.

Top: Maria Jones and Louie. Bottom: Bob Corbin with Maria Jones and Louie.

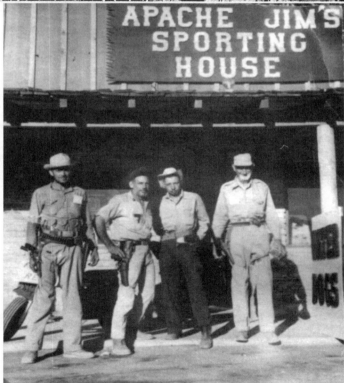

Top: Aerial photo of Weaver's Needle (on left). Bottom: Piper's Army in 1960.

An early photo of the Tumlinson stones purported to show the way to the mine.

An early photo of the backside of one of the Tumlinson stones.

Elisha Reavis, the Hermit of the Superstitions, in a photo taken circa 1894.

379

The mysterious Kinishba Ruins deep in the Fort Apache Indian Reservation.

An old print of primitive mining in the Southwest with its use of log ladders.

7.

NORTHERN ARIZONA

THE EGYPTIAN CITY
OF THE GRAND CANYON

Gold, gold, gold—
They'll do anything for gold.
Gold, gold, gold,
Got to have Mackenna's Gold.
—*Old Turkey Buzzard*, sung by José Feliciano

🌀 🌀 🌀

After spending the night in Greer, we drove south on Arizona Highway 180 through Alpine to New Mexico Highway 180 (I like to call it "Lost Highway 180") on our way to visit the ghost town of Mogollon. The ghost town is along the west side of Mogollon Mountain, a broad peak over 10,000 feet high, and its surrounding peaks. Mogollon Mountain is named after the governor of the Spanish colony of Nuevo Mexico in the early 1700s, Don-Juan Ignacio Flores Mogollon. The proper Spanish pronunciation of Mogollon is "moh-goh-YOHN" but in local usage it is often said "muggy-YON."

In 1870, when the New Mexico and Arizona Territories were part of the United States, a U.S. Army sergeant named James Cooney scouted in the area and discovered a rich vein of silver near Mogollon

Mountain. Cooney kept his find a secret until he finished his military service and then returned to stake his claim and open his silver mine.

His efforts eventually made him rich and created a small mining town named Mogollon deep in the canyons of this remote part of New Mexico, literally straddling the Continental Divide. We took a very scenic but slightly dangerous side road, Highway 159, into town. Mogollon is now basically a ghost town, though some signs of genuine human life can be seen around the few scattered cabins. There are still a few residents, and the town supposedly hosts an art fair on weekends.

Spreading out from Mogollon Mountain is the famous Mogollon Rim. This precipitous ridge of cliffs, canyons, craggy granite mountains and plentiful water is in many ways the defining landmark of the state of Arizona, running from southeast Arizona past Flagstaff. It was my intention to drive from Mogollon Mountain northwest along the Mogollon Rim to the Hopi Mesas and on to the Grand Canyon. My quest was to research a story about Egyptians in the Grand Canyon—a story of a legendary vault of treasures and mummies that had been revealed in a newspaper article in 1909, and, I had begun to suspect, a story that had been kept secret by the ancient and mysterious Hopis.

Why was this treasure never heard of again? It is a mystery that strikes deep into the golden heart of the lost cities of the Southwest: treasure found in man-made caves at a secret location in the Grand Canyon, a secret society that protects this treasure, and the ultimate cover-up of an astounding archeological find. Even today, no clear answers have emerged. Was the newspaper story an elaborate hoax? A confused tale of a more mundane discovery? Or, had the Egyptians, Chinese, Romans, Phoenicians and others actually visited the American Southwest? It was like the plot of a fantasy western movie... indeed, I was to discover this aspect of the story as well!

The Egyptian City of the Grand Canyon Newspaper Story

Had an Egyptian navy crossed the Pacific or Atlantic and come to Arizona? Could they have left an Egyptian tomb in the Grand Canyon, something similar to those found in the Valley of Kings near Luxor, Egypt, and similar to the one supposedly found in the Superstitions? An article published on the front page of the *Phoenix Gazette* on April 5, 1909 claimed that just such an Egyptian rock-cut cave was found!

While many mummies have been found in Egypt, very few were in pyramids—and those that were dated from the later historical periods. The older pyramids dating from the early dynasties (or before!) show no signs of funerary use. Mummies in Egypt are most often found in rock-cut tombs in desert canyons. The tombs often feature tunnels going deep underground with various rooms and passageways along the way. Multiple mummies are often found in one tomb, and the crypts of the wealthy and royalty were filled with precious items and everyday necessities to ease the dead person's continued existence in the afterlife.

According to the article in the 1909 *Phoenix Gazette*, a necropolis of mummies and artifacts similar to an Egyptian tomb was found in the Grand Canyon! An explorer named G. E. Kinkaid apparently discovered a series of catacombs complete with statues, swords, vessels and mummies in 1908 (the exact date of the discovery is not given). As we shall see, Kinkaid may not have been the first explorer to have seen this "cave." The account of Kinkaid's adventure was reproduced as a chapter entitled "Citadel of the Grand Canyon" in Joseph Miller's 1962 book *Arizona Cavalcade*.

The *Phoenix Gazette* article, dated April 5, 1909, starts with four headlines, and then continues through

383

a most amazing account. The story is quoted below in full:

EXPLORATIONS IN GRAND CANYON
Mysteries of Immense Rich
Cavern Being Brought to Light
JORDAN IS ENTHUSED
Remarkable Finds Indicate
Ancient People Migrated From Orient

The latest news of the progress of the explorations of what is now regarded by scientists as not only the oldest archaeological discovery in the United States, but one of the most valuable in the world, which was mentioned some time ago in the *Gazette,* was brought to the city by G. E. Kinkaid, the explorer who found this great underground citadel of the Grand Canyon during a trip from Green River, Wyoming, down the Colorado river, in a wooden boat, to Yuma, several months ago.

According to the story related to the *Gazette,* the archaeologists of the Smithsonian Institute [sic], which is financing the explorations, have made discoveries which almost conclusively prove that the race which inhabited this mysterious cavern, hewn in solid rock by human hands, was of oriental origin, possibly from Egypt, tracing back to Rameses. If their theories are born out by the translation of the tablets engraved with hieroglyphics, the mystery of the prehistoric peoples of North America, their ancient arts, who they were and whence they came, will be solved. Egypt and the Nile, and Arizona and the Colorado will be linked by a historical chain running back to ages which stagger the wildest fancy of the fictionist.

Under the direction of Professor S.A. Jordan,

384

the Smithsonian is now pursuing the most thorough explorations, which will be continued until the last link in the chain is forged. Nearly a mile underground, about 1,480 feet below the surface, the long main passage has been delved into, to find another mammoth chamber from which radiates scores of passageways, like the spokes of a wheel. Several hundred rooms have been discovered, reached by passageways running from the main passage, one of them having been explored for 854 feet and another 634 feet. The recent finds include articles which have never been known as native to this country, and doubtless they had their origin in the orient. War weapons, copper instruments, sharp-edged and hard as steel, indicate the high state of civilization reached by these strange people. So interested have the scientists become that preparations are being made to equip the camp for extensive studies, and the force will be increased to thirty or forty persons.

Before going further into the cavern, better facilities for lighting will have to be installed, for the darkness is dense and quite impenetrable for the average flashlight. In order to avoid being lost, wires are being strung from the entrance to all passageways leading directly to large chambers. How far this cavern extends no one can guess, but it is now the belief of many that what has already been explored is merely the "barracks", to use an American term, for the soldiers, and that far into the underworld will be found the main communal dwellings of the families. The perfect ventilation of the cavern, the steady draught that blows through, indicates that it has another outlet to the surface.

Kinkaid was the first white man born in Idaho and has been an explorer and hunter all his life, thirty years having been in the service of the Smithsonian. Even briefly recounted, his history sounds fabulous, almost grotesque:

First, I would impress that the cavern is nearly inaccessible. The entrance is 1,486 feet down the sheer canyon wall. It is located on government land and no visitor will be allowed there under penalty of trespass. The scientists wish to work unmolested, without fear of the archaeological discoveries being disturbed by curio or relic hunters. A trip there would be fruitless, and the visitor would be sent on his way. The story of how I found the cavern has been related, but in a paragraph: I was journeying down the Colorado River in a boat, alone, looking for mineral. Some forty-two miles up the river from the El Tovar Crystal canyon, I saw on the east wall, stains in the sedimentary formation about 2,000 feet above the river bed. There was no trail to this point, but I finally reached it with great difficulty. Above a shelf which hid it from view from the river, was the mouth of the cave. There are steps leading from this entrance some thirty yards to what was, at the time the cavern was inhabited, the level of the river. When I saw the chisel marks on the wall inside the entrance, I became interested, securing my gun and went in. During that trip I went back several hundred feet along the main passage, till I came to the crypt in which I discovered the mummies. One of these I stood up and photographed by flashlight. I gathered a number of relics, which I carried down the Colorado to Yuma, from whence I shipped them to Washington with details of the discovery. Following this, the explorations were undertaken.

The main passageway is about 12 feet wide, narrowing to nine feet toward the farther end.

About 57 feet from the entrance, the first side-passages branch off to the right and left, along which, on both sides, are a number of rooms about the size of ordinary living rooms of today, though some are 30 by 40 feet square. These are entered by oval-shaped doors and are ventilated by round air spaces through the walls into the passages. The walls are about three feet six inches in thickness. The passages are chiseled or hewn as straight as could be laid out by an engineer. The ceilings of many of the rooms converge to a center. The side-passages near the entrance run at a sharp angle from the main hall, but toward the rear they gradually reach a right angle in direction.

Over a hundred feet from the entrance is the cross-hall, several hundred feet long, in which are found the idol, or image, of the people's god, sitting cross-legged, with a lotus flower or lily in each hand. The cast of the face is oriental, and the carving shows a skillful hand, and the entire is remarkably well preserved, as is everything in this cavern. The idol most resembles Buddha, though the scientists are not certain as to what religious worship it represents. Taking into consideration everything found thus far, it is possible that this worship most resembles the ancient people of Thibet. Surrounding this idol are smaller images, some very beautiful in form; others crooked-necked and distorted shapes, symbolical, probably, of good and evil. There are two large cactus with protruding arms, one on each side of the dais on which the god squats. All this is carved out of hard rock resembling marble. In the opposite corner of this cross-hall were found tools of all descriptions, made of copper. These people undoubtedly knew the lost art of hardening this metal, which has been sought by chemists for centuries without result. On a bench running around the workroom was some charcoal and other material probably used in the process. There is also slag and stuff similar to matte, showing that these ancients smelted ores, but so far no trace of where or how this was done has been discovered, nor the origin of the ore.

Among the other finds are vases or urns and cups of copper and gold, made very artistic in design. The pottery work includes enameled ware and glazed vessels. Another passageway leads to granaries such as are found in the oriental temples. They contain seeds of various kinds. One very large storehouse has not yet been entered, as it is twelve feet high and can be reached only from above. Two copper hooks extend on the edge, which indicates that some sort of ladder was attached. These granaries are rounded, as the materials of which they are constructed, I think, is a very hard cement. A gray metal is also found in this cavern, which puzzles the scientists, for its identity has not been established. It resembles platinum. Strewn promiscuously over the floor everywhere are what people call 'cats eyes,' a yellow stone of no great value. Each one is engraved with the head of the Malay type.

On all the urns, or walls over doorways, and tablets of stone which were found by the image are the mysterious hieroglyphics, the key to which the Smithsonian Institute hopes yet to discover. The engraving on the tablets probably has something to do with the religion of the people. Similar hieroglyphics have been found in southern Arizona. Among the pictorial writings, only two animals are found. One is of prehistoric type.

The tomb or crypt in which the mummies were found is one of the largest of the chambers, the walls slanting back at an angle of about 35 degrees. On these are tiers of mummies, each one occupying a separate hewn shelf. At the head of each is a small bench, on which is found copper cups and pieces of broken swords. Some of the mummies are covered with clay, and all are wrapped in a bark fabric. The urns or cups on the lower tiers are crude, while as the higher shelves are reached the urns are finer in design, showing a later stage of civilization. It is worthy of note that all the mummies examined so far have proved to be male, no children or females being buried here. This leads to the belief that this exterior section was the warriors' barracks.

Among the discoveries no bones of animals have been found, no skins, no clothing no bedding. Many of the rooms are bare but for water vessels. One room, about 40 by 700 feet, was probably the main dining hall, for cooking utensils are found here. What these people lived on is a problem, though it is presumed that they came south in the winter and farmed in the valleys, going back north in the summer. Upwards of 50,000 people could have lived in the caverns comfortably. One theory is that the present Indian tribes found in Arizona are descendants of the serfs or slaves of the people which inhabited the cave. Undoubtedly a good many thousands of years before the Christian era a people lived here which reached a high stage of civilization. The chronology of human history is full of gaps. Professor Jordan is much enthused over the discoveries and believes that the find will prove of incalculable value in archaeological work.

One thing I have not spoken of, may be of

interest. There is one chamber the passageway to which is not ventilated, and when we approached it a deadly, snaky smell struck us. Our lights would not penetrate the gloom, and until stronger ones are available we will not know what the chamber contains. Some say snakes, but others boo-hoo this idea and think it may contain a deadly gas or chemicals used by the ancients. No sounds are heard, but it smells snaky just the same. The whole underground installation gives one of shaky nerves the creeps. The gloom is like a weight on one's shoulders, and our flashlights and candles only make the darkness blacker. Imagination can revel in conjectures and ungodly day-dreams back through the ages that have elapsed till the mind reels dizzily in space.

In connection with this story, it is notable that among the Hopi Indians the tradition is told that their ancestors once lived in an underworld in the Grand Canyon till dissension arose between the good and the bad, the people of one heart and the people of two hearts. Machetto, who was their chief, counseled them to leave the underworld, but there was no way out. The chief then caused a tree to grow up and pierce the roof of the underworld, and then the people of one heart climbed out. They tarried by Paisisvai (Red River), which is the Colorado, and grew grain and corn. They sent out a message to the Temple of the Sun, asking the blessing of peace, good will and rain for the people of one heart. That messenger never returned, but today at the Hopi villages at sundown can be seen the old men of the tribe out on the housetops gazing toward the sun, looking for the messenger. When he returns, their lands and ancient dwelling place will be restored to them. That is the tradition.

390

Among the engravings of animals in the cave is seen the image of a heart over the spot where it is located. The legend was learned by W. E. Rollins, the artist, during a year spent with the Hopi Indians. There are two theories of the origin of the Egyptians. One is that they came from Asia; another that the racial cradle was in the upper Nile region. Heeren, an Egyptologist, believed in the Indian origin of the Egyptians. The discoveries in the Grand Canyon may throw further light on human evolution and prehistoric ages.

And so ends the *Phoenix Gazette* tale of underground chambers, crypts, granaries, copper urns, broken swords plus mummies, poisoned gasses and assorted snakes. What became of these amazing artifacts? Since the find did not become the history-altering event it should have been, one has to wonder what exactly happened.

The few facts given in the story do not check out well. The Smithsonian denies any connection with a G.E. Kinkaid or S.A. Jordan during this time period. The State of Idaho denies that Kinkaid was the first white baby born there, although Kinkaid or Kincaid are common family names in the state. On the other hand, the *Phoenix Gazette* did run a previous story on Kinkaid's journey down the Colorado, a brief account published March 12, 1909 that ends with the sentence, "Some interesting archeological discoveries were unearthed and altogether the trip was of such interest that he will repeat it next winter, in the company of friends."

In addition, John Wesley Powell, who famously navigated the Colorado River in the years around 1870, reported some things that are very interesting in light of Kinkaid's story. In his 1875 book *Exploration of the Colorado River and its Canyons*, he mentions that while passing through the Marble Canyon area of the Grand Canyon he saw up in the cliffs a lot of large, hollowed-out caves, and suggestions of massive "architectural forms." At a later point, he reports:

> I walk down the gorge to the left at the foot of the cliff, climb to a bench, and discover a trail deeply worn into the rock. Where it crosses the side gulches in some places steps have been cut. I can see no evidence of its having been traveled for a long time. It was doubtless a path used by the people who inhabited this country anterior to the present Indian races—the people who built the communal houses of which mention has been made. I returned to camp about three o'clock and find that some of the men have discovered ruins and many fragments of pottery; also etchings and hieroglyphics on the rocks.

So it would seem that the great explorer Powell's accounts corroborate the existence in the Grand Canyon of stone-carved steps that climb the walls, hollowed-out caves in the cliffs and hieroglyphics left by some ancient race!

Did the Smithsonian actually perform the explorations described by Kinkaid, and then engineer some kind of archeological cover-up reminiscent of the last scene in the movie *Raiders of the Lost Ark* (where the Ark of the Covenant is placed inside a crate in one of the Institution's giant warehouses never to be seen again)?

One interesting suggestion is that, while the discovery was real, the archeologists might not have been. These men may not have been working for the Smithsonian out of Washington D.C. at all, but merely claiming to be doing so. This may have been a cover-up for an illegal archeological dig that was raiding the ancient site and claiming legitimacy from a very distant, venerated institution. It may have proved difficult, in 1909, to check on the credentials of the archeologists, and there is no hint that anyone was actually trying to do this. These men may well have disappeared shortly after the article appeared, but not to Washington D.C. as we might suppose, but rather to San Francisco, Los Angeles or Denver.

The Lost Adams Diggings and Mackenna's Gold

I was lost in thought about the 1909 newspaper story when I suddenly caught a glimpse of a rusty old sign out of the corner of my eye.

"Did that sign say Ghost Rock Ranch?" I asked Jennifer, glancing over at her.

"Is that what what said?" she said, looking up from her book.

I glanced back at the pine trees and the sign that was now gone from sight. "I thought that sign on that dirt road said Ghost Rock Ranch."

"I thought that Ghost Rock Ranch was supposed to be in Arizona. We're in New Mexico."

"Well, it's a lot like the old Adams Diggings. It was supposed to be in Arizona, but might have been in New Mexico. What is this town coming up?"

We had left the ghost town of Mogollon about an hour before, winding up and around the hairpin curves out of the remote canyon.

Jennifer glanced at the map. "Reserve. Reserve— but that's still in New Mexico. I thought we were going to back to Arizona."

I took a deep breath and gripped the steering wheel tighter, "Well, I think we'll stop here for a bit."

Small, one-story ranch houses were on either side of the road as I began braking into Reserve. It was here that Ed Adams had first appeared with his remarkable story of a solid gold ledge and other

393

fabulous treasure.

Coming into town I thought about several movies I had watched recently on DVD. One was the 1958 film *The Lone Ranger and the Lost City of Gold* in which the Lone Ranger visits a lost Aztec city inside a mountain where an incredible vein of solid gold is found. Like most of the Lone Ranger stories, it takes place around Reserve and Silver City and the New Mexico-Arizona border. This was the only film to follow the original *The Legend of the Lone Ranger* movie, both starring Clayton Moore and Jay Silverheels. It made me think of Maria Jones and her belief that people lived inside Weaver's Needle, along with the Dutchman's gold. It also reminded me of the 1909 *Phoenix Gazette* story describing the elaborate city carved into the cliffs of the Grand Canyon that could hold 50,000 people.

Another film with even more similarities to the *Gazette* story was *Mackenna's Gold* (1969) starring Gregory Peck, Omar Sharif, Telly Savalas, Edward G. Robinson and others. *Mackenna's Gold* is one of most exciting westerns ever made and it takes place around the Grand Canyon and the area north of Flagstaff and west of the Hopi Mesas. The film combines elements familiar to aficionados of lost treasure lore including: the story of an Egyptian cavern system, a secret canyon, the lost John D. Lee gold mine, and a man named Seth Tanner among others. The film, in the introduction, says it is based on the treasure story of the Lost Adams Diggings, a fabulous vein of gold in a box canyon that "ran for miles." Apaches kept the canyon a secret and killed any prospectors who might ever enter. The legend of Mackenna's Gold is told by a narrator (Edward G. Robinson) at the beginning of the film:

A thousand years ago in the Southwest,
There was an Apache Legend
Told about a hidden canyon, guarded by the Apache

394

Gods, and rich with gold.
As long as the Apaches kept the canyon a secret and
never touched the gold,
They would be strong — powerful.
That was the legend.
When the Spanish Conquistadors came,
They searched for that canyon.
They called it Canyon del Oro, meaning Canyon of Gold.
But they never found it.
Three hundred years later the Americans came.
They heard about the legend.
But they called it the Lost Adams.
That was because a man named Adams
claimed he had seen it.
But whether he did or not—
He never saw anything again,
Because the Apaches burned out his eyes.
Everybody knew about it—that legend,
And a lot of people believed it.
The Canyon del Oro — the Lost Adams.
Then, for awhile back there in 1874,
They called it Mackenna's Gold.

A Vein of Gold and a Secret Canyon

Jennifer and I swung into the local bar in Reserve, an old cowboy watering hole by the name of Uncle Bill's. The bar had a small crowd on that Tuesday afternoon, and a friendly local nodded to me as Jennifer and I took two seats near the door and ordered drinks. Reserve was an interesting town to me, as it was here that history records that Adams stumbled into town in late 1864 and told his now-famous story of a fabulous secret canyon of gold.

Reserve is the county seat of Catron Country, the largest, and least populated, county in all of New Mexico. Almost directly west of Socorro, Reserve was founded by Mormon cattlemen during the early 1860s. Originally, the town was called San

Francisco, as it consisted of three plazas along the small San Francisco River, which ran into the Rio Grande. Each of the plazas was dotted with saloons and shops. The upper plaza area is today's town of Reserve, having taken on that name when the local headquarters of the U.S. forest reserve were located in the town.

Reserve became famous in 1884 when it was the site of one of New Mexico's most notorious gunfights. Elfego Baca, an amazingly tough deputy sheriff from Socorro, had come to town to deal with the unruly cowboys belonging to the large Slaughter Ranch. These Texas cowboys were rough and tough, especially with Hispanics, and had actually castrated a poor Mexican who had wandered into town. The local sheriff felt powerless to deal with the nearly 150 drunk and disorderly cowboys from the Slaughter Ranch. He called for help from Socorro, and Elfego Baca rode into town.

Baca immediately confronted one cowboy, who shot his hat off before being arrested by the deputy. He then confronted a group of cowboys who were demanding their friend's release and would not back down. Baca counted to three and then shot and killed one of the men. The others fled town, but only until the next morning.

The Slaughter Ranch cowboys returned with nearly 80 men to do battle with the stubborn deputy from Socorro. Baca, with both guns drawn, faced the men and then backed into a small log cabin with wide cracks between the logs and a rickety door. One cowboy, named Bert Herne, went forward to get Baca out of the cabin and was shot dead with both guns blazing from Baca's twin pistols. Thus began a 33-hour siege that was to become famous throughout the west.

The Texans alternated between firing into the small cabin and going to a saloon where they bolstered their courage by doing shots of Red Eye. They fired thousands of shots through the walls and door, and even dynamited a corner of the cabin. Elfego Baca fired back at them through the walls and door, killing four of the cowboys and wounding eight. Thirty-three hours after the siege had begun, Baca surrendered on the condition that he did not have to give up his guns, and that the entire group would ride together into Socorro where he would formally surrender. The procession took off with the cowboys in the lead so Baca could keep his guns on them.

After he spent four months in jail, the trial of Elfego Baca was moved to Albuquerque. It was determined in court that the first man Baca had shot during the siege, Bert Herne, had been a Texas outlaw with a price on his head. Further testimony revealed that some 4,000 shots had been fired into the cabin. Everything inside, including a broomstick, had holes through it except for the hero himself and a statue of Saint Ana. The door to the cabin was introduced as evidence, and it alone had almost 400 bullet holes in it. Baca was acquitted of all charges and he remained prominent in New Mexico law and politics as sheriff and later district attorney of Socorro until his death at age 80. Walt Disney produced a film on his amazing life in 1959, *The Nine Lives of Elfego Baca.*

"So is this the bar where the cowboys shooting at Elfego Baca were drinking?" I asked the bartender, an older man with spectacles, as I put down my mug of beer.

"No, that was down at one of the other plazas in Reserve," said the bartender; I suspected that he might actually be the bar owner. "This bar wasn't built until 1920."

"So this isn't the bar that Ed Adams stumbled into with his story of the lost gold canyon?" I asked, a teasing smile on my face.

"Nope," he said wiping the bar, "that would be some other bar, too. A long, long time ago."

The Adams Gold, or Adams Diggings, was a famous "lost" (some wondered if it had ever been found) bend in a stream rich with gold nuggets and sand, plus a vein of pure gold on the canyon wall. This famous lost treasure was generally thought to be in New Mexico, somewhere near the Arizona border. It has generally been placed in the area north of Silver City and Reserve, and south of the Gallup area. However, in the film partially based on the Adams story, *Mackenna's Gold*, they are clearly in the area around present-day Cameron, Arizona, which is at the mouth of the Little Colorado River Gorge.

The story of the Adams Diggings, which I will tell briefly, starts in northwestern New Mexico. According to Ed Adams, he and his partner, Joe Davidson, located gold in August of 1864. Adams said he and Davidson were part of a bunch of men on a beaver hunting expedition that started out from Magdalena, New Mexico (near Socorro) and traveled in a northwesterly direction. Somewhere between Magdalena and old Fort San Rafael (later Fort Wingate), they decided to establish a semi-permanent camp before the cold winter weather set in. They chose a site near a little stream.

Adams reported that one of the men noticed gold in the stream and excitedly revealed his discovery to the rest. Adams, who knew a little more about mining than his companions, thought the gold had probably washed into the stream from a rich outcropping above their camp. The next morning, he and Davidson left camp and traveled up the canyon hoping to discover the mother lode. Not for away, they did indeed find a vein of ore. Shortly afterward, they claimed, their camp suffered a surprise attack by Apaches and, as the men were totally unprepared, the Indians massacred everyone there.

He and Davidson heard the gunfire and, suspecting its cause, took cover in bushes on a nearby hillside. After hiding for several hours, the two men cautiously made their way over the hill and saw that the Apaches had departed, probably believing they had killed all the men of the expedition. All of the mules and horses were gone.

They buried the dead and then knocked a few pieces of gold-bearing ore off an outcropping of quartz they believed to be the mother lode. Adams then claimed they made their way to Fort San Rafael, where they asked for aid to go back and find the gold but were refused by the officer in charge. They then made their way on foot and after perilous hardships and a great deal of suffering, arrived in the small town of Reserve.

They showed off the ore to several people and then, after borrowing some money on the strength of its richness, bought horses and went to Pima, Arizona (near Safford) where Adams had friends who had enough money to properly outfit an expedition to return to the place where he had found the mother lode.

He organized an expedition and traveled from Pima to Alma, between Silver City and Reserve and then to the location where he thought he had found the gold. But through some freak of nature or loss of direction, members of the expedition couldn't find any gold, or even the place where the men had been massacred and buried. What explanation did Adams give for this? He explained that both he and Davidson were notoriously poor in remembering directions.

California Gold from an Apache Massacre

Ed Adams continued to tell his tale to anyone who would listen in the late 1800s. Other exploration parties have set out in search of the riches since then, but to this day, the location of Adams Diggings remains as much a mystery as when Ed Adams first started telling his story.

The famous Texas historian J. Frank Dobie devotes nearly half of his 1928 book *Apache Gold and Yaqui Silver*[32] to a discussion of the Adams Diggings. While he casts some doubt on the story, he generally seems to think that there is such a lost vein of gold being protected by the Apaches. Dobie's book was probably one of the sources for *Mackenna's Gold*.

There is a different version of the story, however.

One of the men who heard old Ed Adams relate his tale in the early 1900s was young Bob Lewis. Ed Adams, by this time, was an old prospector while Bob Lewis was a young one. Bob paid close attention to what Ed Adams said. In 1936, he was interviewed to obtain his oral history, for he had lived his life as a prospector, a cowboy and a frontier peace officer. His version of the Adams Diggings story is now stored at the Library of Congress, and differs substantially from the one told by Adams.

Lewis prefaced his remarks stating, "There never was a bigger old liar than Ed Adams. He'd tell a lie when the truth would fit better. He was used to bragging and stretching the truth."[33]

Lewis proffered different information about what happened at the Adams beaver hunting camp. He maintained that just about dark, in August of 1864, a caravan traveling from California joined the camp the Adams party had set up. Two days before, the caravan had stopped at Fort San Rafael and told the commanding officer they were transporting eighty thousand dollars in placer gold from California to the eastern states. Lewis said this caravan was never seen again after the time the Adams party was wiped out by the Indians. Lewis thought they probably did camp with the Adams party and suffered the same fate as did the Adams men at the hands of the Apaches.

But Lewis believed that Adams and Davidson, taking advantage of the opportunity fortune had provided them, devised a plan that fateful night to ambush the caravan the next morning and make off with the booty. Lewis stated, "I believe Davidson throwed in with Adams and the two of them made plans to hijack the California outfit and steal their gold."

The men in a caravan would usually get up an hour or two before daylight to make an early start, Lewis explained. Adams and Davidson could have made some excuse to leave the camp early in the morning, perhaps saying they were going to gather wood, as wood was scarce in that country.

Adams and Davidson may have gone down country to find a suitable place for waylaying the California outfit. While they were gone, as daylight came (the time Indians usually attacked), Apaches did attack the camp. Every man was killed and all the provisions, including the horses and pack animals, were stolen.

When the caravan didn't show up at the ambush site, Adams and Davidson probably returned to camp and viewed the carnage—and likely congratulated themselves on their luck to be absent from camp! Rummaging around among the disheveled remains of the supplies, Adams must have found at least some of the gold the California outfit had been carrying. As proof of this, Lewis said he later saw a handful of this gold Adams had saved (before he buried the rest) and it was of a quality entirely foreign to that part of New Mexico but identical with gold he'd seen from diggings in California. Lewis remembered, "The pellets were about the size of a pinhead, up to as big as a pinto bean, and I knew that nobody ever found that kind of gold in the parts of New Mexico I have

401

prospected over."

Lewis surmised that Adams and Davidson buried the gold in a secret place. He disputed Adams and Davidson's story that they made their way afoot to Fort San Rafael to report the massacre and to ask for aid to go back and help them relocate the mother lode they'd found.

Lewis said, "I do not believe this part, because in March, 1890, I was at a saloon where Adams, who had been drinking pretty heavy, related his story of how he had gone to Fort San Rafael, in August, 1864, to ask the commanding officer for aid to give decent burial to the massacred party and offer him and Davidson protection while they tried to relocate the rich gold deposits.

"But there happened to be an old, retired Army officer in the saloon who had listened intently to Adams' story—this was Captain Sanborn—who said he was the commanding officer of Fort San Rafael in 1864, and to his knowledge Adams had never set foot in that Fort at anytime in his life."

Lewis concluded that Adams and Davidson never went to Fort San Rafael at all, but traveled a considerable distance to the south to avoid it. Instead, they limped into Reserve, sore-footed and half-starved. It was in Reserve that Adams showed a couple of pieces of ore in quartz form that was exceedingly rich, and stated that it was from the lode he had found before the Indians had massacred his party. He made no mention of the California expedition.

Lewis added that the samples Ed Adams was showing in Reserve were the exact same ones he had earlier shown in Magdalena before he ever left the town on the beaver hunting trip in 1864. Adams told a story in Magdalena that he had given an Indian some whiskey for the samples and had promised him more if he would show him where he got the samples. Lewis said that these samples must have come from one of the richest mines he ever heard of. But to his knowledge, no ore of similar quality has ever been found, and the Indian who gave the samples to Adams would have been long since dead by then. Where the Indian found these samples will probably never be known.

Of course, Adams didn't dare show any of the placer gold he had stolen from the California caravan and buried. At this point, he and Davidson separated, Adams going to Pima, Arizona, to obtain money and supplies from friends to outfit an expedition to return to salvage the gold. Davidson went on a supposed visit to see some relatives in Louisiana. Adams was successful in his attempt to raise an expedition, and he sent for Davidson who returned from Louisiana—the expedition met him in Alma, a town south of Reserve.

This expedition never found any gold, and Adams later made several solitary trips in search of it, but said he never had any luck. Several other expeditions were organized and went forth to find the Adams Diggings, but all met with defeat.

Alma became the gateway to the mining town of Mogollon, which we had just visited in its ghostly remnant. Mogollon wasn't started until the 1890s, so during the time of Ed Adams, it would have been wilderness and it may have been in this area that Adams did some of his prospecting.

A couple of locals heard us talking and told us that there was a place up north of Quemado that was called Adams Diggings on detailed maps.

"Its on County Road 603. It's just the remains of some cabins and fences," said an older lady with white hair and glasses. "Supposedly, Adams lived up around there. But I don't think he found any gold."

Her friend, with black hair in a ponytail said, "Well, Pete Hidalgo said he saw Bigfoot up at Sand

403

Flats. That's something."

"Bigfoot, around here?" I asked. "Where is Sand Flats?"

"It's just past Aragon, about 20 miles east of here," she said.

I looked it up on the map and could see a dirt road going north through Sand Flat Canyon. At the end of the road was a placed called Lost Cabin. "Well, this sounds pretty interesting," I thought. But we weren't headed there right now.

We thanked the ladies, paid our bill and pulled out of Reserve. We headed northwest back to Alpine, just over the border in Arizona. At an elevation of 8,050 feet Alpine is surrounded by the beauty of the Apache-Sitgreaves National Forests. Alpine seems more like northern New Mexico or Colorado, with swift running streams that pass through huge ponderosa pine, aspen and fir forests. The desert is only a few hours away from Alpine, in many directions, but here it is lush and green.

After a night at one the several lodges in town, we headed north on Highway 180 toward the towns of Eagar and Springerville at the headwaters of the Little Colorado River. That was the area of the lost canyon of gold, I felt as I gripped the steering wheel and we passed the small town of Nutrioso. Somewhere up the Little Colorado River was the treasure that was the granddaddy of all Southwest treasure tales.

Ed Adams' stories of a lost canyon of gold and the nuggets that he showed willing listeners in saloons from Socorro and Magdalena to Reserve, Silver City and Safford, were a mixture of fact and fiction. It seems odd that Adams never cashed in those last few gold nuggets—rather, he used them to get people to buy him drinks in every saloon in southwest New Mexico and southeast Arizona. Those nuggets must have bought him a lot of drinks.

But there is another story here, one that goes far

beyond any version of the lost Adams Gold. This is the story of a lost city in the Grand Canyon— the story I think is being told in *Mackenna's Gold*. Though *Mackenna's Gold* says it is about the lost Adams find, I believe it is really about the secret caverns, mines, and artifacts of the Grand Canyon. This story involves the Lost John D. Lee Mine, Seth Tanner, secret Hopi "caves," possible Toltec mines and a leftover Egyptian presence. It is a twisted tale of early explorers, renegade Mormons, tough desert rats, and a wary native population of Hopis and Apache-Navahos who guard in their own ways the ancient secrets.

The Secret Catacombs on the Little Colorado

I braked for one of the few stoplights in the small Mormon farming town of Eagar. Further up was the cowboy town of Springerville and beyond that was the Sacred Zuni Mountain—a place where Zuni spirits are said to go after they die. While the Zuni Reservation is in New Mexico, the sacred Zuni Mountain is in Arizona, near the spot where the Zuni River meets the Little Colorado.

Pulling into the small town of Springerville, we stopped at the local museum and historical society on Main Street. We signed their guest book, and read some of the newspaper clippings on the wall.

One from the *Los Angeles Times-Washington Post* news service was worth quoting. It describes how the archaeologist John Hohmann, now closely associated with the Casa Malpais site, had rappelled down a rope into a fissure of basalt in July of 1990 and discovered an intricate series of passages and rooms that had been modified by the mysterious "Mogollon culture" into underground tombs for the interment of the dead. The remains of these people were apparently mummified, possibly naturally by the dry climate.

Said the article:

> Hohmann had stumbled across a catacomb, an underground burial site composed of chambers and vaults. "We don't expect to see such things in this region," said archaeologist James Schoenwetter of Arizona State University in Tempe. "To my knowledge, this is the only site north of Mexico that has catacombs."
>
> "The discovery is significant because information about how primitive cultures regard their dead sheds light on the groups' religious, social and cultural lives. In the case of the Mogollon and other prehistoric peoples of the Southwest, such information is virtually non-existent," Hohmann said.
>
> "The fact that the Mogollon took such pains to bury their dead suggests a complex culture with a rich spiritual life," he added.
>
> Although Hohmann calls the burial area a catacomb, and dictionary definitions support his terminology, some researchers are less comfortable with the title. "What it conjures up in my mind is something on the order of the Christian tombs under Rome," said archaeologist Bruce Donaldson of the U.S. Forestry Service in Springerville. The Christian catacombs required extensive excavations and feature masonry burial vaults, carved niches and elaborate stonework.
>
> The Mogollon burial ground is nowhere near as complex, Donaldson argued, and calling it a catacomb will evoke a distorted image.
>
> To a certain extent, Hohmann agrees. The Mogollon made only minor modification

inside the catacombs—far less than the early Christians did. But the Mogollon invested a great deal of effort in constructing a vaulted ceiling over many of the fissures and building entryways that restrict access.

"That's always been our focus," Hohmann said, "the amount of architectural work and energy that went into creating the man-made components over this fissure system, and not what was inside the chambers. Just how these chambers were created was an amazing fact to us [along with] the impressive amount of stonework and society effort that went into that creation."

The catacombs lie below a surface area of two to three acres. Some of the rooms are as much as 20 feet high and 30 feet long, while others are substantially smaller. Hohmann said that they contain hundreds of skeletons, but much of the contents have been removed by vandals and pot-hunters.

Hohmann has neither photographed nor mapped the catacombs, and they are not open to the public—or for that matter, anyone else. He is doing his best to keep the locations of the entrances secret. "We need to remember Native American religious concerns," he said. "We're not going to disturb those remains or anything that is in them in any way, shape or form," he said.

The discovery of the catacombs has brought new attention to the little-explored Casa Malpais, which now appears to have been a major trading or religious center built at the height of the Mogollon civilization. It is the largest and most recently occupied village constructed by the Mogollon, hunters and farmers who mysteriously disappeared around

1400, perhaps as the result of a catastrophic drought.

The site, at an altitude of 7,000 feet in the White Mountains near the New Mexico border, also features one of the largest kivas—a religious structure—in the Southwest and three types of American Indian architecture that are not normally found contemporaneously.

Although Hohmann's excavations at Casa Malpais have barely scraped the surface, they are expected to provide new insight into the Mogollons' cultural sophistication and daily life.

The Mogollon inhabited Casa Malpais for perhaps 150 years before moving on, most likely after disease and starvation had sharply reduced their numbers during a severe drought that baked the Southwest for more than a century.

The most distinctive archaeological features are found on the upper-most terrace, which was completely walled in to restrict access. The Great Kiva is about 50 feet square and 10 feet high, constructed of closely fitted rocks and stones.

This curious discovery made national news in the early 1990s, but has largely been forgotten. The catacombs inside the Casa Malpais are described as a burial ground for hundreds of skeletons. Nowhere in the article does it say that the dead are "mummies," but are they? It would not be unusual if the Casa Malpais remains were mummies. Rather, it would be unusual if they weren't. Mummified remains have been found at Mesa Verde in Colorado, at Hovenweep in Utah, and at locations in Arizona.

However, as we talked with the folks at the Springerville Museum, they told us that there hadn't been any mummies found at the site that they were aware of. Basically, they said, the whole burial aspect of the catacomb find had been a big exaggeration on Hohmann's part.

I was stunned by this, as it seemed like something way too detailed to have been completely fabricated. Nevertheless, they insisted, that such must have been the case. Other artifacts had been discovered, and some were on display in the small museum. We were also told that there was some connection with ancient Zuni to the northeast, and that Frank Hamilton Cushing, who lived with the Zuni for many years, was thought to have been brought to Casa Malpais as far back as 1882.

Catacombs, Mummies and "The Thing"

The Springerville case demonstrates the fascination and controversy over mummies found in the American Southwest. I was staggered that there was now a denial of any mummies having been found at Casa Malpais. Had they never been there, or was there some archeological cover-up occurring?

An Arizona mummy that is easy to visit can be found along Interstate 10 near Wilcox, between Benson, Arizona and the New Mexico border. Along this stretch of largely empty desert is the curious roadside attraction called "The Thing." This gas station-museum-tourist trap is the ultimate in the old time billboard advertising phenomenon. Anyone familiar with Wall Drug, South Dakota will recognize the M.O.—pick a spot where nothing else even remotely interesting is located, and put up dozens of billboards over a far-flung area to pique the traveler's interest to stop there (when they finally reach it). Billboards along Interstate 10 for miles in either direction ask the driver and his family, "How far is it to The Thing?" or simply "What is The

Thing?" Other billboards would eventually inform you that it was only ___ (fill in random figure) miles to "The Thing," which was always a relief to hear.

In fact, "The Thing" is a mummified woman, with a child, and according to unofficial literature from the gift shop, was from "around Flagstaff." I believe that the area "around Flagstaff" that the woman and child are from is the Grand Canyon. Incredibly, it is possible that "The Thing" is actually a relic from the Egyptian or Hindu-Buddhist catacombs there! It remains on display to this day. Pay $1 to see "The Thing"!

Were "The Thing" and other mummies of the Southwest part of the early trans-Pacific Egyptian-Hindu-Buddhist-Chinese influence, I wondered as we drove north across the Little Colorado River leaving the town of St. Johns.

We were headed north on New Mexico Highway 191, toward Interstate 40 that runs from Albuquerque through Gallup, New Mexico and on to Holbrook, Winslow and Flagstaff, Arizona. The afternoon was getting late and dark clouds appeared in the sky. Soon it was pouring rain. I turned on my lights and the windshield wipers as I slowed down in the torrent. There were no other cars on the road, but it was hard to see through the driving sheets of rain that were all around us. This was one of the big thunderstorms that the area was famous for—thunderstorms that created flash floods and could be quite dangerous.

Suddenly we saw a lone building in the rainy darkness ahead. A neon light in the window indicated that it sold beer. Lettering on the roof said it was the "Witch Well Bar and Saloon."

"Let's stop here and wait for it to stop raining," suggested Jennifer. Nodding, I pulled off the highway and into the parking lot. There were a few pickup trucks in the small gravel lot.

410

"Strange that there should be a lonely bar out in the middle of nowhere like this," I commented.

"Hmm, the Witch Well. That's a curious name for a bar," said Jennifer.

I could hear a generator running as I stepped out of our 4x4. The door to the saloon was open and we scurried right in.

Inside it was dark and smoky. An attractive woman stood behind a long bar, and in front of a long series of glass door refrigerators. They were, naturally, filled with beer. The woman asked us what we wanted.

I looked around, and then at Jennifer.

"What do you want?" I asked her.

"I'll have a Miller Lite," she said.

"I'll have a Coors," I added.

The bar was dark, and three rowdy guys and a girl were playing pool in the other room. They called out an order for shots of tequila. The sound of billiard balls clacking resounded as our bartender brought us our beers.

I paid and asked her about the sacred Zuni Mountain nearby.

"Oh, I don't know about that," she said. "But I am from Zuni." She looked at the man sitting at the bar with us. He was a nicely-dressed Native American in his 30s. He was drinking a Budweiser.

"Yes, the sacred Zuni mountain is out there to the west," he said. He lifted his cowboy hat and brushed back his thick, black hair. "I'm from Farmington, New Mexico, myself. Just running a power line crew near Eagar. I'm heading back that way, but all this rain and the flooded roads have got me thinking I might spend the night around here instead." Just where he thought he might stay in the middle of this desolation was a fair question, but I didn't ask it.

The rain continued unabated and pounded on

411

the roof. I looked out the window, but there weren't any other buildings as far as I could see. Nor were there any towns around the area. There was just this bar. The Witch Well.

I had a couple of strong swigs of my beer. Boy, this was a strange place. Maybe mummies had been found around this area, years ago, I ruminated. Suddenly a pickup truck with three men crammed into the front seat pulled up to the liquor store take-out window, and the bartender went to serve them. I turned to the power line foreman sitting next to me.

"It looks like there's a flash flood in the road. I guess we'll have to watch it as we head toward the Interstate."

"Are you out here on vacation?" he asked.

"Well, we're driving down the road looking for lost cities and ancient mysteries," I told him, taking a slug of beer. "Have you ever seen 'The Thing'?" I asked him.

"Yeah, I've seen those signs. What is it?" he said, putting his beer down.

"It is a mummy—supposedly from Flagstaff. Do you know any tales of lost treasure or ancient ruins around here?" I asked.

"Yes," he said. "There are some interesting ones in all this area."

We talked for some time, and I brought up the Adams Diggings, and the story from the movie *Mackenna's Gold*.

"Yes, I saw that movie," he said. He agreed that it might have been based on a real story. We discussed the movie and the legend about a lost vein of gold in a secret canyon, and the possibility that it was located somewhere in the Grand Canyon. I told him my theory that this secret canyon might have something to do with the Egyptian caverns in the Grand Canyon, and the fact that Egyptian mummies were not really found inside pyramids, but inside rock-cut tombs and other underground sites.

We speculated that if there was a catacomb of mummies near Springerville, maybe they were ancient Zuni mummies. Why couldn't there be a similar catacomb full of mummies in the Grand Canyon?

"It could be true," he said, taking a swig of beer. "It could be true."

It was now dark and the rain continued to pour down outside. It was time to hit the road and head down that lonesome highway. In this case, our destination was the Hopi Reservation and the canyon of the Little Colorado River.

> *In Xanadu did Kubla Khan*
> *A stately pleasure dome decree*
> *Where Alph, the sacred river, ran*
> *Through caverns measureless to man*
> *Down to a sunless sea.*
> —Samuel Taylor Coleridge, *Kubla Khan*

Seth Tanner and the Secret Hopi Cave

We made our way through the storm to Interstate 40 and went west to Holbrook, passing the Petrified Forest on the way. With the rain thankfully easing up, we checked into a motel and spent a quiet night reading. We didn't have much choice of activity, since the deluge had drowned the cable and there was no TV. The next day, with the sun ablaze, we drove north into Hopi Country.

In *Mackenna's Gold*, Omar Sharif plays the villain, a bandit named, in fact, Colorado. Early in the movie, Colorado has captured Sheriff Mackenna (Gregory Peck), who has seen a map of the route to the secret canyon. With his hands tied, Mackenna and the bandit gang cross a precarious rope-bridge across a narrow, but very deep canyon. With Ray Harryhausen-type special effects in this brief sequence, the group makes its way across the rickety bridge and end up on the north side of what I believe to be the Little Colorado River Gorge. Today, this area is a largely off-limits and roadless part of the Kaibab National Forest, and part of it lies in the Navaho Reservation.

It is somewhere beyond this crossing that Mackenna and Colorado find a secret canyon with a rich vein of gold along one of its walls, and ruins high up on a cliff which must have been part of an ancient mining operation. It is an exciting and imaginative western that claims to be based on fact—but perhaps the facts in this case are even more bizarre than the fictional movie itself.

One of the most important books (in fact, one of the *only* books) on the Grand Canyon and secret mines and tunnels is the book *Quest for the Pillar of Gold*.[86] This compilation of scholarly papers on ancient mines, mineral wealth, and modern-historical mining ventures in the Grand Canyon gives us the tantalizing reality behind all the fantastic stories. One would think that a geological wonderland such as the Grand Canyon would offer a wealth of minerals, including gold. There is definitely an ancient salt mine and other sites that are sacred to the Hopi. And tales of gold, such as the John Lee gold mine, were well-known stories that circulated around the Grand Canyon. Was one of the ancient mines in the Grand Canyon an Egyptian gold mine?

Indeed, with ancient mining, by definition, there would be ancient tunneling! Placer gold could be found on the surface in riverbends, but following a vein of gold—even in ancient times—would mean tunneling into a canyon wall. A number of early

414

pioneer mines in the Grand Canyon were created in this way, sometimes necessitating ladders and walkways on sheer cliffs.

Prospectors were expecting to find veins of gold in the Grand Canyon, but astonishingly, to date no substantiated gold claims have been recorded. Part of the reason for this is that the canyon was difficult to explore on the best day, and deadly during flash floods or chance meetings with Navaho or Hopi warriors.

Among the prospectors was a man who apparently discovered a secret cave in the Grand Canyon or Little Colorado Canyon and was then captured by Hopi warriors. His name was Seth Tanner.

Seth Tanner (1828-1918) was a Mormon miner and trader who had gone west with Brigham Young in 1847 when the Mormons settled Salt Lake City. From Salt Lake City he was sent out to set up a small Mormon colony in San Bernardino, California and it was rumored that he and his brother Myron had some luck in the California gold fields. Tanner also spent some time in San Diego, investing in a coal business that reportedly did not do too well. He returned to Utah and was married; later, he was sent on a scouting expedition to northern Arizona. In 1876, he moved his family to an isolated cabin on the Little Colorado River near Tuba City. The cabin was strategically located on old trade routes, and Tanner, who got along well with both the Hopi and Navajo and spoke their languages, set up a trading post. Because of his burly countenance and extraordinary strength, the Navajos called him "Hosteen Shush" (Mr. Bear).

Tanner became a well-known Grand Canyon character and *Quest for the Pillar of Gold* gives some of his early mining history. He at one time had a mine in an area of heavy quartzite in Seventyfive

Mile Creek. He first filed claims in 1890, and worked several claims in the following years. He improved ancient Hopi trails into the Canyon, and one main access point is called Tanner Trail even today. At some time during his explorations, he discovered a hidden Hopi cave (or mine?) of treasure. Tanner was captured by Hopi warriors at a secret cave in the Grand Canyon sometime around 1896.

His final fate is told in *Grand Canyon Stories: Then and Now*,[87] a book published by the famous magazine *Arizona Highways*. The brief story includes a photo that tantalizes us: Seth Tanner—a grizzly old man who is blind! According to the book, the Hopi blinded Tanner by throwing a potion in his eyes because he was "the discoverer of a cave containing sacred religious treasures of the Hopi tribe, which no white man was allowed to see." The book maintains that it would normally have meant death to see the secret cave, but Tanner was spared because his mother was Hopi. This is highly unlikely, since he was born in New York; it is much more likely he had taken a Hopi wife or had some other significant relationship to cause the tribe to debate his fate. He remained a prisoner off the Hopi, however, and was put in a cave and supplied with daily provisions for years. Supposedly, Tanner became accustomed to his blindness and began to venture out. But because of his alarming appearance, he frightened villagers around Cameron and Tuba City. To scare him off, they would throw water on him. Thinking it was more of the dreaded Hopi potion that had blinded him, he would run back to his cave.

At some point, he must have been released. The photo of him as a blind man is known to have been taken some time shortly after the year 1900. He died near Tuba City in 1918. He is still a famous character in the area, and visitors to the Grand Canyon can see Tanner Springs, Tanner Wash and Tanner

Crossing in addition to Tanner Trail. His children and grandchildren became wealthy trading post owners in the Tuba City and Gallup areas. But part of Seth Tanner remains a mystery and he never divulged the terrible secret or incredible treasure he had seen.

What did he see in the Grand Canyon or Little Colorado Canyon that meant death? Did Tanner discover in the early 1890s the caves full of statues and mummies that were to be reported years later in 1909 by the *Phoenix Gazette*—ancient caves filled with forgotten Egyptian artifacts, now sacred to the Hopi?

The similarities between the real-life Seth Tanner and the fictional Ed Adams in the film *Mackenna's Gold* are striking. As we have seen, Ed Adams was a real historical figure, but the fact that he was not blind and the description and location of the Adams Diggings make it seem unlikely that he was the real person upon which the film character was based. That person is actually Seth Tanner—a man who had seen the "Canyon of Gold" and had his eyes burned out for it.

As we headed up into the Hopi Mesas I caught a glimpse of Holbrook in the rearview mirror. We were headed for Walpi and then Cameron. As we passed through Jeddito and Keams Canyon I looked at the ancient pueblos on the Hopi Mesas and wondered if the Hopi were the descendants of these special visitors from Egypt. The word Djed, or Jedd, is a common word in ancient Egyptian and was associated with the god Osiris. Was the Hopi language possibly derived from ancient Egyptian? Perhaps the ancient Hohokam language as well? To my knowledge, no research has been done on this subject, but Gary David (author of *The Orion Zone* and *Eye of the Phoenix*) has found some evidence that the Hopi language shows some traces of Sumerian, and it has been posited that the Zuni language is derived from Japanese.

One curious thing to note is that, prior to the European expansion into New Mexico and the American Southwest, the Hopi and other Pueblo Indians hunted with boomerangs, as did the ancient Egyptians; modern-day Australian Aboriginals still do. Prior to the Spanish introducing sheep, cattle, and horses, the Hopi hunted jackrabbits and birds with their boomerangs. Jackrabbits are still a popular food in parts of Arizona and New Mexico, and a boomerang can be seen at the museum at the Aztec Ruins in Aztec, New Mexico.

Was the use of boomerangs brought to the Southwest by early Egyptian explorers and settlers? A trunk of boomerangs was found in the rock-cut tomb of Tut-Ankh-Amen, the young Egyptian king discovered at the Valley of Kings in southern Egypt— at a site much like the supposed citadel in the Grand Canyon.

If the Egyptians had sought out the Grand Canyon as some sacred spot where the River Styx disappeared into the underworld of Set, they may have built small outposts and forts for journeys to the Grand Canyon. Exactly such places exist, such as Wupatki and Tusayan, both ancient cities near the Grand Canyon. Wupatki and other nearby ruins are close to the Little Colorado River, and are thought to have been built by the ancestors of the Hopi, though some archeologists dispute this. Signs at the Wupatki Ruins Museum run by the National Park Service are ambiguous as to who the builders of this remarkable little town—complete with a ball court—really were.

But, if there was at one time an Egyptian presence down deep inside the Grand Canyon, one would expect to find some sort of town or outpost down on the canyon floor. And in fact, there is such a place,

418

though to date it has not been tied to the Egyptians. Excavations started in 1967 at an archeological site known as Unkar, where the Unkar stream meets the Colorado River creating the Unkar Delta. Unkar Delta is just downstream (west) of where the Little Colorado meets the main Colorado River, deep inside the canyon.

After years of research and digging, the discoveries were published in a scholarly book called *Unkar Delta: Archeology of the Grand Canyon*[88] by Douglas Schwartz of the School of American Research out of Santa Fe, New Mexico. His team cataloged building foundations, cut stone blocks and broken pieces of pottery. Because of occasional super-floods in the Grand Canyon, much of the Unkar Delta would have been periodically washed away. Schwartz concludes in his book that the Unkar Delta was inhabited circa 900 AD.

One would think that if Unkar had originally been built by Egyptians, it would have been built around 500 BC, if not before. Perhaps earlier dates will eventually come from Unkar, or perhaps this earlier city, if it ever existed, was washed away thousands of years ago, rather than beneath the current Unkar.

And what of the curious name Unkar? It could be an Egyptian word, perhaps a corruption of Ankh-Ka or Ankh-Ra. Is this a reference to the sun god Ra? One of the ancient Southwest legends held that the sun rose and set inside the Grand Canyon, and indeed, one could see the sun set into the canyon if one stood on the eastern rim looking west. Modern maps of the Grand Canyon indicate an Egyptian influence from somewhere—just look at all of the many Egyptian names (and some Hindu) given to the distinctive geological features of the Grand Canyon: Osiris Temple, Tower of Ra, Tower of Set, etc. Is it just a coincidence that the Grand Canyon has been given so many Egyptian names?

❧ ❧ ❧

The river flows, it flows to the sea
Wherever that river goes
That's where I want to be— Flow river flow
Let your waters wash down
Take me from this road
To some other town
—The Byrds, *Ballad of Easy Rider*

Quicksand, the Sipapu and the Hopi Salt Mines

We stopped for a short time to visit the Hopi Villages at Walpi and Oraibi. Old Oraibi is thought to be the oldest inhabited town in the United States, going back to at least 1150 AD. When the early archeologist Victor Mindeleff visited Oraibi in 1882-83, he found that it was the largest of the Hopi pueblos and contained nearly half of the entire Hopi population. In 1968, there were only 167 people living in the ancient town, most Hopis having moved to Hotevilla or to Kiakochomovi, also called New Oraibi, or other small towns closer to schools.[98]

Oraibi is probably much older than originally thought, and it may have been much larger in ancient times. Archeologist Harry James says that wherever a hold is dug, evidence of an ancient city beneath Oraibi is found. He that some years ago a road was being cut through the edge of the village and it exposed a huge trash mound at the bottom of which were found "buried remains of even older and better built houses."[98]

So, the very ancient, pre-1100 AD buildings were larger and better built? Perhaps they were as well made as the Hohokam structures, or even the mysterious buildings at Wupatki and Tuzigoot.

Among the many curious customs of the Hopi is the wearing of an unwed woman's hair in circles on either

420

side of her head. This unusual hairstyle is also found on the ancient statue found in Elche, Spain known as "Our Lady of Elche." E.M. Whishaw gives a drawing of what the full statue looked like in her book, *Atlantis in Spain*.[99]

The woman in the statue, who is associated with Atlantis and Tartessos, according to Whishaw, wears her hair in wheels on either side of her head. Is there some relationship between this statue and the Hopis and their ancient customs? This is also the way that Princess Leah of the *Star Wars* films wears her hair, perhaps a nod from George Lucas to the Hopis and "Our Lady of Elche."

We continued our drive on Highway 264 to Tuba City and then headed west on Highway 160 and then south on Highway 89 to Cameron. As we came into Cameron, I got a good look at the green valley that the Little Colorado was creating. Soon after Cameron, the valley becomes a narrow gorge that the Little Colorado runs through on its way to meeting the Colorado River in the Grand Canyon. We crossed the river on a big steel bridge, the last bridge over the Little Colorado before it sinks into a canyon. We were now in Seth Tanner country. As noted above, because Tanner spent a lot of time in the area, a number of important features are named after him. On the Little Colorado, near Cameron, a rock crossing used in the 1800s was named after Tanner. The Little Colorado is famous for quicksand when water is flowing, and the important crossing was located a mile upstream from the present highway bridge.

Looking west up the canyon of the Little Colorado, I thought of how Seth Tanner must have struggled through quicksand as he scoured this canyon for gold— and had instead found a wondrous cave of treasure (mummies, artifacts and swords?) so hallowed, he was blinded for what he saw. A canyon deep in the Little Colorado Gorge is named after him: Tanner Canyon,

421

a secret box canyon somewhere deep inside those towering cliffs.

As we drove west along the Little Colorado gorge I wondered about the Hopi and their creation stories, which you may remember were mentioned in the 1909 *Gazette* article. The Hopi believe the world has been destroyed several times, but each time certain good people were saved. Twice they were given harbor underground while the earth above was destroyed, and were supported by the Ant People. The Hopis believe that they emerged from the underground world of the Ant People at the end of the Third World from a hole in the Grand Canyon known as the "Sipapu."

The Sipapu is near the Hopi Salt Mines and both areas are off-limits to hikers, generally. The Forest Service has issued a few, rare photos of these places, with little explanation. They are reprinted here. The Sipapu is said to be a lava dome from a hot spot in a volcanic-hot spring area, a bit like a dry geyser at Yellowstone National Park. It is a hole in the ground (sometimes smoking) and could easily help foster creation myths.

The Hopi Salt Mines comprise another ancient area that maintains significance today. Salt was an important trade item within ancient cultures and salt mines, like obsidian mines, were considered highly important. The famous salt mines near Cuzco in Peru were used by the Incas, and the Romans paid their soldiers with a ration of salt. Throughout northern Mexico and the American Southwest, "payment" could be made with turquoise, gold dust (often inside a goose quill), salt, gourds, jade, crystals, fossils and other small trade items. Tanner would have been familiar with the Hopi Salt Mines, and this knowledge may have led him to the secret caves that ultimately became his doom.

Jennifer and I pulled up to the parking lot at Desert View on the southern rim of the Grand Canyon, inside the Grand Canyon National Park. The spectacular view of the meeting of the Grand Canyon and the Little Colorado spread out in front of us.

Nearby were the cliffs where the Tanner Trail begins to descend down the steep canyon walls, switch-backing its way to the bottom. The Tanner Trail starts at Lipan Point on the Desert View Drive. If a hiker were to hike down Tanner Trail to the bottom of the canyon, he would then be in the general vicinity of the Hopi Salt Mines, the Sipapu and the Unkar Delta.

Archeologists largely agree that many sections of the Tanner Trail were originally part of old Anasazi and Hopi Indian routes into the Canyon. As Seth Tanner worked and improved the path, it became known by his name, as did the part of the Grand Canyon first entered by the trail. It is somewhere in the vicinity of Tanner Canyon that Europeans first "discovered" the Grand Canyon. The first of the known European explorers to visit the area was Garcia Lopez de Cardenas, who was shown the canyon by his Hopi guides in 1535, while in search of the fabled Seven Cities of Gold. Today, hikers can visit Cardenas Butte, accessible via the Tanner Trail, named in his honor.

Tanner's mine was just off the trail at a spot near Palisades Creek, upriver from Tanner Delta. The trail was used by other prospectors as well, and a number of small copper mines existed inside the Grand Canyon in the late 1800s.

In the early days prospectors and others also used the trail to cross the Canyon. Most notoriously, horse thieves used the trail to drive horses into the Canyon— so many, in fact, that Tanner Canyon was also called Horsethief Canyon. It is reported that this side-canyon was used by horse thieves to hide stolen horses on their way into Utah. While in this secret canyon, the brands on the horses would be changed; the horse thieves got out of the canyon by taking the Nankoweap Trail up to the North Rim of the Little Colorado. Was this Tanner Canyon-Horsethief Canyon part of the puzzle to the location of the Egyptian catacombs?

We stood on the rim of the Canyon at Tanner Trail. Somewhere out there was a cave entrance, perhaps now with a locked iron door over it that would lead into an underground world of marvelous treasures—so the story goes.

Could the Egyptians have actually made voyages to Mexico and the American Southwest, such as a trans-Pacific voyage? According to an Associated Press story released on January 28, 2006 an Italian-American archeological team announced that it had found the remains of well-preserved Egyptian ships in five caves along the Red Sea. The ships were dated to be about 4,000 years old.

An inscription on some wooden boxes indicated that the artifacts were from the land of Punt. The press release said that artifacts recovered included 80 coils of rope, and that the Supreme Council of Antiquities director in Egypt, Zahi Hawass, said the remains showed that the ancient Egyptians were "excellent ship builders" and had a fleet capable of sailing to remote lands.

It has been suggested that the Egyptians, and other seafarers, voyaged across the Indian Ocean to Australia and Indonesia and then out into the Pacific: to Fiji, Tonga, Samoa, Tahiti and the Americas. Perhaps Punt was Australia or even Mexico or Peru. The mysterious Olmecs would have been part of this oceanic trade and fit into the time frame of 1000 to 2000 BC.

Also related to them are the Champa, or Cham (pronounced Kam) of Vietnam and other areas of Southeast Asia. The Cham were Hindu-Buddhists who built megalithic cities at My Son and other places in Vietnam. They were great seafarers and they maintained a huge navy off the coast of Da Nang (in central Vietnam) called Cu Lao Cham. It is known that these ocean-going traders travelled far up the coast of China and to coastal cities all over Southeast Asia,

Indonesia and India from this island. It is thought that they also traveled across the Pacific and made contact with ports along the Pacific coast of North America. The great city of My Son is thought to have been founded around 200 AD, but the Cham peoples and their ships may be much older than that. King Solomon apparently used a similar navy for the famous journeys to Ophir, where he obtained gold, peacocks, apes and such.

Were the artifacts discovered in the Grand Canyon actually Buddhist artifacts brought by the Champa? They could easily be mistaken for Egyptian artifacts, as there is a strong similarity between the statues of the two cultures, and, in fact, the ancient Egyptians called their country "Kam" or "Kamet." Were the Cham a Southeast Asia version of Egyptian-Phoenician seafarers?

It was amazing that the 1909 story said that the tunnel-vault system goes for "nearly a mile underground... Several hundred rooms have been discovered... The recent finds include articles that have never been known as native to this country... War weapons, copper instruments, sharp-edged and hard as steel, indicate the high state of civilization reached by these strange people."

And what of Jordan and Kinkaid mentioned in the article? In a letter that I received in 2005, signed by a "Colin," I was told that there is a mention of an E.K. Kincaid in correspondence archives for the Smithsonian Institution, Record Unit 189, Box 68 of 151, Folder 8. Said Colin, "These are records dating from 1860-1908, which is in the correct time frame for the Kincaid mentioned in the *Phoenix Gazette*. It is a possibility that different first initials were used and that this is the folder that may contain the valuable information needed to locate the site." Perhaps Kinkaid had gone to Washington D.C. after all. Was Jordan someone else, not actually from the Smithsonian, as he had claimed?

As the great orange ball of fire set over the canyon, a large moon was rising to the north. Soon the Canyon would be lit by the eerie moonlight that makes it glow in a luminescent fashion. For another night, at least, the secrets of the Grand Canyon would be safe from outsiders to her vertical walls and rippling waters.

Ancient Aztec Mines of Jerome and Tuzigoot

We drove back down Highway 89 and stopped at Wupatki, a site of large stone ruins, including a well-made ball court. There are over 800 identified ruins spread around the many miles of desert in the vicinity. Clearly, this was once a major city, very near the Grand Canyon.

The National Park gift shop and museum at the site says that the builders are a complete mystery. Hopi elders claim that Wupatki was occupied by them in the past. Archeologists say that the builders are the Sinagua-Anasazi, but do not know where they came from. It is known that they were connected by major trails, such as the one called the Palatkwapi Trail, with the Hohokam and other cultures even farther south.

We passed through Flagstaff and drove south on Interstate 17 back to the World Explorers Club in Cottonwood, passing through the red rocks and vortices of Sedona on the way. At the clubhouse, I was informed that the Sci-Fi Channel had produced and shown a film in 2008 (released on DVD in May 2009) entitled *The Lost Treasure of the Grand Canyon*. The film starred Shannen Doherty and Duncan Fraser. According to the plot synopsis on Amazon: "In the early days of the 20th Century, an expedition led by Dr. Samuel Jordon traveled deep into the Grand Canyon in search of a long-rumored hidden city. The entire team disappeared. But when Jordon's archaeologist daughter Susan (Shannen Doherty) leads a rescue

426

party into the uncharted valley, she will discover an ancient civilization ruled by savage warriors, human sacrifice and a mythological monster that feeds on carnage. Even if the explorers can survive the deadly trials of the Aztecs, will they find a way to escape the ultimate ritual of evil?"

"Hey, look at this," I said to Jennifer. "They've made a film based on the lost city of the Grand Canyon, and the archeologist who originally found the ruins is named Jordon, just like S.A. Jordan in the original *Phoenix Gazette* article."

"Wow," she said, looking at the computer with me. "They must have taken the idea from that magazine article you wrote. That's great! I'll get you that DVD for your birthday." That sounded good to me.

The next day we visited the nearby ruins of Tuzigoot and I began to unearth evidence that this area was once connected with the Aztecs and their presumed lost gold and silver mines. Nearly any discussion of lost cities and ancient mysteries of the American Southwest needs to include the genuine mystery of where Mexican precious metals and stones came from.

We have seen so far that the location of gold and silver mines—as well as turquoise, jade and obsidian mines—used by the Aztecs, as well as by the Toltecs and the Hohokam, were from the area of Northern Mexico and Arizona.

In fact, it appears that some of the great Aztec-Hohokam gold mines were located around Jerome, Cottonwood, Tuzigoot and the surrounding Blue Mountains. This area of gold, silver and copper was exploited in ancient times and is still being exploited to this day. Jerome has been, in its various incarnations, an ancient mining town, a Wild West boomtown, a ghost town, and now a very special tourist town. Some researchers think that Jerome is the most haunted town in America.

Our story of the Aztecs and their mountain of gold begins when Hernando Cortes (1485-1547) and his band of 400 conquistadors defeated the Aztecs in a series of wars between 1519 and 1521. Montezuma allegedly ordered that what could be saved of the Aztec treasure should be sent to the northern part of Mexico or the American Southwest as this was the location of their homeland, Aztlan. This mysterious homeland has never been positively identified, but many archeologists believe that the Aztecs originally came from the region of what is now Arizona and New Mexico.

Cortez had originally taken the Aztec capital of Tenochtitlán (a city on an island in the center of a lake) without a battle. During a royal audience, Cortez took Montezuma captive, and began to rule Mexico through the captured king. However, Cortez had renounced allegiance to Governor Velázquez of Cuba and in 1520 the conquistador had to return to the Mexican coast to defeat a Spanish army sent by Velázquez under Panfilo de Narváez. This Spanish army had been sent to remove Cortez from power and establish Velázquez's "legitimate" government.

While Cortez and Narváez battled for control of Mexico on the coast, Tenochtitlán was under the control of Cortez's general, Pedro de Alvarado. The Aztecs rallied against the Spanish invaders and drove Alvarado and the Spanish forces out of the city. It wasn't until 1521 that Cortez was able to retake the city, and with that battle the destruction of the Aztec Empire was complete.[1]

It was during this brief period of independence in 1520 that Montezuma ordered his buildings stripped of their gold, silver, and jewels. Gold ingots were supposedly taken from the treasury and seven caravans of one hundred porters, each carrying approximately 60 pounds of gold, were sent to the north. When the plague of the Spaniards had passed, the gold would return to Tenochtitlán.

The mystery of this vast gold treasure, seven caravans with approximately 100 million dollars in treasure apiece, has never been solved. Even the area in which the treasure was deposited is disputed. One account says that the caravans went approximately 275 leagues north from Tenochtitlán, and then turned west into high mountains, where the gold was hidden in various caves in canyons.[12]

The length of a league is disputed and variable (a vague term at best in such a legend as this), and the area in which the treasure may be hidden ranges from the Sierra Madre of Mexico (interesting to think of the Humphrey Bogart film *Treasure of the Sierra Madre* in this connection) to areas even farther north.

The northern part of modern-day Mexico is the very barren Sonora Desert. In ancient times this was a largely uninhabitable place, and included the Sierra Madre mountain range. But beyond this rather bleak desert, with few major rivers, there was a land of cities, ball courts, canyons and temples.

There are many legends that the seven caravans of Montezuma's treasure went into the area of the Four Corners of New Mexico, Arizona, Colorado and Utah—the ancestral home of the Aztecs. This land of the Hohokam, Sinagua, and Hopi included ball courts, large buildings of many stories, and an extensive road network that went all the way to Chaco Canyon and beyond.

Because only a few mines had been found by the Spanish in central Mexico, they sent priests northward into the promising mountains of the Sierra Madre. They carried with them samples of silver, copper and gold, mainly in the form of spoons, buttons, crosses and other small items. They would show these to the local villagers that they met and ask them if they knew where such a metal might be found or if they knew of other tribes who were using such metals.[12]

429

Such was the primitive level of civilization around northern Mexico, Texas, Arizona and California at the time that most of the natives purported not to know much about these metals or where to obtain them. Perhaps this was because their trade system had been curtailed by the Apache invasion hundreds of years before. However, the ruins, ball courts and canals of the Hohokam, plus Chaco Canyon show that the area—which had been rich in gold, copper, silver and turquoise—was well populated by people who were using metals.

This brings us to the treasure of the Blue Mountains—the Sierra Azul. This legendary mountain of gold would spur on the exploration of the west for centuries—and the source of the treasure would ultimately be found in northern Arizona.

The Treasure of the Sierra Azul

If the Aztecs were originally from the area of Arizona and northern New Mexico, then not only was Montezuma's treasure sent back into this area, but much of the treasure may have originally come from this area as well. In fact, legends persisted for hundreds of years of a gold mine in Arizona that contained vast amounts of metals, was very ancient, and was kept by the Apaches as their secret source of gold. The film, *Mackenna's Gold*, as said before, played heavily on this legend.

We have already noted several times that, for centuries, Spanish explorers in the American Southwest called the central part of Arizona "Terra Incognita" because the remote, rugged terrain and hostile Indians (namely Apaches) discouraged exploration and settlement. According to an article in the August, 1993 issue of *Arizona Highways*, a Spanish explorer living in Santa Fe, Antonio de Espejo, after hearing from Indians that a rich gold mine lay far to the west of New Mexico's Rio Grande Valley, entered the Terra Incognita in 1583. Friendly Hopi took Espejo's party on an ancient and well-traveled Indian path—now known as the Palatkwapi Trail—to mines in a mountain range today called the Black Hills. These mountains form the western rim of central Arizona's lush Verde River valley.

The Spaniards called this range the Sierra Azul, the "Blue Mountains," because the Hopi Indians ground the azurite copper ore from mines there into a blue powder they used to color their pottery and themselves. Also, at dawn, the Black Hills, seen from the east, appear to be much more blue than black.

Espejo surveyed the ancient mines, saw the stone ruins of Tuzigoot at the foot of the Sierra Azul, but saw no gold. He took samples of copper and other ores back to Santa Fe and then to Mexico City. Despite the failure to find gold, a report, written by the chronicler of Espejo's expedition, Diego Pérez de Luxán, stimulated a belief in Mexico that rich mines lay somewhere close to a fertile river valley west of the Hopi villages.

In the fall of 1598, another Spaniard, Capt. Marcos Farfán de los Godos, led a party to the Terra Incognita to locate the (by then) wildly rumored gold mines. In the same place that Espejo had visited, Farfán found mineral veins rich in ores so blue that they looked like enamel. Farfán did not seeing any gold either.[80]

Still, these reports prompted stories of rich gold mines in the Sierra Azul, and during the 17th century these tales became widely known in both the New World and in Europe. Out of a confused notion of all of these various accounts evolved the Legend of the Sierra Azul. But stories of the Tierra Incognita's forbidding terrain and menacing Indians discouraged further exploration attempts for many years.

According to the *Arizona Highways* article, in 1662 the governor of Northern New Spain, Don Diego de Peñalosa, led a party that reached the Hopi villages, but word of governmental problems in Santa Fe compelled him to turn back. Peñalosa never did see the Sierra Azul, let alone any gold.

Accused of disrespect toward the Franciscan friars, Peñalosa returned to Mexico City where Church authorities arrested and imprisoned him. On February 3, 1668, a church tribunal of the brutal Inquisition banished Peñalosa from the New World.

Almost ten years later, Peñalosa offered the king of France a plan to conquer the "fabulously rich" Sierra Azul. In what would seem a lie, Peñalosa claimed to have been there himself. Peñalosa created a crude map that clearly showed the Sierra Azul to be central Arizona's Black Hills. In what amounts to uncanny accuracy, considering the information he had to work with, the map shows the Sierra Azul to be only one degree north of where the Black Hills actually exist.

Peñalosa urged the French to allow him to return to North America with LaSalle, the prominent explorer, claiming it would be easy for France to take over sparsely populated Northern New Spain and its great mineral wealth, specifically the Sierra Azul. However, LaSalle made an expedition to the New World without Peñalosa. On the Gulf of Mexico's coastline the ill-fated explorer became lost and he was killed by his angry crew. That same year, 1687, Peñalosa died in France.

Peñalosa's hand-drawn sketch of the Sierra Azul made a great impact on European mapmakers. A highly respected Italian cartographer, Marco Vincenzo Coronelli, stated that he had copied Peñalosa's version in creating his own impressive maps. Coronelli's fame and reputation for accuracy influenced dozens of other European mapmakers. From 1685 until as recently as 1852, many Dutch, German, Spanish, Italian, French, and English maps showed Peñalosa's Sierra Azul.

In 1680 the New Mexico Pueblo Indians, including those from Zuni and Hopi, revolted and drove the region's Hispanics down the Rio Grande Valley to

432

El Paso. Five years later, Father Alonso de Posada, a prominent New Mexico clergyman, wrote a report for the king of Spain concerning the Sierra Azul, which he said was "so famed its ores have been assayed many times, but never possessed because of our negligence and timidity."

According to Posada, the Sierra Azul was 100 leagues west of Santa Fe and 50 leagues north of Sonora. Using 3.45 miles as the distance of a 17th-century Spanish league, we can clearly identify Posada's Sierra Azul as being the Black Hills surrounding the Arizona mining town of Jerome.[80]

In 1691 a new governor of Northern New Spain, Don Diego de Vargas, who had visions of glory and wealth to be gained if the area to the north of El Paso could be reconquered, got approval from the Spanish viceroy in Mexico City, the Count of Galvé, to reoccupy the northern Rio Grande Valley.

Vargas set out from El Paso on August 21, 1692. Meeting no resistance from the Indians, he advanced quickly to Santa Fe. He then went to the Hopi mesas, expecting to find guides to take him to the mines in the Sierra Azul. But the Hopi were hostile, and Vargas' fearful lieutenants talked him into returning to New Mexico. Like Peñalosa, he never did see the Sierra Azul.

We have already introduced the Jesuit priest working in northern Mexico at this time, Father Eusebio Francisco Kino. A well-educated man with a strong and realistic sense of geography, Kino rejected the Sierra Azul gold mines legend. Nonetheless on his famous map of 1701, Kino indicated today's Verde River as the "Rio Azul" because his Indian guides claimed that farther to the north the river flowed near the Sierra Azul.

In the 1700s, other Franciscan missionaries traveling in the region gave glowing reports of the Sierra Azul. One priest wrote: "It is called the Sierra Azul because the earth, rocks, and the whole region is blue... There is a tradition that this mountain is the richest in all New Spain."[79]

Little new information about the mysterious treasure appeared in print after 1800. In January, 1854, Amiel Weeks Whipple, an American Army officer, camped near the source of the Verde River. He wrote in his journal that in the 16th century the Spaniards had discovered a gold mine in an upper tributary of the Verde "near San Francisco Mountain" (outside of present-day Flagstaff).

Four years later, several Mexicans brought word to the celebrated Arizona pioneer Charles D. Poston that rich gold and silver deposits could be found in the hills along the headwaters of the Verde River.

In the 1890s, another tale of a lost gold mine located near the Black Hills was born. This new Anglo-American legend has been known by many names, but its most popular title has been the "Lost Apache Gold Mine." The term "Sierra Azul" never appears on the maps or in the accounts of this more recent lost-mine folklore. According to this legend, several men from Espejo's 1583 expedition to the Terra Incognita, unknown to him, found gold in a canyon seven to 20 miles north-northeast of the Black Hills—in the primitive Sycamore Canyon area.[80]

The Lost Apache Gold Mine and Jerome

The Sierra Azul and the Jerome area are also associated with the Apache chief Geronimo (Spanish for Jerome). While a prisoner of the United States Government in Fort Sill, Oklahoma, in 1886, Geronimo offered to exchange his knowledge of gold deposits for his freedom. He had tricked the army so many times that the acceptance of his offer could not be considered. Furthermore, the military had no stomach for meeting his warriors in the mountain passes again. Treasure author Thomas Penfield in his book, *Dig*

Here!,[12] mentions that some researchers have tried to establish that Geronimo actually made a deal with certain officers at Fort Sill, but he says that this was unlikely, as he never secured his freedom.

It is said that Geronimo told a friend at Fort Sill that his source of gold was located in the Verde River country, which is largely around the towns of Camp Verde and Cottonwood.[80] The vein, according to stories, was first found by the Apaches, and later seized by Spanish soldiers. The main body of these troops moved on to New Mexico, only a few remaining behind to build a smelter for refining the ore. The mine, probably, had been previously worked by the Toltecs and the Aztecs before the Apaches, who, like the Spanish, were newcomers to the area.

The angered Apaches could not stand up to the Spaniards' weapons, even though the remaining contingent was small, so they fought a war of attrition. From the canyon walls, they rolled boulders into the camp. They attacked from ambush when they were certain of success. They made frightening sounds at night, and generally did everything they could to keep the Spanish in a constant state of turmoil. Nevertheless, the Spaniards refused to be driven away. They tunneled into the canyon wall where the vein became so rich that the ore could be taken directly to the smelter.

When a large number of gold bars had been smelted, it was decided to carry them to Mexico on mules and return with sufficient force to drive the molesting Apaches from the canyon. As the contingent was packing out of the canyon, the Indians attacked furiously, killing all of the Spaniards with the exception of two.

The two surviving miners awaited their chance and returned to the canyon. They hid the bars of gold in the tunnel and closed the mine. At night they made their way out and after days finally reached Tubac, where they rested for the long trip to Mexico City. There they

435

told of the mine and supplied maps to others. It is said that a party of prospectors later found the remains of an old stone building and evidence of mining activity in one of the many small canyons emptying into Sycamore Creek, but they found no mine.[12]

Apparently, however, the Lost Apache Gold Mine, the Sierra Azul, and the copper mine at Jerome, near Tuzigoot, were all one and the same.

During the past 100 years, historians have speculated as to exactly where Espejo and Farfán found their well-publicized mines and whether these were the same as Geronimo's lost gold mine. According to the *Arizona Highways* article referenced above, in 1889 Hubert Howe Bancroft, a historian of the far West, said the mines were situated near Bill Williams Mountain, 28 miles north of Jerome. But his book contains a map that shows the routes of both Espejo and Farfán going to and stopping in Sycamore Canyon, about 20 miles southeast of Bill Williams Mountain. This map provides graphic evidence that ties the 19th and 20th centuries' Lost Apache Gold Mine story to the Sierra Azul legends of the 17th and 18th centuries.

In 1942 a more realistic and precise location of the mines appeared in print. In a geographically sensitive essay, Katharine Bartlett of the Museum of Northern Arizona in Flagstaff demonstrated that the mines Espejo and Farfán had visited in the late 1500s were indeed located at a site that three centuries later would become Jerome. She showed that the explorers had come to Jerome by a route far to the south of Sycamore Canyon.

Her argument was so knowledgeable and logical that among historians it became the definitive statement on the subject. Recent research specifically identifies this route as the Palatkwapi Trail—going from the Hopi villages of Awatobi and Walpi to Jerome.

On this pathway, both Espejo and Farfán descended the Mogollon Rim into the Verde Valley. They crossed

Oak Creek and the Verde River and then ascended the Black Hills up to copper-rich Jerome. No evidence exists to suggest that the Spanish expeditions from Hopi to the Black Hills traveled on any other route. The documents that do exist clearly establish Jerome as the only site in Arizona where the Spaniards found substantial mineral deposits.

Seems like I've always been looking for some other place
To get it together
Where with a few of my friends I could give up the race
And maybe find something better.
But all my fine dreams,
Well thought out schemes to gain the Motherland
Have all eventually come down to waiting for everyman.
—Jackson Browne, For Everyman

An Ancient Mummy Found inside the Jerome Mines

As proof that the Jerome mines were the ancient mines of the Aztecs, later appropriated by the Apaches, comes the discovery of a mummy within the mines— which were apparently being worked many hundreds of years before the Jerome mining companies were created. The following story appeared in the *Jerome Mining News* on Dec. 8, 1900:

A MUMMY FOUND IN AN AZTEC CAVE
One of the Most Wonderful Relics of the Lost Race Which Inhabited Arizona 1,000 Years Ago

The finding of a mummified man by workmen at the United Verde Mines on Monday, December 3, created some little excitement in Jerome. The body is undoubtedly that of a man who, during life was a giant, at least everything surrounding the find would signify that such was the case, as beside him was found a fire arm somewhat similar to the shot-gun used at the present time, but so large and of such weight that the average man of today could not pose it for shooting; besides the gun there were found near him working tools all of which were manufactured of tempered copper, showing that the man must have been buried over 1,000 years ago—during the first age of copper. The body is well preserved but has evidently shriveled, yet many of the most important parts have undoubtedly remained their natural size.

The numerous articles found with the body would signify that he was a chief or king of some renown.

The find was made in a cave exposed by the late caving in of the Verde mines. It was with wonder and awe that the workmen first entered the cave and handled the relics that must have been laid away for centuries.

Our informant regarding the above find, who is somewhat of an authority on the Aztec period, says that the body is that of an Aztec, the people who inhabited this part of Arizona about the period that he claims the mummy was laid away. He says from certain hieroglyphics on the cloth taken from the body, he has no doubt but that the body is that of the Aztec King Montmezoma [sic], who became famous under the Spanish Conquests and in whose honor the wells near Camp Verde was named, also the castle near the wells. It was about this period that the Aztecs became so predominant and from which time they became a power in the history of Arizona which was then a part of Old Mexico. If not the king, our informant says he certainly was a high priest from the temple of Huitzilopochtli [sic] which was located at one time near where Bob Mitchell's office is at present. Huitzilopochatli was the war god of the Aztec. He was also said to be a relative of Neyahual coyotli, king of Tezcuco [Texcoco], whose son Nezahualpilli made Tezcuco so celebrated for its intellectual culture and who for years continued to take tolls out of Quanhnahuac, Miztec and the Xicalance countries until he brought them into the fold. He insisted on telling us a great deal more but we prevailed upon him to drop off and give us a little time to think over what we had been told and thus we give it to our readers.

The mummy with the gun and tools are now on exhibition in the "Fashion" where the proprietors will be pleased to show it to any who may call. It is certainly worth a visit.

The Aztec authority cited in the article goes a little overboard speculating that the mummy found was that of Montezuma. It is well established that he died at the hands of the Conquistadors in Mexico. More likely, this was the mummy of one of the ancient Aztec miners who had died at the Sierra Azul and was mummified and interred in the mine. With the invasion of the Apaches into Texas, New Mexico and Arizona circa 1250 AD, the Aztecs were forced south into Mexico where they wandered for several hundred years until they founded Tenochtitlan. It was not until after the conquest that the Aztecs attempted to send the remains of their treasure back to their ancestral homeland. While they may have succeeded in getting their treasure out of Tenochtitlan and away from the conquistadors, they did not succeed in ever recovering the treasure for themselves.

Instead, the vast treasure of the Aztecs remains lost. If it is to be ever found, it will be found a long, long way from Tenochtitlan.

The Lost Pyramid of Sycamore Canyon

On another day, we drove up a dirt road past the Tuzigoot ruins outside Cottonwood, and followed the winding track to its end. This took us to the lower section of a vast wilderness known as Sycamore Canyon. This little-known canyon goes north from near Tuzigoot up to Williams on the Mogollon Rim. Running through it is Sycamore Creek, though this creek is dry for part of the year. Also in Sycamore Canyon is rumored to be a lost pyramid, covered with bushes and small trees.

This lost pyramid was first reported by Tom Babbitt, who was living at the Rockin' B Ranch in Cottonwood some years ago. Around the year 2001, Babbitt created his own web pages, on which he put a photo of the pyramid and a brief story about it.

Babbitt said, "After descending in a side canyon off of Sycamore Canyon my companion and I decided to head out up to the north ridge of the canyon, affording us a better view of the area. While ascending to the rim I spotted the pyramid shape of these limestone cliffs. I have traveled all over this area and would normally dismiss this feature as a visual oddity only visible from one perspective, but the shape remained consistent over a vertical distance of some 1500 or more feet."

Babbitt theorized on his web pages that the pyramid was part of an ancient gold mining city, and may have been the ancient mine being searched for by Captain Espejo, mentioned above. Babbitt thinks that the pyramid was partly covered in ash from the last volcanic explosion in the nearby Flagstaff area, when Sunset Crater erupted in 1065 AD.

Babbitt's photo is interesting (see photo section) but I think it is inconclusive. From talking with other people around Cottonwood, I gathered that the best place to view the area where the pyramid is supposed to be is the Sycamore Canyon Overlook, which is approached

440

from Williams. Heading south on Perkinsville Road, a left turn on Forest Road (FR) 110 will take you on a wild ride to a northern rim of Sycamore Canyon, where the Overlook gives a great view into the vast wilderness. Babbitt, however, told friends that he was on FR527 and FR527A, which are on the east side of the canyon, and more easily reached from Flagstaff, going past Rogers Lake on FR321.

We drove back to Cottonwood, and went to the Sycamore Canyon Overlook the next day. It was a spectacular scene, but we could not see Babbitt's pyramid. Is there a lost pyramid in Sycamore Canyon? Perhaps on some future trip, we will hike in and find out.

The Sphinx of the Grand Canyon

We were getting ready to leave for the drive north to Monument Valley when a package I was expecting arrived in the mail. Darrell Lane had called me a few days before to tell me that he had an interesting photo to send me.

"It's amazing to see this face on a mesa in the Grand Canyon! I think that, if you look closely at the photo, you can see other caves and catacombs below the face. It was part of a stereograph view of the Grand Canyon that was probably a souvenir in the early 1900s. It was originally a card with two similar photos on it that you would view through a kind of 'View-Master' to get the stereo effect. But, it had been torn in half, so we only have one side—but it's enough!" he told me over the phone.

When I got the package a few days later, I was very interested in the color photocopy he sent me of the stereograph photo (see illustrations). It showed what seems like a northern bluff in the Grand Canyon with a series of steadily rising rock cliffs that came to a rounded but sharp point. In the middle of the very top is a face, and it has a canopy on either side of the head

441

in the manner of an ancient Egyptian headdress. On the right side of the photograph were the stereograph instructions, which ironically tell the reader to hold the *face* of the photograph to the glass of stereograph viewer.

I scanned the photo at 1200 dpi and made the best blowup of the old photo (circa 1910) that I could. I looked at a printed version of my high-resolution scan and pondered the photo. The peak did have a face at the top, and at least viewed at this angle at this time of the day, it could serve as a landmark of sorts. It looked very similar to the famous Face on Mars. Was it just a trick of the light? Had ancient man actually carved this mesa to look like a man—or a sphinx?

This had certainly been done before, notably by the ancient Egyptians, whose most famous example of such work are the four gigantic statues of a seated Ramses II hewn into the rock face at Aswan. The Chinese, Hindus and Buddhists also produced such monuments—witness the giant statues at Bamiyan in central Afghanistan that were destroyed by the Taliban in the 1990s. They were giant depictions of Buddha standing hundreds of feet high, chiseled into the massive cliff faces. I was glad I had seen them years ago, before they were lost forever in the name of Muslim fundamentalism.

I wondered if features like this played a part in the decision to give many of the features of the Grand Canyon Egyptian and Hindu-Buddhist names. This did not seem to be a well-known feature at the Grand Canyon—do tourists rarely get this view? Was it a man-made attempt to make a sphinx or other signal for mankind's pilgrims—or just a natural formation that was a simulacra (something that is natural but has a resemblance to something else). Was it still there? I looked at it for some time, and then contemplated it some more. It was odd, but considering the other strange stories concerning the Grand Canyon, seemed like it somehow fit in with whole milieu.

At around the same time, I received a different photo from a man in Albuquerque named Robert, who sent me a picture of Canyon de Chelly taken by the famous photographer of the old Southwest, Edward S. Curtis. Robert told me that it showed a very faint statue of a standing or sitting Buddha that was colossal in size. I could faintly see the outline of what he was talking about, and if it is an artificially carved image, it would have to be absolutely monumental in scope. It was a fascinating idea that huge Buddhist figures rivalling those in Asia might have been carved in the American Southwest!

Finally, it was time to hit the road again. We headed out of Cottonwood and drove north to Flagstaff, and from there passed through Cameron again on north Highway 89. We continued on through the huge Navaho Nation, following Highway 160 to Tuba City and Kayenta. There, we turned north on Highway 163 to Monument Valley. We camped for the night in a Navaho Nation Campground situated on a bluff overlooking the features of the famous landscape.

We pitched our tent on the edge of campground, directly in front of the famous Mittens monument that was featured in so many westerns, including John Wayne's breakout movie, *Stagecoach*.

The sun was setting and the Mittens of Monument Valley were silhouetted in an orange glow. We lay back against our rolled up sleeping bags and relaxed while looking out at this classic desert scene. The ghosts of Egyptians, Toltecs, Chinese, Buddhists, Romans, Aztecs, Hopis, Navahos and dusty cowboys still trod those ancient trails, seeking out the small creeks that still flowed drip by drip along the thirsty sands.

Lost Cities & Ancient Mysteries of the Southwest

EXPLORATIONS IN GRAND CANYON

Mysteries of Immense Rich Cavern Being Brought to Light.

JORDAN IS ENTHUSED

Remarkable Finds Indicate Ancient People Migrated From Orient.

The latest news of the progress of the explorations of what is now regarded by scientists as not only the oldest archaeological discovery in the United States, but one of the most valuable in the world, which was mentioned some time ago in the Gazette, was brought to the city yesterday by G. E. Kinkaid, the explorer who found the great underground citadel of the Grand Canyon during a trip from Green river, Wyoming, down the Colorado, in a wooden boat, to Yuma, several months ago. According to the story related yesterday to the Gazette by Mr. Kinkaid, the archaeologists of the Smithsonian Institute, which is financing the explorations, have made discoveries which almost conclusively prove that the race which inhabited this mysterious cavern, hewn in solid rock by human hands, was of oriental origin, possibly from Egypt, tracing back to Ramses. If their theories are borne out by the translation of the tablets engraved with hieroglyphics, the mystery of the prehistoric peoples of North America, their ancient arts, who they were and whence they came, will be solved. Egypt and the Nile, and Arizona and the Colorado will be linked by a historical chain running back to ages which staggers the wildest fancy of the fictionist.

A Thorough Investigation.

Under the direction of Prof. S. A. Jordan, the Smithsonian Institute is now prosecuting the most thorough explorations, which will be continued until the last link in the chain is forged. Nearly a mile underground, about 1480 feet below the surface, the long main

fect ventilation of the cavern, the steady draught that blows through, indicates that it has another outlet to the surface.

Mr. Kinkaid's Report.

Mr. Kinkaid was the first white child born in Idaho and has been an explorer and hunter all his life, thirty years having been in the service of the Smithsonian Institute. Even briefly recounted, his history sounds fabulous, almost grotesque.

"First, I would impress that the cavern is nearly inaccessible. The entrance is 1486 feet down the sheer canyon wall. It is located on government land and no visitor will be allowed there under penalty of trespass. The scientists wish to work unmolested, without fear of the archaeological discoveries being disturbed by curio or relic hunters. A trip there would be fruitless, and the visitor would be sent on his way. The story of how I found the cavern has been related, but in a paragraph: I was journeying down the Colorado river in a boat, alone, looking for mineral. Some forty-two miles up the river from the El Tovar Crystal canyon I saw on the east wall, stains in the sedimentary formation about 2000 feet above the river bed. There was no trail to this point, but I finally reached it with great difficulty. Above a shelf which hid it from view from the river, was the mouth of the cave. There are steps leading from this entrance some thirty yards to what was, at the time the cavern was inhabited, the level of the river. When I saw the chisel marks on the wall inside the entrance, I became interested, secured my gun and went in. During that trip I went back several hundred feet along the main passage, till I came to the crypt in which I discovered the mummies. One of these I stood up and photographed by flashlight. I gathered a number of relics, which I carried down the Colorado to Yuma, from whence I shipped them to Washington with details of the discovery. Following this, the explorations were undertaken.

The Passages.

"The main passageway is about 12 feet wide, narrowing to 9 feet toward the farther end. About 57 feet from the entrance, the first side-passages branch off to the right and left, along which, on both sides, are a number of rooms about the size of ordinary living rooms of today, though some are 30 or 40 feet square. These are entered by oval-shaped doors and are ventilated by round air spaces through the walls into the passages. The walls are about 3 feet 6 inches in thickness. The passages are chiseled or hewn as straight as could be laid out by an engineer. The ceilings of many of the rooms converge to a center. The side passages near the entrance run at a sharp angle from the main hall, but toward the rear they gradually reach a right angle in direction.

The Shrine.

"Over a hundred feet from the entrance is the cross-hall, several hundred feet long, in which was found the idol, or image, of the people's god, sitting cross-legged, with a lotus flower or lily in each hand. The cast of the

The Sipapu volcanic dome inside the Grand Canyon, sacred to the Hopis.

GAZETTE, MONDAY EVENING, APRIL 5, 1909.

EXPLORATIONS IN GRAND CANYON

(Continued from Page One.)

which indicates that some sort of ladder was attached. These granaries are rounded, and the materials of which they are constructed, I think, is a very hard cement. A gray metal is also found in this cavern, which puzzles the scientists, for its identity has not been established. It resembles platinum. Strewn promiscuously over the floor everywhere are what people call 'cats' eyes' or 'tiger eyes,' a yellow stone of no great value. Each one is engraved with a head of the Malay type.

The Hieroglyphics.

"On all the urns, on walls over doorways, and tablets of stone which were found by the image are the mysterious hieroglyphics, the key to which the Smithsonian institute hopes yet to discover. These writings resemble those on the rocks about this valley. The engraving on the tablets probably has something to do with the religion of the people. Similar hieroglyphics have been found in the peninsula of Yucatan, but these are not the same as those found in the orient. Some believe that these cave dwellers built the old canals in the Salt River valley. Among the pictorial writings, only two animals are found. One is of prehistoric type.

The Crypt.

"The tomb or crypt in which the mummies were found is one of the

contain a deadly gas or chemicals used by the ancients. No sounds are heard, but it smells snakey just the same. The whole underground institution gives one of shaky nerves the creeps. The gloom is like a weight on one's shoulders, and our flashlights and candles only make the darkness blacker. Imagination can revel in conjectures and ungodly day-dreams back through the ages that have elapsed till the mind reels dizzily in space."

An Indian Legend.

In connection with this story, it is notable that among the Hopis the tradition is told that their ancestors once lived in an underworld in the Grand Canyon till dissension arose between the good and the bad, the people of one heart and the people of two hearts. Machetto, who was their chief, counseled them to leave the underworld, but there was no way out. The chief then caused a tree to grow up and pierce the roof of the underworld, and then the people of one heart climbed out. They tarried by Paisisvai (Red river), which is the Colorado, and grew grain and corn. They sent out a message to the Temple of the Sun, asking the blessing of peace, good will and rain for the people of one heart. That messenger never returned, but today at the Hopi village at sundown can be seen the old men of the tribe out on the housetops gazing toward the sun, looking for the messenger. When he returns, their lands and ancient dwelling place will be restored to them. That is the tradition. Among the engravings of animals in the cave is seen the image of a heart over the spot where it is located. The legend was learned by W. E. Rollins, the artist, during a year spent with the Hopi Indians. There are two theories of the origin of the Egyptians. One is that they came from Asia; another that the racial cradle was in the upper Nile region. Heeren, an Egyptologist, believed in the Indian origin of the Egyptians. The discoveries in the Grand Canyon may throw further light on human evolution and prehistoric ages.

The Hopi and Little Colorado River country circa 1870.

A poster for the film *Mackenna's Gold*.

Seth Tanner late in his life, after he had been blinded.

446

Top: The Hopi village of Walpi in 1870.. Bottom: An aerial photo of Casa Malpais near Springerville. It may have been an early Zuni city.

447

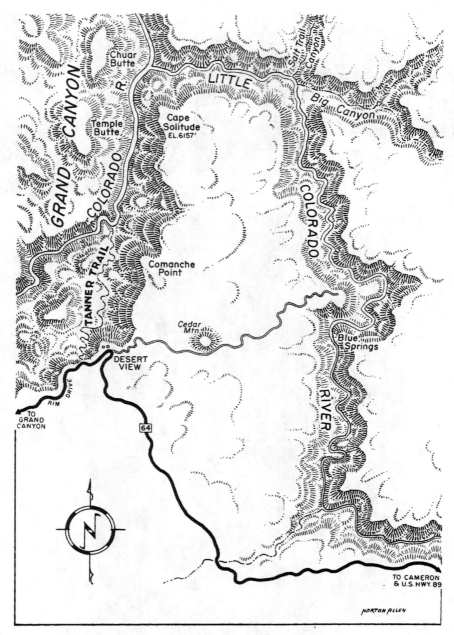

Tanner Trail in the Grand Canyon.

448

The Hopi village of Walpi drawn by Powell's team in 1870.

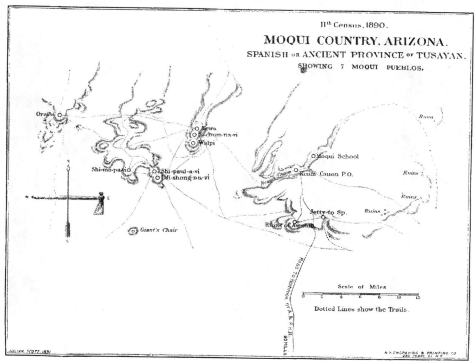

Map of Tusayan, the site of the Hopi Mesas.

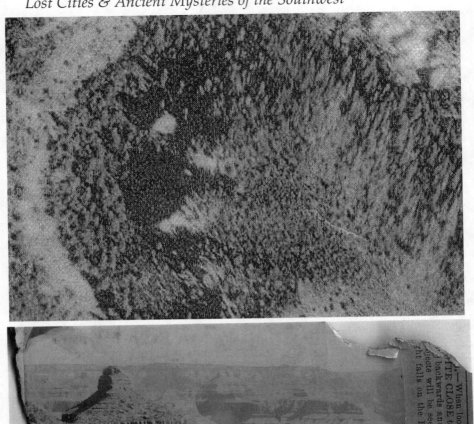

Top: The photo of a pyramid in Sycamore Canyon taken by Tom Babbitt. Bottom: The Grand Canyon "Sphinx" from half of a stereograph slide from circa 1910.

The Grand Canyon "Sphinx" from a stereograph slide from circa 1910 enlarged.

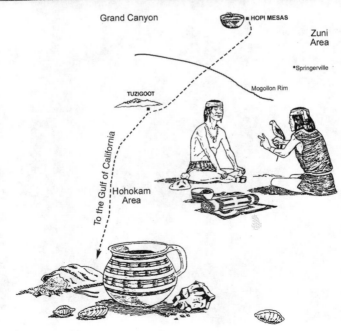

Top: Hopi ceremony inside a kiva. Bottom: Hopi Mesas-Tuzigoot map.

8.

CALIFORNIA

UNDERGROUND CATACOMBS AND DRIED LAKES

Crossroads seem to come and go,
The Gypsy flies from coast to coast…
Freight train—each car looks the same.
No one knows the Gypsy's name,
No one hears his lonely sound,
There are no blankets where he lies…
—Allman Brothers, *Melissa*

Towers and a Twilight World

The full moon was rising over the desolate buildings of Hovenweep National Monument in southeast Utah as Jennifer and I walked around the site. It was a large area, with settlements scattered over several miles, mainly around the rim of a small side canyon of Montezuma Creek, off the San Juan River. The buildings were well made, and often perched along the edges of sheer cliffs.

The most extensively excavated settlement is called The Square Tower Group, aptly named since it is the site of numerous square towers. These structures are nearly identical to the ones near Gallina, New Mexico. Were the towers, which seemed defensive in nature, part of a last ditch effort of the early people of this area—called the Anasazi Indians— to stem the advance of some powerful invader?

The name Hovenweep is a Paiute word meaning deserted valley. It was given to the region by the photographer William Jackson while he was exploring the area in 1874. The site became a national monument in 1923. Many of the structures are D-shaped and some were at least four stories high. Archeologists are largely in agreement that the Paiutes of California, Nevada, Utah and western Colorado were not the original inhabitants of these buildings. The builders were "the people before"—the Anasazi—who had also occupied Chaco Canyon, Aztec, Pecos and other large stone settlements in northwestern New Mexico. Connected integrally with the Anasazi farmers of Mesa Verde in southwestern Colorado, both these major sites were apparently abandoned by the end of the thirteenth century. This area, on the edge of the desert, may have been stricken by drought, but probably always had some water.

Ancient Mines in Utah

We continued down the highway, the full moon arcing over the craggy rocks of southern Utah. I thought of some of the strange stories I had heard of ancient caves and ancient mines that were occasionally discovered.

In 1953 miners of the Lion coal mine of Wattis, Utah, broke into a network of tunnels between five and six feet in height that contained previously mined coal of such vast antiquity that it had become weathered to a state of uselessness for any kind of burning or heat production. A search outside the mountain in direct line with the tunnels revealed no sign of any entrance. Since the tunnels were discovered when the miners were working an eight-foot coal seam at 8,500 feet, the evidence strongly suggests that miners from some unknown civilization conducted an ambitious mining project so far back in time that all exterior traces have been eroded away.

Professor John E. Wilson of the department of engineering at the University of Utah says in regard to the mystery mines of Wattis in the February 1954 issue of *Coal Age:* "Without a doubt, both drifts were man-made. Though no evidence was found at the outcrop, the tunnels apparently were driven some 450 feet from the outside to the point where the present workings broke into them... There is no visible basis for dating tunnels."

Jesse D. Jennings, professor of anthropology at the University of Utah, said that while he was unable to identify the ancient miners, he knew that the vast tunnels and coal-mining rooms were definitely not the work of any American Indian people. Such a vast mining network would have required an immediate and local need for coal, and Professor Jennings pointed out, "There is no reported extensive burning of coal by aboriginals in the region of the Wattis mine."[144]

During the evening we drove west on Utah Highway 95 going toward Hanksville and the vast desert areas of Glen Canyon National Recreation Area and the Capitol Reef National Park. Capitol Reef National Park is a nearly 100-mile long warp in the Earth's crust, known as the Waterpocket Fold. Geologists say that this is a classic monocline: a regional fold with one very steep side in an area of otherwise nearly horizontal layers. A monocline is a "step-up" in the rock layers. The rock layers on the west side of the Waterpocket Fold have been lifted more than 7,000 feet higher than the layers on the east. Major folds are almost always

associated with underlying faults. The Waterpocket
Fold formed between 50 and 70 million years ago
when a major mountain-building event in western
North America, the Laramide Orogeny, reactivated
an ancient buried fault. When the fault moved, the
overlying rock layers were draped above the fault
and formed a monocline.

The most scenic portion of the Waterpocket
Fold, found near the Fremont River, is known as
Capitol Reef: *capitol* for the white domes of Navajo
Sandstone that resemble the Capitol Building dome
in Washington D.C., and *reef* for the rocky cliffs which
are a barrier to travel, like a coral reef. We camped
for the night somewhere near Caineville, and visited
the strange rock formations the next morning. As we
looked at the weird water-worn rocks, I wondered
if the fold had happened millions of years ago, as
geologists insisted, or had it happened much more
recently than that? As we shall see, there is a great
deal of evidence that the western basin and range
of Utah, Nevada and California was once part of a
very recent series of large seas and finger lakes.

Soon, we were headed west to Cedar City and
south to Zion National Park, and cutting across
a small corner of Arizona to reach the Nevada
border town of Mesquite, where, naturally, there
were several casinos. We drove on to an area of
petroglyphs, called the Valley of Fire because of the
stunning red hue of the cliffs, and then on to the
nearby Lost City Museum. This enticingly named
spot is dedicated to the mysterious natives who
inhabited the area, where the Virgin River flowed
out of the Virgin Mountains of the far northwest
corner of Arizona and met the Colorado River near
the Muddy Mountains.

This entire area has now been flooded by the
Hoover Dam and the subsequent Lake Mead. The
lake now occupies nearly all of the lowland that

once surrounded the lower portion of the Virgin River. Because the original adobe, stone and cement buildings of the "Lost City" tribe, are now under water, it is fortunate there is a museum dedicated to these now vanished people.

As Jennifer and I toured the museum, I asked the woman who was the curator if the people had used boomerangs as did many of the Pueblo peoples. The lady was not aware of any boomerangs being found in the area, and it was the first she had heard of their use in the Southwest.

Later that night we were driving down the Las Vegas Strip, checking out the lights of the various casinos. It was some sort of modern Babylon in the desert: bright lights flashing to alert us to various attractions; crowds of people intent on enjoying themselves; giant pyramids lit up with sparkling lights; a thousand and one lives living a fantasy of glittering glory. Las Vegas was like a parody of a lost city that wasn't dead yet—still holding the desert at a comfortable distance—but how long could that last?

Area 51 and the Extraterrestrial Highway

The next morning, with a slight hangover and a lighter wallet, we met up with an old friend, Doug, who owns an art gallery in Los Angeles. We all had a big casino breakfast and talked about the good times that we had had together in Peru, Bolivia, Mexico and Central America on various trips with the World Explorers Club over the years. Doug had traveled considerably in the south Pacific, and we had in common our love of remote islands and their mysterious megalithic ruins.

We checked out of the hotel and then drove in a caravan of two vehicles out of Las Vegas north on Highway 93 to the small town of Ash Springs. At a lonely crossroads we went north on Highway 318

457

to look for some petroglyphs that Doug had found mentioned in a guidebook. We had a great time looking for them, but we never actually found them. We turned around and went back to the crossroads, where we would now head west on Highway 375— the Extraterrestrial Highway. The state of Nevada decided to name this 98-mile section of highway after aliens in 1996 when Area 51 UFO fever had reached its height.

At the beginning of this historic highway was nothing more than the empty desert crossroads and a big green Nevada highway sign announcing that this was the Extraterrestrial Highway. We stopped our vehicles to take the obligatory photos of the bullet-ridden sign. I guessed that if gun-toting locals couldn't actually take potshots at real extraterrestrial aliens, they could at least shoot at the signs.

After consulting our maps and synchronizing our watches, we jumped back in our cars and began the journey along this unusual stretch of desert highway. This stretch goes northwest along the northern edge of a top-secret military base that is larger than many Eastern States; parts of the base carry such famous name as Area 51, Groom Lake, Mercury, the Nevada Test Site and others.

It was only 39 miles to the tiny town of Rachel, where we planned to spend the night (in fact it is the only place to stop along the Extraterrestrial Highway), so we had some time to take some side roads. We stopped briefly at the famous "black mailbox" that stands on the south side of the road near Coyote Summit, a pass just before Rachel. This black mailbox (which, in late 2008 was actually painted white) belongs to a rancher named Steve Medlin, who moved into the area in 1973.

The lone mailbox is something of a magnet for tourists wanting to see UFOs or other strange phenomena and it is possible to drive south on a dirt road from here for a few miles until one gets to a military-controlled gate that says that entry is forbidden, as well as photography. As we stopped by this sign, we could see a military vehicle on a nearby hill; the driver was watching us with binoculars. Since photography was forbidden (and we were being watched), we did not take any photographs. We got out of our vehicles, briefly, looked around, and left. We drove back to the mailbox and then continued northwest on the Extraterrestrial Highway to Rachel.

Rachel became a tourist spot in 1989 when a man named Bob Lazar claimed in an interview with a Las Vegas television station that he had worked as a physicist in Area 51 retro-engineering alien spacecraft. He also claimed to have watched test flights of flying saucers in Tikaboo Valley, which is near Groom Lake within the military reservation.

Because of the fame that Area 51 gained as a spot to see flying saucers and possibly meet the extraterrestrials that people imagined were flying them, visitors sometimes camped out for weeks at the black mailbox, often leaving messages for the aliens inside. Some took to shooting at the mailbox, putting bullet holes through Medlin's bills and junk mail. Eventually, he bought a bulletproof mailbox for his own mail, and put up a second box for tourists to leave messages for the aliens. Some actually put dollar bills in this box, apparently hoping to fund further extraterrestrial activity.

"Good idea," I thought as we accelerated down the highway toward Rachel. It was just starting to get dark and a dull glow could be seen to the south; perhaps it was some flying saucer being tested in the dark.

Shortly, we pulled into Rachel, something of a one-horse town (maybe we should say a one-spaceship town) that had an abandoned gas station, a few trailer homes, and the famous Little A'Le'Inn, a bar, café, motel and quirky gift shop. A faded sign on the café said, "Welcome earthlings and/or aliens. Please specify planet."

We checked in with Pat Travers, the owner, who was a friendly gal in her 60s. She set us up with a couple of rooms in the trailers behind the café that comprised the motel. Soon we were sitting at the bar inside the café, having a cold beer among the jars of alien ooze, fake Area 51 ID cards, and assorted alien key chains, mugs, pens and shot glasses. There were books and DVDs, as well, and even a few video poker and slot machines for the gamblers.

"What a great place," I said to Doug, taking a swig of beer. "I suppose this is as good a spot as any to see a UFO."

"One would think that," said Doug. He turned to the bartender, a young attractive woman who had moved to Rachel from California. "What have you seen around here?" he asked her.

"Oh," she said, wiping down the bar, "people see orange glows and strange lights out there from time to time. I suppose most folks have seen some pretty weird things out there over the years."

"Has anyone ever seen any aliens or been abducted?" I asked.

"Not that I am aware of," she said. "But there are plenty of strange lights in the sky."

More people came into the bar, and soon Doug, Jennifer and I were surrounded by various denizens, including two flamboyant gay fellows who had come from Tennessee in their snazzy mobile home, an old couple from Seattle, and even a few State Troopers. The night wore on as we had dinner, mingled and drank beer. This was all followed by a late drive along the Extraterrestrial Highway to look for lights in the sky and such.

The orange glow far to the south over the

mountains, inside the military reservation somewhere, had grown brighter. Something was definitely lighting up the sky about 10 miles to the south, or more, perhaps the powerful lights of an airfield, or the powerful lights of a giant USAF flying saucer. Perhaps it was both!

I've been from Tucson to Tucumcari
Tehachapi to Tonopah
Driven every kind of rig that's ever been made
I've driven the back roads so I wouldn't get weighed
—Little Feat, Willin'

The Search For the Lost City of Death Valley

We had a big breakfast at the Little A'Le'Inn, cooked by the same busy ladies who run the café-bar-bookstore-gift shop from early in the morning till late at night. After taking some photographs around the tiny town, we were packing up the car for more driving across central Nevada on the Extraterrestrial Highway.

In a few seconds we were out of town and the vast desert terrain and the road of burning tar and hot cement was all there was to see. Behind us I could see Doug in his 4x4. I played with the radio but there was nothing but static.

"So, what's ahead?" I asked Jennifer.

She grabbed the map of Nevada from between the seats and said, "Tonopah."

"Tonopah, huh? Like in that Little Feat song. Well, we'll have to take the back roads, I suppose."

"Uh, I think we might be *on* the back road. At any rate, there aren't any other roads out here—except the ones that go through Area 51 out there."

She was right about that, and with static on the radio and Tonopah over a hundred miles away across the sand, my thoughts drifted to our ultimate destination—Death Valley and its many side roads, rock formations and strange places. There were rumors of an ancient city, an ancient lake, fabulous gold treasure and tunnels with strange mummies and other artifacts.

Researcher Rene Noorbergen, in discussing the evidence for a cataclysmic war in the remote past that included the use of airships and weapons that vitrified stone cities, says of Death Valley in his book *Secrets of the Lost Races*[92]:

> The most numerous vitrified remains in the New World are located in the Western United States. In 1850 the American explorer Captain Ives William Walker was the first to view some of these ruins, situated in Death Valley. He discovered a city about a mile long, with the lines of the streets and the positions of the buildings still visible. At the center he found a huge rock, between 20 to 30 feet high, with the remains of an enormous structure atop it. The southern side of both the rock and the building was melted and vitrified. Walker assumed that a volcano had been responsible for this phenomenon, but there is no volcano in the area. In addition, tectonic heat could not have caused such a liquification of the rock surface.
>
> An associate of Captain Walker who followed up his initial exploration commented, "The whole region between the rivers Gila and San Juan is covered with remains. The ruins of cities are to be found there which must be most extensive, and they are burnt out and vitrified in part, full of fused stones and craters caused by fires which were hot enough to liquefy rock or metal. There are paving stones and houses

torn with monstrous cracks... [as though they had] been attacked by a giant's fire-plough."

Other vitrified ruins have been found in parts of Southern California, Arizona and Colorado. The Mojave Desert is reported to contain several circular patches of fused glass.[92]

These vitrified ruins in Death Valley and their discovery by William Walker, who later went on to fame and fortune as the mercenary-adventurer President of Nicaragua, are also mentioned by Peter Kolosimo in his book *Timeless Earth*.[124] These mysterious ruins sounded fascinating—but did they really exist?

Perhaps, as most modern archeologists would surmise, Walker was looking at some of the bizarre rock formations found in Death Valley, and assumed that they were the ruins of a great and ancient city, rather than natural contortions of the earth. A similar such natural, though artificial-looking, spot is Rock City in southern New Mexico, near Silver City.

We finally left the Extraterrestrial Highway and arrived in Tonopah. From there we drove south, with Area 51 now to our east. Soon we were passing the old mining town of Goldfield—still alive but something of a quasi-ghost town.

Death Valley and its mysteries straddle the state line between Nevada and California. We were arriving by turning at Scotty's Junction where Highway 95 meets Highway 267. As we sped down the road into the National Park, I thought of the traces of ancient civilizations that had been reported here. There are numerous petroglyphs and inscriptions in Titus Canyon in Death Valley made by unknown prehistoric hands. The current Paiute Indians seem to know nothing of the origin of the glyphs, and therefore they appear to be from some vanished people now long gone.

The Underground Land of Shin-au-av

I had with me a 1932 book entitled *Death Valley Men*[130] by Bourke Lee that mentions an underground land called *Shin-au-av*, and tells of bizarre caverns and lost treasure that would make Indiana Jones jealous. Lee tells a number of interesting stories of Death Valley in the 1920s and '30s. His last chapter is entitled "Old Gold" and describes some encounters and conversations he had with a small group of Death Valley residents.

The conversation between the men eventually turned to the subject of Paiute Indian legends that describe an underground world. The Paiute legend, as told by Lee in *Death Valley Men*, is as follows:

> Several thousand years ago a noted Paiute chief lost his greatly beloved wife. Sorrow overcame him. He mourned his wife for a long time. At last he felt that life without his wife was not worth the living; and he took his earthly body into the spirit land. His journey into the land of the dead was a long ordeal. He passed through an endless underground passage following the trail of all brave Indian spirits. He was beset by fierce beasts, evil spirits, supernatural demons. But the courageous chieftain fought his way onward through the ghoulish cavern. He won through to the sunlight at the far end and his feet resolutely carried him across the narrow ribbon of rock arched over a bottomless chasm. He stepped from the bridge of rock into the green meadows of the land of the dead, a great kingdom ruled by Shin-au-av. The chief had survived all his

trials.

One of the many beautiful daughters of Shin-au-av welcomed the Paiute chief to the land of bounty and happiness. She was an ample *houri* with shining eyes and no fault of limb or curve or character. Like all of Shin-au-av's daughters, she was a presumptive virgin. This beautiful and miraculous maiden offered herself freely to the brave chieftain who had dared to venture into the valley of the dead in his earthly body, but the chief would have none of her. He wanted to know where he could find his wife. The maid stood before the chief in awe. It was the first rebuff she had known in thousands of years.

Certain that the new arrival must be greater than some of the gods, the daughter of Shin-au-av took the chief by the hand and led him to a vast natural amphitheater. It was a dancing place and many thousands of dead and happy Paiutes were dancing in a huge circle.

The chief looked at the great assemblage of dancers and said, "I'll never find my wife in that crowd."

"Oh, yes, you will," said his kindly guide. "Just sit here on the edge of the circle until your greatly beloved wife passes." She left him for a moment and then returned with baskets of food and wicker vessels of cactus wine. "Be comfortable, great chief," she said. "When your wife comes by, you must carry her off quickly. And beware! Once you have seized your wife, you must both leave the valley without a single, backward glance."

The chief promised that once he found his wife he would leave the valley at once. And he sat down to watch the great pageant of the dancers revolve before him. He watched them for several days and nights. He saw a lot of his old enemies, but he did not see his wife. Whenever he began to despair of finding his wife, he comforted himself with the wine. He drank enough wine to empty the vessel many times, but the wicker flagon was still full of wine. The chief drank the wine steadily for three days and nights and was still happy. It was miraculous wine.

Late on the third night the Paiute chief saw his wife approaching. He ran to her and dragged her from the circle of dancers. Together, they fled across the valley to the rock arch which spanned the bottomless chasm and joined the land of Shin-au-av to the long cavern and the world of human life. Close to the edge of the chasm, the chief stopped to caution his wife about crossing the narrow bridge. As he talked, his wife's glance strayed back to the happy dancers in the valley. The chief followed the example of his wife. He turned to look at the joyous festival and the bountiful valley. The chief's wife vanished. The chief had forgotten that he must leave the land of the dead without a single backward glance.

Alone, and sorrowing, the chief returned to his own country and rejoined his tribe. He spent the remainder of his days describing the beauties and luxuries of the land of Shin-au-av. His story became well known to all the Paiutes. Even after all the Paiutes had heard the chief tell of his adventure enough times to remember his account word for word, the chief continued to tell his story. He became rather a bore to the entire Paiute nation. His life ran on through the years to a greatly advanced old age. He died one day when he was in the middle of his story. The Paiutes thought this unfortunate. Other storytellers took up the tale where the chief left off. They have been telling it ever since.[130]

☙ ☙ ☙

Modern Tales of the Death Valley Underworld

And so we have a strange Paiute legend involving an underground world somewhere around Death Valley. But what was the origin of this myth? Had a Paiute chief once explored some actual bizarre underground world that had been abandoned thousands of years ago? Was his strange adventure into a frightening world of mummies and dusty ancient gods one that lived on for hundreds of years in the form of a Paiute myth? In fact, much stranger tales than this would be told about Death Valley, as we shall see.

Jim Brandon in says in his book *Weird America*,[94] "Piute legends tell of a city beneath Death Valley that they call *Shin-au-av*. Tom Wilson, an Indian guide in the 1920s, claimed that his grandfather had rediscovered the place by wandering into a miles-long labyrinth of caves beneath the valley floor.

"Eventually the Indian came to an underworld city where the people spoke an incomprehensible language and wore clothing made of leather."[94]

At one point in Lee's book, *Death Valley Men*,[130] Lee meets two men, Jack and Bill, who describe to Lee their conversation with two other men named White and Thomason about an 'underground city' which they claimed to have discovered. White and Thomason claimed that they found the catacombs after one of them had fallen through the bottom of an old mine shaft near Wingate Pass, which is in the southwest corner of Death Valley. Wingate Pass was the old route the mule teams took when hauling

467

borax out of Death Valley in the 1800s.

The men, Thomason and White, said they found themselves in a natural underground cavern that they claimed went for about 20 miles north into the heart of the Panamint Mountains. To their amazement, they allegedly found themselves in a huge, ancient, underground cavern city. They claimed that they discovered within the city several perfectly preserved 'mummies,' which were clad in fine leather and wore thick gold armbands and wielded gold spears. The city had apparently been abandoned for ages, except for the mummies, and the entire underground system looked very ancient. It was formerly lit, they found out by accident, by an ingenious system of lights fed by subterranean gases.

They claimed to have seen a large, polished round table which looked as if it may have been part of an ancient council chamber, giant statues of solid gold, stone vaults and drawers full of gold bars and gemstones of all kinds, heavy stone wheelbarrows which were perfectly balanced and scientifically-constructed so that a child could use them, huge stone doors which were almost perfectly balanced by counterweights, and other incredible sights.[130]

Thomason and White further claimed that they followed caverns upward to a higher level that ultimately opened out onto the face of the Panamints, about halfway up the eastern slope, in the form of a few ancient tunnel-like quays. They realized that the valley below was once part of a series of lakes and they eventually came to the conclusion that the arched openings were ancient 'docks' for sea vessels. They could allegedly see Furnace Creek Ranch and Wash far below them.

They told Jack and Bill that they had brought some of the treasure out of the caverns and tried to set up a deal with certain people, including scientists associated with the Smithsonian Institution, in order to gain help to explore and publicize the city as one of the 'wonders of the world.' These efforts ended in disappointment, however, when a 'friend' of theirs stole the treasure (which was also the evidence) and they were scoffed at and rejected by the scientists when they went to show them the 'mine' entrance and could not find it. A recent cloudburst, they claimed, had altered and rearranged the entire countryside and the landscape did not look like it had before.[130]

A Lost City of Gold Worth Billions

In Lee's book *Death Valley Men* he recounts the fascinating conversation Bill and Jack had with Thomason and White. I have excerpted below certain parts of the conversation that give further description of the fascinating find:

> "It's too bad you were delayed by your car," said Jack with a carelessness he did not feel. "That's the way it is. As soon as you have serious business that should be attended to, your car breaks down. That's one of the many reasons why I have never purchased a car. Most of the other reasons were lack of the purchase price."
>
> "No harm done by the delay," said Thomason. "Our business is safe. And you can buy your car very soon if you want to. What brought us down here to Death Valley was millions and millions of dollars! Uncounted millions of dollars!"
>
> "Millions and millions!" echoed White, bobbing his bald and shining head...
>
> Thomason said, "I've been in and out of the Death Valley country for twenty years. So has my partner. We know where there is a lost treasure. We've known about it for several years, and we're the only men in the world

who do know about it. We're going to let you two fellows in on it. You've been good to us. You're both fine fellows. You haven't asked us any questions about ourselves, and we like you. We think you can keep a secret, so we'll tell you ours."

Jack blew smoke and asked, "A lost mine?"

"No, not a mine," said Thomason. "A lost treasure house. A lost city of gold. It's bigger than any mine that ever was found, or ever will be."

"It's bigger than the United States Mint," said White, with his voice and body shaken with excitement. "It's a city thousands of years old and worth billions of dollars! Billions of dollars! Billions! Not millions. Billions!"

...Bill's voice was meek as he asked, "And this place is in Death Valley?"

"Right in the Panamint Mountains!" said Thomason. "My partner found it by accident. He was prospecting down on the lower edge of the range near Wingate Pass. He was working in the bottom of an old abandoned shaft when the bottom of the shaft fell out and landed him in a tunnel. We've explored the tunnel since. It's a natural tunnel like a big cave. It's over twenty miles long. It leads all through a great underground city; through the treasure vaults, the royal palace, and the council chambers; and it connects to a series of beautiful galleries with stone arches in the east slope of the Panamint Mountains. Those arches are like great big windows in the side of the mountain and they look down on Death Valley. They're high above the valley now, but we believe that those entrances in the mountainside were used by the ancient people that built the city. They used to land their boats there."

"Boats!" demanded the astonished Bill, "boats in Death Valley? "

Jack choked and said, "Sure, boats. There used to be a lake in Death Valley. I hear the fishing was fine."

...Thomason explained quietly, "These ancient people must have been having a meeting of their rulers in the council chamber when they were all killed very suddenly. We haven't examined them very closely because it was the treasure that interested us, but the people all seem to be perfect mummies."

Bill squinted at White and asked, "Ain't it dark in this tunnel?"

"Black dark," said White, who had his voice under control again. His outburst had quieted him. "When I first went into that council room I had just some candles. I fumbled around. I didn't discover everything all at once like I've been telling you. I fell around over these men, and I was pretty near almost scared out of my head. But I got over that and everything was all right and I could see everything after I lit the lights."

"Lights? There was lights?" It was Bill asking.

"Oh, yes," said White. "These old people had a natural gas they used for lighting and cooking. I found it by accident. I was bumping around in the dark. Everything was hard and cold and I kept thinking I was seeing people and I was pretty scared. I stumbled over something on the floor and fell down. Before I could get up there was a little explosion and gas flames all around the room lighted up. What I fell over was the rock lever that turned on the gas, and my candle set the gas off. Then was when I saw all the men, and the polished table, and the big statue.

...White polished his shining pate with a grimy handkerchief. "After I got the lights going I could see all the walls of this big room and I saw some doors cut in the solid rock of the walls. The doors are big slabs of rock hung on hinges you can't see. A big rock bar lets down across them. I tried to lift up the bars and couldn't move them. I fooled around trying to get the doors open. It must have been an hour before I took hold of a little latch like on the short end of the bar and the great big bar swung up. Those people knew about counterweights and all those great big rock doors with their barlocks—they must weigh hundreds of tons—are all balanced so you can move them with your little finger, if you find the right place."

Thomason again said, "Tell them about the treasure."

"It's gold bars and precious stones. The treasure rooms are inside these big rock doors. The gold is stacked in small bars piled against the walls like bricks. The jewels are in bins cut into the rock. There's so much gold and jewelry in that place that the people there had stone wheelbarrows to move the treasure around."

... "Yes," insisted White, pleasantly sure of himself. "A small boy could fill one of those stone wheelbarrows full of gold bars and wheel it around. The wheelbarrows are balanced just like the doors. Instead of having the wheel out in front so that a man has to pick up all the weight with his back, these wise old people put the wheel almost in the middle and arranged the leverage of the shafts so that a child could put in a balanced load and wheel the barrow around."

…Bill asked, "Did you ever bring anything out of the cave?"

"Twice," said Fred Thomason. "Both times I went in we filled our pockets with gems, and carried out a gold bar apiece. The first time we left the stuff with a friend of ours and went to try and interest someone in what we'd found. We thought the scientists would be interested or the government. One government man said he'd like to see the stuff and we went back to our friend to get the gold and jewels and he told us he'd never seen them; and dared us to try and get them back. You see, he double crossed us. We were in a little trouble at the time and the loss of that stuff just put us in deeper. We couldn't get a stake because we were having hard work making anyone believe us. So we made another trip out here for more proof. That time we brought out more treasure and buried it close to the shaft entrance to the underground city before we went back to the Coast. I persuaded some university officials and some experts from the Southwest Museum to come out here with me. We got up on the Panamints and I could not find the shaft. A cloudburst had changed all the country around the shaft. We were out of luck again. The scientists became unreasonably angry with us. They've done everything they can to discredit us ever since."

Jack watched Thomason and White across the rim of his coffee cup. Bill said, "And now you can't get into your treasure tunnel. It's lost again. That's sure too bad."

Thomason and White smiled. "We can get in all right," said Thomason in the genial voice his cold eyes did not support.

...Thomason turned to White: "How high do you think those galleries are above the bottom of Death Valley?"

White said, "Somewhere around forty-five hundred or five thousand feet. You looked out of them; what do you think?"

"That's about right," agreed Thomason. "The openings are right across from Furnace Creek Ranch. We could see the green of the ranch right below us and Furnace Creek Wash across the valley. We'll find those windows in the mountains, all right."

"You goin' down there now?" asked Bill.

"That's what we came in for," said Thomason. "We're going to take out enough gold to finance ourselves, and we'll open that underground city as a curiosity of the world."

"That's it," said White. "We're through with the scientists. We tried to make a present of our discovery to science because we thought they would be interested. But they tried to rob us, and then laughed at us and abused us. Now, we'll make ourselves rich!"[130]

When Lee again heard from the two men, Bill and Jack, they were preparing to climb the east face of the Panamints to locate the ancient tunnel openings or quays high up on the side of the steep slope. Bourke Lee was fascinated by the story and eventually tried to find the entrance in the Panamints himself.

Thomason mentions a "government man" that they tried to interest in their startling find. Is it possible that the government did indeed become very interested in the underground catacombs of Death Valley? The southwestern portion of Death Valley around Wingate Pass did, in fact, become part of the China Lake Naval Weapons Center. Had the government possibly explored the Wingate Pass underground passages themselves and then decided to take the area over?

Here we have the possibility that a similar lost treasure snatch by the military was made at Death Valley as was made at Victorio Peak in New Mexico, and possibly at the Egyptian caverns excavated in the Grand Canyon in 1909. If the American military can deal with extraterrestrials at Area 51, then they could certainly deal with some Atlantean—or Lemurian—tunnels discovered in Death Valley. One would think that if there was something to find around Wingate Pass, the military has found it.

One has to wonder at this curious story and its claim that Death Valley had been a lake with the Panamint Mountains running along the western shore like the faces of cliffs. It is a fascinating idea, and in fact, at one time, there was exactly such an lake where Death Valley is today. It is called Lake Manly and it was connected to whole series of lakes that once existed in southern California. If seafarers had come into this lake system, they may well have carved a series of docks, linked with stone-cut tunnels going north and south along the cliffs.

However, geologists say this ancient lake system existed from 1.8 million years ago to 10,000 years ago—the end of the Pleistocene. Could geologists be wrong about the slow geological changes in North America, and perhaps these lakes existed—and vanished—within the last 10,000 years or so? The stories of the mummies and other artifacts would seem to place them within the last 5,000 years, though the extremely dry climate of Death Valley may have preserved them even longer than that.

Let a man talk a very long time
A hole he will bore in a cliff.
—Paiute Saying

The Mystery of Death Valley Scotty

At the northern end of Death Valley, on the east side, in the Grapevine Mountains is Scotty's Castle, a massive mansion in a secluded valley oasis. It is named after a local character known as Death Valley Scotty. It cost millions of dollars to build, and is a tourist attraction today. Where did the money come from to build this villa in the desert? According to some sources, it came from an ancient stash of gold somewhere underground in Death Valley.

In *Weird America*[94] Jim Brandon sums up the mystery of this enigmatic desert rat:

> During his lifetime, there was endless speculation on the source of wealth enjoyed by Walter Scott, an eccentric local character who built the "castle" and racetrack still located at the far north end of the valley. Those who knew him claimed that, when funds were running low, "Death Valley Scotty" would check out for a few days of wandering in the nearby Grapevine Mountains bringing back suspiciously refined-looking gold that he claimed he had prospected. Many believe that Death Valley Scotty, who spent millions on a huge castle-estate, got his gold from the stacked gold bars in the tunnel system beneath Death Valley.[94]

Death Valley Scotty was born Walter E. Scott in Cynthiana, Kentucky, on September 20, 1872. He spent his early childhood traveling the harness racing circuit with his family. At the age of 11, he left home to join his two brothers on a ranch near Wells in northeastern Nevada.

Because of his experience with horses, Walter signed on with a horse drive to California in 1884.

When he joined a crew surveying the California-Nevada boundary later that year, he made his first visit to Death Valley, beginning his lifelong love for this hot, barren region. In 1885, he took a job with the Harmony Borax Works on the 20-mule teams that hauled borax across the Mojave Desert. After this there was a short stint working for the Southern Pacific.

When only 16, Scott joined Buffalo Bill Cody's Wild West Show as a stunt rider. Here he learned how to perform, touring the U.S. and Europe for the next 12 years. In 1900, while in New York City, he met Ella Josephine Milius, whom he called "Jack." They married six months later and moved to Cripple Creek, Colorado where Walter unsuccessfully tried his hand at gold mining.

During the winter of 1901-1902 Scotty had collected a few samples of the high grade ore being mined at Cripple Creek. Using these samples he convinced Julian M. Gerard, third vice president of the Knickerbocker Trust Company, that it came from a mine that he and a partner owned in Death Valley. Gerard was fascinated with cowboys and had met Scotty when he attended the Wild West Show. He had studied mineralogy at Yale and recognized the ore as being very valuable. On April 23, 1902, Gerard and Scotty became partners and Gerard gave Scotty $750 in cash and a promise of more later.

Jack and Scotty moved to Los Angeles and Scotty focused on selling shares or partnerships in his "secret Death Valley mine." On two separate occasions Gerard sent mining engineers west to investigate the mine, but Scotty managed to turn them away and keep Gerard's money flowing. In 1904 Gerard himself visited, but returned to New York without having seen the mine. Even so, he continued to send funds to Scotty and by the end of 1905 when he decided to write the mine off as a bad investment, he had lost close to $10,000.

Scotty cultivated mystery, told tall stories about his activities, and sought publicity wherever and whenever possible. In December 1904, his mysterious ways resulted in his being suspected for a time of having robbed a Wells Fargo messenger near Daggett. The press, particularly Hearst's *Examiner*, began to print stories about him and he became something of a celebrity. Death Valley was in the news as well because legitimate mines there were producing real gold and making real profits.

Did Scotty really have a secret gold mine in Death Valley? Was he really a millionaire? Had he really ridden with Buffalo Bill Cody when he was only 16? Had he discovered a lost civilization in Death Valley? Scotty told many a tall tale—but some of it was apparently true. Cartoons in California newspapers called him the Sphinx of the Desert because he was so inscrutable. In one cartoon, he was depicted (wearing his signature cowboy hat and red tie) as the head of the Great Sphinx in Egypt with the headline, "Modern Sphinx of the Desert Who is a Riddle Yet Unsolved."

Walter was soon boasting he could break the rail speed record from Los Angeles to Chicago. On July 9, 1905, with backing from a Los Angeles mining engineer, he chartered a three-car train, the *Death Valley Coyote Special*, at a cost of $5,500. Arriving in Chicago in just 44 hours and 54 minutes, his train did indeed break the existing record for the 2,265-mile journey.

"We got there so fast that nobody had time to sober up, " was the way Scotty often described the feat. During the trip, speeds of 106 miles per hour were recorded—faster than any train had ever run before. "Death Valley Scotty" was front-page news around the nation. Wild Bill Cody even paid his former employee a compliment by hiring an impersonator to play him in the Wild West Show. It is said that Scotty got his lifelong nickname during this trip to Chicago, when he signed a hotel register as "Scott, Death Valley."

❧ ❧ ❧

Scotty's Camp Hold Out

When Scotty had money he spent it lavishly, often buying drinks for people and telling them stories. When he was broke, he would disappear into Death Valley where he had a secret hideaway in the Black Mountains which he called Camp Hold Out. Apparently he did not spend much on his now ex-wife, Jack, because she moved to Stockton, California, where she was able to get work.

One of the people who met Scotty after his arrival in Chicago with the *Death Valley Coyote Special* was Albert M. Johnson, a man who Scotty had bilked the previous winter. Johnson was the owner and President of the National Life Insurance Company and was still interested in Scotty's mine. At the time, with Johnson re-interested, Scotty was worried about his original mark, Gerard. In order to avoid trouble, Scotty signed over to Gerard all rights to the imaginary "Knickerbocker claim" in return for $100.

In September 1905, Scotty took Azariah Y. Pearl into the desert to see a likely claim near his mine. After briefly showing Pearl another man's mine, Scotty and his brother, Bill, staged a gunfight that forced the group to flee to Barstow. For most of the rest of the year he was involved in trying to promote a play in the New York Opera House that would tell the story of his life. Late in the year he went out into the desert and disappeared. When his mule and blood stained saddle appeared in camp, Death Valley Scotty was again newsworthy. Later it was determined that he had accidently shot himself in the leg.

Then, Azariah Pearl lined up some financing from T. Coleman du Pont for the new mine that Scotty had shown him. In connection with this deal, Scotty agreed to take Daniel E. Owens, a qualified mining engineer, to the mine to verify its worth for the du Pont investment. Scotty invited Johnson to come along and, using Johnson's and du Pont's money, Scotty organized a luxurious expedition that set out from Lone Willow Spring on February 25, 1906. That evening a planned ambush that had been designed to scare the party and force them to turn back went sour and Scotty's brother, Warner, was accidently wounded. The next morning the party turned back to Barstow. The newspapers referred to it as the "Battle of Wingate Pass" and headlined that Scotty had escaped death.

On March 11, 1906 Scotty's play about his secret gold mine opened in Seattle at the Third Avenue Theater with standing room only crowds clamoring to see Scotty play himself in the leading role. After a successful run in Seattle it was to play in California but Scotty was arrested instead. Owens had brought suit against him for $152,000 in assorted charges associated with the affair at Wingate Pass. Bail was set at $2,000 and was paid by the writer of the play. The suit was thrown out on a technicality, but the court proceedings made it clear that Scotty was a fraud. The press covered the trial extensively and Scotty was publicly exposed as a charlatan, and the mystery of his mine was destroyed. Public interest in the "Death Valley Fraud" faded quickly and the play closed soon thereafter.

Scotty ignored the bad press, and somehow managed to keep Johnson interested in his mine. In 1908 Johnson sent Alfred MacArthur to visit the mine. After the usual runaround, MacArthur concluded that there was no mine and so informed Johnson.

480

Johnson refused to believe it and the following year went to Death Valley himself to finally get to the bottom of things, but left again without seeing the mine.

During this period Scotty was said to have started fencing high-grade ore stolen from other mines in the area. As a front for this operation he left Death Valley and leased a mine in northern Nevada in the Humboldt Mountains. He then returned to Death Valley in 1912 to announce that he had sold his mine for a million dollars. This claim landed him in court when his creditors sued for old debts. This time he actually went to jail and was forced to admit that his mine did not exist and that the money that he had spent over the years had come primarily from Gerard and Johnson. The press branded him a cheat.

This time Scotty moved to Twentynine Palms and lived quietly until 1915 when Johnson decided that he wanted to visit Death Valley again and see his old comrade Death Valley Scotty. Johnson purchased the Staininger Ranch in Grapevine Canyon as a base camp and permitted Scotty to use it when he was not in residence. Scotty received a modest allowance and immediately returned to his old ways. Once again the mystery of his mine was the subject and once again the tales were unbelievable. Johnson regarded it as entertainment and did nothing to inhibit Scotty. He claimed that Scotty paid him back in laughs for every cent that he gave him. One of Johnson's closest associates believed that he actually admired Scotty for the way in which he had fooled him.

A Great Villa in the Desert

In 1926, Johnson decided to build a splendid ranch in Death Valley and began construction in 1927. Before construction was complete, Scotty was referring to the ranch as "my Castle." In 1929, Scotty went on another self-promotion binge, claiming among other things that he would set a new world airplane speed record, break the bank at Monte Carlo and purchase an entire string of polo ponies for his personal use at his Castle. After a week of speeding around Hollywood and Beverly Hills in a new car, his red necktie blowing in the breeze, reporters proclaimed him "America's number one mystery man."

Scotty rarely stayed in the castle itself, preferring to stay in a small bungalow that Johnson built for him at Grapevine Springs on the edge of the valley. His ex-wife, Jack, and their son, Walter Junior, stayed in another bungalow provided by Johnson in Reno. Work on the castle continued until 1931, when it was discovered that, because of a surveying error, Johnson did not own the land on which the castle had been built. The error had been discovered in the run-up to making Death Valley a national park at the close of President Herbert Hoover's term in office in 1933. The problem was finally resolved in 1935, but too late for Johnson to finish the building. His insurance company had gone into receivership in 1933 and he did not have the funds necessary to complete the plans.

Meanwhile, various victims of Scotty's past mining swindles attempted to sue him for his ownership of the Castle. It became necessary for Johnson to prove that he, not Scotty, owned and financed the construction of the Castle. He also paid off some of the litigants, including Jack, Scotty's ex-wife.

Johnson and his wife willed Death Valley Ranch to a religious organization and wrote into the will that Scotty should live there as long as he wished.

Meanwhile, after hospitalization for an illness in 1951, Scotty returned to live in the Castle and each night regaled paying guests with his exploits over the past eighty years. He had reached the pinnacle of his fame, becoming a tourist attraction in his own right. Tales of the underground, lost city of gold were told nightly, along with Scotty's many other adventures.

The castle was never completed, but Scotty continued to live there until his death on January 5, 1954. He is buried at Death Valley Ranch on a hill above "his" castle as per his express wish.

Today, as one walks through Scotty's Castle on guided tours, one is told that Scotty was basically a con artist who told tall tales of gold mines and a lost city of gold. But could Scotty have actually known about an ancient site that was not actually a gold mine, but had treasure in it? Like some sort of underground galleries carved just inside a cliff face—a cliff face that was once the shoreline of an ancient lake?

This might explain a number of strange things concerning Scotty. It is easy to dismiss him as a colorful character whose charm and charisma allowed him to con people over a lifetime. But I tend to think that "where there's smoke, there's fire." He was often gone for long periods of time "at Camp Hold Out." He did sometimes have some high-grade ore. He claimed he knew of a source of ancient gold, telling a story similar to one told by others. And he actually did many amazing things—his tall tales were usually based on some sort of fact.

Scotty tried to get people to invest in a secret gold mine, but perhaps what he actually had was a treasure trove. In an earlier chapter we discussed the bizarre story of Victorio Peak and Doc Noss, who similarly claimed that he had a gold mine, while what he really had was a treasure trove inside a mountain. Doc Noss, who had access to, and sold real gold ingots, was also accused of being a con artist and a swindler. He dared not tell the truth about the incredible discovery he had made, so he made up a different story about it. Some parts of the story were actually toned down, while others were artificially inflated. Doc Noss was ultimately shot to death because of the convoluted tales he told.

Could Death Valley Scotty have been part of some similar plot involving a forbidden treasure, an ancient civilization with mummies and gold artifacts to loot—but with all the curse and danger that that would entail? It is interesting to note that Lester Dent, the creator of the fictional hero Doc Savage, used Scotty as a model for his protagonist—Doc Savage had a secret gold mine in Central America guarded by a lost tribe of Mayans. During his long sojourns into Death Valley, what did Scotty do? As any desert rat will tell you, you don't just lie under a tree for months at a time, you go out and explore every nook and cranny of those rugged volcanic mountains until you find your bonanza. Perhaps Scotty's El Dorado was an underground world that remains a secret today.

And what of the Johnsons? Why would they have wanted to build such a grand and expensive villa out in the desert? Though this couple was fairly wealthy, was it their idea to build this grand villa near Scotty's old homestead? Could there have been an ideal partnership between someone who had millions from a business venture and someone who had millions wrapped up in a secret treasure trove? Remember, it was illegal to own or sell large amounts of gold at the time. Perhaps the Johnsons somehow "laundered" money for Scotty, keeping his actual wealth a secret from his many creditors.

There was things which he stretched,
but mainly he told the truth.
—Mark Twain, *The Adventures of Huckleberry Finn*

The Strange Underground Vaults Known Only to Scotty

At the end of his book, *Death Valley Men*, Bourke Lee tells of Death Valley Scotty's claim to know of the underground, lost city of gold that people were constantly seeking. Says Lee in the final pages of the book:

> Someone did not keep the secret of the jewel-encrusted gold-lined caverns of the Panamints. When winter came around again the entire Death Valley region knew of the golden cavern. The story of the fabulous treasure buried deeply under thousands of tons of rock and sealed with the weight of tall Telescope Peak was being told in San Francisco and Salt Lake City. An entirely sane, level headed business man, a minor pillar to Pacific Coast industry headed an amateur expedition in search for the Panamint caves. He did not find the cavern. An enterprising amusement man reached Bill and sent Bill forth to find the caves. Bill needed no urging. Bill persuaded Tom Wilson, the Indian whose grandfather had been through the cave, to guide him. Far south in the Panamints, Tom and Bill found a shaft in the mountain where no shaft had a right to be. Bill and Tom rushed across the desert to a telegraph office and wired for all the rope on the Coast. They got enough rope to find the bottom of the shaft. It was not a deep shaft. And it did not go anyplace.
>
> ...Others have searched for the entrance to the golden city of the Panamints. Tom Wilson has been in great demand as a Panamint guide. Tom's grandfather, you see, went through the cave. Tom has overcome his reluctance to approach the sacred portals of the shaft which

probably leads to the Indian hereafter. When John Thorndike set out to investigate the shaft, Tom's superstitions checked him a long way from the shaft. John finally located the shaft himself. It was an old abandoned mine shaft with an unknown history. John told Tom the cave through the Panamints was an Indian fairy tale and went back to his camp in the timber at the head of Wildrose Cañon. John found visitors at Wildrose Camp awaiting his return.

Automobiles and trucks stood about the buildings of John Thorndike's camp. One of Death Valley Scotty's men from the Death Valley Ranch was sitting on the cookhouse doorstep.

Maxfield said, "Scotty's partner, Johnson, is up on Telescope Peak with the horses. Scotty's camped down the road. We been wondering where you were. Heard you were hunting this lost city."

John said he had been hunting it, but had given it up. He walked down the road past the trucks which had brought the horses several hundred miles overland from the Death Valley Ranch in Grapevine Cañon so that Scotty and his partner, Albert Johnson, would be able to ride up on Telescope Peak from Wildrose. John found Scotty camped at his favorite spot beside the trail. Scotty always camps at that little fireplace under the junipers and mountain mahogany. The rest of the cañon may be hot, but a little breeze about ten feet wide blows across that fireplace in the warmest weather. Scotty pushed his sombrero back on his head and snapped his bright shrewd eyes at John Thorndike. Scotty had to laugh at John and his looking for the golden Panamint caverns.

Scotty pulled up his pants and his well-knit body shook with strong inward laughter, some of which escaped.

"Humph!" said Scotty. "So you didn't find it." "No," said John. "We didn't find it."

"Humph!" said Scotty. "I can go right to it." Death Valley Scotty knows his country.[130]

So, the last few paragraphs of Lee's book say that Scotty claimed to know the location of the secret underground world of Death Valley and its contents. By inference, one would think that this was the source of his wealth. Was it? Sometimes truth is stranger than fiction.

End of the Road: Death Valley's Racetrack Playa

Our little caravan of two SUVs came into the junction at Grapevine at the northern end of the park, and then drove up a rough and rocky road to Teakettle Junction where dozens of old teakettles are hung from a post. From here, it was 28 more miles of bad road to the Racetrack Playa. Rangers at the park warn people to have two spare tires and a lot of time to make this trek. We thought they spoke from an "overabundance of caution," but soon found out they spoke from experience.

We were to have met our friends Greg and Sigrid Bishop (Greg is the author of the books *Wake Up Down There* and *Weird California*) at Teakettle Junction, but we were running late. Since they were not at the Junction when we arrived, we pressed on, time being of the essence. After a few bumpy miles, we were flagged down by a couple of women who needed tools to fix a flat tire on their stranded SUV. As we pulled over, Greg shimmied out from beneath their vehicle! We all joined in the effort, and after we'd

487

seen the women on their way, it was discovered that my SUV now had a flat. We quickly changed the tire, but since we had not brought two spares, Jennifer and I piled in with Greg and Sigrid for the further journey to the Playa, planning to pick up our car on the way back.

The Racetrack Playa is a dry lakebed ("playa" means "beach" in Spanish) where large rocks mysteriously move about on their own, as evidenced by trails in the ground on which these rocks lie. Scientists have wondered for years just how these stones move for hundreds of yards across the desert.

According to Mike Marinacci in his book *Mysterious California*,[116] rocks of various sizes and shapes lying on the lakebed move silently and secretively across its surface, cutting furrows in the earth and leaving trails up to 1,200 feet long. The rocks range in size from pebbles to 600-pound boulders. No one has ever actually seen the rocks moving, but careful recordkeeping by rangers and researchers shows that some unknown process does indeed roll and slide them over the alkaline flat lakebed.

Says Marinacci, "The most popular theory says that high winds push the rocks across a thin film of ice formed by rainwater. However, this doesn't explain why some rock trails are zigzagged, while others are straight, curved, irregular or even full circles. Also, some formerly adjacent rocks have moved in completely opposite directions."[116]

Indeed, as we looked out across the playa in the late afternoon sun, we could see scores of rocks at the southeast part of the dry lakebed that had come off of a cliff at that end of the playa. These rocks had clearly fallen off onto the lakebed, and many had just taken off, apparently on their own, across the flat terrain.

There is no doubt that the lakebed would be at

times quite slippery with a thin layer of wet mud, and perhaps ice. With high winds, the conditions could be right to move the stones around the lake. But it is curious that no one has ever seen them move, and that they move in quite odd directions, often in spirals of a sort. Curiously, one method the ancient Egyptians used to move their megalithic statues was to place them on sleds, and have people pour water in front of the runners to turn the earth into a slippery surface.

As we stood out in the dry lakebed, it seemed like a pretty strange place. We were nearly 6,000 feet up in the Inyo Mountains, while the floor of Death Valley was below sea level. "Maybe we should camp here for the night, and see if these rocks move. Nobody else has ever seen it," I suggested. Everyone was too busy taking photos to really notice. But the sun was setting, and soon we would have to head back down the mountain to Stovepipe Wells or Furnace Creek, where there were a couple of small motels and gas stations.

As an interesting aside, Marinacci also tells the following curious tale of a discovery in the Amargosa Range, nearby in the southern part of Death Valley:

> Years ago, a desert rat was driving through this range in his Jeep when he came to a group of boulders blocking the road. He parked his Jeep, found a narrow pass between the rocks and walked down into a sandy valley, where he saw about 30 wooden buildings half-covered by sand dunes.
>
> Too big and elaborate to be miners' shacks, the structures were laid out like a planned community. The explorer went inside some of them and found wooden tables set for meals, brass candlesticks, cloth and even an empty picture frame on a wall. There were no human

remains and no signs of violence or natural disaster.

No record exists explaining this settlement, and the unnamed explorer's story could very well be another wild-goose chase designed specifically for desert neophytes. [116]

Ancient Objects Imbedded in Stone

A most interesting discovery that was definitely not made up occurred on the other side of Death Valley, to the west, in 1961. Wally Lane, Mike Mikesell, and Virginia Maxey, co-owners of the LM&V Rockhounds Gem and Gift Shop in Olancha, California, went into the Coso Mountains in the Inyo National Forest to look for unusual rocks. Near the top of a 4,300 foot peak overlooking the dry bed of Owens Lake they found a fossil-encrusted geode. When they opened the geode, which are generally hollow with crystals inside, they found something that resembled a spark plug. This object became known as the Coso Artifact.

In the middle of the geode was a metal core, about .08 inches (2 millimeters) in diameter. Enclosing this was what appeared to be a ceramic collar that was itself encased in a hexagonal sleeve carved out of wood that had become petrified. Around this was the outer layer of the geode, consisting of hardened clay, pebbles, bits of fossil shell, and "two nonmagnetic metallic objects resembling a nail and a washer."[16] A fragment of copper still remaining between the ceramic and the petrified wood suggests that the two may once have been separated by a now-decomposed copper sleeve. Based on the fossils contained in the geode, the object was estimated to be at least 500,000 years old! [16,18]

The geological dating of objects like this may

establish them as being much older than they actually are, largely because geologists tend to assume great dates for almost everything, plus dating rock by the fossils in it has many problems. One of these can be illustrated by the case of the Coelacanth. This fish began showing up live off Southern Africa in the 1930s, when it was thought to be extinct. The only known fossils of the Coelacanth are 85 million years old (so geologists and paleontologists claim) but why are there not other more recent fossils of the ancient fish? If the Coso Artifact was found with a fossil of a Coelacanth it might be thought to be 85 million years old. So, the Coso Artifact may only be 15,000 to 30,000 years old, rather than half a million years old.

There are probably hundreds of reports of anomalistic items like this, reports of artifacts that are unquestionably man-made, yet, according to uniformitarian geology, must be hundreds of thousands, if not millions of years old! A book by the famous 1950s and '60s radio personality Frank Edwards entitled *Strangest of All*[159] recounts the discovery of several similar "out-of-place" objects, and is a fascinating read.

Geological dating of coal, fossils, geodes, etc., is done on a scale of geological strata. On the assumption that geological change is slow and uniform, the strata are assigned dates, such as "five million years old," for example. Lower strata are, of course older than the strata above them.

But there is a distinct possibility that uniformitarian geology and dating are completely erroneous. There is a large (and growing) body of evidence that suggests that the Earth periodically undergoes violent cataclysmic changes. If this is the case, various parts of the strata could be lurched up or down, destroying their uniformity. This would allow for objects that would initially appear to have a startlingly ancient date, according to the strata dating method, to be of a much more recent manufacture. I suggest that this is the case with most of "out-of-place" artifacts. While it seems that most of them are authentic, they are probably closer to tens of thousands of years old, rather than millions of years old. This is still pretty amazing!

An interesting thing to note here is that the mechanism for burying artifacts in coal, stone and geodes is the same mechanism that creates fossils— not slow geological change, but sudden geological cataclysms, like the one that supposedly sank the ancient continents of Atlantis and Mu. It appears that such cataclysms are not isolated, rare events, but occur with alarming regularity!

The Manson Family in Death Valley

Jennifer and I headed out of Death Valley the next morning, having spent the night in one of the few motels at Stovepipe Wells. We stopped briefly at the Devil's Hole National Park and went by the Barker Ranch where Manson and his family took up residence back in the 1960s.

Tales of underground worlds around Death Valley ultimately brought Charles Manson and his clan from San Francisco and Los Angeles out into this remote desert area on the Nevada border. Manson was arrested here in 1969, and has been in jail ever since.

Bob Murphy tells much of the tale in his book *Desert Shadows*.[134] Murphy details the apocalyptic existence of Manson and his family, with their off-road vehicles, and commune living at the various ranches where they squatted. Murphy briefly tells of Manson's plan to escape the chaos of a projected race war in the cities, which Manson called "Helter Skelter" after the Beatles tune of the same name:

Charlies' plan was to lead selected whites

into the desert, where they would multiply until they reached a population of 144,000. Charlie got this idea from interpreting the Bible passage of Revelation 7, which mentions the twelve tribes of Israel, each numbering 12,000. In Revelations as well as the Hopi Indian legends, Charlie learned about a bottomless pit. According to Charlie, the entrance to this pit was a cave underneath Death Valley that led down to a sea of gold the Indians knew about. There was a river through the bottomless pit, filled with milk and honey, and there was a tree that bore 12 kinds of fruit, a different variety for each month. The place would not be dark, because the walls would glow to furnish light, and it would not be too cold or too hot. There would be warm springs and cold fresh water.

Charlie believed there were people already down there waiting for him. Family members listened attentively to Charlie's sermonizing about this underground sanctuary, a veritable paradise. Not only did they believe such a place existed, they had spent days searching for the entrance to it in Death Valley in late 1968. Because it was here they intended to wait out Helter Skelter, there was an urgency in their search.[134]

Says Marinacci in *Mysterious California*:

Manson, who had been involved with some of Southern California's most sinister and evil cults, was searching Death Valley for a passageway to a legendary underground world, where he hoped to lead his followers after starting a cataclysmic race war. He thought he'd found it at Devil's Hole, a deep, water-filled cavern on the park's Nevada side, but was arrested before he could figure out how to get his gang of killer flower-children through several hundred feet of hot, salty water where two skin divers had drowned just a few years earlier.

Manson may have learned of the underground world from the story of Tom Wilson, a Cahroc Indian who was a Death Valley guide in the 1920s.[116]

Manson believed that Devil's Hole, on the Nevada side of Death Valley, was some sort of entrance to the hollow earth, or at least the underground world of *Shin-au-av*. Devil's Hole is a surviving bit of the inland sea that was around Death Valley only a few thousand years ago. In the caves, which go to an unknown depth into the earth—presumably connecting with other underground lakes and tunnels—is a unique type of fish called the Devil's Hole Pupfish (*Cyprinodon diabolis*) that only lives in Devil's Hole. It is thought to be 22,000 years old— isolated from the other pupfish that exist in other parts of the Southwest.

If there is an underground world around Devil's Hole, it is a wet one!

Dr. Russell, Howard Hill and Amazing Explorations, Inc.

We headed directly south now, on California Highway 127 toward Baker. It was a two-lane blacktop stretching out over the rolling desert hills. There was not another car in sight. With Death Valley now in the rearview mirror, I wondered about the strange stories surrounding that remote and forbidding place. We hadn't seen the vitrified city that was described in the mid-1800s. Did it ever exist? Had it been dismantled or otherwise used by early prospectors? There were many ghost towns around; maybe they were built on top of some ancient settlement.

I continued my musing as a roadrunner suddenly darted across the pavement. *Death Valley Men* had been written in 1932, and covered largely events from the 1920s. The stories of underground catacombs complete with mummies and artifacts just would not go away, however. Witness this press release from Los Angeles on August 4, 1947, concerning a group called Amazing Explorations, Incorporated, that appeared in a number of newspapers in California and Nevada. Says the *San Diego Union* version of the story:

TRACE OF GIANTS FOUND IN DESERT

Los Angeles, Aug 4. 1947. (AP) — A retired Ohio doctor has discovered relics of an ancient civilization, whose men were 8 or 9 feet tall in the Colorado Desert near the Arizona-Nevada-California line, an associate said today.

Howard E. Hill of Los Angeles, speaking before the Transportation Club, disclosed that several well-preserved mummies were taken yesterday from caverns in an area roughly 180 miles square, extending through much of southern Nevada from Death Valley, Calif. across the Colorado River into Arizona.

Hill said the discoverer is Dr. F. Bruce Russell, retired Cincinnati physician, who stumbled on the first of several tunnels in 1931, soon after coming west and deciding to try mining for his health.

Mummies Found

Not until this year, however, did Dr. Russell go into the situation thoroughly, Hill told the luncheon. With Dr. Daniel S. Bovee, of Los Angeles—who with his father helped open up New Mexico's cliff dwellings—Dr. Russell has found mummified remains together with implements of the civilization, which Dr. Bovee had tentatively placed at about 80,000 years old.

"These giants are clothed in garments consisting of a medium length jacket and trouser extending slightly below the knees," said Hill. "The texture of the material is said to resemble gray dyed sheepskin, but obviously it was taken from an animal unknown today."

Markings Discovered

Hill said that in another cavern was found the ritual hall of the ancient people, together with devices and markings similar to those now used by the Masonic order. In a long tunnel were well-preserved remains of animals including elephants and tigers. So far, Hill added, no women have been found.

He said the explorers believe that what they found was the burial place of the tribe's hierarchy. Hieroglyphics, he added, bear a resemblance to what is known of those from the lost continent of Atlantis. They are chiseled, he added, on carefully-polished granite.

He said Dr. Viola V. Pettit, of London, who made excavations around Petra, on the Arabian Desert, soon will begin an inspection of the remains.

Another version of this story appeared in the *Hot Citizen*, a Nevada paper, on August 5, 1947. The story is here reprinted in full:

EXPEDITION REPORTS NINE-FOOT SKELETONS

A band of amateur archaeologists announced today they have discovered a lost civilization of men nine feet tall in Californian caverns. Howard E. Hill, spokesman for the expedition said the civilization may be "the fabled lost continent of Atlantis."

The caves contain mummies of men and animals and implements of a culture 80,000 years old but "in some respects more advanced than ours," Hill said. He said the 32 caves covered a 180-square-mile area in California's Death Valley and Southern Nevada.

Archeologists Skeptical

"This discovery may be more important than the unveiling of King Tut's tomb," he said.

Professional archaeologists were skeptical of Hill's story. Los Angeles County Museum scientists pointed out that dinosaurs and tigers which Hill said lay side by side in the caves appeared on earth 10,000,000 to 13,000,000 years apart.

Hill said the caves were discovered in 1931 by Dr. F. Bruce Russell, Beverly Hills physician, who literally fell in while sinking a shaft for a mining claim.

"He tried for years to interest people in them," Hill said, "but nobody believed him."

Russell and several hobbyists incorporated after the war as Amazing Explorations, Inc. and started digging. Several caverns contained mummified remains of "a race of men eight to nine feet tall," Hill said, "they apparently wore a prehistoric zoot suit—a hair garment of medium length, jacket and knee length trousers."

Cavern Temple Found

Another cavern contained their ritual hall with devices and markings similar to the Masonic order, he said.

"A long tunnel from this temple took the party into a room where," Hill said, "well-

497

preserved remains of dinosaurs, saber-toothed tigers, imperial elephants and other extinct beasts were paired off in niches as if on display.

"Some catastrophe apparently drove the people into the caves," he said. "All of the implements of their civilization were found," he said, "including household utensils and stoves which apparently cooked by radio waves."

"I know," he said, "that you won't believe that."

This is an amazing story indeed! Nine-foot mummies in zoot suits were hardly typical news stories back in 1947! One has to wonder, if this story were true, what ever happened to these caves, artifacts, and mummies? The extinct animals on display in the caves sound particularly fascinating, and it was this portion of the tale that caused the Los Angeles County Museum officials to lose interest in the story, as it was too incredible to be believed.

But, the last comment about cooking food with radio waves being unbelievable is ironic. That is the one thing that modern readers of the story could believe *was* true, considering the widespread use of microwave ovens today (who had heard of them in 1947?).

Dr. Russell apparently died near his car, another victim of one of the harshest deserts in the world. According to Mike Marinacci in *Mysterious California*, "The desert can be very deceiving to anyone not used to traveling it. Month's later Russell's car was found abandoned, with a burst radiator, in a remote area of Death Valley. His suitcase was still in the car."[116]

Marinacci hints that there has been some sort of cover-up involving the supposed discoveries around Death Valley and concludes, "For now, these stories will have to be shrouded in mystery, along with the 21,000 year old bones found in California's Imperial Valley, also rumored to have been spirited off by the Smithsonian."[116]

As Jennifer and I got into Baker, California, where we could catch Interstate 15 into Los Angeles, I pondered how the military had taken over parts of Death Valley, the southwest portion, to be exact. This is the area of Wingate Pass where one story claimed that an entrance to the tunnels could be found.

I also thought about the fact that Russell and Hill said that the area of the discovery was the Nevada-California-Arizona triangle, which is actually a bit south of Death Valley. Was the area that Russell and Hill had explored actually in the Nopah Range, the Providence Mountains or the Castle Mountains? All these areas are known to have lava tubes, and therefore, plentiful underground tunnels.

Indeed, this seems to be what is described by Russell and Hill, and by Thomason and White before them: an abandoned mine (or what seems like one) that leads into an extended lava tube which leads into a large room. This large room then had several passageways that led to other rooms. It all seems incredibly fantastic, but such were the stories told by the Paiutes and many others who came after them.

Excavations of Giants in Death Valley 1898

There are yet more stories of mummified giants that were discovered in our around Death Valley. Brad Steiger tells the interesting story of H. Flagler Cowden and his brother Charles C. Cowden. These men, who were said to be scientists dedicated to the study of desert antiquity, conducted an archaeological dig in desolate Death Valley in 1898. In that year they are said to have uncovered the skeletal remains of a human being believed to be the largest ever found and documented in the United States.

The fossilized human remains were those of a giant female, seven and a half feet tall, and the Cowdens stated their theory that she had been a member of "the race of unprecedented large primitives which vanished from the face of the earth some 100,000 years ago."[11] The Cowdens made the determination of age by the amount of silica in the soil and sands, by the state of petrification of the skeleton, and the crystallization and opalization of the bone marrow. The fossilized remains of the seven-and-a-half-foot woman were found at a depth of five feet in a "hard-rock formation of conglomerate containing small amounts of silica, which required a longer time to petrify than normal desert sands."[11]

Says Steiger:

> Ed Earl Repp, a writer, told of the "honor and privilege" that were his in working with the Cowden brothers; in the June 1970 issue of *Wild West* magazine he recalled that "in the same earth-strata where the giant female skeleton was found, they also recovered the remains of prehistoric camels and mammals of... an elephant-like creature with four tusks... With them were the remains of petrified palm trees, towering ferns, and prehistoric fishlike creatures."
>
> The Cowdens theorized that in times of vast antiquity when the lost race of giants lived there, Death Valley may have been an inlet of the Pacific Ocean, for in the same pit in which they found the skeleton of the giant female they also unearthed the petrified remains of marine life.
>
> The two brothers also found that the giant woman's skeleton bore a number of anomalous

physical appendages and attributes not found in contemporary humans. The existence of several extra "buttons" at the base of the woman's spine indicated that she and her people were endowed with tails. They also discovered that her canine teeth were twice the length of modern humans.'

The Cowdens theorized that when the California we know today was formed, together with the rising of mountains and the retreat of the seas, the tropical climate left the valley regions. The steaming swamps were replaced by vast wastelands, which still remain over much of the southern portion of the state.[11]

Here we have one of the earliest accounts of the strange giants and ancient seas that once existed around Death Valley.

Mummified Giant Woman Found in 1895

In July 1895 a party of miners working near Bridlevale Falls found the tomb of a woman whose skeletal remains indicated that she had stood six feet, eight inches.

Says Brad Steiger in his book, *Montezuma's Serpent*:

G. E Martindale, who was in charge of the miners, noticed a pile of stones that seemed to have been placed against the wall of a cliff in an unnatural formation. Assuming that the rock had been stacked by human hands, Martindale ordered his men to begin removing the stones in order to investigate what might lie beyond the formation.

The miners were astonished when they found a wall of rock that had been shaped and fitted together with apparent knowledge of

501

fine masonry technique. Convinced that they had stumbled upon some lost treasure trove, they set about tearing down the wall so that they might claim their riches.

Instead of ingots of gold or trunks of jewels, the men found a mummified corpse of a very large woman lying on a ledge that had been carved from natural stone. The corpse had been wrapped in animal skins and covered with a very fine powder. She was clutching a child to her breast.

When the mummy was taken to Los Angeles, scientists agreed that the woman was a member of a giant race that had thrived on this continent long before the American Indian had become the dominant inhabitant. They concluded that the mummy's height of six feet, eight inches would have represented a height in life of at least seven feet. Figuring the classic height difference between men and women, they supposed that the males of the forgotten species would have been nearly eight feet tall. [11]

Yet More Mummies

Giants have been occasionally discovered in other parts of California in the last few hundred years. In his book *Stranger Than Science*,[52] Frank Edwards describes how, in 1833, soldiers digging a pit for a powder magazine at Lompock Rancho (near San Luis Obispo) hacked their way through a layer of cemented gravel and came up with the skeleton of a man about twelve feet tall. The skeleton was surrounded by carved shells, huge stone axes, and blocks of porphyry covered with unintelligible symbols. The giant was noteworthy in still another respect: he had a double row of teeth, both upper and lower.[52] When local Indians began to attach a religious significance to the skeleton and artifacts, the authorities ordered it secretly buried, so it is lost to science.

Edwards also mentions that another giant man was found off the California coast on Santa Rosa Island in the 1800s. He also had a double row of teeth. These giants may have been the ones who roasted the dwarf mammoths on the island thousands of years ago.[52]

Mescalito has opened up my eyes
Mescalito has set my mind at ease
Mescalito has opened up my eyes
Set my mind at ease...
—James Taylor, *Mescalito*

Mescalito and the Black Dog

People have long been attracted to the Death Valley desert for a number of strange reasons. According to an article written by Robert Marshall for Salon.com in April of 2007, the famous author Carlos Castaneda may have caused his closest followers to flee to Death Valley and commit suicide after his death in 1998.

According to Marshall, at the heart of Castaneda's movement was a group of intensely devoted women, all of whom were or had been his lovers. They were known as the witches, and two of them, Florinda Donner-Grau and Taisha Abelar, vanished the day after Castaneda's death, along with Cleargreen president Amalia Marquez and Tensegrity instructor Kylie Lundahl. A few weeks later, Patricia Partin, Castaneda's adopted daughter as well as his lover, also disappeared. In February 2006, a skeleton found in Death Valley was identified through DNA analysis as Partin's.

Marshall says, "Former Castaneda associates say they suspect the missing women committed

503

suicide and cite remarks the women made shortly before vanishing, and point to Castaneda's frequent discussion of suicide in private group meetings. Achieving transcendence through a death nobly chosen, they maintain, had long been central to his teachings."

According to Marshall, Castaneda enrolled at UCLA in 1959, where he signed up for California ethnography with archaeology professor Clement Meighan. One of the assignments given to the class was to interview a Native American and Carlos wrote his paper about speaking with an unnamed man about the ceremonial use of jimson weed. Castaneda had money troubles and soon dropped out of school, working in a liquor store and driving a taxi. Marshall says that he began to disappear for days at a time, telling friends he was going to the desert. For seven years, Castenada worked on the manuscript that was to become *The Teachings of Don Juan*, published in 1968.

Says Marshall:

> This book begins with a young man named Carlos being introduced at an Arizona bus stop to Don Juan, an old Yaqui Indian whom he's told "is very learned about plants." Carlos tries to persuade the reluctant Don Juan to teach him about peyote. Eventually he allows Carlos to ingest the sacred peyote cactus buds. During his "trip" Carlos sees a transparent black dog, which, Don Juan later tells him, is Mescalito, a powerful supernatural being. His appearance is a sign that Carlos is "the chosen one" who's been picked to receive "the teachings."
>
> "The Teachings" is largely a dialogue between Don Juan, the master, and Carlos, the student, punctuated by the ingestion of carefully prepared mixtures of herbs and

mushrooms. Carlos has strange experiences that, in spite of Don Juan's admonitions, he continues to think of as hallucinations. In one instance, Carlos turns into a crow and flies. Afterward, an argument ensues: Is there such a thing as objective reality? Or is reality just perceptions and different, equally valid ways of describing them? Toward the book's end, Carlos again encounters Mescalito, whom he now accepts as real, not a hallucination.

Castenada withdrew from the public eye in 1973 and purchased a compound on Pandora Avenue in the Westwood area of Los Angeles. He continued to write books and with his inner core of witches, he ran an organization called Cleargreen which promoted a technique that he called Tensegrity.

According to Marshall, Castaneda died sometime in April 1998, at age 72 (the exact date is uncertain). He was cremated at the Culver City mortuary, but no one knows what became of his ashes. Within days, Donner-Grau, Abelar, Partin, Lundahl and Marquez had their phones disconnected and vanished. A few weeks later, Partin's red Ford Escort was found abandoned in Death Valley's Panamint Dunes. Castaneda's ashes may have been scattered in Death Valley.

It is believed that Castenada had earlier sent Partin into Death Valley to identify abandoned mines in the desert, which could be used as potential suicide sites. Apparently, there is an abandoned mine not far from where her remains were discovered.

On its web site, Cleargreen maintains that the women didn't "depart." They are instead "traveling" and "for the moment they are not going to appear personally at the workshops because they want this dream to take wings."

According to the Salon.com article, there seems to

have been no investigation into at least three of the disappearances. Marshall says that the Los Angeles Police Department and the FBI confirm to him that there's been no official inquiry into the disappearances of Donner-Grau, Abelar and Lundahl.

Marshall then says that in 2002, Janice Emery, a Castaneda follower and workshop attendee from Taos, jumped to her death in the Rio Grande gorge. According to him, the *Santa Fe New Mexican* said that:

> Emery had a head injury brought on by cancer. One of Emery's friends told the newspaper that Emery "wanted to be with Castaneda's people." Said another: "I think she was really thinking she could fly off." A year later, a skeleton was discovered near the site of Partin's abandoned Ford. The Inyo County sheriff's department suspected it was hers. But, due to its desiccated condition, a positive identification couldn't be made until February 2006, when new DNA technology became available.

Marshall says that one follower recalls how Castaneda had told Partin that "if you ever need to rise to infinity, take your little red car and drive it as fast as you can into the desert and you will ascend ...that's exactly what she did: She took her little red car, drove it into the desert, didn't ascend, got out, wandered around and fainted from dehydration."

Another odd victim of the desert was the former Ultimate Fighting Championship middleweight titleholder Evan Tanner who was found dead in the mountain area near Palo Verde, on September 8, 2008. Only 37 years old, Tanner wrote in his blog on Spike

TV's website on August 10, that it was his desire to start an adventure in the desert east of his new home in Oceanside. An avid outdoorsman and wandering spirit, he wanted to escape civilization for a while.

"I'm not just going out into the desert, I'm going out into the desert to hunt for lost treasure," he wrote. "I'm going on a pilgrimage of sorts, a journey to solitude, to do some thinking, and to pay my respects to the great mysteries."

Fox News reported on August 16 that Tanner wrote about collecting supplies for his journey, and wrote about the dangers he might face. "I plan on going so deep into the desert, that any failure of my equipment, could cost me my life," he said. "I've been doing a great deal of research and study. I want to know all I can about where I'm going, and I want to make sure I have the best equipment."

This led followers of his blog to fear for his safety, as they often did when Tanner reported his frequent by-the-seat-of-his-pants adventures. Then in a blog dated August 27, Tanner tried to calm his audience. "This isn't a version of 'Into the Wild,'" he wrote. "I'm not going out into the desert with a pair of shorts and a bowie knife, to try to live off the land. I'm going fully geared up, and I'm planning on having some fun." He further said, "I do plan on going back pretty far, so I did mention in one of my posts that I wanted to make sure to have good quality gear," he said. "Any failure of gear out in the desert could cause a problem."

Unfortunately, according to Fox News, Tanner was discovered by a helicopter after the Marines were called in to help with the search for the missing man. A spokesman then said that Tanner had trekked into the desert on a journey to "cleanse" himself. "Kind of like 'Survivor Man.'"

Officials said that they believed his motorcycle had run out of gas, so he attempted to walk out in 115 to

118-degree temperatures. His body was apparently found miles away from his motorcycle and it was assumed that he succumbed to the heat.

As we got on Interstate 15 in Baker and headed west for Barstow and the strange ghost town of Calico, I wondered what it was about the desolate desert of the Southwest that made people want to challenge their survival skills in the remotest spots—or just plain find a place to end it all. Was it the splendid isolation of the sand, rocky peaks and billions of stars? Perhaps it is a place where we can easily imagine our "return to the stars." For that matter, it is a seemingly good place for spaceship to suddenly land and pick us up. According to the many reports: there's a lot of UFO activity out there!

The Ancient Seas of Central California

Much of central California was a great inland sea at one time. This huge sea was connected to many finger lakes that went up into Nevada, and was connected even to Lake Tahoe and Pyramid Lake. Other bodies of water in the region were much larger, also, in the not-too-distant past. The existence of this vast system of waterways is more evidence to me that ancient seafaring expeditions could easily have made their way to Nevada and other areas that would seem inconceivable today. I cover this whole subject in more detail in my book *Lost Cities and Ancient Mysteries of North and Central America.*[18]

The inland sea was so huge, even at the time of Spanish exploration, that early visitors to the area thought that California was an island. Confusion over the extent of the Salton Sea and the Colorado River delta area contributed to this false impression.

In 1625, Henry Briggs, a noted English mathematician who developed the concept of logarithms and who also studied navigation and astronomy, drew what is believed to be the first map of the New World that showed California as an island. This endeavor was a seminal work, and *Insula California* was placed on many subsequent maps.

Maps drawn from 1600 to 1700 by the Spanish showed California as being separate from the mainland. They did not yet realize that the Sea of Cortez and the Salton Sea did not actually connect with the huge Tulare Lake Basin in central California.

Later, after some of the water boundaries had been better established, detailed Spanish maps showed a huge inland sea that started at the San Francisco Bay and went inland. Even as late as 1753, a map published by the famous French cartographer Philippe Buache shows a large inland sea, which he named on the map *"Mer de l'Ouest."*

Buache even has his *Mer de l'Ouest* washing the shores of the fabled kingdom of Quivera. On the map, Quivera lies on the southeastern shore of this sea, approximately in the area of the extensive ruins at Chaco Canyon, New Mexico. The kingdom of Cibola can be found in the Casa Grande area, the site of the present day metropolis of Phoenix, which I believe is probably a correct placement.

Buache's map also demonstrates quite nicely how the Cibola area was an ideal meeting place on the navigable rivers, the Colorado, the Gila and the Rio Grande. In drawing *Mer de l'Ouest*, Buache seems to be combining the Great Salt Lake in Utah, which was probably larger in the 18th century and may have included some of the dried up lakes in Nevada, with the Tulare Lake in California.

A map published in 1830 by Jose Maria Narvaez entitled *Plano del Territorio de la Alta California* showed the remains of an inland sea, and labeled it a huge marsh-lake. On this map, central California is called *Cienegas de Tulares,* or the Marshes of Tulares. The Tulare Lake Basin was one of the largest vestiges of the ancient sea, the lake extending for 1,000 square miles in the mid-1800s. Sailboats and steamships trafficked the waters, but by 1895 the lake had dried up because the streams that fed it had been diverted for irrigation. In an interesting turn of events, a few years later, after a winter of heavy snows in the mountains, the streams delivered abundant water and the lake reappeared (destroying crops that had been planted in the meantime). Today the lake is a tiny body of water, and the basin is crisscrossed with freeways and housing developments.

There is evidence that there is a great subterranean lake beneath California, similar to the large underground river beneath the Nile discovered by ultrasound in the 1960s. According to Jim Brandon in *Weird America*,[94] "Early in February of 1952, well-drillers found artesian water on a ranch near Fresno at a depth of 580 feet. But at the same time, fish two and one-half inches long with small spikes on their backs began gushing up with the water and fell flopping to the ground. A biologist at California State Polytechnic College knew of no underground streams in the area. The fish were identified as sticklebacks by Dr. Earl S. Herald, curator of the aquatic biology at San Francisco's Steinhart Aquarium, who said there had been similar incidents earlier in California: 1870—unidentified fish from a well in San Jose; 1874—thousands of young freshwater trout from a 143-foot well at Port Hueneme, near Ventura; 1884—sticklebacks from 191-foot well at San Bernardino; 1951—five squawfish from a 543-foot well in Lincoln. Other well-drilling surprises have happened in Boise, Idaho; Peoria County, Illinois; and Norfolk, Virginia."[94]

I couldn't help wondering where are all these fish were coming from. The disappearance of the huge inland sea of California probably had something to do with it, I figured. Most of the water probably drained out into the Pacific through the San Francisco Bay and the "Golden Gate." The Golden Gate of California provides an interesting parallel with the Pillars of Hercules that feature in Socrates' story of Atlantis. A legend exists that there was once a land associated with the narrow sea passage defined by those headlands, a paradisical country similar in climate and geography to the Mediterranean, which is now lost.

❧ ❧ ❧

At night, deep in the mountains I sit in Zazen.
The affairs of men never reach here.
In the stillness I sit on a cushion
across from the empty window.
The incense has been swallowed up
by the endless night;
My robe has become a garment of white dew,
Unable to sleep, I walk into the garden;
Suddenly, above the highest peak,
the round moon appears.
—*Ryoken*

The Calico Early Man Site

We pulled off the Interstate at the Minneola Road Exit and drove north to the old ghost town of Calico. This seemed like someplace Scooby and his gang might have visited once. It was just a few miles further to the archeological site and the small shack where a caretaker mans the Visitor's Center and gift shop, with assorted stones, booklets and desiccated lizards. We then took the self-guided walking tour.

This old mine is a controversial spot in North American archeology. It is the oldest known American archaeological site, according to many scientists. Opinions differ as to whether it is 200,000 years old, 100,000 or 50,000 years old—or just an elaborate hoax. The age of the site would indicate when the ancient Calico Lake, and other lakes in the area, actually existed, because the archeological evidence is that people were living around these lakes making tools, arrowheads and spearheads. Up to 60,000 stone tools have been found at the Calico site alone.

When this area was inhabited—whenever that was—the climate was much cooler and moister than it is today. About 20 inches of rain per annum made this location a giant series of lakes and swamps. At one point, one of the Ice Age ice sheets was only about 500 miles away. Forests of pine and oak covered what is today a desert of Joshua Trees and sagebrush. A 200 square mile lake covered the valley floor around Calico. It was a productive environment for the local people to find and process food. Geologists believe that seismic actions caused the lake to drain into what is now Death Valley. Shortly after this, the glaciers retreated.

Excavations at Calico Early Man Site began on November 1, 1964. Because of a high concentration of artifacts found in the northwest corner of Master Pit #1, a second pit was begun a short distance northwest. When a high concentration of artifacts was found in the southeast corner of pit 2, this indicated that they were probably digging at the edges of a work site, so a third pit was begun between them. Over the years, many atifacts have been found.

So, when did Calico Lake and the others contain water that could support the thousands of people living around them? Early excavations suggested that humans had been at the site as early as 200,000 years ago! The esteemed anthropologist Louis Leakey was the project director at Calico until his death in 1972, and it was the only New World site he worked on. The working dates of 50,000 to 200,000 years ago were given by Leakey based on the age of the sediments containing the artifacts. These sediments were most recently confirmed by thermoluminescence to date to 135,000 years BP. Another test called uranium/ thorium analysis gave a date of 200,000 years.

It was thought that ancient man could not have been in North America that long ago, and still today a debate rages among the "experts" as to whether man has been in the Americas for 12,000 years (the most popular theory), 30,000 years or 100,000 years or more.

Since it could not be denied that the artifacts were very old, archeologists looked into the question of whether they were artifacts at all. The controversy then became the interpretation of features found on small stone artifacts. According to the online encyclopedia Wikipedia, in 1979, James G. Duvall and William Thomas Venner published a statistical analysis of the stone objects, stating that they were "not modified by man but, rather, were form selected by the archaeologists. Form selection . . . is the selection of naturally fractured lithics that resemble man-made tools and therefore create a biased sample of lithics from the total population of naturally fractured lithics at that site."

Dee Simpson, the site's primary archeologist for 40 years until her death in 2000, staunchly claimed that the rough points on some of the rocks were formed by man, but others continued to maintain that they were naturally formed—not artifacts at all, but geofacts.

Some folks still say that it was only 30,000 years ago, or even 15,000 years ago, that Calico had a large inland lake. In fact, it is possible that the many lakes of southern California had been full—and then dried up—many times. We have just seen how quickly that process can occur with the example of Tulare Lake. But exactly when the lakes were there is not the crux of the issue with the Calico site—the problem is all the dates coming from geologists are too old to fit into the currently promulgated theory that men came to North America over the Bering Land Bridge 12,000 years ago. But we have already pointed out the vagaries of geological dating.

Perhaps the strata had shifted in cataclysmic earth changes that disturbed the geologic layers, affecting the dating process. Perhaps the seas had come and gone numerous times. As is often said, the only constant is change. California's landscape had certainly changed over the years, and there would be more change in the future.

Goin' down the road feelin' bad.
Goin' down the road feelin' bad.
Goin' down the road feelin' bad,
I don't want to be treated this ol' way.
Goin' where the climate suits my clothes.
—Grateful Dead, *Goin' Down the Road Feeling Bad*

The Round Spheres of Los Angeles

It was evening when we pulled into metro Los Angeles, getting a hotel in Burbank. We would be in the area for a few days, seeing some filmmakers, and then we would be driving down to Oceanside to visit a friend.

I was curious about the strange round stone spheres that had been discovered during the building of an electric tram through Santa Monica to downtown Los Angeles. I looked at an old book from 1908 in my collection called *Trolleys to the Surf* by Myers and Swett. The book is about the Los Angeles Pacific Railway that ran through Hollywood, Santa Monica, Venice, and along Sunset Boulevard.

The last page was fascinating, with two photos

taken in 1907 by Russell Westcott. The bottom photo was of an electric shovel excavating along the north side of Sunset Boulevard. The other, larger photo on the top of the page was quite amazing! It showed a partially excavated portion of a hill along Sunset, just west of Silver Lake Boulevard. A wagon with two horses stood along the upper part of the excavation. Below, in a hollowed out area of excavated earth from the hill, were dozens of perfectly round stones. Some appeared to be quite large—several feet in diameter—while others were smaller.

The caption read: "Giants' Marbles, or—as was popularly believed—dinosaur eggs? In excavating to straighten Sunset Blvd. just west of Silver Lake Blvd. in 1907, a treasure trove of these huge rock spheres was uncovered."

This was all there was to go on, but a picture tells a thousand words. The spheres seem to be, for the most part, perfectly round, not oval or flattened. Some other rocks in the picture appeared to be broken.

Strangely enough, the discovery of round stones is not entirely unheard of. The giant stone spheres of Costa Rica come immediately to mind. There is also a stone sphere on Easter Island that is associated with the magic that made the statues walk in popular legend. Easter Island's stone sphere is said to be foreign to the island, brought from another place, such as South America. It is the most sacred thing on the island and is said to be the "navel of the world."

Other stone spheres have been found in Malta, Brazil, New Zealand and elsewhere. Some are known to be artificial, such as those in Costa Rica, Easter Island and Malta. Others are thought to be bizarre natural spheres, such as those in New Zealand and Brazil. What category do the California spheres fall in?

It is interesting that it was a popular thought at the time of the discovery that the stones were dinosaur eggs. The La Brea tar pits with their wooly mammoth and saber-tooth tiger bones are nearby. Fossilized dinosaur eggs are known as well, and found in Mongolia, Montana, Argentina, and elsewhere. They are often amazingly round and well formed. Could this have been a nest of fossilized dinosaur eggs? Current scientific dogma would place these "dinosaur eggs" as at least 65 million years old—if that is what they were.

Well, we can only speculate since the stones appear not to have been examined or saved. If they were man-made stone spheres, like the mysterious Costa Rican spheres, they might be only ten to fifteen thousand years old, or even more recent. If they were man-made, we would have to wonder what they were for, and how they got buried in the desert hills of southern California. George Erikson and Ivar Zapp, authors of *Atlantis in America*,[13] speculate that the stone spheres of Costa Rica were used to recreate constellations used in navigation, to aid seafarers. In this case, the stones being found near the Pacific Coast would tend to fit in with this theory—though they seem more like a giant pile of stones, rather than a star map. Another theory is that some cataclysm may have washed them a shore and buried them in the hills. Was it millions of years ago, 10,000 years ago—or some other date, entirely?

Other curious round stones, possibly washed up in a Pacific Ocean catastrophe can be found at Point Loma on the southern side of San Diego. Here hundreds of "traveled boulders" lie at the low-tide line and along the bluffs near Cabrillo National Monument.

According to Mike Marinacci in *Mysterious*

California, "The huge rocks are not native to the Point Loma soil. The nearest source for similar rock is across 18 miles of ocean, on North Coronado Island. How the rocks, some of which weigh 50 tons and lie 350 feet above sea level, got to the point is a mystery."

Orthodox geologists usually explain away such "erratics" as glacierborne rock, however, Marinacci points out that glaciers never touched this area. He concludes that a more likely theory is that they were carried here by massive oceanic flooding.[116]

As we headed south on Highway One through Huntington Beach, I wondered whether these rock spheres were artificial or natural? Part of some Lemurian trove of stone balls that got washed up on the California coastline? Anything was possible in California it seemed.

Believe nothing,
no matter where you read it,
or who said it,
no matter if I have said it,
unless it agrees with your own reason
and your own common sense.
—Gautama Buddha

The Hemet Maze Stone

We stayed in Oceanside for the night with our friend, Giorgio Tsoukalos. Giorgio was originally from Switzerland and Greece, but now was living in the United States, planning to become a citizen. He had started out as a student in upstate New York, and now had his own magazine and book club called *Legendary Times*. It was fun to get together with Giorgio at his house near the beach and talk about our various adventures. Giorgio had traveled to many of the same places as I had, and we were both interested in ancient mysteries, archeology, extraterrestrials and other oddball topics.

"You've got to go see the Hemet Maze Stone," said Giorgio, finishing off his wine. "It was probably made by Buddhist explorers who wanted to find the Grand Canyon and the great Middle of what they called the Turtle Island. If you look at North America, it looks like a turtle, with Florida and Baja as the back legs."

"Turtle Island, huh?" I said. "Maybe the Zunis are the remnants of ancient Buddhist explorers who voyaged to the Southwest and made it to the area around the Grand Canyon."

After a late night at Giorgio's, we arose fasionably late and he made us a great breakfast of scrambled eggs with toast. Then we packed up the SUV to head back into the desert. Our first stop was, as Giorgio suggested, Hemet, north of Oceanside and Temecula. We pulled up a mountain road to a spot where it was blocked by several large boulders. From here we walked the rest of the way up to large granite block that is known as the Hemet Maze Stone. Today, the stone is surrounded by a fence to protect it from vandals and wild weekend parties.

The maze etched into the stone is in the form of a swastika, a sacred symbol for numerous Native American tribes across the continent. It is also an ancient symbol of Buddhism. No one knows who carved the Hemet Maze Stone. No one is sure how old it is, either. One website associated with the town of Hemet said that the petroglyph was 15,000 years old. I discovered that this assertion stemmed from a theory that the stone was a 15,000 year-old remnant of the "Cascadians," the alleged ancestors of the Maya. Another, more popular theory, was that it was a religious symbol left by Chinese Buddhist monks about 500 AD. This theory is especially favored by historians seeking to prove that the Chinese beat Columbus to North America by at least 1,000 years, and were searching for "The Middle" and "Where the Sun was born."[183]

They reportedly found all this at the Grand Canyon and the area around the Hopi and Zuni Pueblos. Perhaps they were the ones to supervise the construction of Chaco Canyon and the first of the Zuni Pueblos. The Springerville, Arizona site is now thought to be an early Zuni structure as well.

With regard to the Hemet Maze Stone, accumulation on its surface of a light patina known locally as "desert varnish," suggests to mainstream archeologists that it is many hundreds of years old, but they have no idea who might have carved it. Others think the incised carving was executed between 3,000 and 4,000 years ago, and the desert varnish helps them prove it. Certainly it is ancient.

About 50 other ancient maze stones have been identified throughout Riverside, Imperial, Orange and San Diego counties. There are at least 14 examples of labyrinthine rock art known in the remote area of Palm Springs. They are all attributed, like the Hemet stone, to the "Maze Culture." All of them have been found within 150 miles of each other, and virtually every one is rectangular, although varying in size from four inches to several feet in diameter. Typically, they are located on boulder-strewn mountainsides. They may be the remnants of a pilgrimage route dedicated to commemorating a special sacred event in the remote past, or perhaps marking a special route that was used from the California coast to the deserts that lay inland. The Hohokam Indians of southern Arizona also used the maze symbol in their finely-woven baskets.

The swastika is a common symbol, one used by the Hopi Indians, to whom the hooked cross signifies the migration of their tribe from the east following a

519

great flood that overwhelmed early mankind. Hopi sand paintings, spiritual devices for the removal of illness, are often formed into swastikas, with the patient made to sit at its center. Frank Joseph points out in his book *The Atlantis Encyclopedia* (New Pages Press, 2006) that in the bottom-left corner of the square outline of the Hemet Maze Stone is a simple, much smaller, reversed (or right-oriented) hooked cross, known in Buddhism as the *sauvastika*.

The Lost Peg Leg Mine and the Anza Borrego Desert

Our next stop was the Anza Borrego Desert. We drove down Highway 79 through Oak Grove and on to the crossroads of Highway S22. We turned east on S22 and began our drive through the bizarre Anza Borrego wilderness.

The earliest track through this wilderness was a footpath that Juan Bautista de Anza and his men built as the first trail through California in the 1770s. The trail was eventually adopted by the Mormon Army of the West, battling Indians and the elements.

After that, it became part of the route for the Butterfield Overland Stageline, a 2,000-mile trip that began in Tipton, Missouri, and took 24 days. It is said that passengers often lost 20 pounds along the way, especially as they crossed the desert.

When the Mormon Battalion first came through in 1847, they brought the first wagons to the area, but lost their picks and shovels while crossing the Colorado River. They had to use axes and pry bars to carve a route through solid rock to accommodate the wagons where the trail entered Box Canyon in what is now the state park.

Box Canyon was still too deep for the stage, so the Butterfield route detoured to the south so as to circumvent the canyon. Stage stations were generally about 20 miles apart (about the distance a stage traveled in a day) and were located in oases, canyons, and by streams where old Indian villages had been.

At Foot and Walker Pass, in the northwestern end of Blair Valley, the stagecoach passengers usually had to get out and walk and sometimes even push, so the stagecoach could cross the mountain ridge leading out of the dry lake bed.

In 1932, the year before the area became a state park, Marshall South and his wife Tanya used mostly indigenous material to build an adobe home on top of Ghost Mountain above Blair Valley.

The South family lived a subsistence existence above the valley for more than a decade, raising three children, using the desert for food, shelter, and building materials, and writing articles for *Desert Magazine*. But Tanya eventually left and the family broke up.

Their adobe house can be reached today by hiking up a steep, but manageable one-mile trail. Visitors can see the frame of their home, the underground cisterns they used to store water, the remnants of their sundial, and the outdoor oven in which they baked bread. Their strange story is told in the 2005 book, *Marshall South and the Ghost Mountain Chronicles*,[121] which includes his complete writings for *Desert Magazine*.

Out in the Borrego Badlands is the reputed site of the Lost Peg Leg Mine, which lured hundreds of prospectors in search of its fabled cache of blackened gold nuggets. A brass plaque at the site is dedicated to all those who have searched for the lost gold mine.

Many strange stories were told of this area, involving giant, glowing skeletons, huge apemen, and other terrifying phantoms that supposedly chased people in the desert. Some locals believe that

521

the grotesque skeleton protects a hidden entrance to the gold mine.

This "lost mine" is perhaps the one that has been searched for more than any other in southern California. The Lost Peg Leg Mine is not actually a mine, but rather a placer deposit. The actual name of its discoverer "Peg Leg" was Thomas Long Smith, who allegedly dabbled in horse thievery and telling tall tales.

Born in Kentucky in 1801, he left home while young and wandered throughout the Old West, traveling through the Anza Borrego desert in 1829 with pelts he snagged in Utah.

Peg Leg is said to have climbed one of the buttes that were close by in his desperation for water. Tired from his unsuccessful searching, he sat down to get some rest. At that point, he noticed that the butte was covered with black rocks that were the size of walnuts. He picked some of the rocks up and was impressed at how heavy they were and decided to put a few in his pocket. He emerged from the desert with the rocks he said he had found near the springs. He claimed that experts in Los Angeles said the rocks were pure gold.

But instead of going back to mine his find immediately, he moved to Idaho and became a horse trader until 1850, when he organized the first of several unsuccessful expeditions to find his mine.

Not being able to find his gold mine again, he became famous earning drinks by telling stories until dying in 1866. He inspired legions of gold seekers, but no one found his treasure. Instead a bizarre Peg Leg cult began to grow.

In 1916, Borrego Springs resident Harry Oliver organized the first Peg Leg Club, which initially organized expeditions to search for the gold and even was rumored to have salted the desert with fake wooden legs to enhance the legend.

On February 12, 1949, a man named "Desert Steve" built a monument to Peg Leg and his lost gold by piling up stones into a heap almost six feet high and about 25 feet around. A sign nearby notes: "Let he who seeks Peg Leg's gold add 10 stones to this monument."

The strange story of a glowing skeleton in the desert is mentioned in Mike Miranacci's *Mysterious California*.[116] He tells the story of how the area around Borrego Springs and the Borrego Badlands took on a legend of being haunted by phantoms and dangerous monsters. According to Marinacci a curious story of a terrifying phantom in the Borrego Badlands began appearing around the turn of the century. The story was that that some monster was chasing away prospectors and lost-mine seekers from the Badlands area. At that time there were still many prospectors and adventurers voyaging into this remote desert area in search of the Lost Peg Leg Mine. Says Marinacci:

> The first man to see the phantom was Charley Arizona, a wise old desert hand who thought he'd seen everything the land could throw at him. One night, Charley was camped on the western edge of the Badlands, when something scared his burros. Walking over to investigate, the prospector spotted an eight-foot tall skeleton stumbling around just 200 yards to the east. The skeleton had a lantern-like light flickering through its ribs, and Charley swore he "could hear his bone a-rattlin'" as it disappeared over a ridge.
>
> The phantom showed up again two years later, when two prospectors saw it in the Superstition Hills to the south. They forgot about the incident until a year afterwards, when another prospector told them he'd seen

a giant skeleton with a light in its chest loping aimlessly around the Badlands.

Soon, almost all of Borrego's regulars knew about the strange phantom. Stories and speculations about it made the rounds of the prospectors' fraternity for several years. Eventually, two men, whose names are now lost, set out to track down the skeleton for themselves.

They weren't disappointed. On the third night of their hunt, they spotted an eerie light bobbing around in the Borrego Badlands. They approached it, and sure enough, it was the skeleton, running around crazily in the black night. The pair took off after it, chasing the wraith at top speed over hills and through arroyos. One of the men even took a shot at the shambling phantom. But after about three miles, the skeleton lost his pursuers in the dark desert.

The skeleton was seen infrequently afterwards, usually in the Badlands, and a story began to grow up around it. It was said, [it was] the spirit of a man who had found and worked the appropriately named Phantom Mine, and had died on the desert, his body reduced to bones by scavengers and heat. And his ghost, in the form of a huge skeleton, wanders the night desert around his old claim, chasing off all intruders.[116]

This strange story seems like a tall tale—perhaps one to be told to greenhorn prospectors. Had someone actually seen this? Maybe it was a practical joke, with the perpetrator using a skeleton made of wood with lanterns hung on it to scare off folks who were known to be poking their noses around in the area.

The last thing ever heard about the Lost Peg Leg

Mine was contained in a letter received at *Desert Magazine,* a now extinct magazine that dealt with desert lore and lost treasure in the Southwest, in February of 1965.

In the letter, the writer claimed to have found about $315,000 in black gold nuggets between 1955 and 1965 (about $4 million at today's price of gold). He says he accidently found the nuggets within 30 miles of the Salton Sea, while looking for rocks and flowers in the desert. The gold nuggets were coated with a black varnish that may have been created from the oxidation of copper. He did not mention a glowing skeleton or giant apemen.

The Apemen of the Borrego Desert

Only four or five miles Southeast of Borrego Springs is the Borrego Sink area. The Borrego Sink is the lowest part of Borrego Valley, receiving runoff from Coyote Canyon. Vegetation on its flanks is typical of desert growth in alkaline soil such as mesquite, desert thorn and bunch grass.

Choral Pepper, in her book *Desert Lore of Southern California,*[122] says that on a dark night while camping alone in 1939, a prospector was confronted by a pack of gigantic silver-haired beasts with red eyes that glowed in the dark. Although they menaced him for some time, they appeared to fear his blazing fire and kept a distance.

Mike Marinacci, in a slightly different version of the same story, says that Southern California Bigfoot expert Ken Coon once interviewed a man who said he'd seen Sasquatches in the tangle of dry gulches known as Borrego Sink. The witness was a local storeowner who wished to remain anonymous, and he told Coon that back in 1939 he was prospecting around the Borrego Sink and camped there alone at night, when he was confronted by a pack of hairy, two-legged creatures. The apemen were covered with white or silver fur, and had red eyes that glowed in the dark. They surrounded him at his camp and threatened him for a bit, but were frightened by the blazing campfire.[116]

Pepper says that no one took the prospector's story very seriously until 30 years later when Harold Lancaster, "a well-respected desert wanderer," confirmed to skeptics that some kind of strange beast was roaming the Anza-Borrego desert. He claimed that while camped in that same area, he was startled to see a "giant apeman" approaching. Lancaster grabbed his shotgun and fired a warning shot. The apeman "jumped a good three feet off the ground," then hightailed it back into the early morning shadows.[122]

Other apemen, or perhaps the same ones, were lurking in the nearby Deadman's Hole. According to Marinacci:

> Back in the 19th century, this wooded hollow witnessed a string of unsolved murders that were blamed on a rampaging Sasquatch.
>
> It all began in 1858, when an unidentified man was slain here. Twelve years later, a Frenchman who had just settled in the Hole was murdered in his cabin. Two more locals were killed at the Hole: prospector David Blair, who was found dead of "knife wounds" in June 1887; and a young woman named Belinda, who was either shot, strangled or mutilated three months later.
>
> The rest of the story is vague and controversial. In March 1888, two hunters from Julian went up into Dark Canyon, just west of the Hole, and were allegedly attacked by "an immense unwieldy animal" that was over six feet tall, covered with black hair, with huge feet and a humanlike face and head. The

hunters had been exploring a little cave full of human and animal remains when the creature surprised them. Cornered, they shot it dead.

The beast's body was then supposedly taken to either Julian or San Diego, and exhibited publicly at a police station on April 1. The *San Diego Union* covered the story, and blamed the beast for the recent murders at Deadman's Hole. The next day, though, the paper ran a retraction, dismissing the whole thing as an April Fool's Day joke and belittling credulous readers who had trudged down to the police station to see the monster. If the whole incident was a joke, it was in extremely poor taste, considering that it made light of real, recent murders.

Ugly rumors and feelings still surround Deadman's Hole. Local sportsmen tell of "bad vibes" around the hollow, and Indians give the area a wide berth. Nobody quite knows why the wooded glade still inspires such feelings of dread.[116]

Coral Pepper tells of a man named Victor Stoyanow who also searched for the Abominable Sandman:

A manuscript written by Victor Stoyanow, a retired marine major, passed across my desk at *Desert Magazine* in January 1964. I had met the writer. In fact, I had suggested that he try his hand at writing when he had dropped into the office to compare notes on desert explorations. At every opportunity Stoyanow sought adventure in the most out-of-the way areas he could find. As it turned out, he wrote very well and we published several of his stories. And then came the one about the "Abominable

Sandman!"

Our marine major had been tramping around one of the more remote canyons in the Borrego Sink when he came across some incongruous tracks. Splay-toed and immense with clearly definable digits terminating in tiny depressions made by claws, they pointed downhill, each pair falling at an interval of approximately forty inches. Upon reaching the desert floor, the tracks disappeared into wind-blown sand. Continuing his search, the major found identical prints on a nearby hill among some bunch grass where the ground was softer. These tracks were about seven feet apart and slightly larger than the others. From this, the major deduced that the monster was capable of prodigious leaps.

Returning to his home in San Diego, the major went through *San Diego Union* files at the library. He found no reference to a desert bigfoot, but he did learn that some years earlier a monster had been killed by a Frank Cox at Deadman's Hole near Warner Hot Springs on the northern fringe of the park. This monster was described as having feet twenty-four inches long, weighing about four hundred pounds and with a small head and buckteeth. It appeared to be a cross between a man and a bear. Satisfied with his research, the major neglected to read a subsequent edition of the newspaper which revealed that the story had been published as an April Fool's joke.[122]

Well, I wasn't so sure that these desert Sasquatch were just an April Fool's joke. I couldn't help thinking that there was something to this. I looked on the detailed map we had of Anza-Borrego, and saw that Deadman's Hole is seven miles northwest of Warner

Springs on Highway 79. However, we were headed east to Ocotillo Wells and then east on Highway 78 to the Salton Sea.

> *Oh, Peyote*
> *She tried to show me*
> *You know there ain't no cause to weep*
> *At Bitter Creek*
> *—Eagles, Bitter Creek*

The Strange Oriflamme Mountain and Superstition Mountain

Jennifer and I were driving along Highway S2, going south toward Superstition Mountain and were passing Ghost Mountain to the east. To the west was Oriflamme Mountain. It is said that on dark desert nights, mysterious "ghost lights" often play over the slopes of the mountain, the name of which means "golden flame."

For a long time, it was thought that Oriflamme's lights were signal flares from bootleggers. But the mountain is an exposed, barren ridge of little use to moonshiners, and its glowing balls have long outlived Prohibition.

Mike Marinacci says that mystery lights have been seen in other parts of the Borrego Desert. He says that back in the 1880s, miners said that "burning balls" often lit up the night sky like fireworks over the Vallecito Mountains, in the center of the park. Also, a "spirit light' that bobbed along nearby San Felipe Creek in the 1930s was written up in the Journal of the American Society for Psychical Research.[116]

Like the Marfa Mystery Lights, the strange lights on Oriflamme Mountain are probably caused by some natural process. One theory is that dry desert winds blow sand against quartz outcroppings on the mountain, and this produces static electricity that lights the dark slopes with bright flashes. More

529

probably, pressure on quartz deposits are creating a piezoelectric effect that includes flashes of light and glowing balls.

Then there is the "money light" belief that is popular in the Andes of South America and other parts of Latin America. The general belief is that the lights mark a gold treasure, or perhaps some major ore deposit. This is a popular belief among prospectors and desert wanderers, as well.

Ghost lights can be fairly common and certain mystery lights, like the ones in Marfa, occur virtually every night. If the presence of ghost lights on Oriflamme isn't strange enough, the local scene gets totally weird with the addition of the hollow granite mountain known as Superstition Mountain. It was directly to the east of us as we drove to Ocotillo.

Choral Pepper discusses the strange case of Superstition Mountain, which some historians believe was the Aztlan of the Aztecs. In 1965 a California graduate geologist, who was also a member of the California Bar Association, introduced a provocative concept. After years of searching throughout Mexico and the Southwest for the mysterious Aztec homeland described in the pre-Columbian *Codex Boturini*, Ralph Lawrence Caine concluded that this seemingly insignificant range called the Superstitions was in reality the fabled Aztlan from whence came the Aztec nation. Caine built a strong case. Some of his colleagues took it seriously; others praised his imagination. In 1962 Caine published his book on the theory, *Historic Aztlan and the Laguna del Ora*.[123]

Caine said that according to the Aztec calendar, in the year one these people who called themselves "the Crane People," began their wanderings from a homeland far to the north of Mexico. An ancient codex describes this place, the Vale of Aztlan ("place of reeds and herons"), as an island with seven caves amid a lake surrounded by mountains and much swampy land.

Historians have been interested in the location of the mysterious Aztlan for centuries, and it was generally agreed to have been north of the Valley of Mexico where the Aztecs ultimately built their capital, Tenochtitlan, on an island in the middle of a volcanic lake. Aztlan has been placed from Texas to the Mississippi River Valley—and even Wisconsin. Many thought it was in Utah, New Mexico or Arizona, but now Caine placed it in the very southern part of the California desert.

Caine contended in his book that the best possible clues are the Aztec's recorded description of the place itself and legends of creation that the Pueblo Indians of the Southwest had in common with the Aztecs. One similar legend was that the mother earth gave birth to their early ancestors in a dark underground world (cave) surrounded by land-locked waters. The vast cavern was roofed by a tremendous stone, "solid and resting upon the earth like an inverted bowl." Mountains to the west were blue, those to the north red, ones to the south white, with yellow to the east.

Coral Pepper met Caine and wrote an article about him when she was the editor of *Desert Magazine* in the 1960s. She says that a naturalist named Lowell Lindsay suggested a regional parallel between the Superstion area and the mountains described in the Aztec myth. The Superstition area is surrounded by the yellowish Algodones sand dunes to the east; the reddish sandstones of Mecca Hills to the north (or perhaps Red Rock Canyon in the Fish Creek Mountains); the bluish Laguna Mountains to the west; and the snow-capped Sierra San Pedro Martir (Baja's highest mountains) to the south.

Caine is convinced that Superstition Mountain is Aztlan and in his book *Historic Aztlan and the Laguna del Ora*, he reveals further clues derived from Pueblo

531

Indian legends. In the lower level of this cave lived a water serpent that caused floods and earthquakes. These disasters ultimately drove the people from the cave world. A severe earth shock crumbled their walls and water in the lake began to disappear, leaving soft marshy ground around its perimeter which eventually hardened into rock.

Because of this last catastrophe, they had to dig out of their cave world before the big overhanging rock fell. After this final emergence into the "upper world," the Indians migrated eastward "across a great river"—the Colorado River. An almost identical passage appears in the retraced migration route for Aztec souls retuning back to their cave heaven after death. On top of this, says Caine, both Aztec and Pueblo Indians share a legend about Montezuma sending his priceless hoard of gold north to escape the plundering of Mexico City. [123]

Choral Pepper thinks that Superstition Mountain "may well be the real Aztlan. The mountain at one time jutted into the great Lake Cahuilla, indicated by white calcium carbonate deposits marking a shoreline against surrounding mountain ranges. Protruding above the surface of those waters near the western shore would have been a peninsular mass consisting of Superstition Mountain and its associated hills. And most importantly, this relic island consists of a solid granitic 'stone cover, like an inverted bowl' over fifty feet thick, resting upon lower sediments due to the fault rift character of the district." [122]

It all seemed amazing that some granite mountain out in the desert was somehow hollow and held a lost civilization. Part of it is now a U.S. Naval Reservation. Had it been taken over by the military, much as Victorio Peak in New Mexico had? What might they have found inside this ancient mountain?

"Do you suppose that Superstition Mountain has lots of caves and tunnels in it?" asked Jennifer.

532

"It sounds like it, doesn't it?" I responded. We could not find out anything more in this regard. As we came around a bend in the desert highway, I wondered about it all being a vast inland sea with lakes and marshes around it. Was it hundreds of thousands of years ago? Or had it only been a few thousand years ago? Lost ships in the desert might provide an answer to that question.

The Mystery Ships in the Desert

We were passing through Agua Caliente Springs north of Ocotillo on Hwy S2. Today, the hot and cold springs in this desert region are maintained as a county park. Sufferers of arthritis and rheumatism park their mobile homes here for up to six months at a time, to enjoy the springs' soothing waters. As Jennifer read aloud from Choral Pepper's book, we realized we were in the area of the lost ships in the desert, found up some of the numerous canyons.

Pepper, in her book *Desert Lore of Southern California*,[122] mentions several interesting ships found in the desert. One persistent story concerns Senora Petra Tucker who, before she married her prospecting husband, was the widow of a man named Santiago Socia. It was Santiago who first found an "ancient ship of the desert."

Santiago had recently moved from Mexico City to Tecate where his new wife Petra was to join him. While awaiting her, he met a local with a map to some gold ore buried about forty kilometers northeast of Tecate. Armed with the map, which he had purchased from the man with his last pay, he set forth immediately after Petra's arrival. Santiago came back a month later, poorer but wiser. However, he was not empty-handed. The souvenir he brought home was a shield made of metal in the shape of a round tortilla, only larger. Says Pepper:

> Santiago had a strange story to tell. While searching for the treasure, he had entered several canyons near the floor of the desert. In the bottom of one with high sheer walls stood an ancient ship with round discs on its side. Only a portion of the ship projected from the sand. There was strange writing on the wall above the ship which Santiago didn't recognize as Indian, Spanish or English. The bow of the ship was curved and carved like the long neck of a bird. It was one of the discs attached to the ship's side that he had brought home to Petra. When she remarried after Santiago's death, it was discarded, but she often spoke of the strange ship.
>
> An intriguing record turned up in Guadalajara, Mexico, in the mid-'50s that revealed an official inquiry held by the Spanish court in 1574. A strange fleet of three large and five small vessels had been sighted sailing north in the Gulf of California. The vessels resembled Galician caravels with carved pelican figureheads. Because they obviously were not of Spanish origin, the Crown had ordered an investigation. Witnesses included Spanish soldiers and Indians who lived in pueblos along the western coast of Mexico. All described the vessels in a similar manner. One of the witnesses was a Franciscan friar who was brought up in a European seaport and was familiar with the sailing vessels of many nations. Never had he seen vessels such as these.[122]

I thought this pretty interesting, especially the idea of a mystery fleet that was sailing around the west coast of the Americas in 1574.

The Phoenicians were famous for being very secretive about their trade routes, and they were one of the "Lost Tribes of Israel"—the tribe of Dan. Indeed, Denmark may be named after the tribe of Dan, for it is alleged some of the vanquished Phoenicians ended up in Northern Europe when they fled the Mediterranean. Certain Viking voyages setting forth from Denmark may have had special purposes and been far flung in nature—there are reports of Vikings actually exploring the coasts of British Columbia, California, Mexico and other areas. The ship with the curved, carved bow found by Santiago sounds like it would resemble a Viking ship. Apparently, many of the inland seas of California still had water in them even some 1,500 years ago, or less—could a remnant Viking ship have been marooned while exploring some channel, now dry?

The idea of a Viking ship stranded in the Borrego Desert may not be quite as preposterous as it sounds. During the great Norse expeditionary period from 900-1100 AD, high temperatures in the Northern Hemisphere melted away much of the Arctic ice north of Canada. At least one Viking ship may have sailed through the Northwest Passage and down through the Bering Strait, although there would be no guarantees that the adventurers would ever make it back to Scandinavia.

A curious Indian legend implies that Vikings may have strayed as far south as Mexico. The Seri Indians of the Gulf of California's Tiburon Island still sing the song of the "Come-From-Afar-Men" who landed on the island in a "long boat with a head like a snake." They say the strange men had yellow hair and beards, and a woman with red hair was among them. Their chief stayed on the island with the redheaded woman while his men hunted whales in the Gulf. When they had finished hunting, the strangers went back aboard their ship and sailed away.

One version of the legend says their ship sank in the Gulf, and the survivors swam ashore and were taken in by the Mayo Indians. Even today, the Mayos sometimes produce children with blond hair and blue eyes, and say that they are descendants of the strangers that married into the tribe in ancient times.[116, 143]

Pepper and Marinacci both tell of how, back in the 1930s, the Agua Caliente Springs were known only to a few locals, such as Myrtle and Louis Botts of nearby Julian. Myrtle, an amateur botanist, was especially fond of the springs, since brilliant wildflowers grew in the canyons above them.

The story goes that in early 1933, she and her husband, on a wildflower hunt here, were camped at the mouth of a canyon. Myrtle had just prepared a campfire meal when an old desert rat came up to them from out of nowhere. They invited him to share their dinner and he began to tell them a few stories. A few days earlier, he told the Bottses, he had been far into a canyon where he had seen an old ship sticking right out of the side of a mountain. Because he also claimed to know where the Peg Leg gold was, the Bottses laughed and went on with their dinner.

The next morning, the Bottses hiked into the canyon. As the grade got steeper, they took a rest. Then, they saw, jutting out of the canyon wall, almost immediately overhead, the forward portion of a large and very ancient vessel. A curved head swept up from its prow. Along both sides of the vessel were clearly discernible, circular marks in the wood, quite possibly left by shields that at one time had been attached to the vessel. Near the bow, on one side of the ship, were four deep furrows in the wood. The craft was high enough to hide its interior from the Bottses' view and the side of the canyon was so steep that it could be scaled only by an expert mountain climber.

For a long time, the Bottes studied the curious sight. Then they retraced their steps back to their camp, taking careful note of the landmarks in order to experience no difficulty in returning to the ship. Suddenly, the big earthquake of 1933 struck southern California just as they were returning to their camp. Both were thrown to the ground and their car was bounced along the desert in front of them. The canyon they had just exited became a disaster of landslides. If they had lingered there any longer, they would have been buried in tons of earth.[116, 143]

Myrtle was tantalized by the mysterious wreck, and immediately began to read up on ancient ships at the library where she worked. After several days of study, she decided that the craft most closely resembled one of the old Viking sea raiders, though she couldn't bring herself to believe that Norsemen sailed the ship over 40 miles of mountains to Agua Caliente. Other ancient ships looked like this as well, and it could have been Phoenician or Roman.

Myrtle and her husband resolved to visit Agua Caliente Springs the following weekend, and take pictures of the craft to prove it existed. But when they returned to the canyon, they were (not surprisingly) stopped short by a slide that blocked the trail where they had hiked a week earlier. There was no trace of the ship or the canyon wall that held it. The Bottses decided that the great 1933 earthquake had shaken tons of earth loose from the mountain, and buried the ancient ship beneath it.[116]

Coral Pepper's book, *The Mysterious West*,[143] gives several curious accounts of mystery ships in the desert, and Indian or Spanish legends concerning them. There is the tale of a rancher named Nels Jacobsen, of California's Imperial Valley, who reportedly found a skeleton of an ancient boat near his house some six miles east of the Imperial Valley in 1907 and salvaged the lumber from it to build a pigpen.[143]

There are also records of a Spanish expedition led by Captain Juan de Iturbe in 1615 to command a pearling station off of La Paz in the Gulf of California. Iturbe sailed through a wide channel at high tide and found himself in another sea, the Salton Sea, but was unable to get his ship back out afterwards. Iturbe was then forced to abandon his ship with its valuable cargo of pearls, and walk back to Mexico, where he filed his report on what had happened.[143] Presumably, this ship is still somewhere out there.

According to the book *Geology of Anza-Borrego: Edge of Creation,*[137] Lake Cahuilla last evaporated in 1600 AD, leaving a high-water mark at 40 feet above sea level at numerous locations around the Salton Trough. The present surface of the Salton Sea is 225 feet below sea level. So… geologists are telling us that only 400 years ago there was a body of water in the Salton Sea-Anza-Borrego area that had a potential water level 265 feet higher than the Salton Sea is now.

If the huge Lake Cahuilla existed until 1600 in southern California, what about the other dried up lakes to the north, such as those around Calico and Death Valley? These lakes supposedly dried up over 100,000 years ago—could remnants of them still have existed shortly before 1600 AD when Lake Cahuilla still existed?

What had drained this lake? Did a powerful earthquake alter the geology of southern California (and that of the lower Colorado River) around the year 1600 and create the desert that we see today? This major geological change may have affected the civilizations in Arizona and even New Mexico, what little may have remained of them. In fact, if this lake existed around 1600 AD, it could have been possible for early Spanish explorers sailing north of Acapulco

538

to have sailed into Lake Cahuilla, and perhaps have been unable to sail back out again if an earthquake had occurred during their voyage. Furthermore, any ships that may have made the voyage in pre-Columbian times when the lake apparently held water (ships of the Olmecs, Mixtecs, Mayans, Phoenicians, Polynesians, Chinese or Vikings, just to name a few), could have entered into the inner California lake system via the same Lake Cahuilla. Indeed, it would seem quite possible to have gone even as far north as Death Valley during those times. My, how things have changed!

We had a late lunch in El Centro at one of the many Mexican restaurants. We were just north of the infamous border town of Mexicali, known for its many bars. It was founded in 1903, combining the names of Mexico and California. During Prohibition in the U.S., many Chinese laborers and farmers came to the town to open bars, restaurants and hotels to cater to American clients. Chinesca (Mexicali's Chinatown) eventually housed just about all of the city's casinos and bars, and had an underground tunnel system to connect its bordellos and opium dens to Calexico on the U.S. side.

After lunch we got on Highway 78 going east through the Imperial Sand Dunes Recreational Area. We stopped at the big store in the dune buggy capital of Glamis, on the eastern edge of the dunes, and bought some postcards and cold drinks.

Is there anything a man don't stand to lose
When the devil wants to take it all away…
He just might find himself out there on
horseback in the dark
Just ridin' and runnin' across those desert sands.
—Grateful Dead, *Mexicali Blues*

Suddenly, we came to an immigration checkpoint in the desert, going north on Highway 78 to Palo Verde and Blythe. It seemed to be manned by soldiers, who motioned to us to come to a stop. Not another car could be seen for miles in any direction.

"Where are you coming from?" asked a uniformed young man with a rifle in his hand, as he came to the driver's window.

I looked him in the eye and said, "We're coming from Oceanside." We were being watched by another soldier who was standing with a rifle a few yards in front of us.

"Where are you going?" asked the soldier, looking around in the back of the SUV. We had boxes of food and camping supplies, plus luggage and such.

"We are going back to Arizona," I said. "Back to the World Explorers Club."

"The World Explorers Club?" he said. "What do they do?"

"Oh, they look for lost cities and ancient mysteries," I said, smiling.

"Lost cities and ancient mysteries, eh?" he said, and broke into a smile. "Good luck," he said waving us forward.

With thoughts of lost ships in the desert and glowing skeletons and apemen lurking at some remote oasis swirling in our heads, we drove north through the Imperial Valley, an agricultural area that had been disastrously flooded by the Colorado River overflowing its banks from time to time. Boats had come into the desert that way as well.

South of us was Yuma, and that turned my thoughts to the subject of giants. Early reports from Jesuit missionaries along the Colorado River described the Yuma Indians as literal giants. In September of 1700, Father Kino was exploring the area and was hailed by thousands of Yumans, who greeted him in peace as he rode along the southern section of the Colorado River.

Says Charles Polzer in his book, *A Kino Guide,* "The Yumans were gigantic in stature, and one of them was the largest Indian Kino had ever seen. It must have been a little nerve-wracking to be the willing captive of such giants. But Padre Kino's own good will and understanding of the Indian ways won a whole new nation in friendship."[71]

In the theory that mankind has been getting progressively shorter over history, mainly due to constant warfare, the Yumans may have been the descendents of a race of giants, and by the 1700s were still quite tall by normal standards of the time. Today the Yumans are of normal height, as far as I know.

Another interesting tale of California giants comes from one of the state's most famous desert rats, a blonde-haired adventuress named Choral Pepper. I have already quoted extensively from her numerous books on remote back-country spots and their associated legends. Choral, with her husband Jack, published *Desert Magazine* in the 1960s and wrote books up until the 1980s. She was also a friend of Erle Stanley Gardner who wrote many of the Perry Mason novels, as well as many of the scripts for the television show starring Raymond Burr.

Choral and Jack accompanied Gardner on some of his expeditions into Baja California, and she chronicled their adventures in her 1973 book *Baja California: Vanished Missions, Lost Treasures, Strange Stories Tall and True.*[136] In her chapter on central Baja missions, she mentions a curious story from Mission San Ignacio de Kadakaman, known usually as simply San Ignacio, an oasis of the Cochimi Indians. The Jesuit priest Juan Bautista Luyando, a wealthy man in his own right, donated dozens of Arabian date palms to the oasis, where they still thrive today.

Pepper says that the village became alarmed when sometime after 1752, Padre George Retz "dug up a gigantic skeleton at Rancho san Joaquin, about ten miles to the south. He reported that the bones exactly resembled those of a human being, with the dimensions of the skull, vertebrae and leg bones representative of a man over eleven feet tall. This find caused the missionaries to have second thoughts about the natives' report that the cave paintings in the region's canyons were executed by giants."

Concludes Pepper in the story of the San Ignacio giant, "There was no further investigation along this line so far as I know, although ranchers in isolated places occasionally reported to Earle Stanley Gardner that they had come upon abnormally large skeletal remains."[136]

Researcher Joseph Jochmans tells of the remains of another giant discovered in the area in his booklet *Strange Relics from the Depths of the Earth.*[126]

The long drive north through the Imperial Valley had us crossing numerous canals, but there was hardly a car in sight. We drove through the small quasi-ghost town of Palo Verde; it had several closed cafés and rock shops. It seemed like maybe one store was actually open. The Colorado River could just be seen to the west, a ribbon of blue water cutting through some of driest desert in the world.

> *The river flows*
> *It flows to the sea*
> *Wherever that river goes*
> *That's where I want to be*
> *Flow river flow*
> *Let your waters wash down*
> *Take me from this road*
> *To some other town.*
> —The Byrds, *Ballad of Easy Rider*

❧ ❧ ❧

Giant Drawings in the Desert

Shortly, we reached Interstate 10 and drove east for a few miles to Blythe, where we turned north on California 95. Our next stop was the Blythe Intaglios one of the most spectacular ancient creations in California. The gigantic figures are etched in the desert a few miles north of Blythe and are similar to the enigmatic figures in the Nazca area of southern Peru. There are no lines stretching for miles across the desert such as those at Nazca, however, only figures.

Just like the Nazca figures of Peru, they were made by removing a layer of the topsoil to expose the lighter soil underneath. And just like the Nazca figures, they are hard to see from ground level and are best viewed from the air. According to a *Literary Digest* article of November 12, 1932, Army Air Corps flyers in California photographed shapes of giant human and animal figures ranging from 50 to 167 feet in length. George Palmer, who spotted the figures while flying from Hoover Dam to Los Angeles, wrote, "Near two of the human shapes are figures of serpents and four-legged animals with long tails. One giant, or god, appears just to have stepped out of a large dance ring."[17]

Shortly afterward, Arthur Woodward, ethnologist of the Los Angeles Museum, made "...efforts to find out who made the figures, but to no avail. The Mojave and Chemehuevi Indians who once frequented this area said they had no knowledge of them. But he found new hope upon learning that there was another similar figure near Sacton, Arizona, on the north branch of the Gila River, which the Pima call *Haakvaak*, or 'Hawk-Lying-Down.' "[17]

Ancient artists, for unknown reasons, created the figures using the intaglio process. They scraped away a shallow layer of dark surface soil and rock to reveal the light colored soil underneath, and piled dark gravel around the figures to outline them. Though portions of the effigies can be seen if one is standing right next to them, they are virtually invisible just a few feet away.

The larger of the human figures is about 175 feet long and is thought to be the outline of a woman. Her outstretched arms span 158 feet. Her male companion is about 95 feet tall. The coiled-snake figure has been mostly obliterated. Off-road vehicle drivers have ground it into dust, and nearly destroyed the other figures as well. Fortunately, today, the Blythe Intaglios are protected by two lines of fences, and are open to the public at all times as a State Historic Monument.

The figure that has been of most interest is the 53-foot long representation of a four-footed creature that has been alternatively identified as a panther, a coyote or a horse. The latter interpretation is especially popular among revisionist anthropologists who insist that horses lived on the North American continent long before the Spanish brought their mounts here.

Choral Pepper and Brad Williams comment in their book *The Mysterious West*,[143] "a covering of 'desert varnish' on rocks scraped aside to outline the figures suggests a date preceding that of the arrival of the Spanish conquistadors, who introduced the horse to North America. However, the animal figure ...appears to be a horse."

Richard Pourade, of the San Diego Museum of Man, says in his book *Ancient Hunters of the Far West*:[144] "In the desert near Blythe, California, are raked gravel 'pictographs' of the Mojave Indians. One of them is a crude representation of a man;

the other of a horse. The horse clearly places these gravel arrangements in the historic Indian period, as the original Western horse vanished from the continent many thousands of years ago and only was reintroduced by the Spaniards arriving from Europe."

It would then be reasonable to agree with Pepper and Williams that the intaglios pre-dated the Spanish Conquistadors, but it is not so surprising that the four-footed figure is that of a horse, as it might have come with other earlier explorers.

Pourade says that the intaglios were made by the Mojave, but Arthur Woodward, ethnologist of the Los Angeles Museum, has said, "…The Mojave and Chemehuevi Indians who once frequented this area said they had no knowledge of them."[143, 144]

We hiked around the area, ascending some small hills to get a better look at the huge figures. As I tried to find the best angle for taking some photos, I noticed that the sun was starting to set in the western sky. We decided to camp that night just over the Arizona border in Quartzite. Shortly, we were driving on a bridge over the Colorado River to Ehrenberg.

It was another 17 miles to Quartzite, a tiny desert gas station town that has been a rock hound's paradise since the 1960s. These days, it is also a Mecca for well over a million visitors each year, most of whom converge on this small town in a wave of RVs during the months of January and February.

During those months, over 2,000 vendors of rocks, gems, minerals, fossils and everything else imaginable create one of the world's largest open-air flea markets. Eight major gem and mineral shows are held, and vendors of raw and handcrafted merchandise peddle their wares to snowbirds, collectors and enthusiasts.

We walked past the wooden pelicans and wharf-posts that line the entrance of the Quartzite Yacht Club and plopped down on a couple of bar stools. Indeed, we were in a Yacht Club in the middle of the desert, with the compulsory décor of fisherman's nets, glass floats and wooden anchors. A Jimmy Buffet song was even playing on the jukebox. Surreal. We ordered some basic sandwiches and French fries, plus a couple of beers to wash it all down.

"I guess this part of the journey is coming to an end soon," sighed Jennifer.

"Yes, I suppose so," I replied. "Tomorrow we should be back at the World Explorers Club in Cottonwood."

"Well, maybe we should have a shot of tequila to celebrate," she suggested.

Moments later the bartender handed us each a shot glass and a slice of lemon.

"Here's to lost cities and ancient mysteries," I said. After a lick of salt, we took our shots and bit into the lemons. I shook my head and shivered at the rush of alcohol and the sour taste of lemon. "Yow!" I said.

That night we camped out in the desert, past the trailers and campers of the many rock hounds parked along the dusty dirt roads of Quartzite. The stars were out in great number. It was the great star-fest in the sky.

I lay back in my sleeping bag as Jennifer suddenly produced a small bottle of tequila from her pack and began slicing a lemon.

"Ready for another tequila to watch the stars with?" she asked, handing me a shot of tequila and a slice of lemon without waiting for an answer.

I drank the shot and lay back in my sleeping bag.

Much change had come over the Southwest in the past few thousand years. Cities and cultures had come and gone, lakes and inland seas had dried up, sacred caves and hollow mountains had been walled up or otherwise hidden from the average man. What mysteries were there left to solve?

As I looked up at the stars in the clear desert sky, they were telling me: "billions and billions."

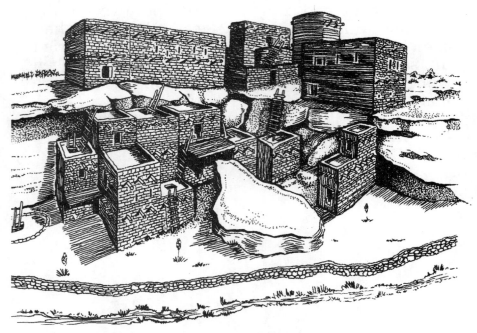

Top: A drawing of some of the buildings at Hovenweep. Bottom: Death Valley Scotty on the trail with his mules in this old photo.

548

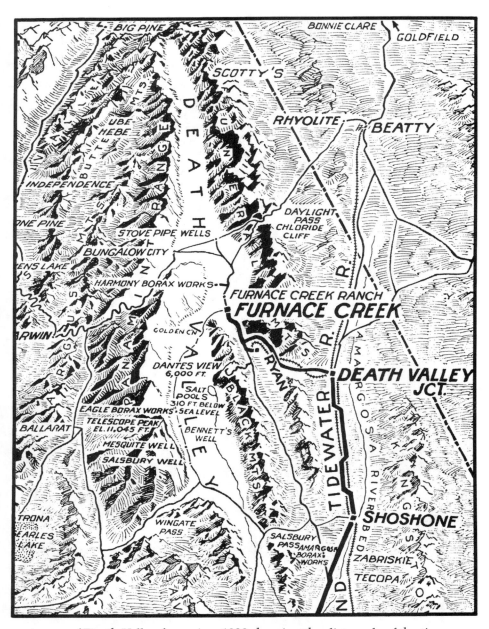

A map of Death Valley from circa 1930 showing the dirt roads of the time.

The strange Pumpkin Patch formation in Death Valley.

An early map of California showing it as an island.

A Los Angeles Times cartoon about Death Valley Scotty.

Al Johnson and Death Valley Scotty.

Death Valley Scotty: He liked to look you in the eye.

The "Coso Artifact"—a spark plug imbedded in a geode?

The giant mummified body of a woman found at Bridlevale Falls in 1895.

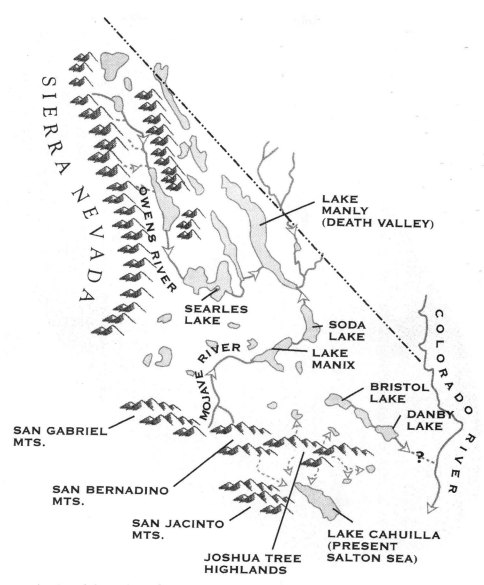

Ancient lakes of southern California include Searles Lake, Lake Manly, Lake Manix, Bristol Lake, Danby Lake and Lake Cahuilla.

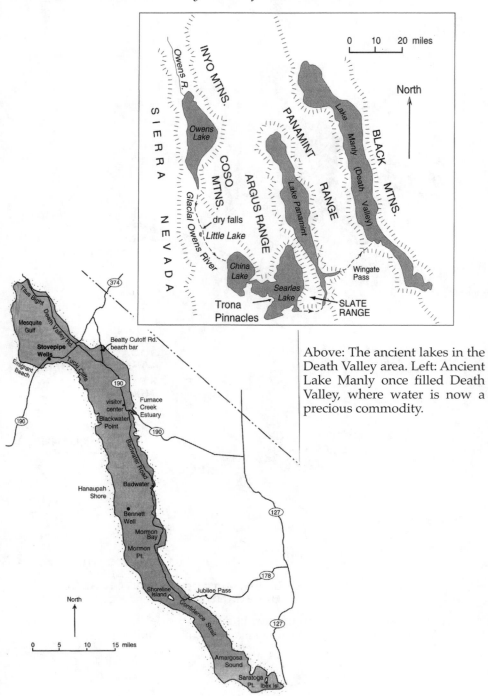

Above: The ancient lakes in the Death Valley area. Left: Ancient Lake Manly once filled Death Valley, where water is now a precious commodity.

556

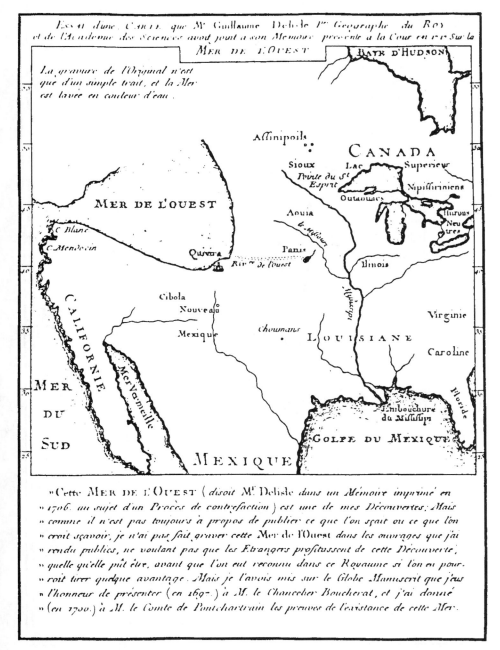

The 1753 Philippe Buache map showing an inland sea, the Mer de l'Ouest, with a city called Quivera as the port to a land called Cibola.

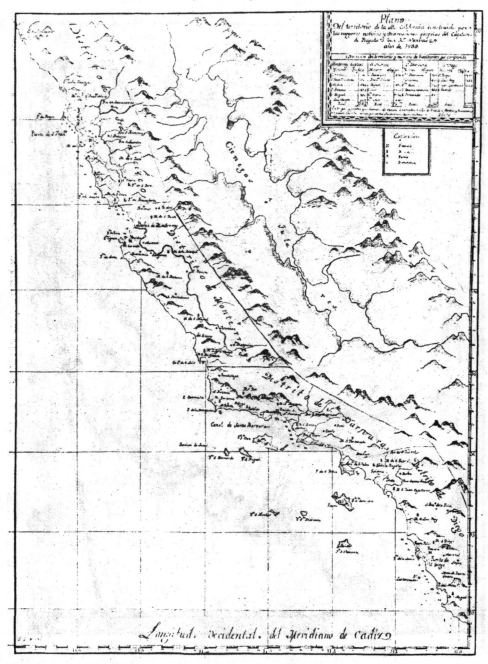

An 1830 Spanish map of California showing inland lakes.

The sign at the Barker Ranch in Death Valley in 1969.

Flints from the Calico site: Man-made or natural?

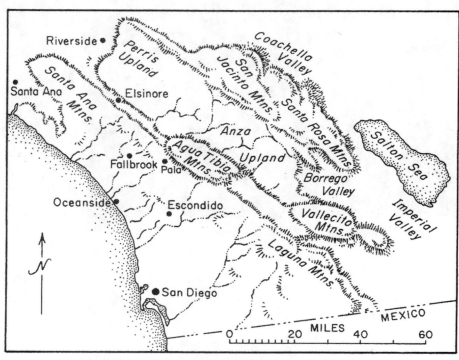

The Peninsula Ranges of southwestern California.

The "Dinosaur Eggs" discovered in Los Angeles in 1907.

The Hemet Maze Stone.

561

The skeleton (fossilized?) from the Ocotillo Conglomerate in the Borrego Badlands. Photo by J. Johnstone.

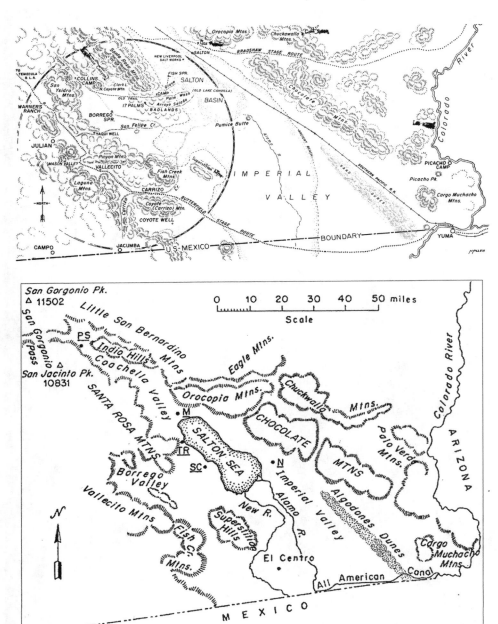

Top: A map of the Borrego Desert and Peg Leg Treasure from *Desert Magazine*. Bottom: Map of the Salton Sea area.

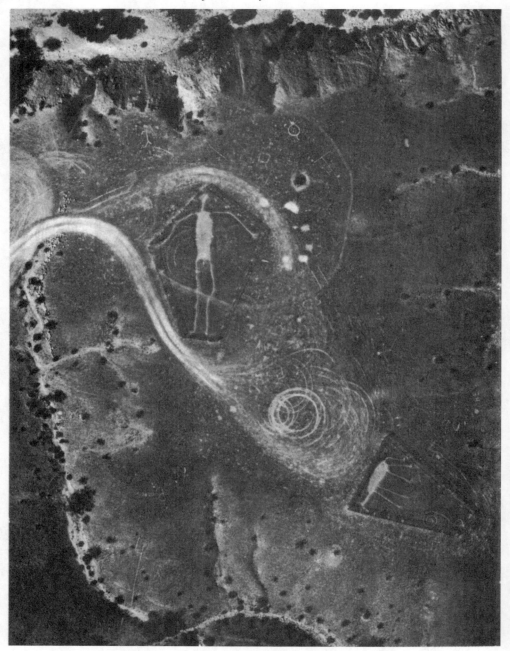

The Blythe Intaglios. Is the figure in the lower right a pre-Columbian horse?

BIBLIOGRAPHY & FOOTNOTES

1. **Cortés and Montezuma**, Maurice Collis, 1954, Harcourt Brace Jovanovich, New York.
2. **The Ancient Kingdoms of Mexico**, Nigel Davies, 1982, Penguin Books, Middlesex, England.
3. **A History of Mexican Archaeology**, Ignacio Bernal, 1980, Ignacio Bernal, Thames & Hudson Ltd., London.
4. **The Discovery and Conquest of Mexico**, Bernal Diaz del Castillo, translated by A. P. Maudslay, 1956, Farrar, Straus and Cudahy, New York.
5. **The Olmec World**, Ignacio Bernal, 1969, University of California Press, Berkeley.
6. **Zone of Silence**, Gerry Hunt, 1986, Avon Books, New York., Cyrus H. Gordon, 1974, Crown Publishers, NYC.
7. **Ancient Infrastructure**, compiled by William R. Corliss, The Sourcebook Project, 1999.
8. **The Crystal Skulls**, David Hatcher Childress and Stephen S. Mehler, 2008, Adventures Unlimited Press, Kempton.
9. **The Mystery of the Olmecs**, David Hatcher Childress, 2007, Adventures Unlimited Press, Kempton.
10. *"Ancient Mariners: Strong Evidence of Andean-Mexican Seagoing Trade as Early as 600 AD,"* David L. Chandler, Aug. 14, 1995, *Boston Globe*.
11. **Montezuma's Serpent**, Brad Steiger & Sherry Hansen-Steiger, 1992, Paragon House, New York.
12. **Dig Here!**, Thomas Penfield, 1962, Reprinted 2004, AUP, Kempton, IL.
13. **Atlantis In America**, Ivar Zapp and George Erickson, 1998, AUP, Kempton, IL.
14. **The Aztec: Man and Tribe,** Victor Von Hagen, 1958, New American Library, New York.
15. **Mexico**, Michael D. Coe, 1962, Thames & Hudson, London.
16. **Mysteries of Time & Space**, Brad Steiger, 1974, Prentice Hall, Englewood Cliffs, NJ.
17. **Ancient Man: A Handbook of Puzzling Artifacts**, William Corliss, 1978, The Sourcebook Project, Glen Arm, MD.
18. **Lost Cities of North and Central America,** David Hatcher Childress, 1994, Adventures Unlimited Press, Kempton, Illinois.
19. **Tales of the Big Bend**, Elton Miles, Texas A&M Press, College Station, 1976.
20. **Mysteries & Miracles of Texas,** Jack Kutz, Rhombus Publishing,

Corrales, NM, 1994.

21. **The Marfa Lights**. Judith M. Brueske, Alpine, Texas. Ocotillo Enterprises. 1988. Revised 1989.

22. **The Desert Candle**. Judith M. Brueske, Alpine, Texas. Ocotillo Enterprises. May-June, 1993.

23. **Handbook of Unusual Natural Phenomena**, William R. Corliss, New York, Arlington House, Inc. 1977.

24. **Electric UFOs**, Albert Budden, Blandford Press, London, 1998.

25. **Night Orbs,** James Bunnell, 2003, Lacey Publishing, Cedar Creek, TX.

26. **Stray Tales of Big Bend**, Elston Miles, 1993, Texas A&M Press, College Station, TX.

27. **Big Bird!**, Ken Gerhard, 2007, The Centre for Fortean Zoology, UK.

28. **Legends of Texas**, J. Frank Dobie, 1924, Texas Folklore Society, Austin, TX.

29. **100 Tons of Gold**, David Chandler, 1978, Doubleday, Garden City, NY.

30. **Mysteries & Miracles of New Mexico,** Jack Kutz, 1988, Rhombus Publishing, Corrales, NM.

31. **More Mysteries & Miracles of New Mexico,** Jack Kutz, 1998, Rhombus Publishing, Corrales, NM.

32. **Apache Gold and Yaqui Silver**, J. Frank Dobie, 1928. Little and Brown Co., New York.

33. **Treasure Trails of the Southwest,** Marc Simmons, 1994, University of New Mexico Press, Albuquerque.

34. **Unfound Treasures of Mexico**, Charles Kenworthy, 1995, Quest Publishing, Encino, CA.

35. **Saga America**, Barry Fell, 1980, New York Times Books, New York.

36. **America BC**, Barry Fell, 1976, Demeter Press, NYC.

37. **Bronze Age America**, Barry Fell, 1982, Little, Brown & Co., Boston.

38. **Strange Artifacts**, William Corliss, 1974, The Sourcebook Project, Glen Arm, MD.

39. **Coronado's Children**, J. Frank Dobie, 1930, Literary Guild, New York.

40. **Lost Mines of the Great Southwest**, John D. Mitchell, 1933, Rio Grande Press, Glorieta, New Mexico.

41. **A Guide To Treasure in New Mexico**, Thomas Penfield, 1981, True Treasure Library, Demming, NM.

42. **Treasure of Victoria Peak**, Phil A. Koury, 1986, Schiffer Publishing, West Chester, PA.

43. **Secret Cities of Old South America**, Harold Wilkins, 1952, reprinted by AUP, Kempton, IL.

44. **Death Valley Men**, Bourke Lee, 1932, Macmillan Company, New York.

45. *"The Big Bend Mystery Tablet,"* *True West,* July-August 1972, Western Publications, Austin, TX.

46. **Lost Cities & Ancient Mysteries of South America**, David Hatcher Childress, 1987, AUP, Kempton, IL

47. **The Mysterious Past**, Robert Charroux, 1973, Robert Laffont, NYC.

48. **Living Wonders**, John Mitchell & Robert Rickard, 1982, Thames & Hudson, NYC.

49. **Enigmas**, Rupert Gould, 1945, University Books, NYC.

50. **"Things" and More "Things"**, Ivan T. Sanderson, 1968, Pyramid Books, NYC. Reprinted 2007 Adventures Unlimited Press

51. **Strange World**, Frank Edwards, 1964, Bantam Books, NYC.

52. **Stranger Than Science**, Frank Edwards, 1959, Bantam Books, NYC.

53. **On the Track of Unknown Animals**, Bernard Heuvelmans, 1958, MIT Press, Cambridge, MA.

54. **Rattlesnake Blues**, Leo W. Banks, 2000, Arizona Highways Books, Phoenix.

55. **UFOs Over Galisteo**, Robert J. Torrez, 2004, University of New Mexico Press, Sante Fe.

56. **Superstition Mountain: A Ride Through Time**, James Swanson and Tom Kollenborn, 1981, Word Publishing, Apache Junction, AZ.

57. **Quest For the Dutchman's Gold,** Robert Sikorsky, 1983, Golden West Publishers, Phoenix.

58. **The Curse of the Dutchman's Gold**, Helen Corbin, 1990. Foxwest Publishers, Phoenix.

59. **The Sterling Legend**, Estee Conatser, 1972, Gem Guides Book Company, Baldwin Park, CA.

60. **The Lost Dutchman Mine of Jacob Waltz**, T. E. Glover, Ph.D., 1998, Cowboy-Miner Productions, Phoenix.

61. **The Story of Superstition Mountain and the Lost Dutchman Gold Mine**, Robert Joseph Allen, 1971, Pocket Books, New York.

62. **The Treasure of the Superstition Mountains**, Gary Jennings, 1973, W.W. Norton & Company, New York.

63. **Superstition Mountain and its famed Dutchman's Lost Mine**, Barney Barnard, 1954 (revised 1964), Self Published at Rancho del Superstition, Apache Junction, Arizona.

64. **Mysteries & Miracles of Arizona**, Jack Kutz, 1992, Rhombus Publishing, Corrales, NM.

65. **Thunder God's Gold**, Barry Storm, 1945 (reprinted 1967), Schoose Publishing, Goldfield, AZ.

66. **The Peralta Stone Maps** (20 page booklet), Jim D. Hatt, 2005, Apache Junction, AZ.

67. **Hiker's Guide to the Superstition Wilderness**, Jack Carlson and Elizabeth Stewart, 1995, Clear Creek Publishing, Tempe, AZ.

68. **Superstition Treasures**, Travis Marlowe, 1965, Tyler Printing, Phoenix.

69. **Apache Junction and the Superstitions Mountains**, Jane Eppinga, 2006, Arcadia Publishing, Charleston, SC.

70. **Bizarre America**, Gerry Hunt, 1988, Berkley Books, New York.

71. **A Kino Guide: A Life of Eusebio Francisco Kino and a Guide to His Missions and Monuments,** Polzer, Charles, S.J., 1974, Tucson: Southwestern Mission Research Center.

72. **Canyon of Gold**, Barbara Marriott, 2005, Catymatt Productions, Tucson, AZ.

73. **From Khyber (Kheeber) Pass to Gran Quivira (Kheevira), NM and Baboquivaria, AZ**, Gene D. Matlock, 2002, iUniverse, Lincoln, Nebraska.

74. **The Last Atlantis Book You'll Ever Need**, Gene Matlock, 2001, Dandelion Books, Temple, AZ.

75. **Death Comes for the Archbishop**, Willa Cather, 1927, Alfred A. Knopf, Inc., New York.

76. **Roadside History of New Mexico**, Francis and Roberta Fugate, 1989, Mountain Press, Missoula, Montana.

77. **The Lost Americans,** Frank C. Hibben, 1946, Thomas Y. Crowell Company, New York.

78. **Prehistoric Man in Europe**, Frank C. Hibben, 1959, University of Oklahoma Press, Norman, OK.

79. **Arizona Highways**, July, 1992.

80. **Arizona Highways**, August, 1993.

81. **New Light on Chaco Canyon**, Edited by David Noble, 1984, School of American Research Press, Santa Fe.

82. **El Morro: Inscription Rock**, New Mexico, John M. Slater, 1961, The Plantin Press, Los Angeles.

83. **The Zuni Enigma,** Nancy Yaw Davis, 2001, W.W. Norton & Company, New York.

84. **Acoma: Pueblo In the Sky**, Ward Alan Minge, 1991, University of New Mexico Press, Albuquerque.

85. **The Dene and Na-Dene Indian Migration 1233 A.D.**, Ethel G. Stewart,

1991, ISAC Press, Columbus, Georgia.

86. **Quest For the Pillar of Gold**, Billingsley, Spamer and Menkes, 1997, Grand Canyon Association, Grand Canyon.

87. **Grand Canyon Stories: Then and Now**, Leo Banks and Craig Childs, 1999, Arizona Highways, Phoenix.

88. **Unkar Delta**, Douglas Swartz, with Chapman and Kepp, 1980, School of American Research Press, Santa Fe.

89. **The Great Temple and the Aztec Gods**, Doris Heyden & L.F. Villaseñor, 1984, Editorial Minutiae Mexicana, Mexico City.

90. **Oaxaca: The Archaeological Record**, Marcus Winter, 1989, Editorial Minutiae Mexicana, Mexico City.

91. **The Oaxaca Valley**, 1973, Instituto Nacional de Antropología e Historia, Mexico City.

92. **Secrets of the Lost Races**, Rene Noorbergen, 1977, Barnes & Noble Publishers, NYC.

93. **Hindu America?**, Chaman Lal, 1960, Bharatiya Vidya Bhavan, Bombay.

94. **Weird America**, Jim Brandon, 1978, E.P. Dutton, NYC.

95. **The Rebirth of Pan**, Jim Brandon, 1983, Firebird Press, Dunlap, IL.

96. **The Santa Fe Trail,** William E. Hill, 1992, Caxton Printers, Caldwell, ID.

97. **The Pima-Maricopa**, Henry F. Dobyns, 1989, Chelsea House Publishers, New York.

98. **Pages From Hopi History**, Harry C. James, 1974, University of Arizona Press, Tucson.

99. **Atlantis In Spain**, E.M. Whishaw, 1928, Rider & Co., London. Reissued by Adventures Unlimited Press.

100. **Grand Canyon Geology**, edited by Stanley S. Beus and Michael Morales, 1990, Oxford University Press, New York.

101. **Megalithic Man in America?**, George F. Carter, 1991, The Diffusion Issue, Stonehenge Viewpoint, Santa Barbara, California, USA.

102. **Arizona Cavalcade**, Edited by Joseph Miller, 1962, Hastings House Publishers, NYC.

103. **Navaho & Tibetan Sacred Wisdom**, Peter Gold, 1994, Inner Traditions, Rochester, VT.

104. **Aboriginal Monuments of the State of New York**, E.G. Squier, 1850, Smithsonian Institution, Washington D.C.

105. **Ancient Monuments of the Mississippi Valley**, E.G. Squier & E.H. Davis, 1848, Bartlett & Welford, NYC. (originally a Smithsonian Publication).

106. **Atlantic Crossings Before Columbus**, Frederick Pohl, 1961, Norton,

NYC.

107. **They All Discovered America**, Boland, 1961, Doubleday, NYC.

108. **Vanished Cities**, Hermann & Georg Schreiber, 1957, Alfred Knopf, NYC.

109. **Calalus**, Cyclone Covey, 1975, Vantage Press, NYC.

110. **Mysterious America**, Loren Coleman, 1983, Faber & Faber, Boston.

111. **Quest For the Pillar of Gold**, Bilingsley, Spamer and Menkes, 1997, Grand Canyon Association, Grand Canyon, AZ.

112. **Grand Canyon Geology**, edited by Stanley S. Beus and Michael Morales, 1990, Oxford University Press, New York.

113. **The Exploration of the Colorado River and Its Canyons**, John Wesley Powell, 1895, reprinted 2002, National Geographic Society.

114. **The Grand Canyon of the Colorado**, John C. Van Dyke, 1920, Charles Scribner's Sons, New York. Reprinted 1992, University of Utah Press.

115. **Unkar Delta: Archeology of the Grand Canyon**, Schwartz, Chapman and Kepp, 1980, School of American Research Press, Sante Fe, New Mexico.

116. **Mysterious California**, Mike Marinacci, 1988, Pan Pipe Press, Los Angeles.

117. **They All Discovered America**, Charles Boland, 1961, Doubleday, Garden City, New York.

118. **The Atlas of Archaeology**, K. Branigan, consulting editor, 1982, St. Martin's Press, NYC.

119. **Nu Sun, Asian American Voyages 500 B.C.**, Gunnar Thompson, 1989, Pioneer Press, Fresno, California.

120. **Conquistadors Without Swords**, Leo Deuel, 1967, St. Martin's Press, NY.

121. **Marshal South and the Ghost Mountain Chronicles,** edited by Diana Lindsay, 2005, Sunbelt Publications, San Diego.

122. **Desert Lore of Southern California**, Choral Pepper, 1994, Sunbelt Publications, San Diego.

123. **Historic Aztlan and the Laguna del Ora**, Ralph Lawrence Caine, 1962, Los Angeles.

124. **Timeless Earth**, Peter Kolosimo, 1974, University Press Seacaucus, NJ.

125. **Lost Tribes & Promised Lands**, Ronald Sanders, 1978, Harper, New York.

126. **Strange Relics from the Depths of the Earth**, Joseph Jochmans, 1979, Forgotten Ages Research Society, Lincoln, Nebraska.

127. **Legends & Lore of the American Indians**, edited by Terri Hardin, 1993, Barnes & Noble, NY.

128. **Men Out of Asia**, Harold Gladwin, 1947, McGraw-Hill, NYC.

129. **Digging Up America**, Frank C. Hibben, 1960, Hill & Wang, New York.

130. **Death Valley Men**, Bourke Lee, 1932, MacMillan Co., New York.

131. **An Unnatural History of Death Valley**, Paul Bailey, 1978, Death Valley '49ers, Death Valley.

132. **Death Valley Scotty**, Mabel (Bessie Johnson), 1978, Death Valley Natural History Association.

133. **Geology Underfoot In Death Valley and Owens Valley**, Robert Sharp and Allen Glazner, 1997, Mountain Press, Missoula, MT.

134. **Desert Shadows: A True Story of the Charles Manson Family in Death Valley**, Bob Murphy, 1993, Sagebrush Press, Morongo Valley, CA.

135. **The Anza-Borrego Desert Region**, Lowell and Diana Lindsay, 1978, Wilderness Pres, Berkeley, CA.

136. **Baja California: Vanished Missions, Lost Treasures, Strange Stories Tall and True**, Coral Pepper, 1973, Ward Ritchie Press, Los Angeles.

137. **Geology of Anza-Borrego: Edge of Creation**, Paul Remeika and Lowell Lindsay, 1992, Sunbelt Publications, San Diego.

138. **Geology and History of Southeastern San Diego County**, Edited by Carole L. Ziegler, 2005, Sunbelt Publications, San Diego.

139. **Incidents of Travel in Yucatan**, John L. Stevens, 1843, Harper & Bros. NY.

140. **Mysteries of Ancient South America**, Harold Wilkins, 1946, Citadel, NY. (Reprinted by AUP, Kempton, IL).

141. **Death Valley: Geology, Ecology, Archeology**, Charles B. Hunt, 1975, University of California Press, Berkeley.

142. **In Quest of the White God**, Pierre Honoré, 1963, Hutchinson & Co. London (Reprinted 2007, by AUP, Kempton, IL).

143. **The Mysterious West**, Brad Williams & Choral Pepper, 1967, World Publishing Company, Cleveland, Ohio.

144. **Ancient Hunters of the Far West**, Richard Pourade, editor, 1966, Union-Tribune Publishing Co., San Diego, California.

145. **Exploring Death Valley**, Ruth Kirk, 1956, Stanford University Press.

146. **Mysteries of the Mexican Pyramids**, Peter Tompkins, 1976, Harper & Row, NYC.

147. **The Cities of Ancient Mexico**, Jeremy Sabloff, 1989, Thames & Hudson, New York.

148. **Conquest of Mexico**, William Prescott, 1843, London & New York.

149. **The Conquest of New Spain**, Bernal Díaz, (1492-1580), 1963, Penguin Books, London.

150. **The First Americans**, G.H. Bushnell, 1968, Thames & Hudson, London.

151. **The Search For Lost America**, Salvatore Trento, 1978, Contemporary Books, Chicago.

152. **Ancient Celtic America**, William McGlone & Phillip Leonard,1986, Panorama West Books, Fresno, California.

153. **Ogam Consanine & Tifinag Alphabets**, Warren Dexter, 1984, Academy Books, Rutland, Vermont.

154. **The Norse Discovery of America**, Paul Chapman, 1981, One Candle Press, Atlanta, Georgia.

155. **Exploring the Fremont**, David Madsen, 1989, Utah Museum of Natural History, University of Utah.

156. **Unknown Mexico**, Carl Lumholtz, 1902, Charles Scribner's Sons, NYC.

157. **The Natural and Aboriginal History of Tennessee**, John Haywood, 1959, McCowat-Mercer, Jackson, Tennessee.

158. **Before Columbus**, Cyrus Gordon, 1971, Crown Publishers, New York.

159. **Strangest Of All**, Frank Edwards, 1956, Ace Books, New York.

160. **America's Ancient Treasures**, Franklin & Mary Folsom, 1971, University of New Mexico Press, Albuquerque.

161. **The Lost Cities of Cibola**, Richard Petersen, 1985, G & H Books, Phoenix.

162. **The Hohokam**, Edited by David Noble, 1991, School of the American Research Press, Sante Fe, New Mexico.

163. **Psychic Archaeology**, Jeffrey Goodman, 1977, Berkley Books, NYC.

164. **Quetzalcoatl**, Joes Lopez Portillo, 1965 (English Translation ©1977), James Clark & Co., Cambridge, England.

165. **Explorations In Grand Canyon**, *Arizona Gazette,* April 5, 1909, Phoenix, Arizona.

166. **The Ancient Sun Kingdoms of the Americas**, Victor von Hagen, 1957, World Publishing Co. Cleveland, Ohio.

167. **Mexico Mystique**, Frank Waters, 1975, Swallow Press, Chicago.

168. **Explorations of the Aboriginal Remains of Tennessee**, Joseph Jones, 1880, Smithsonian Institution, Washington, D.C.

169. **Madoc & the Discovery of America**, Richard Deacon, 1966, George Braziller Co. New York.

170. **Brave His Soul**, Ellen Pugh, 1970, Dodd, Mead & Co., New York.

171. **Curious Encounters**, Loren Coleman, 1985, Faber & Faber, Boston.

172. **Thunderbirds! The Living Legend of Giant Birds**, Mark A. Hall, 1988, Hall Publications & Research, Bloomington, Minnesota.

574

173. **Children of the Sun**, W.J. Perry, 1923, London, reprinted by Adventures Unlimited Press.

174. **Axis of the World**, Igor Witkowski, 2008, Adventures Unlimited Press, Kempton, IL.

175. **The Ancient Aztalan Story**, Helen Schultz, Ed., 1969, Aztalan Historical Society, Lake Mills, Wisconsin.

176. **The Lost Pyramids of Rock Lake**, Frank Joseph, FATE, Oct. 1989.

177. **Preliminary Catalogue of the Comalcalco Bricks**, Neil Steede, 1984, Centro de Investigacion Precolombina, Tabasco, Mexico.

178. **The Smithsonian Book of North American Indians**, Philip Kopper, 1986, Smithsonian Books, Washington, D.C.

179. **Metallurgical Characteristics of North American Prehistoric Copper Work**, David Schroeder and Katharine Ruhl, American Antiquity, Vol. 33, No.2, 1967.

180. **New York Times**, March 17, 1992.

181. **The Secret: America In World History Before Columbus**, Joseph Mahan, 1983, ISAC Press, Columbus, Georgia.

182. **Man: 12,000 Years Under the Sea**, Robert F. Burgess, 1980, Dodd, Mead & Company, New York.

183. **Pale Ink**, Henriette Mertz, 1953 (1972, revised, 2nd edition), Swallow Press, Chicago.

184. **Atlantis, Dwelling Place of the Gods**, Henriette Mertz, 1976, Swallow Press, Chicago.

185. **The Wine Dark Sea**, Henriette Mertz, 1964, Swallow Press, Chicago.

186. **The Mystic Symbol**, Henriette Mertz, 1986, Global Books, Chicago.

187. **The Dictionary of Imaginary Places**, Alberto Manguel & Gianni Guadalupi, 1980, Macmillan Publishing Co., New York.

188. **Ancient America**, John Baldwin, 1872, Harper & Brothers, New York.

189. **Archaeology and the Book of Mormon**, Milton Hunter, 1956, Deseret Book Company, Salt Lake City.

190. **Book of Mormon Evidences in Ancient America**, Dewey Farnsworth, 1967, Deseret Book Company, Salt Lake City.

191. **Man's Rise To Civilization As Shown by the Indians of North America from Primeval Times to the Coming of the Industrial State,** Peter Farb, 1968, E.P. Dutton & Co., NYC.

192. **Relación de las Cosas de Yucatan**, Friar Diego de Landa, 1579, (published as **Yucatan Before & After the Conquest**, 1937, The Maya Society, Baltimore, reissued 1978, Dover Publications, NYC).

193. **Time & Reality in the Thought of the Maya**, Miguel León-Portilla, 1988, University of Oklahoma Press, Norman, OK.

194. **No Longer On the Map**, Raymond H. Ramsay, 1972, Viking Press, NYC.

195. **Legendary Islands of the Atlantic**, William Babcock, 1922, New York.

196. **The Ancient Stones Speak**, Dr. David Zink, 1979, E.P. Dutton, NYC.

197. **Danger My Ally**, F.A. Mitchel-Hedges, 1954, Elek Books, London.

198. **The Crystal Skull**, Richard Garvin, 1973, Doubleday, NYC.

199. **Sacred Mysteries Among the Mayas & the Quiches**, Augustus LePlongeon, 1886, Kegan Paul (Agent), London & NY.

200. **Queen Moo & the Egyptian Sphinx**, Augustus LePlongeon, 1900, Kegan Paul (Agent), London & NY.

201. **Popul Vuh**, Translated by Dennis Tedlock, 1985, Simon & Schuster, NYC.

202. **Indian Masks & Myths of the West**, Joseph H. Wherry, 1969, Funk & Wagnalls, New York.

203. **Lost America**, Arlington Mallery, 1951, Overlook Co., Washington, D.C.

204. **Historical Sketch of the Spiro Mound**, Forrest Clements, 1945, Museum of the American Indian, Heye Foundation, Volume XIV, New York.

205. **Old West Adventures In Arizona**, Charles D. Lauer, 1989, Golden West Publishers, Phoenix.

206. **Into the Unknown**, Susan Hazen-Hammond, 1999, Arizona Highways Publications, Phoenix.

207. **Frauds, Myths, and Mysteries: Science & Pseudoscience in Archaeology**, Kenneth Feder, 1990, Mayfield Publishing Co., Mountain View, California

208. **Fantastic Archaeology: The Wild Side of North American Prehistory**, Stephen Williams, 1991, University of Pennsylvania Press, Philadelphia.

209. **Men of the Earth**, Brian Fagan, 1974, Little, Brown & Co. Boston.

210. **Elusive Treasure**, Brian Fagan, 1977, Charles Scribner's Sons, New York.

211. **Incidents of Travel in Central America, Chiapas and Yucatan**, John L. Stevens, 1841, Harper & Bros. NY (reprinted by Dover, 1969, NYC).